WE INSPIRE AND ENABLE PEOPLE
TO IMPROVE THEIR LIVES
AND THE WORLD AROUND THEM.

www.Rodale.com

The PGA TOUR
Complete Book of Golf

Michael Corcoran

A MOUNTAIN LION BOOK

Henry Holt and Company

New York

Henry Holt and Company, Inc.
Publishers since 1866
115 West 18th Street
New York, New York 10011

Library of Congress Cataloging-in-Publication Data
Corcoran, Mike.
The PGA Tour complete book of golf / by Michael Corcoran.—1st ed.
    p.   cm.
"A Mountain Lion book."
Includes index.
ISBN 0-8050-6377-3
1. Golf—United States. I. PGA Tour (Association) II. Title.
GV965.C664   1999   99-10390
796.352—dc21

Henry Holt books are available for special promotions and premiums.
For details contact: Director, Special Markets.

Designed by Max Crandall

Printed in the United States of America
All first editions are printed on acid-free paper. ∞

10 9 8 7 6 5 4 3 2 1

This book is dedicated to my wife, Angela, and
my kids, Michelene, Elaine, and Michael, none of
whom complained for one second during the time
I took from our life together to write this book.
Every writer should be so lucky.

Acknowledgments

The author would like to thank John Ledesma for his help in conducting interviews with players at PGA TOUR events; all of the TOUR players who graciously gave their time to be interviewed; John Monteleone, Randy Voorhees, Mark Gola, and Joan Mohan of Mountain Lion, Inc., who put years of work into this project; David Sobel, the book's editor at Henry Holt; photographers Leonard Kamsler, Marc Feldman, and Michael Plunkett; illustrator extraordinaire Barry Ross; John Morris, Wesley Haynes, Cindy Reid, and Chuck Adams from the PGA TOUR; and Joseph Passov, Kenneth Fretz, Sr., Scotty Burns, and Fran Luther.

Foreword

The PGA TOUR Complete Book of Golf may not solve all your problems on the golf course, and it certainly is not intended to take the place of lessons from the professional at your local club or course.

What we hope to achieve with this book is to give you some insight into how the best players in the professional sport of golf approach a game that most of the rest of us play for the fun and challenges it offers.

A substantial number of players on the PGA TOUR, SENIOR PGA TOUR and NIKE TOUR have contributed their advice and counsel for this book. They have been motivated to do so in part because the TOUR's royalties from this book will be donated to the PGA TOUR Caddie Benevolent Fund.

Few people have been blessed with the physical skills to compete at the level of playing ability that is on display week-in and week-out on the three tours under the auspices of the PGA TOUR; however, all of us can benefit from the knowledge and experience those players have gained during their successful competitive careers.

We hope that you will enjoy reading this book and applying its principles to your own games.

—Tim Finchem, Commissioner, PGA TOUR

Foreword

It is the glorious uncertainty of golf that makes it the game it is.
— P. G. Wodehouse

Clearly, Mr. Wodehouse, one of the most prolific and entertaining writers of the twentieth century, had a true understanding of golf.

It is that uncertainty, that constant wonderment, that makes golf a challenge and a great deal of fun. Whether you play golf as a game or as a sport, the challenge remains the same—hitting the perfect shot, playing the perfect hole or the perfect round.

Even the game's best players, those of us fortunate enough to play on the PGA TOUR and the SENIOR PGA TOUR, have moments when the club feels like a foreign object in our hands and the ball seems to have a mind, and sense of direction, of its own.

And so golfers of all skill levels spend countless hours—and dollars—in quixotic attempts to master the game. No sport has been the subject of as much literature as golf. Most of that verbiage has come in the form of books and articles promising that you will "drive it straighter and longer," "develop a golden touch on the greens," or "cut ten strokes off your score."

This book won't make any such promises, but it should give you some great insight into how the game is played at its highest level. It will be up to you to apply the lessons contained in the following pages to your own game.

But the number one suggestion I have for you is a simple one: Enjoy the glorious uncertainty of the greatest game in the world.

— Hale Irwin

Contents

Introduction

Everywhere you turn, it seems, somebody is trying to sell you advice on how to improve your golf game. Books, magazines, television shows, videos—all contribute to this veritable deluge of information. The reader may well wonder then: Why this book?

The answer is simple. Most of the instructional information currently available focuses on or promotes a specific theory or school of thought. Many of these competing theories have great value. However, no single approach to the game is automatically or necessarily better than any other, and golfers at all levels can and will benefit from exposure to a great variety of techniques. Certainly there are fundamentals that no successful player can do without, but no two players apply all of these fundamentals in the same way. From basic shot-making and course management to mental preparation, each individual player succeeds or fails according to his or her own personal approach. To deny this is to deny that Tiger Woods and Jim Furyk are both superb players despite the fact that they do very few things the same way.

Thus you will learn from this book that there are countless ways to skin a cat. PGA TOUR players are like all great hand-eye performers, from fighter pilots to major-league baseball hitters. Some choose a more methodical approach to their shot-making, while others prefer to hit their shots more by feel or instinct, with less of *how* they do it, but totally confident that they *can* do it. In style of play some PGA TOUR players are aggressive and some conservative. It's the difference between Nick Faldo and Lee Trevino, Tom Kite and Mark Calcavecchia. The playing styles of these players differ, but to be sure, on any given day, any one of them can be the best.

The PGA TOUR Complete Book of Golf describes the fundamentals in a way that allows you to easily apply them to your own game. To this end, *The PGA TOUR Complete Book of Golf* provides the unique insights on fundamentals of several leading PGA Teaching Professionals, and it offers the applied knowledge of the world's greatest tournament players. The hundreds of photographs reveal as much as the words of the game's great players—men who have faced (and many who have overcome) the pressure of winning PGA TOUR events, Players Championships, U.S. Opens, PGA Championships, British Opens, the Masters, the Ryder Cup and, perhaps the most daunting, the PGA TOUR Qualifying School. And so it is with your game: Adapt the fundamentals to your personality; practice and experiment; grasp the tip that will help bring about that breakthrough; and ultimately, become the best player you can be.

A quick note on the text: The fundamentals, swing mechanics and situational tactics in this book are written as they would apply to a right-handed golfer. Apologies to any left-handed players offended by this.

— M. C.

1

Golf in America and the PGA TOUR

Golf, or some version of it, has been in existence for a remarkably long time. Mentions of the game being played in Scotland, the country universally regarded as the home of golf, date back at least as far as the twelfth century, and there can be little question that the game was being played for some time before that. Although it has never been established when golf was brought to the United States or who brought it, it is generally accepted that the game was not played in an organized format until the late 1800s. The oldest championship in golf, the British Open, was first played in 1860, but the first official championships in the United States did not occur until 1895, when the U.S. Open and the U.S. Amateur both were played at Newport Golf Club in Rhode Island. Horace Rawlins was the winner of the U.S. Open, with a score of 173 (for thirty-six holes). Charles B. Macdonald won the U.S. Amateur.

At the dawn of the twentieth century, golf certainly was not a game of the masses, and the concept of a man being a profes-

The King, Arnold Palmer.

sional golfer (as opposed to a golf professional) was still relatively novel. In 1900 the legendary British champion Harry Vardon made an exhibition tour in the United States, sparking, perhaps for the first time, a modicum of interest in the game among the general public. At the time, Vardon was one of the most famous players in the world, and along with J. H. Taylor and James Braid formed the Great Triumvirate, a tag the men earned by winning sixteen British Open Championships among them in the twenty-one Opens from 1894 to 1914. Vardon won six, and Taylor and Braid each won five. Thirteen years after his turn-of-the-century tour, Vardon would figure prominently in an event that forever changed the game in America.

The 1913 U.S. Open: David versus the Goliaths

As the game moved through its infancy, its appeal to the man on the street remained rather limited. That began to change in 1911, when Johnny McDermott became the first American-born player to win the U.S. Open. McDermott's victory, although historically significant, did not do much to bolster the game's popularity because Vardon and most of the other elite British professionals were not in the field. Two years later, at The Country Club in Brookline, Massachusetts, Vardon was on hand and was considered a sure thing to take the title. By the end of the week, Vardon found out the same thing every golfer does eventually: There are no sure things in golf. In an upset, the proportions of which have never been matched in golf, Francis Ouimet, a twenty-year-old amateur who lived in the Brookline neighborhood and caddied at the club, defeated Vardon and fellow Englishman Ted Ray in an eighteen-hole play-off after the three ended regulation play in a tie. The event made the papers nationwide and in Great Britain. For the first time, all of America was talking about a golfer.

At the time of Ouimet's victory, the standard of play between the top professional golfers and the top amateur players was on the same level. There were no regularly scheduled events for professionals, and the men who played competitively for money and the men who made their living working at golf and country clubs were often one and the same. The interest sparked by Ouimet's triumph caused more than a few citizens to pick up clubs for the first time and head for the links. As for those who made their living off the game, changes were also at hand.

The Evolution of Golf as a Profession

The appearance of Ouimet on the American golf scene coincided with the arrival of Walter Hagen, who was also in the field at The Country Club in 1913. The following year, the twenty-two-year-old Hagen won the U.S. Open at Midlothian Golf Club just outside Chicago. It was the first of eleven major championships for Hagen (including six PGA Championships, a record still shared with Jack Nicklaus), making Hagen the first American professional golfer of any significance. Hagen is handed down to us in the popular history of the game as a wily match player and *bon vivant*—a guy who would beat you in a match with one hand while chilling a bottle of champagne with the other. Although there is little question that "The Haig" had a certain zest for life, he was also a monumental figure in American golf. He was an advocate for the rights of professionals—both playing and club—at a time when pros were treated with mild contempt by the financially fortunate who made up the membership of golf and country clubs.

It was a time in sports, particularly golf, when it was considered ungentlemanly to devote one's life to a game. If you could be good at the game in your spare time, that was fine. To excel at a game because you pursued it with vigor exceeding that devoted to a hobby was considered bourgeois. Hagen, by dint of his competitive genius and indomitable personality, did more to gain acceptance for professional golfers than any other figure in the game's history. He made it acceptable to be a great player—he gave professionals a reason to hold their heads high.

In 1916, just two years after Hagen's Open victory and three years after Ouimet's, the PGA (Professional Golfers' Association) of America was founded. Today, the PGA of America represents more than 23,000 golf professionals in the United States who serve the golf population as club professionals, teaching golf and performing a myriad of services—from selling equipment and apparel to fitting players for equipment. At its founding in 1916, the PGA of America represented every professional. Within three years there occurred three hugely significant events in American golf.

As Hagen and Ouimet had captured the public's imagination, so did twenty-year-old Gene Sarazen, when he won the U.S. Open at Skokie Country Club in Illinois and the PGA Championship at Oakmont Country Club outside of Pittsburgh, to become the first to win both events in the same year, 1922. Sarazen eventually went on to become the first player to win all four of the major professional championships (the Masters, U.S. Open, British Open, and PGA Championship) at least once. To date, only three players—Ben Hogan, Jack Nicklaus, and Gary Player—have matched Sarazen's achievement. Together, Hagen and Sarazen laid the foundation for the public's perception of the professional golfer, a process that was not fully refined until the phenomenal Arnold Palmer appeared in the late 1950s.

Gene Sarazen, a dominant player in the '20s and '30s, was the first to win all four professional majors at least once.

The End of the Amateur Era:
Bobby Jones and the Slam

Amateur golfers have always and will always make up the overwhelming majority of the golf population. However, the competitive significance of the nonprofessional reached its zenith in the 1920s in the person of Robert Tyre Jones, who successfully completed a single-season sweep of the major championships. Today, the four major championships in golf are (in order of play in a typical year) the Masters, the U.S. Open, the British Open, and the PGA Championship. In Jones's day, however, the U.S. Open and Amateur and the British Open and Amateur were considered the primary championships. In 1930 Jones managed to win them all, an accomplishment that has come to be known as the Grand Slam. (More colorful accounts of the day noted how Jones had succeeded in conquering the "Impregnable Quadrilateral.")

By 1930, Bobby Jones already had amassed a collection of championships that was unrivaled in the game's history, having won a total of nine Opens and Amateurs in the United States and Great Britain. For the sake of perspective, it is important to note that Jones was in a unique position to establish this record. Of all the monumental players of his time, including Hagen and Sarazen, Jones was the only player eligible to compete in all four championships in a given year. Therefore, in events of any magnitude, he bumped heads with the best professional players only twice a year. Nonetheless, Sarazen and other professionals of the time routinely acknowledged that Jones was the greatest player of his day and in the game's history to that point.

When Jones put the finishing touches on his sweep by winning the U.S. Amateur at Merion Golf Club in Ardmore, Pennsylvania, he did more than simply cap off an amazing year. He once again embedded the game in the national consciousness. In an era known as the Golden Age of American Sports, Jones was the biggest sports star in the country (perhaps the world) with the exception of Babe Ruth. Jones's Grand Slam earned him a ticker-tape parade up Broadway in New York and set the standard against which any golfer must measure a great season.

Having concluded the only perfect season anyone has ever had in golf, Bobby Jones retired immediately saying, in effect, that he had accomplished everything a man could hope to in the game: There were no worlds left to conquer. A serious run at the Slam would not be mounted for twenty-three years, when Ben Hogan won three of the four majors in a single season. Jones's record of thirteen major championships stood until 1973, when it was surpassed by Jack Nicklaus. After retiring, Jones returned to practicing law in Atlanta and, along with stock baron Clifford Roberts, founded the Augusta National Golf Club and, in 1934, the Masters. When Jones passed from the competitive scene, so, too, did the days when amateur golf was considered near the level of professional golf. The public eye turned toward the pros.

Bobby Jones, shown here hitting a tee shot in the first Masters (1934), won golf's only Grand Slam in 1930 as an amateur, and then retired from competitive golf. He built the Augusta National Golf Club and started the Masters Tournament.

The Masters and Other Legends of the Game

Even after his retirement, Jones was still very much on the minds of golfers. His adoring public was able to see him in a series of instructional movie shorts he made for Warner Bros., and he busied himself with the construction of Augusta National Golf Club on a property that had formerly been a nursery. Jones partnered with Dr. Alistair Mackenzie to design the course, which would go on to become one of the most famous in the world as a result of the tournament played there each spring, the Masters. The first Masters Tournament was played in 1934 and was called the Augusta National Invitational Tournament. It was won by Horton Smith. The following year, Sarazen won the event in dramatic fashion, forging a tie with Craig Wood in the fourth round when he holed out his second shot on the par-5 fifteenth hole. Sarazen was nearing the end of his run as one of the world's top players, and when he won the play-off the following day it was the final of his seven major championships (three PGA Championships, two U.S. Opens, one British Open, and one Masters).

With the birth of the Masters and the decline in significance of the U.S. and British Amateur Championships, golf had its modern four major professional championships.

Determining exactly when they became considered the four majors is a dicey proposition. The PGA Championship was started in 1916 as a match-play championship for professionals. Although it was considered a significant event and is legitimately counted among the major championship totals of players such as Hagen and Sarazen, it was not considered a Grand Slam event until the birth of the Masters. The Masters made it an even four major championships for the professionals, and four apparently was the magic number required for a Slam. Its status as Jones's event instantly qualified the Masters as one of the four.

Together, Hagen, Sarazen, and Jones had established the United States as the home of the finest championship golfers in the world. If there was any question as to who would carry that mantle forward, it was answered by three young men, one from the hills of West Virginia and two who had known each other since boyhood in Texas.

Three American Icons of the Game

The first of them to burst upon the scene was the West Virginian, Samuel Jackson Snead, who holds the all-time PGA TOUR record with eighty-one tournament victories and who is credited with 135 wins worldwide. With just about the sweetest swing anyone had ever seen, Snead won the West Virginia PGA in 1936 and picked up five more victories in 1937. When he won the Oakland Open in 1937, the papers played it up big, and golf had a hillbilly star—at least that's how the newsmen wrote it. Snead was managed by the wily promoter Fred Corcoran, who knew a good thing when he saw it. Corcoran determined that the more Snead played up his country boy image, the more the public would adore him. He was right. Snead was still winning titles thirty years after his first, his fluid swing never changing.

The fans could not get enough of the gregarious Slammin' Sammy, as he came to be known. The "Slammin'" part of his nickname was justified, for it can be argued that Snead hit the ball farther than any player ever had up to that point. He was a tremendously strong player and arguably the most natural athlete ever to play the game. The only unfortunate bit of Snead's career was that he never managed to win the U.S. Open, although he came painfully close on a number of occasions. He did win each of the other three major championships, however.

Golf fans could argue forever which of the fifty states has produced the best players, but you can be certain that anyone hailing from Texas has a

Sam Snead in his trademark hat. One of the most naturally gifted players of all time, Snead won his first professional tournament in 1936. In 1979, at age 67, Snead became the first player on Tour to shoot his age or better when he shot rounds of 66 and 67 at the Quad Cities Open.

pretty solid claim that his home state is tops. At the same time Snead began wowing the fans, two strong, silent types emerged from the Lone Star State, Byron Nelson and Ben Hogan. The names Nelson and Hogan would go on to become synonymous with ball-striking excellence. Nelson found his game a little sooner than Hogan, winning the 1937 Masters and the 1939 U.S. Open. (The 1939 Open, on the Spring Mill Course at Philadelphia Country Club, was one Snead let slip away from him. With just one hole to play, Snead needed only to par to win the championship. He mistakenly believed otherwise, and played as if he needed to birdie. Instead he made an eight, and Nelson beat Craig Wood and Denny Shute in an eighteen-hole play-off.)

In the storied history of the PGA TOUR, no one has ever had a season like Byron Nelson had in 1945, and it is hard to imagine that it will ever be matched. In that magical year, Nelson won eleven consecutive events. It seems almost unbelievable that he could do so, but he also won seven more official events that year and one unofficial title, for a total of nineteen tournament victories in a single season. In the course of his career, Nelson would finish first fifty-two times (officially), placing him fifth on the all-time victory list. That he won more than a third of those events in 1945 emphasizes how remarkable that season was for Nelson.

In a game where the consistently fine striking of the ball is considered a hallmark of the greatest players, Nelson's ball-striking ability has been immortalized in a rather intriguing manner: The mechanical device that the United States Golf Association uses to test equipment, a hulking machine that swings a club time and time again to the same impact position, is nicknamed Iron Byron. Nelson made a bit of iron history himself when, in the 1930s, he became the first great player to use steel shafts in his clubs. Until that time, the shafts in clubs had been made of hickory wood.

In the record book, the second name on the list of consecutive victories would be that of Ben Hogan, who won six consecutive tournaments in 1948, just three years after Nelson's streak. All professional golfers strive for perfection of their art, but few would argue that Hogan was driven like none before him. Hogan began his streak by winning the U.S. Open at Riviera in Pacific Palisades, California. Later that year he won the PGA Championship in St. Louis. It was Hogan's second TOUR victory in the PGA (his first had been in 1946). After years of struggling on the TOUR, fighting a sometimes wild hook, Hogan had arrived at the point he had so doggedly sought. And then the roof fell in. In 1949, on a foggy, rainy night, Hogan's car collided with a Greyhound bus. Hogan threw himself across his wife's body to protect her, and by so doing probably saved his own life as well. The car was crushed, and so were Ben Hogan's legs.

Byron Nelson (left) who in 1945 won 11 consecutive tournaments and a total of 18 for the year.

Ben Hogan, a four-time U.S. Open champion, won the British Open in 1953, the only time he ever entered that event. But for a schedule conflict that year (the PGA Championship was played at the same time as the British Open), Hogan might have swept all four majors.

The prognosis for Hogan after the accident was straightforward: He would be very lucky to walk properly again, and there was little chance he would ever play golf. The story of Hogan's comeback is a book unto itself: Ben Hogan walked again, played golf again, and, indeed, played championship golf again—the best golf of his or just about any other golfer's career. Against staggering odds, Hogan returned to the pinnacle of the game at the 1950 U.S. Open. At Merion, on the same course where Jones completed his Grand Slam, Hogan shot 69 in an eighteen-hole play-off to defeat Lloyd Mangrum and George Fazio and captured the Open. Hogan won it again the next year, at Oakland Hills in Michigan, forever labeling that course as one of the fiercest in the world when he said, "I'm glad I finally brought this course—this monster—to its knees." Before winning the 1951 Open, Hogan had also won the Masters.

In 1953, however, Hogan's performance in the major championships was at a level so remarkably high that no player save Jack Nicklaus has ever approached it in a single season. In a stretch that began in April and ended in July, Hogan won the Masters, the U.S. Open, and the British Open, the latter his only appearance in that event. The travel time back to the United States after the British Open at Carnoustie prevented him from playing in the PGA Championship and completing his Grand Slam bid. His level of play that year, however, is the standard against which all TOUR players since have measured their ball striking. In his one visit to Scotland, the natives dubbed him the "Wee Ice Mon," because despite his lack of physical stature, the people in the home of golf had never seen anyone so focused, deliberate and precise in performance. Hogan stands third on the PGA TOUR's all-time victory list with sixty-three.

The King and the Bear

The 1947 U.S. Open at St. Louis Country Club was noteworthy for two reasons. The first is that Sam Snead once again came close to winning, but lost in a play-off to Lew Worsham when Snead three-putted the final hole after a bit of controversy over whose turn it was to putt. Less noticed at the time, but much more significant in the explosion of the game's popularity among the American public, was the fact that portions of the event were broadcast locally on television. It was the start of something big. In 1954 the U.S. Open was broadcast nationally for the first time. That very year there appeared on the golf scene a man who forever altered the public's perception of golf. His name was Arnold Palmer, and in 1954 he won the U.S. Amateur.

It can be safely stated that Palmer is one of the finest championship golfers of all time, but his impact on the game of golf cannot be measured in championships and titles. For the record, he won seven major championships and sixty professional events. He owned the Masters for a seven-year stretch, winning in 1958, 1960, 1962, and 1964. He won the U.S. Open in 1960 by coming from six strokes off the lead at the start of the final round. He breathed fresh life into the British Open, an event that had grown stale and in which the best Americans did not bother to play. In 1960, at St. Andrews, he finished one stroke behind Kel Nagle, but returned the following year to win at Royal Birkdale, and again in 1962 to win at Troon.

From 1958 to 1964 Palmer came to personify golf like no other before or since. He was born to be a television star: strong, handsome, emotional,

A sign of the times: Arnold Palmer took golf to the people, and the people took to him.

Jack Nicklaus walking tall at Pebble Beach in the '72 U.S. Open, which he won. All told, Nicklaus won 18 professional majors and was runner-up in 19 more—a competitive record that set the standard for major championship performance.

a risk-taker, with a magical way of making eye contact with every person. When things went well for him, they went well for all who watched either in person or on television. At the same time that television was establishing itself as an integral part of the American home, golf began to establish itself as part of the American lifestyle, for Palmer was Everyman. Granted, he was Everyman with talent and remarkable putting prowess, but he also offered something that viewers could connect with—he was a sports hero/movie star from a small town (Latrobe, Pennsylvania), the son of a PGA Professional (Deacon Palmer), and he tried so damned hard to win that the outcome did not matter to his legion of fans. "Arnie's Army" they called themselves, with justifiable pride. He was the champion of the people, their King, and fans and peers referred to him as such.

No one ever called Jack Nicklaus "the King." In fact, Nicklaus was the polar opposite of Palmer when he won his first tournament as a pro, the 1961 U.S. Open at Oakmont Country Club, outside of Pittsburgh. Nicklaus, a burly bear of a young man, sporting a crew cut and the same pair of, as he described them, "iridescent green khaki pants" over five rounds, defeated Palmer in a play-off. This turn of events did not sit well with Arnie's Army, but even they could not deny that Nicklaus had a game that was simply awesome.

To almost anyone who watched him play, Nicklaus' talent was just plain scary. Watching him play in the Masters, an aging Bobby Jones was moved to say, "He plays a game with which I am not familiar." No golfer in history had ever combined colossal length and power with accuracy in the manner of Nicklaus. His drives were so powerful that, in one season early in his career, Nicklaus pulverized the face inserts on three separate wooden drivers. This power allowed him to hit his shots high in the air and softly land his iron approach shots on the green, a characteristic that came in handy at the Masters and the U.S. Open. By his own admission, his favorite club was the 1-iron, a straight-faced knife of a club with a head barely larger than the ball itself. To play such a club so effectively required extraordinary precision and attention to detail, two things Nicklaus had in abundance.

His game had one more quality, which has yet to be matched: In the big events, he could elevate his game to the level necessary to win on a consistent basis. He did so a record eighteen times in professional majors (six Masters, five PGA Championships, four U.S. Opens, and three British Opens). When you add his two U.S. Amateur victories, his total of major titles stands at twenty, seven more than the great Jones. Nicklaus played at a championship level longer than any other player, spanning from his first U.S. Amateur victory in 1959 to his sixth Masters title, at age forty-six, in 1986. When he was not winning majors, he was close, finishing runner-up in nineteen of them. Nicklaus stands second on the all-time tournament victory list with seventy, more than a quarter of which were major titles. By the time of his final Masters victory in 1986, Nicklaus was no longer the anti-Palmer. Nicklaus was the beloved Golden Bear, and the fans cheered as vociferously for him as they did for the King.

In the era dominated by Nicklaus and Palmer, roughly the late 1950s through the early 1970s, three other players made huge marks on the game and deserve noting. Gary Player won his first major championship in 1959 at Muirfield and would go on to be one of the four men to capture each of the major professional titles at least once. He won more than 100 titles worldwide and was very much an international player. The month before Player's victory at Muirfield, Billy Casper won the U.S. Open at Winged Foot. Casper would go on to win the 1966 U.S. Open and the 1970 Masters on the way to collecting fifty-one professional victories, placing him sixth on the all-time victory list. Finally, between 1954 and 1965, Australian Peter Thomson won five British Open Championships, a total second to Vardon's six that he shares with J. H. Taylor, James Braid, and Tom Watson.

The Birth of the PGA TOUR

Back in 1932, the men who made a living from golf strictly as players formed a group known as the "Playing Pros" organization. It was the first inkling that there eventually would be a distinction between the PGA of America members who served the public as teachers and product suppliers and those who played the game in national and worldwide competition. Thirty-six years later, in 1968, an autonomous tournament players division broke away from the PGA of America, dubbing itself the Association of Professional Golfers (APG). The following year, Joe Dey, long the top man at the United States Golf Association, became the first commissioner of the APG, which eventually changed its name to the PGA TOUR. Dey was succeeded in his role in 1974 by Deane Beman, a former TOUR player and the man responsible for building the PGA TOUR into what it is today: a nearly year-long calendar of events contested by the world's best players vying for titles and huge amounts of prize money. Beman, in turn, was succeeded by Tim Finchem in 1994. The PGA TOUR does more than entertain golf fans on a weekly basis, however. By 1997 the TOUR had donated more than $400 million to charity, a number not approached by any other professional sports organization.

The tournament that highlights the PGA TOUR schedule each year, The Players Championship, was first played in 1974 at the Atlanta Country

Joe Dey (left) and Deane Beman, the first two commissioners of the PGA TOUR. Dey helped start the organization after years of heading up the USGA. Beman, a long-time TOUR player, grew the TOUR into what it is today.

Club. Befitting of the status the tournament would quickly attain, the event was won by Jack Nicklaus. Originally known as the Tournament Players Championship, the tournament moved to its permanent home at PGA TOUR headquarters in Ponte Vedra Beach, Florida, in 1982, to be contested over the Pete Dye-designed Tournament Players Club at Sawgrass Stadium Course. The field includes no amateurs and no club professionals and is the biggest event of its kind to feature strictly touring professionals. The course itself is historic, being the first in a series of TPCs constructed not only to challenge the world's best but also to provide maximum viewing pleasure for those in attendance. This is accomplished via the "stadium" aspect of the architecture, in which key viewing locations are set on hills overlooking the field of play.

The Arrival of Tom Watson (and Company)

As the years rolled by, Nicklaus, the first Players champion, began to compete in fewer and fewer events each year. The question was asked, "Who will pick up the mantle as the man to beat?" The answer came in the form of a gutsy, scrambling, boy-faced man from Kansas, Tom Watson. Watson proved fearless, his Huck Finn looks belying a warrior's nature. He locked horns with Nicklaus on two memorable occasions and came out the victor. The first was the 1977 British Open at Turnberry, where the two left the field in their dust and fought a pitched battle over the final two rounds. Nicklaus shot 65-66 over those two rounds. Watson triumphed with a pair of 65s. Back across the ocean in 1982, at the far western reaches of the United States, the two faced off again at the U.S. Open at Pebble Beach. The Bear roared to life in the final round, making birdies at five of the first six holes. Undaunted, Watson, playing behind Nicklaus, soldiered on, finally wresting the title from Nicklaus with a historic pitch-in for birdie 2 at Pebble's seventeenth hole.

Like all great players, Watson was a demon with the putter. Watson's putts gathered speed as they bounded across the greens, seemingly going full tilt when they reached the hole, where they would swiftly disappear. He was unfazed by a miss that would go barreling past the hole, for in his heyday no one made more comeback putts than Watson, and he knew he would make them. As of this writing, Watson has racked up thirty-three TOUR victories and is still capable of winning more. A five-time PGA of America Player of the Year (1977–80 and 1982), Watson left his indelible print on history at the British Open. His mind-set and imagination seemed perfectly tailored for the rugged, quirky links over which the Open is played, and he won the championship five times.

Tom Watson, triumphant at the Masters. A six-time player of the year, Watson emerged in the mid-70s to tumble Nicklaus as the king of the majors.

The Explosion of the International Game

Watson, of course, was not the only hugely successful player during this period. In Europe and Australia the level of play had risen, and the major championships and the PGA TOUR itself had developed an international quality. In the mid-1970s Seve Ballesteros of Spain captured two Masters titles and three British Opens; Bernhard Langer of Germany won the Masters twice; from Australia there was Greg Norman, twice British Open champion and once a Players champion and a gigantic presence on the PGA TOUR; from Scotland there was Sandy Lyle (one British Open, one Masters), from England Nick Faldo (three Masters and three British Opens); and from Wales Ian Woosnam (one Masters).

The Ryder Cup, a biennial match-play event that matches a team of America's best pros against a similar team from Europe, initiated the renaissance of the international game. Originally the Ryder Cup featured American players versus players only from Great Britain, and was therefore a rather one-sided affair. From its first official playing, in 1927, through 1979, Great Britain could squeak out only three victories and one tie. In 1981 the format was changed to include all of Europe, and the event and world golf have never been the same. Led by the inspirational captaining of England's Tony Jacklin (1969 British Open and 1970 U.S. Open champion) and the bravado and fiery demeanor of Ballesteros, Europe consistently gained ground on the United States, eventually winning for the first time as Team Europe in 1985. Since the decision to include all of Europe, the European team has held the upper hand, winning four times and halving once.

Phil Mickelson was an integral cog in the Americans' 1995 Ryder Cup victory.

The tremendous amount of interest generated by this international festival raised a question: What about players from Australia, such as Greg Norman and Steve Elkington, and players such as Nick Price of Zimbabwe? In response, in 1994, The President's Cup was established as a biennial competition that pits a team of the best players from the United States against an international team of players not born in Europe. Still young, The President's Cup is certain to evolve into an event with a rich history, and has already become a closely contested battle. The United States won the inaugural event handily in 1994, but managed just a one-point victory (16½ to 15½) in 1996.

In 1978, while the Ryder Cup was still mired in disinterest, a bunch of old pros got together to tee it up at the Onion Creek Golf Course in Austin, Texas. The event was called the Legends of Golf, and it featured such glorious names as Sam Snead, Tommy Bolt, Julius Boros, Gardner Dickinson, and Roberto DeVicenzo. At the time no one quite knew what the first Legends of Golf would lead to. The idea behind it was that these fellows could still play and that a lot of people would enjoy still seeing them play. That year, the seed was planted for the SENIOR PGA TOUR, which officially made its debut with four events in 1980.

What occurred next was indicative of the widespread appeal of golf's champions. As the SENIOR PGA TOUR grew, the nation was experiencing nearly unprecedented economic bliss, which may have accelerated the growth of the SENIOR PGA TOUR. By 1985, the SENIOR PGA TOUR had grown to twenty-seven events worth more than $6 million in prize money. Five years later, the SENIOR PGA TOUR consisted of forty-two events worth more than $18 million in prize money.

Beyond all the numbers, beyond all the growth, the SENIOR PGA TOUR did something that meant more to golf fans than anything else: It gave them a chance to watch their heroes carry on. The truth was that fans were not ready for golf without Palmer, Nicklaus, or Lee Trevino. Or maybe they were ready for it, but if they could still get it, that just made things all the better. It was a smorgasbord of golf—the best of the younger players on the PGA TOUR and the legends on the SENIOR PGA TOUR. It gave fans a chance to appreciate fully a superb player such as Hale Irwin, who won his third U.S. Open at age forty-five and was clearly playing some of the best golf of his life as he approached age fifty, the magic age to compete on the SENIOR PGA TOUR. In 1997, Irwin recorded the single finest year in the history of the SENIOR PGA TOUR, with nine victories (tying Thomson's 1985 record) and an all-tours record $2,343,364 in earnings.

Before Irwin, in the late 1980s, the SENIOR PGA TOUR allowed players such as Orville Moody to compete again. Moody, affectionately known as "the Sarge" from his army days, won the 1969 U.S. Open—the only event he won during his pre-senior playing career—and, for the most part, vanished from the public eye. His fellow TOUR players considered him one of the best ball-strikers of his era, but the Sarge could never break through after that Open victory. The SENIOR PGA TOUR gave him new life. A gregarious sort, popular with the fans, Moody wielded his long putter like a magic wand from 1984 to 1989, during which time he won nine events and was a dominant player on the senior circuit. With his daughter Michelle caddying for him, Moody was a fan favorite.

In the end, the SENIOR PGA TOUR gave fans the chance to relive past glories. Arnold Palmer won again. Jack Nicklaus and Lee Trevino fought it out down the stretch again. And wasn't it grand, all of it? To watch Trevino work the ball like no other—Trevino, who won the 1968 and 1971 U.S. Open, two British Opens (1971, 1972), and two PGA Championships (1974, 1984). To watch Nicklaus stalk the landscape, the Bear in

Lee Trevino, the man with an ungainly swing and uncanny knack for winning. Trevino raised shotmaking to an art form.

search of a title. To watch Raymond Floyd, a masterful player, hard-nosed competitor—perhaps the greatest chipper ever—take his funky swing and big-time game (he won the 1986 U.S. Open, 1969 and 1982 PGA Championships and the 1976 Masters) and take on all comers. To drink in the precision of Irwin's long irons and fairway woods, for there was never anyone better than Irwin with these clubs. And it gives the fan hope as the years roll by. If you grew up watching Johnny Miller scorch the desert courses in the early 1970s, or shoot 63 to win the U.S. Open in 1973; if you watched Watson at his peak; or the gritty Larry Nelson, or the quirky Hubert Green—if you delighted in them when they were your age, they will always be your age, and the SENIOR PGA TOUR makes certain you can watch them play.

Tiger Woods (left) receives the green jacket emblematic of a Masters victory. Woods won the event in 1997, his first year on Tour. Making the presentation is Nick Faldo of England, three times the Masters and British Open champion.

Into the Future

The brevity of this history makes going into the details of every player and listing the name of every great champion an impossibility. The list of champions who have played and won the admiration of the people is endless: Lee Trevino, Raymond Floyd, Johnny Miller, Paul Azinger, Lanny Wadkins, Ben Crenshaw, Tom Kite, Fred Couples, Greg Norman, Mark O'Meara, Davis Love III—it could go on for hundreds of pages. These names have been joined in more recent years by players such as Tiger Woods, who captured the attention of the world with his runaway victory at the 1997 Masters, and Justin Leonard, who won the 1997 British Open. Phil Mickelson and David Duval are yet two more of the newest generation who will lead the PGA TOUR into the next century. How history will treat the latest wave of golf talent remains to be seen. One thing is certain: Watching their progress over the years will be a lot of fun.

The hunter.

The hunted.

2

What's in *Your Bag?*

Clubs are to the golfer what paintbrushes are to an artist: The golfer uses them to transmit his thoughts and actions to the ball. In this metaphor, of course, the ball is the canvas. Just as an artist is finicky about brushes, using different ones to achieve various results, so should the golfer be discerning in the selection of clubs. This chapter will provide some guidance, clear up confusion, and give you a plan for putting together the set of equipment that is best for you. It is vital to understand your equipment before you play a shot, because aiming the club is an integral part of that preparation.

The three basic types of clubs are woods, irons, and putters. The word "basic" is a bit misleading because each club can have a wide array of uses: You can putt with a wood, play shots off the green with a putter, and use irons from the tee on long holes to play for accuracy. Only your imagination limits what you can do with any club in your bag. It is helpful, however, to understand the purpose behind the design of each club so you can realize the full potential of each club.

Lee Janzen consults his caddy and his yardage book.

Club Construction

All three types of clubs have three parts: the *clubhead*, the *shaft*, and the *grip*. The clubhead is the part that comes in contact with the ball, the shaft is the "stick" that connects the clubhead with your hands; and the grip is the rubber or leather "glove" that covers the top of the shaft, and around which you place your hands. The clubhead is glued to the shaft with epoxy, and the grip is attached to the shaft with double-sided tape and solvent. The solvent and tape meld together to keep the grip attached to the shaft. Unless you are familiar with the various areas of the clubhead, it is difficult to aim the club when you prepare to play a shot, and getting yourself and the club properly aimed at your target is more than half the battle in golf.

The area that makes contact with the ball is the *clubface*, and the area of the club that rests on the ground as you prepare to play a shot is known as the sole. The point at which these two areas meet—at the very bottom of the clubface—is known as the *lead edge* (sometimes referred to as the leading edge) of the club. Throughout this book are many references to the lead edge of the club, because the lead edge is used as your aiming reference. Even though it might not always appear to be a perfectly straight line, always think of the lead edge as a straight line.

The other important areas of the clubhead are all on the clubface. The *toe* is the area of the clubface farthest from the point where the shaft joins the clubhead. The *heel* is the part of the clubface closest to the point where the shaft joins the clubhead. The *sweet spot* is the center of the clubface, ideally the place where you want to contact the ball (with the exception of some rarely used specialty shots).

The modern golf club comes in all shapes and sizes. From top to bottom: A persimmon driver with a graphite shaft; a metal driver with a steel shaft; a perimeter-weighted iron with a steel shaft; a perimeter-weighted iron with a graphite shaft; two types of putters, the mallet and the blade.

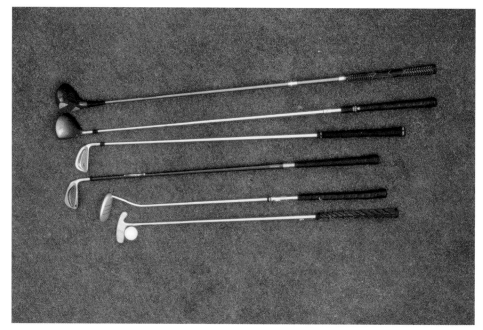

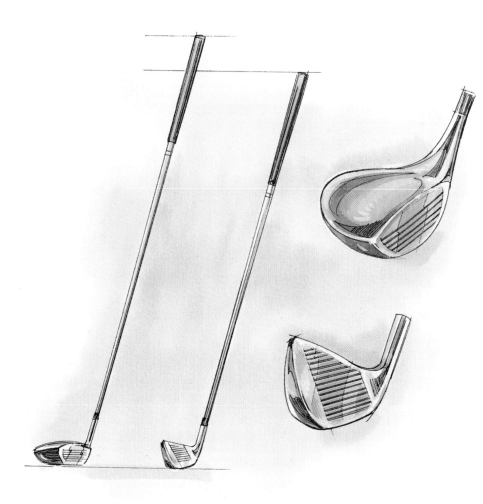

As a set of golf clubs progresses from driver down through the irons, each club is shorter than the previous one. The shorter the club, the easier it is to control the ball. Modern clubhead designs (at right in the illustration) give more favorable results on off-center hits than clubs did for the first few hundred years the game was played.

Shafts

The shafts of your clubs have properties that must be coordinated with your swing to achieve maximum performance. Whether they be steel, graphite, titanium, or some other substance, shafts all bend and twist when you swing. How much they bend and twist depends on how fast they are moving and the properties of the particular shaft. How do you make sure the shafts in your clubs are a good match with your swing? That is, how can you be certain that the shafts are not too resistant to bending (too stiff) or that they do not allow too much bending (too weak)? This is a crucial and frequently overlooked aspect of putting together a set of clubs that is right for you. You do not want a shaft that does not flex at all, but you want to make sure that the shaft has the right amount of flex.

Jim Gallagher   *Experiment with new equipment before buying it.*

Ranked fourteenth in driving distance in 1995, with an average drive of 275.4 yards.

"Often the everyday golfer makes the decision to buy a new club without ever hitting a putt or a shot with it. They give the thing a few waggles and go buy the club. I know that I cannot tell anything by simply waggling the club a few times. Now I realize that most everyday players don't have the opportunity that we do to practice and try out new equipment. On TOUR, every time you turn around on the practice tee, someone wants you to try a new club. If you are thinking of buying a new club, see if your PGA professional has a demo you can try, because it's really important to hit balls with a club so you know how it will perform before you make that big purchase. If you find a club you really like and it does not match your set, and you can afford it, go ahead and get it. I'm not talking about irons, but wedges and putters and woods. No matter how much the equipment companies say they can match everything, they cannot, and it's up to you to find the clubs that work best for you.

"Another big concern for the everyday player is what type of ball to use. A better player is going to be able to play a balata ball. They can spin it better and have better feel around the greens. A lot of amateurs play a real hard ball and wonder why they can't spin it. It's because of the ball. But you might get more distance out of that type of ball, so you have to decide if you want to sacrifice maximum distance for maximum spin. Most folks ought to go with the tougher cover—it's certainly a lot cheaper game to play that way!"

How much flex you need depends on how fast you get the club moving on a typical swing. This factor is typically referred to as *clubhead speed*. Figuring out your clubhead speed has been made easier by computer devices that monitor the actual speed of the club. Still, there is no exact science to determine which shaft properties are best for you. There are subtleties involved, and more important, shafts vary from manufacturer to manufacturer. In other words, what company A considers a stiff shaft will differ from the stiff shaft manufactured by company B.

The hosel is the point where the shaft and the clubhead are joined. The lead tape that has been added to the back of the clubhead adds to the overall weight of the club.

Many golfers feel that they should play the stiffest shaft they can find because they hear or assume that TOUR players use extra-stiff shafts. This faulty logic will hurt your game. The smartest thing you can do is to ask a PGA professional to assess your swing and your game and to recommend the shaft flex you should be using. The professional will probably be aware of the various subtleties among the various shafts on the market at any given time.

Putting the Clubhead and the Shaft Together

Almost all modern clubhead designs for irons and woods feature *perimeter weighting*, which means that the weight of the club is evenly distributed around the outer edges of the clubhead. This provides a more forgiving club—that is, it widens the margin of error in striking the ball on the clubface. Does this mean that you can buy a better golf game? Not exactly, because perimeter weighting really does not improve good shots that much. A shot struck in the center of the clubface with a quality forged iron manufactured in the 1960s would be just as good as a shot struck in the center of the clubface with a modern club. The big difference is in shots that are struck off center.

In older club designs, the majority of a club's weight lay behind the center of the clubface, and, as a result, striking the ball off center caused it to fly away from the club weakly and often dramatically off target. Perimeter weighting allows off-center hits to fly with much more force and reduces somewhat the off-line flight. In golf parlance, it increases your chances of getting away with a less than perfect swing and keeping the ball in play. As you might imagine, this can greatly reduce the frustration level, making the game a much more pleasant experience for the everyday golfer.

Everyday golfers benefit from the combination of metal woods and graphite shafts. The lighter shaft and lighter clubhead allow you to pick up a little more clubhead speed without swinging harder. This can help you pick up a few more yards on shots in which distance is a primary consideration. The same can be said of graphite shafts paired with modern iron clubhead designs, but in most cases maximum distance is not a primary concern with a shot played with an iron. Some people feel that steel shafts have a more consistent feel from club to club, which is important with your irons.

For the everyday golfer, economics play a role as well. Graphite and other nonsteel shafts are more expensive than steel. Although it might make sense to splurge on graphite for a driver and maybe a 3-wood, it can be very costly to outfit an entire set of irons with graphite shafts. For golfers who suffer from arthritis or similar discomforts in the hands and arms, however, graphite definitely helps soften the rattling effect of off-center hits.

Once you have determined the type of clubhead and shaft you prefer, you should consider an often overlooked but important element of your club's makeup, the *lie angle.* When the sole of the club is resting flat on the ground, the angle at which the shaft protrudes from the clubhead is the lie angle. The biggest factor in determining the proper lie angle for your clubs is your height and the length of your arms. Once again, your best bet is to have a PGA professional help you determine the best lie angle.

Pulling shots on a straight line left of your target—they don't hook, they fly straight—may indicate that the lie of your clubs is too upright, or too steep; and pushing shots on a straight line to the right of your target may indicate a lie angle that is too flat, or not steep enough for you. If you have either of these problems, visit a PGA professional, who will put your clubs on a loft-and-lie measuring device and make a recommendation to you.

Finding a Comfortable Grip

Along with the clubhead and the shaft, the third element that completes the club is the *grip.* (The word "grip" has two meanings in golf. It refers to the rubber or leather tube that slips over the end of the shaft of the club, and it also refers to the placement of your hands on the club.) Grips come in various styles and are made of rubber or leather. Most new clubs come with rubber grips. The style of grip you use is purely a personal preference. If you are playing with secondhand clubs, however, the size of the grip does matter. Grips come in various sizes, and players often put extra layers of tape under a grip to make it thicker.

A simple test can determine whether the grip is the right size for you: If the tips of your fingers just reach the palms of your hands when you hold the club, the grip is the right size. If your fingers do not reach your palms, the grip is too big and you will probably put too much pressure on the club, achieving poor results. If the club feels thin in your hand, the grip is probably too small; this will result in overactive hands during your swing, which also can lead to problems.

Inside the Ropes

Loren Roberts   *Building up grips can help stop hooking.*

Ranked seventh in scoring average in 1994 (69.61) and twelfth in 1997 (69.88).

"I've never built my grips up with extra layers of tape underneath the grip, but it does make your grips fatter— bigger around in diameter. You might do this if you have big hands or if you want to lessen the effects of your hands during the swing. The fatter the grips, the slower your hands are going to turn over, so if you have problems hooking the ball, you might want to consider bulking up your grips. You probably won't hook the ball quite as badly."

Which Clubs to Carry

The Rules of Golf allow you to carry fourteen clubs in your bag during a round. There is no single correct method of selecting which clubs to carry. Each player has different needs, and your clubs should complement your strengths as a player and help you cover your weak points as well.

Start considering which fourteen clubs you carry by first acknowledging that every golfer should carry a putter and a sand wedge. The reasons why you have a putter are obvious, and the reason why you must carry a sand wedge *should* be obvious: Although its first function is extracting balls from the sand, a sand wedge is a valuable tool in all areas of the short game. Once you have these two clubs (discussed below), twelve clubs remain to make up the rest of the set.

David Edwards *When selecting clubs, use your playing experience.*

Tied for thirtieth in scoring average in 1993 (70.32) and seventh in driving accuracy in 1997.

"I'm not sure if I can fully explain why I would choose to add a new club to my set. It's really just experience and results. Anyone who has played for any length of time has hit enough shots to know the feel that's comfortable. It's like when I go skiing every year. You get to the resort, and they tell you to try out all the new demo skis. I do, and I get down the mountain okay, but I can't really tell the difference in most of them. For most people, it's probably the same with golf equipment. Unless you play practically every day, you are not going to notice a lot of small differences from club to club. It might sound like a cliché, but it's really a matter of personal preference and experience—as is almost everything else in golf."

In selecting the remaining twelve clubs, you are striving for a combination that gives you range from various distances and, more important, control over the direction of the shots. Start with the distance clubs, the woods and long irons.

The king of all distance clubs is the driver. The everyday golfer most often uses a driver to put the ball in play. A TOUR player may or may not use a driver to put the ball in play, depending on the characteristics of the course and of the individual holes. Suffice it to say that TOUR players do not automatically reach for the driver on every par-4 and par-5 hole. Later chapters discuss strategy and club selection for tee shots.

The marketing efforts of golf equipment manufacturers consistently try to make a connection between the equipment used by TOUR players and their performance. Because PGA TOUR players are the best in the world and the everyday golfer wants to play his or her best, common sense suggests that everyday players should use the same equipment as the TOUR players. What does this mean to you? You must be careful about how you interpret the messages used in an attempt to sell you golf clubs. First, there is nothing disingenuous about the basic message delivered to you by reputable equipment manufacturers. They all make superb equipment, all of which is worthy of your consideration. Nonetheless, you cannot take a TOUR player's endorsement of a golf club to mean that you should play the same club with the same specifications. This is truer for a driver than for any other piece of equipment. To explain why requires some digression.

Club Loft

As advancements were made in equipment design, golfers became more and more aware of the different aspects of clubs. One example of this is the club specification known as *loft*, which describes the angle at which the clubface leans away from the target. Loft is the property of the club that controls how high the ball flies in the air. Before the popularization of metal woods, all golfers knew that clubfaces of their

woods had loft, but in general they did not know how much loft. In other words, a driver was a driver, and you found one you could hit well and that was that. As metal woods gained in popularity, manufacturers began marketing the clubs based on various factors including loft. Because TOUR players can effectively play clubs with low lofts (because of their swing mechanics and the tremendous clubhead speeds they generate), it became widely known that TOUR players favored drivers with a single digit's worth of loft—that is, drivers with as little as seven, eight, or nine degrees of loft. Sure enough, clubs with single-digit lofts started to become popular among everyday golfers, and now the most common mistake in selecting a driver is choosing one without enough loft.

On the surface, having a minimal amount of loft on your driver might make sense. Not only do TOUR players use drivers with low lofts, but also it seems logical that less loft means you would hit the ball farther. In fact, for the everyday golfer, using a driver with less than twelve degrees of loft makes very little sense indeed. First, consider that TOUR players use low-lofted drivers because they can do so effectively. Their talent, endless hours of practice, and tremendous clubhead speed allow them to handle easily all low-lofted clubs.

The second reason—less loft means longer shots—is not necessarily true of the everyday golfer. Using a driver of minimal loft does not keep the ball in the air long enough to achieve any substantial distance. More important, the less loft a club has, the more likely you are to hit it off line. In general, an everyday golfer consistently hits short irons straighter than a

Metal woods come in a great variety of lofts, which allow the everyday player to take the difficult-to-hit long irons out the bag if he so chooses. From left to right: driver, 2-wood, 3-wood, 4-wood, 5-wood, and 7-wood.

driver because of the loft of the club. The more loft on the club, the more likely you are to hit a shot with backspin and the less likely you are to hit a shot with sidespin. The reverse is also true: The less loft on the club, the more likely you are to hit a shot with sidespin—that is, a hook or a slice. This effect is magnified with each degree of loft you take off a club.

When you are considering making a driver part of your set, remember that although the distance you can hit it is an important factor, you should be able to hit it consistently on target as well. (Another reason why you can consistently hit short irons straight is that the shafts are shorter, and the resulting shorter swing is easier to control. Keep this in mind when consider-

Inside the Ropes

Fuzzy Zoeller *Make sure your clubs fit you.*

The 1984 U.S. Open Champion, ranked first in greens-in-regulation on the PGA TOUR in 1993 and second in 1996.

"The number one equipment problem for everyday golfers is that they go into a shop, buy a set of clubs off the rack, and start playing with them. The lie of that club has a lot to do with how the ball performs. That's why on TOUR we're always

tweaking our clubs—we bend them flatter or more upright depending on what we need, how we swing, and how that clubface hits the turf. In this day and age, with the preponderance of club repair places and PGA professionals who can help you out, it is most wise to make sure your clubs fit you no matter what kind of game you play."

ing any driver with an extra-long shaft. The longer the shaft, the harder the club is to control.)

Your final decision should be based on a balance between distance and control. Only a small percentage of golfers can handle a driver with single-digit loft. Use a metal driver that gives you the most distance you can get without losing control over the majority of your shots. To play it safe, you should probably not use less than ten-and-a-half degrees of loft. Drives that travel 230 yards and straight are better than drives that fly 260 yards and thirty yards off line.

The Other Long Clubs

As subsequent chapters show, how you put together the rest of the long clubs in your bag (other than your driver) is one way of making the game a lot easier to play. The design of modern fairway woods makes them incredibly easy to hit—much more so than long irons. The trade-off involving the many choices in fairway woods is that the more woods you carry, the fewer irons you can carry.

It is, of course, a personal choice, but a 3-wood offers so many advantages that it is almost silly not to carry one. Modern designs have made it easier to get a 3-wood off the ground, and its versatility on tee shots is irreplaceable. More detail is given in subsequent chapters, but when you use the 3-wood as a driving club, the ball flies only slightly shorter than it would with a driver (somewhere between eight and ten yards); the ball flies straighter than it does with a driver; and, because a 3-wood has more loft and a shorter shaft, the ball comes into the ground at a steeper angle and does not run along the ground as far as a ball struck with a driver. All of this means that the 3-wood gives you far greater control than the driver without sacrificing distance. This is also why nearly every TOUR player carries a 3-wood. When the premium is on accuracy, the 3-wood is frequently the club you should be using from the tee.

The recommendation here is to play a metal 3-wood. It is more forgiving, and the design helps get the ball airborne with a minimal amount of effort—you won't have to try to lift the ball into the air. In addition, modern sole plate designs have made these clubs playable from lies that a generation ago would have allowed only the most expert players to use a wood.

The availability of so many choices in the fairway-wood category has made it possible for the everyday player to make up a set without using any long irons at all. You need to know your own game to decide where to draw the line: A particular long iron may allow you to carry the ball a greater distance than with a fairway wood. However, the modern 4-wood, 5-wood, and 7-wood are such terrific clubs—effective from all but the worst lies in the rough—that you should carry as many of them as you want in your bag.

Fairway Wood or Long Iron?

When choosing between fairway woods and long irons, you need to consider several questions. How far does the ball carry with a particular wood and the comparable iron? Which one is easier to hit? Which one offers more versatility in terms of lies you can play it from? Where you play most of your golf, is it an advantage to hit the ball high and have it stop (favoring the woods) or low and have it run (favoring the irons)?

You must hit various woods and irons on the practice range to arrive at an understanding of how far you hit each club and how it reacts once it is on the ground. Then the decision comes down to the needs of your particular game. This area of your set—the woods and long irons-gives you the most choices, but you will have to give up one or two of the clubs if you decide to carry more than two wedges.

Scoring Clubs

The middle and short irons and the putter are clubs that you should have tremendous control over—you should know exactly how far you are going to hit the ball when you have one in your hand. With the long clubs, you can only estimate how far you are going to hit the ball because there is more room for error, and more things happen to the ball when it hits the ground.

A ball played with a fairway wood (red line) will typically carry farther and fly higher than a shot played with the comparable long iron (orange line).

Nearly every golfer carries 5-, 6-, 7-, 8-, and 9-irons, and a pitching wedge. (With a driver, 3-wood, sand wedge, and putter, this brings the total number in the bag to ten clubs. The four remaining open spots in the set can be filled with any combination of fairway woods, long irons, and wedges.) With these irons, you have clubs over which you should have great control and consistency in terms of both accuracy and distance. Any irons you carry, up to and including the pitching wedge, should produce shots of a consistent distance increase/decrease from club to club. In other words, if you hit your 7-iron 150 yards, you should hit your 8-iron 140 yards, your 9-iron 130 yards, etc. The pattern here is 10 yards of variance from club to club on a full swing. (This does not mean that you *should* hit your 7-iron 150 yards. You may hit it 160 yards, 165 yards, or 120 yards, but the *spread* of distance from club to club should be consistent.) This assumes that from your lowest numbered iron you have no gaps until you reach the sand wedge in your set.

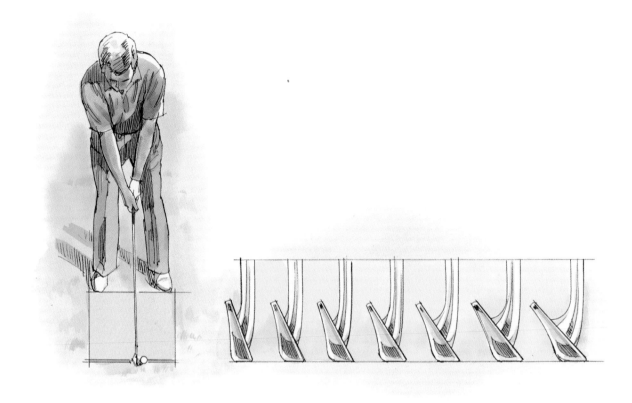

In a matching set of irons, each club has more loft than the one preceding it (from left to right). Ideally, there should be an 8–10 yard distance between each club. If you hit your 7-iron 150 yards, then your 8-iron should travel 140 yards, and so on. From left to right: 3-iron (23 degrees), 4-iron (26 degrees), 5-iron (30 degrees), 6-iron (34 degrees), 7-iron (38 degrees), 8-iron (42 degrees), and 9-iron (46 degrees).

Achieving this consistency in yardage differential from club to club is fairly simple if you play with irons that are all the same model from the same manufacturer. It is the easiest way to be certain of the consistency of the shafts and the *gapping* of the lofts of your irons. Most major club manufacturers gap their irons ten yards from club to club. Some golfers may produce a nine- or eight-yard difference from club to club, but it does not really matter as long as the gap is consistent from club to club. If you happen to have a mixed set of irons and are not in a position to buy new clubs (or if you just happen to like them), or if your irons are old and have been banged around a lot, take them to a PGA professional to have the loft and lie measured on each club to find out whether they are consistent from club to club. If they are not, the pro may be able to make the necessary adjustments on the spot.

Wedges

No that long ago, "wedges" meant the pitching wedge and the sand wedge. Today, however, that notion has gone the way of persimmon woods, and the idea of having only two wedge options is outmoded. The reasons for this are twofold. First, the everyday golfer has trouble getting the ball up in the air quickly (if need be), and by producing clubs with more loft on them than traditional sand wedges (fifty-six degrees), manufacturers have helped golfers more readily accomplish short, lofted shots. Second, many golfers, including TOUR players, find that shots played with a full swing are easier to execute than shots requiring a partial swing. Adding loft to wedges allows shorter shots to be played with fuller swings.

Raymond Floyd prepares to play a chip shot. Note the steel shaft in Floyd's iron. Most top level players still use steel shafts in their irons.

Fred Funk   *The bounce on the wedge helps make it a keeper.*

In 1995 got up and down from greenside bunkers 60.6 percent of the time, tying him for thirtieth on TOUR.

"I use a sixty-degree wedge a lot. Around the greens it's a great trouble club. I use it out of bunkers and deep rough around the greens. Anytime you have a flop shot, you want a lot of loft. The thing with the wedge is you want it to be versatile—I'm looking for a wedge that does not have too much bounce, so I can hit it from the fairway, but one without any bounce would be no good from the rough or the sand. So it's a combination club for me."

The availability of wedges with sixty degrees of loft (commonly referred to as lob wedges or L wedges), and some as high as sixty-four degrees of loft, is not just a trend among everyday players. Many TOUR players carry more lofted wedges to play lofted shots around the greens. Another recent trend favors *gap* wedges that fill the distance gap between pitching wedges and traditional sand wedges. It is not uncommon for a TOUR player to carry three (or even four) wedges, depending on the course he is playing.

Highly-lofted wedges (sixty degrees or more) are tremendously useful if you struggle with your short game. If you have trouble getting the ball up in the air quickly for shots around the green, you should at least consider making an L wedge part of your arsenal. (Nearly any shot played with an L wedge can be made with a traditional sand wedge, but an L wedge makes the job easier, because playing very high, very short shots with a sand wedge requires adjustments and a tremendous amount of skill and touch.)

The pitching wedge in your set is really just a "10-iron." In other words, it should, with a full swing, produce shots of about ten yards less than your 9-iron. In fact, in the past, it was not uncommon for this club to be stamped with the numeral "10" rather than the now universal "PW." The pitching wedge is very versatile, and you definitely should have it in your bag. It is not only for full shots. Sometimes around the green the bulky bottom of sand wedges and other loftier wedges is a hindrance, and your pitching wedge can help in these situations.

Of all the wedge options, the traditional sand wedge, with fifty-five or fifty-six degrees of loft, is still an invaluable weapon. First, it is not only for shots out of the sand. With a full swing, it can be used to produce approach shots that land softly on the green. Around the green it can be used to play any number of shots. With the exception of extraordinary conditions it is *the* club of choice from the sand. When you play a shot from the sand, you want the club to enter the sand, but you do not want the club to get stuck in the sand or to go in too deep. The sand wedge is designed to deflect upward once it enters the sand. In short, this allows you to hit the proper amount of sand

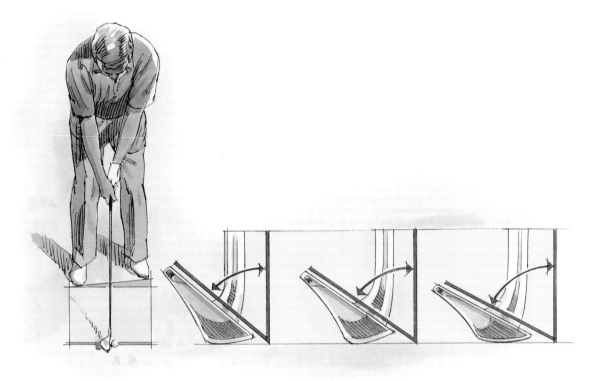

From left to right, a pitching wedge, sand wedge and lob (or L) wedge. Each serves a different purpose. The 52 degree pitching wedge is designed to play shots from the turf inside of 9-iron range. The 56 degree sand wedge is designed specifically for sand shots, but can be used for other shots. The 60 degree L-wedge is designed for short, high pitch shots.

without hitting too much. Higher-lofted wedges also have these properties, but you do not always want to play the highest possible shot out of the sand. Usually you want the ball to roll at least a little bit, and the traditional sand wedge strikes the best balance between height and distance for playing out of the sand.

Inside the Ropes

Dave Eichelberger   *Be patient with the new clubs in your set.*

Four-time winner on the PGA TOUR and owner of two victories on the SENIOR PGA TOUR.

"Right now I'm in transition as far as my set makeup goes. I've just added a third wedge, an L wedge. I've been using it for almost a year now, and I'm still trying to get familiar with it. I added it to my set because I didn't have any use for my 1-iron anymore, and with my shots around the green I was having a hard time making the ball stop. My sand wedge was about fifty-five or fifty-six degrees, so I decided to experiment

with a club that was about sixty degrees. But even after all of these months, it's still a work in progress. I haven't quite mastered the club yet. At times I hit the ball too far, or chili-dip it, or whatever. I'm still learning to play with it, and I think that's a big key for the everyday player. If you're introducing a new club into your set, don't expect it to be a miracle club the first time out. You've got to give yourself some time to get acquainted with its quirks."

Putters

Putters are the most diverse clubs in terms of design. They come in various shapes and sizes, and unlike woods and irons, the clubhead sometimes connects with the shaft at points other than the heel section of the clubhead. Just as with woods and irons, there are putter designs that distribute the weight around the edges of the clubhead and designs that distribute the weight in various other ways. Although there are clear-cut recommendations for the type of wood and iron you should play, that is not true for putters. There are too many variables in the design of putters, and too many effective personalizations you can add to a putting stroke for any general recommendation to be made.

The type of putter you use is predicated on the type of stance and stroke that feels comfortable to you. Do not let your putter dictate the stance you take. You should determine what stance and body position feels best for you and then find a club that fits that posture. The mechanics of putting are not so rigid that they eliminate room for you to customize your putting stroke. As a result this is the one area of the game where

Lee Janzen lines up a putt. Note the insert in the face of his putter, a technological development used by many TOUR players who want a softer feel at impact.

Inside the Ropes

Jim McGovern   *With putters and wedges, if it looks and feels right, it probably is right.*

An eight-year veteran of the PGA TOUR and winner of the 1993 Shell Houston Open.

"The putter I'm using now has felt good from the moment I first grabbed it. I'm comfortable with it—I've made more than a few putts with it. Sometimes you just look at a putter, and it doesn't look right or feel right. If that's the case, you shouldn't try to force it. There's no question that the aesthetics of the club play a big part in whether you're comfortable with it. The same is true for wedges. I don't make many changes in my clubs, but if it looks great and feels great, I'll try it out."

Rocco Mediate *A long putter helped me overcome a bad back.*

A TOUR veteran and one of the few players to successfully use the long putter. He finished twenty-eighth in scoring average in 1996 (70.45).

"SENIOR PGA TOUR player Jim Ferree helped me start using a long putter when I had a bad back. At the time I couldn't practice my putting because of my back, and I was frustrated because putting is so important to our games out here [on TOUR]. I don't have the bad back anymore, but I still use the long putter because I feel like I can practice putting forever, and my back never gets tired or sore. I don't quite know how to explain it, but I feel like I have an advantage over everyone else out here. Whether I actually do or not is *another story! It does take a few weeks of time and effort to get used to the long putter, but the stroke itself just seems more efficient. I use a shoulder motion just like you would with a regular putter; I just try to lessen the importance of my hands in the stroke. I can feel them, but I don't feel like they have total control over the club. Some guys anchor the club against their chest with the left hand and use the right arm as a sort of piston back and forth. That works for some guys, but that's not what I do. If a typical golfer wanted to try it, my advice is to do what I did—just start doing it and kind of teach yourself along the way."*

whatever feels right probably is right. You should take advantage of this by finding a putter that fits your setup and stroke.

The basic design elements you need to consider are a putter's weighting and the point at which the shaft joins the clubhead. The weight distribution on the clubhead of a putter is not quite so crucial as that of the other clubs. Because of the shorter, more controlled stroke used in putting, you have a much higher probability of making contact somewhere near the center of the clubface. However, perimeter-weighted designs compensate for any hiccups in a given stroke that might cause a wildly off-center hit and also offer some other elements of versatility.

The point at which the clubhead and the shaft are joined has some effect on the movement of the clubhead during the stroke. When the shaft is connected to the club at the rear of the club (commonly referred to as a heel-shafted putter), it creates a swinging-gate effect. In other words, the shaft acts as a sort of hinge and the clubhead swings—very slightly—around it. When the shaft of the putter joins the clubhead somewhere near the center (a center-shafted putter), the putter is designed to move on more of a "straight back/straight through" line. Which shaft-to-clubhead connection you use depends on your stroke and setup.

In the past ten years or so, the long putter has been introduced into the game. The long putter is gripped with the hands far apart, the left hand anchored near the chest, and the right hand pulling the club back and pushing it through down around waist level. There are also putters of an in-between length, splitting the distance between the standard-length putters (thirty-five inches or so) and the chest-high putters. Both types of long putters have proved popular on the SENIOR PGA TOUR, and a few PGA TOUR players use them as well. In this chapter, PGA TOUR player Rocco Mediate explains why he switched to a long putter.

Offsets and Inserts

Because there are very few PGA TOUR players and approximately 25 million everyday golfers in the United States, the goal of manufacturers is to design clubs that will benefit the everyday player. These designs may be used by TOUR players, but the impact they have on players of TOUR level is minor compared to the impact they can have on *your* game.

One new club design method is offset woods, irons, and putters. An offset design places the shaft and, subsequently, your hands, in front of the lead edge of the clubface without your having to think about it. This is especially effective with putters, where you almost always want your hands to be out in front of the clubhead.

Offset woods and irons produce an effect that makes the club appear to be somewhat closed, which is a nice psychological effect for players who suffer from a chronic slice. Whether it actually helps can be determined only by the individual player. You can decide what works for you by "test driving" clubs that your local professional may have available.

Another popular trend has been the addition of inserts to the faces of putters. Made of various soft-feeling materials, these inserts create a softer feel at impact with the ball. Do they help your game? Like every other equipment development, it depends on your game and your sense of feel, and you should try various samples to see how they work. A lot of players were great putters before inserts came along, and a lot of great putters currently use clubs with inserts. Only you can decide.

Golf Balls

In the mind of the everyday golfer, equipment means clubs and balls. Just as marketing messages about clubs flood magazines and televised TOUR events, so does advertising about golf balls. Some balls are claimed to travel great distances; others are supposed to fly straighter; and others are touted as having a tremendous amount of spin. The point is not whether all of these claims are valid. As with clubs, a ball from a reputable manufacturer is a quality golf ball. You must consider what type of ball is best for your game.

There are two basic ball types. One type is designed for maximum distance with every club in the bag. This type of ball used to be referred to as a hard ball because it lacked feel or a two-piece ball because it consisted of two parts, a solid rubber core and the cover. The cover on a two-piece ball typically resisted damage when struck with the lead edge of an iron on a misplayed shot.

The second ball type was referred to as a soft ball because it offered better clubface-to-ball feel; a balata because that was the name of the material used to make the cover; and a three-piece because it consisted of a small rubber ball, rubber bands, and a cover.

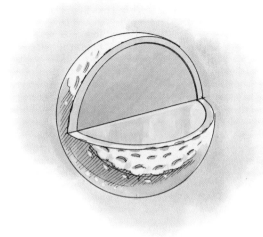

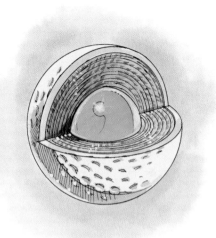

Left: A basic illustration of a two-piece ball. This type of ball was originally designed for distance and endurance, but in recent years the amount of spin on two-piece balls has been improved. Right: A three-piece ball. The middle layer of tightly wound rubber bands provides advanced players with more control of the ball around the greens.

Traditionally this type of ball was very susceptible to damage when hit with the lead edge of the club. A term not used much anymore, but once very popular, was "smile," because hitting a three-piece ball with the lead edge of an iron would create a smile-shaped crease in the ball cover.

Distance vs. Spin

Today the two types of ball have merged, and balls can be roughly categorized as distance balls and spin balls. Which type you use depends on your game, but both types share characteristics, and the old names no longer apply.

What was once considered a hard ball—a ball without much spin that ran a lot when it hit the ground, but was hard to stop on the green—is now in many cases covered with a material that allows it to spin and stop on the green. And it still offers the resistance to damage it always did.

The former soft ball is still soft, and still produces great spin for control on approach shots, but is now covered with synthetic balata, making it much more resistant to damage than the older balls.

Which type of ball you play depends on personal preference and the type of performance you want from your ball. If you want maximum spin on the ball on approach shots, a balata ball is probably still your best bet. But a lot of spin may not be advantageous—you may want a ball that rolls as far as possible. On the other hand, the current models of the two-piece ball spin enough to give you sufficient control on approaches and short shots around the green. What it all comes down to is what type of feel you prefer at impact. Balata balls still offer the softest feel you can get. The dis-

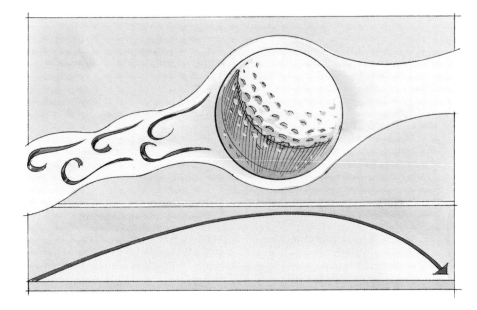

tance balls sacrifice a little bit of feel, but modern manufacturing techniques make the differences between the two types of balls very slight. Finally, it all comes down to what feels best to you.

Ten Equipment Blunders That Can Cost You Strokes

Simply having the right clubs and balls does not free you from equipment problems. Once you have equipment, you need to take care of it from season to season and from round to round. Here are the ten most common equipment failures that plague the everyday golfer:

1. Worn-out grips. Some players buy clubs and leave the same grips on for years at a time without ever cleaning or changing them. The grips are not intended to last a lifetime. In fact, they do not last long at all, depending on how often you play. Always clean your grips with soap and water and a dry towel after every round (or before the next one you play). This prevents gooey buildup that becomes slick and hardens after a few weeks. Whenever your grips feel hard and slick (and they are not wet), it is time for new ones. You also need new grips if you feel you have to squeeze the club very tightly to get good traction between the grip and your hands. Grips are fairly inexpensive to have changed, and you can do it yourself if you buy the necessary supplies. No matter what, you should have new grips put on every club (with the possible exception of your putter) at the beginning of every season.

2. Dirt in the club grooves. Plain and simple, the grooves on your clubs are important. They help the club get airborne and they provide spin. If the grooves of your club are filled with dirt, it is the equivalent of hitting the ball with a smooth-faced club.

3. No towel. This may seem crazy, but one of the most important equipment accessories you can have during a round is a towel—and not one of those little things you clip to your bag. You need a full-size towel you can use to clean your clubs, wipe your grips, and clean your ball. (You should *never* lick your ball to clean it. The fertilizers and other substances put on the grass at golf courses are *not* meant to be ingested.)

4. A damaged ball. The Rules of Golf allow you to remove a damaged ball from play under certain circumstances. Be familiar with the Rules.

5. A sweaty glove. If you use a glove and count on it as part of your overall feel for the game, you should do two things: On very hot days, remove your glove between shots and give the leather a chance to breathe and dry out. Also, carry more than one glove, keeping your backup glove in the packaging until you need it.

6. Unprepared to play in the rain. Whether you play in the rain is up to you, although you should *always* get off the course immediately if there is even a hint of lightning in the area. However, if you find yourself in a club tournament where you have to play in the rain to stay in the event, you must be prepared.

- You should have a rainsuit or, at the least, a rain jacket. The jacket should be lightweight so you can layer sweaters under it if it gets cold, and it should offer you the same freedom of movement you have when you are wearing only a shirt.

- You should have an extra towel, maybe even two. They should be stored in a plastic bag inside your bag. This helps keep them dry when moisture soaks through the bag, which is quite common with today's lightweight bags.

- You should have an umbrella, and you should keep the towel you are using hanging down from the inside spokes of the umbrella while you play. You can also use the Velcro fastener to attach your glove to the inside spokes between shots. When the towels or gloves are too wet, replace them with dry ones, and put the wet ones in your golf bag, but not inside the plastic bag with the extra dry ones. Carry a separate empty plastic bag for wet towels and gloves.

- Wear a hat, especially if you wear glasses. In fact, you should almost always wear a hat to help prevent overexposure to the sun.

- You should have a cover for the top of your bag that goes over your clubs. The cover should have a zipper and repel water.

- You should take the headcovers off your woods so you can avoid dealing with the soggy covers on every hole.

- Whenever possible, you should take a caddie in the rain if you are serious about shooting the lowest score. It is easier to keep your equipment dry and handle the umbrella if you work with a teammate.

7. Too many clubs. If you are playing in any type of competitive event, you cannot have more than fourteen clubs in your bag. Count them before you go out.

8. The wrong clubs for the course. If you are familiar with a course, you should make sure every club in your bag is going to serve some purpose. If you are not familiar with the course, get advice from people who are.

9. An extra ball in your pocket. This advice is not for TOUR players, whose caddies are always by their side. If you are an everyday golfer, however, you should have two balls on you at all times in case you need to hit a provisional. Depending on where you parked your cart or how far away your caddie is, you can waste a lot of time and hold up play if you need to hit a provisional and do not have an extra ball.

10. Using the wrong club to measure club length. In many instances, when you take relief or declare a ball unplayable, the Rules dictate that you may drop within two club lengths of a given point. When it is beneficial to move the ball as far as you can, always use your driver, which is generally the longest club in your bag. It will provide as much as twelve more inches in relief as opposed to some other clubs in your set.

The making of a yardage book.

Larry Laoretti and his signature cigar.

The Pre-Shot Setup and Routine

3

For the everyday golfer, the search for lower scores begins and advances farthest in the process that occurs before the club ever moves an inch. More avoidable mistakes and more ball-flight inconsistencies arise as a result of miscues in *preparation* to swinging the club than as the result of anything that happens when the club is actually being swung. Trying to fix a mistake in midswing is simply not feasible for the everyday player, but trying to fix a mistake before your swing has begun is a very attainable goal indeed. The good news is that properly setting up to the ball is a fairly simple process, and this chapter will provide all the salient points. Once you understand all the checkpoints, the biggest potential pitfall is getting careless in monitoring yourself as you set up to play a shot. The best way to avoid this is to have a pre-shot routine you go through before every shot you play with a full swing. As Steve Pate mentions later in this chapter, "It's so easy to focus on the results and lose sight of what you have to do to get the result you want."

Andrew Magee takes one last look at the target before striking his shot.

Your Connection to the Club

With all the turning and shifting and swinging that go into playing a shot, your hands are the only part of your body that come in contact with the club. The position of your hands on the club is the first fundamental you must grasp, because once you start to swing, tremendous momentum begins to build up. If you do not position your hands perfectly on the club, you adversely affect the position of the clubface at impact, and when the clubface is off square by even the tiniest of margins, the resulting shot is exponentially off target.

Consider four things when you are positioning the club in your hands: where the club sits in your hands; whether your hands are in a *strong*, *weak*, or *neutral* position; how your hands work together; and the amount and placement of pressure on the club.

The club should rest in the fingers of the hand as you prepare to take your grip. Holding it in the palms will reduce your feel for the club and create tension.

Hold the Club with Your Fingers

When you are gripping the club, the shaft should rest in your fingers. Specifically, it should rest at the point where the fingers join your palm. The top of the shaft should rest against the fleshy, padded part of your left hand—what would be the lower right quadrant of your left palm if you held your hand up in front of your face. You never want to feel like the club is resting in your palms, because this will reduce your sense of feel of the weight of the clubhead and also hinder the action of your hands throughout the swing.

Strong, Weak, or Neutral?

Once you are comfortable with the idea of the club resting mainly in your fingers, the next step is to position your left hand properly on the club or, more precisely, position your left *thumb* properly. If you place your thumb directly on top of the shaft so your thumb runs straight down the middle of the shaft, you are placing your hand in a *neutral* position. If you were to turn your hand (and your thumb) slightly to the right—say, one-quarter inch to one-half inch—you would be placing your hand in what is known as a *strong* position. If you did the opposite, and turned your hand and thumb so the thumb rested to the left of the center of the shaft, you would be setting a *weak* grip position. The obvious question is, "Which one is best for me?"

To answer that question, it helps to know what each of the three terms—neutral, strong, and weak—means. The following descriptions are a bit of an oversimplification, but they provide the basic information:

- In the neutral position, the position of your left hand and thumb does not exert any extraneous influence on the angle of the clubface at impact. In other words, if you set the clubface square at address, took a neutral grip, and made a perfect swing, the clubface would be perfectly square at impact.
- In the strong position, with your left hand and thumb turned to the right of the center of the shaft, the tendency is for the clubface to be slightly *closed* at impact, even if you start from a square position at address. *Closed* refers to the idea that the lead edge will be aimed left of your target.
- In the weak position, with your left thumb sitting slightly to the left of the center of the shaft, the tendency is for the clubface to be slightly open at impact. Again, this is true even if you have the clubface squarely aimed at address. When the clubface is open at impact the lead edge is pointing to the right of your target.

Three basic grip positions: A weak grip (1), with both hands turned toward the left, creates an open clubface at impact. A strong grip (2), with both hands turned to the right, creates a closed clubface at impact. The neutral grip (3) has little or no effect on the clubface at impact.

You can easily see the impact of each of these left hand/thumb positions without making a full swing. Pick up a club and turn your left hand so the thumb is on the right side of the shaft at the three-o'clock position. You don't even need your right hand on the club to do this. Swing the club back in slow motion, as if you were going to swing, and you will see immediately that the clubface turns down or, in effect, closes. With a strong grip and a real swing, this initial closing effect stays with the clubface through impact. Next, turn your left hand so the thumb is on the left side of the shaft. Repeat your slow-motion drill and you will get the sense of the club fanning up or open. With your thumb in the neutral position, you can move the club straight back from the ball without feeling like it wants to turn one way or the other.

Still, the question remains, "Which one is best for me?" The strong grip gets its name from the tendency to produce shots that curve from right to left—a ball-flight pattern considered more powerful than a left-to-right ball flight, which is the type of shot you would likely get with a weak grip. A neutral grip has no effect on the flight of the ball. Throughout the history of the game, great players have employed each of these grips. Players such as Fred Couples, Paul Azinger, and John Daly use very strong grips. Ben Hogan swung with a neutral grip. Corey Pavin uses a grip that leans toward the weak side. Although each of the grip positions can work and has worked for various players, you must consider what the majority of great players do and what your needs are. A vast number of great players use a *slightly* strong grip—nowhere near as extreme as the one suggested above. They probably position the left thumb in approximately the one-o'clock to one-thirty range. This moderately strong position helps to generate a slight

Jim Furyk *Take your grip behind the ball as part of your routine.*

Ranked fourth in scoring in 1998 (69.50), following a ranking of eighth in 1997 (69.64).

"Before I play any shot I go through the same routine. I take a practice swing from next to the ball to get a feel for the lie. On the tee it doesn't matter, but if you have a funky lie in the fairway, it can help you get a feel for what your swing is going to feel like. Then I go behind the ball—about five yards or so—and I start to think about how I'm going to hit the shot and what it's going to look like. I pick out a spot in front of the ball that I'm going to aim over, and then I take my grip with my left hand while I'm still standing behind the ball. I like

to make sure I set my left hand correctly. A lot of everyday golfers probably put both hands on the club at the same time, but I put the left hand on first and then I put my right hand on as I'm walking up to the ball.

"After that, I check my distance from the ball, and I make sure my left foot is fanned out a little—that helps make it easier for me to turn through the shot. Then I make sure I take a waggle—that's a big part of feeling comfortable over the ball. With the waggle you don't throw in a lot of excess movement—don't use your wrist a lot if that's not how you swing the club."

draw and to create more roll when the ball hits the ground, but it is not so strong as to create problems for most players.

Even though players such as Couples, Azinger, and Daly use very strong grips, the everyday player would be in error in attempting to duplicate their grips. For the typical everyday player who is continually striving for more distance, a *moderately* strong grip is probably best. If you consistently hit off-line shots in the same pattern, checking your grip might be the place to start the cure. Consistently wild hooks could be caused by an excessively strong grip, whereas frequent wild slices may be the result of a weak grip.

What about the neutral grip? If you feel your swing mechanics are so sound that you can repeatedly reach the impact position with the clubface perfectly square, it's a valid option. Otherwise, if you are a tad erratic, the moderately strong grip at least allows you to develop a tendency for impact.

Davis Love III in a perfect setup position. Note that his feet are wide enough to give him a stable base, but not so wide as to hinder his turn away from the ball. The right shoulder is lower than the left because you have to reach down farther with the right hand to grip the club.

Making Your Hands Work Together

With all the emphasis that has been placed on the left hand, you might think that your right hand has nothing to do with your golf swing. As you probably already know that's not true. Because the left hand is placed on the club first and because it also dictates the position of the right hand, it always precedes the right hand in any discussion of grip.

To swing the club most effectively you need both hands to blend together and act as one. There are a few ways to accomplish this. The two main ways are the *overlapping* or *Vardon* grip, and the *interlocking* grip. Both grips start by placing the "V" in the right palm and, as a result, the right thumb, over the top of the left thumb. In the overlapping/Vardon grip, the union of the hands is completed by placing the right pinkie finger directly on top of the left index finger. Some players place the left pinkie finger in the crease between the right index finger and the right middle finger. (This is sometimes called the *Vardon grip* because it was popularized by the great English professional Harry Vardon, one of the game's first dominant players.)

With the interlocking grip you take the notion of coupling the hands literally by looping the right pinkie finger through the gap between the left index finger and the left middle finger.

The overlapping grip and the interlocking grip are the two most commonly used grips, but an overwhelming majority of TOUR players use the overlapping grip. There are some notable exceptions, such as Jack Nicklaus and Tom Kite. Some everyday golfers who have fingers on the short side prefer the interlocking as well, because it gives them a more solid sense of connection between the two hands.

Like so many other things, how you choose to link your hands is a matter of personal preference. Many great players through the years have personalized their grips. Gene Sarazen chose to not place his left thumb at the top of the shaft and did not fit it into the "V" in his left hand at all. Instead, it hung to the side, underneath his right hand. Greg Norman uses a hybrid of the overlapping and interlocking, slipping his right pinkie finger between his left index finger and left middle finger. Bob Rosburg, the 1959 PGA Championship winner and longtime ABC Sports golf commentator, held the club like a baseball bat, placing all ten fingers on the club without joining his hands in any way. In other words, there is more than one way to skin a cat.

Once you have both hands on the club, one classic tip for checking the position of your hands is this: The "V" formed by the left thumb and index finger should point at your left shoulder. The "V" formed by the right thumb and index finger should point at your right shoulder.

An example of the Vardon or overlapping grip, the type used by nearly all TOUR players.

An example of an interlocking grip, which is often more effective for players with smallish fingers. Jack Nicklaus and Tom Kite both use this grip.

Grip Pressure

The final element of the hands-to-club relationship is the amount of pressure you apply—that is, how tightly you hold the club. Although this is perhaps the most overlooked piece of the grip puzzle, it is just as important as the other elements of the grip. There is little question that the everyday golfer squeezes the club too tightly and that this has a negative influence

When holding the club, the pressure should be applied mainly with the last three fingers of the left hand and the middle two fingers of the right hand.

on performance. The downside of squeezing the club is twofold: It reduces your sense of feel for the clubhead, and it creates tension in your arms, restricting freedom of movement during the swing. These are both significant drawbacks because it is essential to have a sense of where the clubhead is at all points during the swing, and tension of any form turns the swing into more of a whack or hack, replacing fluidity with awkward, stiff-limbed lunges.

Consider these two points in relation to grip pressure: how much to apply and where to apply it. How much pressure you apply is the more important of the two, and the answer is simple: as little as possible. Apply only enough grip pressure to keep the club from flying out of your hands when you swing. If you can feel any tension at all in your forearms, you are squeezing the club far too much. An image that works well is to think of holding something rather soft in your hands as you grip the club. For example, imagine you are gripping a hotdog bun rather than a golf club. If you apply any excess pressure to that bun, you will squash it—and squash your chances of making a good swing.

Lee Janzen   *Grip pressure varies from person to person*

The 1998 and 1993 U.S. Open Champion was sixteenth in the All-Around Ranking in 1998 and fifteenth in scoring average in 1997 (69.96).

"I think everyone is a little different when it comes to grip pressure. I know that [Ben] Hogan practiced gripping the club as tightly as he possibly could so that when he was under pressure he wouldn't be able to grip the club any tighter than he was accustomed to. I hold the club as lightly as I can—just enough pressure to hang on to it."

Correctly positioning your hands on the club is another important thing Hogan used to talk about, and I think his advice is super. He said he worked on it for five minutes at the beginning of every practice session, and he didn't worry about it after that. If you check your grip for the first five minutes of every practice session, you won't have many problems with it. You should end up with a consistent grip and end up with the club in the right spot in your hands.

"I try to keep my grip as close to neutral as I can. If you get your hands turned too far in either direction you can get into trouble. I always try to make sure that my grip is not too strong.

"Hold the club so that it's mostly in your left hand. The calluses on my left hand are all on those last three fingers. The grip is tighter toward what you would consider the heel of your hand, and on the right hand the pressure is closer to your index finger and thumb."

Where you apply the pressure is something that happens quite naturally based on the way you grip the club. For the most part, the top three fingers on your left hand (pinkie, ring finger, and middle finger) apply the most significant amount of pressure. On your right hand, you squeeze mainly with two fingers, the middle and ring fingers. Knowing where to apply the pressure is useful only to the extent that when you are trying for the lightest possible grip, it helps to know where you should feel the pressure.

Preparing Your Body for the Swing

Once you have placed your hands on the club, the next step in preparing to play a shot with a full swing is to put your body in a position that allows the swing to happen efficiently and productively. The word typically applied to this element of preparing to play a shot is *posture*, but it helps to think in terms of assuming an athletic position. (*Posture* makes most people think simply of the angle of the back, but setting your body to swing a golf club involves more than that.)

There is a universal athletic position that applies to nearly every sport, including golf. That position consists of the following things: the feet spread apart for balance and the body weight evenly distributed on the balls of both feet, the knees flexed, the upper body angled forward from the hips, the arms hanging loose and free of tension, and the head steady at the center. If this position does not *sound* familiar to you, it should at least *look* familiar. It is the position a linebacker takes as he prepares for the snap of the ball; it is the position of a tennis player as he awaits service; it is, with the exception of the arms hanging down, the position a baseball player takes when awaiting a pitch; it is the position a basketball player takes just before shooting a free throw. In a more extreme form, it is the position a swimmer takes on the starting blocks waiting for the gun to sound. What do all of these examples have in common? Each athlete assumes this position while waiting for the action to begin. They are not simply waiting, however. They are preparing themselves to react quickly and smoothly to the action. This state of preparedness is just as vital as the action itself.

In golf, of course, you do not react to anything; you initiate the action. It is hard to say which is more difficult, reacting to someone else or initiating the action yourself. Your body needs to do whatever is necessary to make the play. Therefore, it is important to put yourself in the same "ready" position in golf as you do in any other sport. Here are the basic elements of that position for golf:

A golfer in the "ready" position (top) which is ideal for playing golf shots. The knees are flexed, the arms hang loose and the player is balanced. There is little difference once the club is placed in his hands.

- A solid base, which means your feet are separated and your weight is evenly balanced between both feet. The basic reference point for how wide to spread your feet is your shoulders. For a full shot played with your driver, the insides of your feet should be approximately the width of your shoulders. The width between your feet narrows as the clubs (and your swing) get shorter. However, your shoulders always serve as the reference points.

  Your weight should be toward the balls of your feet, but not so much that you tip forward as you stand ready to play a shot. Similarly, you do not want so much weight toward the rear of your feet that you feel as if you are falling backward as you stand ready to swing. The key is to feel well balanced—not tilting forward, falling back, or leaning to either side. For certain specialty shots it helps to place more weight on your left foot than on your right. For full shots, however, balancing your weight is always the standard.

- Flex in your knees; this reduces tension and allows your lower body to do what it needs to do. Flexing the knees also helps to lower the clubhead to the ball without compromising the angle of your back and shoulders—that is, it allows you to reach the ball without slouching your shoulders. How far should you bend your knees? If you picture a line from the side of the ball of your foot going straight up—perpendicular to the ground—it should go directly through the center of the side of your knee. If it helps, draw that mental line while you are standing straight, and you will get a sense for how much you should flex your knees.

- Your arms should hang straight down and be tension-free. Watch any TOUR player and you will see very little stretching out of the arms to reach the ball. (Occasionally, in a unique setup, you may see something that contradicts this notion. By and large, however, this is true in the setups on TOUR.) Even with your knees flexed and your arms hanging down and free of tension, however, your hands would still be too close to your body to swing freely and allow full extension of your arms.

- To create enough separation between your hands and body, bend forward slightly from your hips while keeping your back straight. In this sense, "straight" means that, as you bend forward from the hips, you are careful not to droop your shoulders. Remember when your teacher used to say, "Sit up straight and put your shoulders back!"? The key part is your shoulders—no slouching!

  Once again the question is: How far forward from your hips should you bend? Think of the line that started straight up from the ball of your foot and through the center of your knee. If you continue that line straight up from the knee until the point where it goes directly through the center of the side of your armpit, you should be close to getting the correct amount of flex forward from your hips.

- Your head should be steady, set in a position that allows you to see what is happening. In other words, don't drop your chin down onto your chest just because the ball is on the ground! You must tilt your head down a tiny bit to see the ball, but don't tip it down any farther than necessary to see the ball. It helps to remember that your left shoulder must pass under your chin during a full swing, and that is not possible if your chin is on your chest.

  Once you are comfortable assuming this position, you should have an understanding of how to hold the club and how to get set to swing it. Golf at its essence as a ball-striking game is a target challenge. Just like any other target game, your accuracy depends on how well you aim. In almost every game that requires proper aim, the main element of the aiming process is the alignment of your body to the target. Once your body is in proper relationship to the target, you have done nearly all you should to achieve accurate aiming. The second element is properly aiming your club, the object that actually launches the ball.

With the driver and longer clubs, the feet are set shoulder-width apart in order to create a solid base for a big swing. With the shorter irons, the stance is narrowed for a tighter turn and shorter backswing.

Now It's Time to Aim

Aiming your club. Aiming your body and your club to play a shot consists of two separate parts: the checkpoints of proper body and club alignment, and the sequence of events required to achieve these checkpoints most effectively. You must first understand the aiming checkpoints for the

Ernie Els   *Sit on a high stool to set your hips.*

The 1997 U.S. Open Champion, he has ranked in the top fifteen in scoring average every year since 1993.

"When I settle into my shot, I give a slight 'shake, rattle, and roll.' My hips are a big part of my swing—both the angle of the tilt from them and their alignment with the target. When I get them where I want them it feels like I'm sitting on a high stool, and then when it feels right, I start to swing.

"Like almost everyone out here on TOUR I visualize the shot before I play it. We've got the ball standing still, whereas

in tennis or another game, there is something to react to, so we have to have a trigger point. Some guys make a little forward press with their hips or legs, and that's their trigger to go. When I get set, I feel a little flex in my knees, and then I just try to slide the club away from the ball very slowly. I would say almost everyone out here does it the same before every shot, and that it's a good idea for the everyday player to use the same routine every time as well."

body/target relationship before moving on to the sequence of events in playing a shot. The first step in understanding the aiming process is to understand *your target.*

There are numerous variables in exactly which point you choose as your target for a given shot, all of which are covered in various portions of this book. The one absolute is that the target for a shot played with a full swing is always *where you want the ball to land.* Where the ball runs to after it strikes the ground, or what it does while in the air, are irrelevant to the selection of your target. For the purposes of aiming, your target is the point where you want the ball to first strike the ground after its flight.

For almost every shot you play with a full swing—especially as it relates to this fundamental discussion—the *lead edge* of the club should be aimed directly at the target. (The *lead edge* is the straight edge or straight line at the bottom of the clubface, the point where the clubface and the sole of the club join.) In other words, from the lead edge of the clubface, a straight line—perpendicular to the lead edge—extends to your target. You should think of the relationship between your clubface and your target as a straight line known as the *target line.* (Getting the club aimed on that straight line while your body is standing to the side of the ball—and not directly behind it—is the most difficult element of aiming the club. That problem is discussed and solved later in this chapter, in the sequential part of your setup.)

Aiming your body. Aiming your body is perhaps the most difficult part of getting set to play a shot. Because you are standing to the side of the ball, and because you are not aiming your body at the target, it is not uncommon for some visual confusion to take place. This is complicated because you are not, at least in the final address position, looking at the target with both eyes. This problem is overcome by following the proper sequence of setting your body to play a shot, which is covered later in this chapter.

The alignment of your body is related to the alignment of your clubface. More specifically, the alignment of your body is related to the target line, the straight line from the clubface to the target. The key thing to remember about aiming is: Do *not* aim

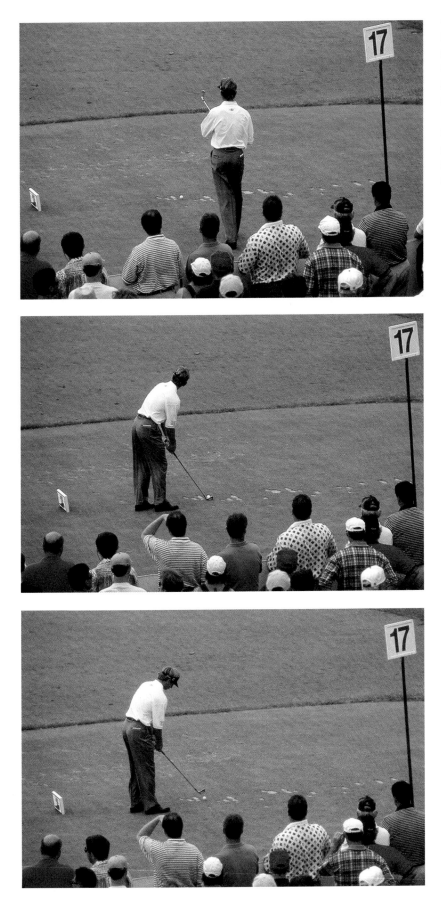

PGA TOUR player Brad Faxon executing a perfect pre-shot routine. Note how he stands behind the ball (frame one) to select his target and pick an intermediate target. In frame two, notice how he initially "steps into" his setup with his right foot, thus giving him a clear view of the target as he gets his body into position and aims his clubface. Once all that is finished, Faxon completes his setup (frame three).

your body directly at the target. Aim your body along a line parallel to the target line.

The idea of aiming your body parallel to the target line is important. If you aimed your body directly at the target, it would create problems in your swing. Here, however, it is best to consider exactly how to aim your body.

When you aim the clubface at the target, you have a reference point: the leading edge of the clubface. You have reference points for aiming your body, too. Specifically, your feet, hips, and shoulders form the lines that you set parallel to the target line. There are all sorts of individualized setups both on TOUR and with the everyday golfer, but the basic reference for a fundamentally sound setup is as follows: A straight line across the tips of your toes, a straight line from hip to hip, and a straight line from shoulder to shoulder should all be parallel to your target line.

You might wonder how, if you aim your clubface directly at your target and aim your body at a point left of (but parallel to) your target, the ball ends up where you want it to. Some simple visualization can put this into perspective. At the center of this discussion of alignment stand two straight lines that run parallel to each other from the ball to (and beyond) your target. The line farthest from you—which extends from the clubface and the ball to the target—is your target line. The other line is formed by your body: those straight lines across your toes, your hips, and your shoulders. You can think of these as your *body* lines. For a moment, think of these two lines as the two rails on a railroad track. Don't visualize this from the perspective of your address position— that is, next to the ball—but visualize it from a vantage point behind the ball. In other words, the ball is directly between you and your target. As you mentally picture yourself standing between the two rails, you will see that the farther you look down the line, the closer the two rails appear to be. Eventually the two rails visually merge into a single rail or a single line. This is precisely the way you need to consider aiming your club and your body: They travel along different lines, but they eventually come together at a common destination.

Inside the Ropes

Fuzzy Zoeller   *You can use your setup to remind you to do something in your swing.*

1979 Masters Champion. Made a birdie every 3.73 holes on TOUR in 1993, tying him for eleventh in that category.

"I think anyone who has ever seen me play has probably noticed that I slide the club out so that the ball is setting off the heel of the club before I start my swing. I do that because when I get to the top of my swing, I want to feel like the first move down is the heel of the club moving toward the ball.

Making that move in my setup reminds me to do it during my swing. That's all it means—it doesn't mean to take the club outside or pull it inside or any of that. You have to do little things like that when you play as much golf as we do in order to prevent going brain dead over the ball. Some guys hitch their pants, others check a spot in front of the ball for alignment—everybody has his own little nooks and crannies in his setup."

The key to aiming your body lies in getting your feet, hips, and shoulders parallel to your target line. The key to aiming your club is to select an intermediate target (in this example the leaf) along your target line and close to your clubface.

Getting Your Body into Position to Play a Shot

Many of the difficulties people encounter playing golf arise because of the ball-to-body-to-target orientation. Properly aiming your club and body depends heavily on straight lines. Straight lines appear straight only if you observe them directly from behind. This is where you are at a disadvantage in golf, because you are not behind the ball as you play it. You can, however, properly aim yourself and the club by following a certain sequence of events, one that allows you to gain orientation to the target from *behind* the ball before you move around to the side of the ball to swing the club.

The start of that sequence of events begins like everything else in golf—with the selection of a target.

Exactly which point you pick as a target varies from shot to shot and from club to club, because you must consider what the ball will do once it strikes the ground—an often overlooked aspect of playing a shot. The ball reacts differently depending on the angle at which it strikes the ground. The steeper the angle at which the ball hits the ground, the less it rolls once it has landed. Remember, however, that for aiming purposes, your target is always the point at which you wish the ball to hit the ground. Where the ball will stop is not a consideration in aiming your body. (The variables of selecting your target are covered in later chapters, which are divided according to the height and length of the shots.) It is assumed from this point forward that "target" refers to the point where the ball first strikes the ground.

One of the few rules of golf that you should never violate is: *Always decide on your target from a point behind the ball.* In fact (reverting to the straight lines again), once you decide on a target for your shot, you should be standing on a straight line that runs from the target to (and through) your ball.

Here is a step-by-step breakdown of the process of selecting a target and aligning your body to that target:

- Before you select a club, stand behind the ball and get acquainted with the shot you are about to play. If that shot is played from the tee box, you know you are going to have a good lie because you should tee the ball up for every tee shot. For any other shot, the first thing you should do is assess the lie of the ball. *This is important: You cannot decide on your target (or your club) until you have assessed the lie of your ball.* If the lie is clean—there is no long grass around the ball, it is not in a divot, and the ground is relatively flat—you can safely assume it won't affect your shot much.

- Once you are sure that the lie will not affect your shot very much, you can select a target. At this point you are standing behind the ball and looking down the line toward your eventual destination. At this moment you should be thinking about three things: *your actual target; a landmark in the distance beyond that target (if there is one); and, most important, an intermediate target—that is, a spot between your actual target and your ball.* You should be very precise in selecting a target.

Inside the Ropes

Steve Pate   *Routine gets you focused on hitting the shot rather than the results.*

Ranked seventh on TOUR in greens-in-regulation in 1996.

"A pre-shot routine is important for every golfer because it's so easy to focus on the results—the flight of the ball—and lose sight of what you have to do to get the result you want. If you are focused on doing the same thing before every shot you can block out that type of results-oriented focus. That's why you want to spend the majority of your pre-shot time picking a close target—about eighteen inches in front of the ball—then getting the clubface aimed squarely at that target. Finally, set your body parallel to the club."

A superb example of Jack Nicklaus getting oriented to his target. In the first frame, he is looking at his actual target in the distance. In the second, he is checking his intermediate target to which he will align the lead edge of his clubface.

Brent Geiberger   *Imagery is important to a good shot.*

Was twenty-fourth in driving distance in 1997 (276.9) and tied for fifteenth in total driving.

"When I am playing well I try to picture the shots as they are going to come off, and what I want to do to make them happen. If I don't have a set plan for what I want to do, or if I don't go through my routine with a given shot, I know I don't have as good a chance of hitting the best possible shot.

"What you visualize depends on the situation. Sometimes you see the ball in flight, sometimes you see your swing. For example, if the wind is blowing a certain way and I want to take a little bit off of it and cut it into the wind, I picture the swing I need to make as opposed to the ball in flight. I just do that in my head and then try to make a few practice swings like the one I am visualizing."

You should not think, "I'm sort of aiming at that," or "I want to hit this one in that general direction." You should choose a specific spot on the ground toward which you wish to play the shot.

- Once you pick your target, you return to those straight lines. Because the ball is rather tiny and your target is rather far away, it can be difficult to put the two—the small ball and the faraway small target—into perspective. Therefore, it is a good idea to pick a big target that lies beyond your actual target—for example, a tree, bush, hill, building, cloud, or anything that lies on a direct line beyond your target. Simply speaking, it's easier to align with a bigger target.

- Now that you've selected your big target, you can greatly increase your chances of accurately aiming your club and yourself by selecting an intermediate target, a point that is closer to you but along the same line as the big target. How do you do that? The answer is more lines. Mentally draw a straight line from your ball to your big target. Along that line select something on the ground within three feet of your ball. It can be anything—a twig, a leaf, a discolored blade of grass, a divot, a piece of clover, anything that will serve as a visual reference. Selecting an intermediate target is the most important thing you do in preparing to play a shot.

- You have done all of the above while standing behind the ball. While you are still standing behind the ball, make a visual connection (draw a straight line) from your ball to your intermediate target to your actual target. The reason the intermediate target should be as close as possible to the ball is that it is the point at which you aim your clubface. Once you aim your clubface, you can set your body in place as well.

- Now you start to move into position. As you move up next to the ball, you step into the setup position with your right foot first, keeping your head and shoulders directly facing your target. You do this so you can aim the club while you are looking at your target with both eyes. This keeps you from peering at the target out of the corner of your left eye, which is quite often disorienting.

- You aim your club by setting the lead edge square (perpendicular) to your target line. At this point you should be comfortable with your target line, because you have selected the intermediate target close to the ball. Aim your club at the intermediate target. Although many TOUR players never actually set the club on the ground, the everyday golfer should do so. It makes things simpler, and it helps reduce the amount of tension in your arms.

- Once you have aimed the club, you can step into your setup position with your left side. Because the club is already aimed, you can concentrate on making your body lines parallel to your target line. It is easiest to start with your feet, because they are closest to the target line. Next, set your shoulders parallel to the target line. Once your feet and shoulders are set, you have accomplished what you need to do to aim your club and body. Now it is simply a matter of assuming the athletic position described earlier in this chapter.

- Once the club is set, the shaft should be leaning slightly toward the target, with your hands slightly ahead of the clubhead. At the very least, your hands should be even with the clubhead and the shaft should be straight. You never want to be in a position where your hands are behind the clubhead or the shaft is leaning away from the target.

The Ball, Your Stance, and Other Things to Consider

No two shots in golf are alike, so preparing each shot involves changes in your setup. Those changes are covered in depth in the following chapters, but some basic rules will make these little adjustments easier to remember. Here is a little checklist of things to think about as you set up to the ball for full shots:

- Longer shots require longer clubs. The longer clubs—driver, fairway woods, and long irons—require you to set your feet fairly wide apart to stay balanced during your swing. With your longer clubs, the insides of your feet should be as wide as your shoulders. As the clubs get progressively shorter, your stance becomes progressively more narrow.

- The longer the club, the farther forward (toward your left foot) the ball should be in your stance. With the longer clubs, the ball should sit along a straight line extending from the inside of your left heel.

With the middle and short irons, the ball is positioned toward the center of the body and feet. In this case, the feet belong to Tom Lehman.

Ian Woosnam playing the ball well back in his stance. For certain specialty shots in the short game, this helps to keep the ball very low and allows it to run along the ground quite a bit.

Shorter clubs require the ball to be moved back in your stance. With the shortest clubs, the wedges, the ball should be roughly in the center of your stance, in the middle of your feet. You never want the ball to be to the right of the center of your stance except for certain specialty shots.

• The longer the club, the farther you stand from the ball. The shorter the club, the closer you stand to the ball. As the clubs get shorter, the posture you assume to play a shot changes. The way you lower yourself to the ball is equal parts knee flex and tilting forward from your hips, as described earlier in this chapter. You should never reach for the ball with your arms and shoulders.

Developing a Routine

Without question, preparing to play the shot is more important than anything you do once the club is in motion. If the beginning is not right, there is not much chance of achieving the hoped-for end result. Chances are you have heard or read a description of a TOUR player's pre-shot routine and how important it is to his game. It can be—and should be—just as important to your game. The word *routine* is used here in the purest sense—that is, a sequence of thoughts and movements that are repeated with great efficiency. The routine is significant and should not be glossed over.

The basic elements of a pre-shot routine are:

- An assessment of the lie of your ball. Is it going to interfere with clean contact?
- The selection of a target.
- Accurate determination of the yardage between your ball and the target.
- The selection of an intermediate target (from behind the ball) to aid in aiming the clubface.
- The setting of your body into place.
- A single key swing thought—for example, "Take the club away low and slow." You should have only one swing thought as you prepare to play a shot.

Inside the Ropes

Tom Lehman *Waggling the club makes it easier to start your swing.*

In 1996 won the British Open and led the TOUR in scoring average (69.32).

"I think the most important thing about my pre-shot routine is that it always takes the same amount of time. I think if someone were to time me on every shot over the course of a season, there would be a variation of no more than one second—which means the same number of waggles, the same number of looks at the target, etc.

"You should be completely comfortable with your routine. It should be second nature so that you're not even conscious of how you do it. I couldn't tell you exactly what I go through to play a shot. It's one of those things like, 'How do I breathe?' I know it's the same every time, because I've done it so many times that I just know I'm doing it right.

"If I don't do my routine correctly, I'm aware of it because I've done it thousands and thousands of times. There's an immediate feedback that says, 'Hey, this isn't right!' At that point you should always step back and start over. Everyday players seem reluctant to do this, but on TOUR the players don't hesitate to back off if something doesn't feel right.

"I start from behind the ball, and I take a couple of practice swings and visualize the ball in flight. When I walk up to the ball, I take a little half swing and then get over the ball and shuffle around until I feel comfortable. I waggle the club a few times and look at the target and then I swing.

"When my wife is watching me play, she says she knows exactly when I'm about to hit the ball because my last waggle is always a little bigger than the others. I never come to a complete stop between that final waggle and the start of my swing. I've always found that if I get to a point where I'm totally static—where I'm not moving at all—that the chances of my hitting a good shot are dramatically decreased.

"If you watch any athlete who is good at something—someone shooting free throws or getting ready to steal a base—they're always wiggling their hands or bouncing the ball or looking at the basket. They bend their knees, they breathe, they shrug their shoulders—they do something so that they don't become totally frozen. I think it's because it's easier to get a big motion going if you already have a little motion going. I know I take the big waggle, make a little forward press with my hands, and away I go. It's just my way of initiating my swing without coming to a dead stop."

TOUR players often say things such as "I wasn't really thinking about anything when I played that shot," because they concentrate on choosing the right club and getting aimed properly. After that, they trust their swings to get the job done.

- A practice swing that matches the swing you would like to make when actually playing the shot.
- A visualization of the shot as you expect it to fly. "Seeing" the shot before it is played is a hallmark of almost every great player.

Waggles, Practice Swings, and Other Ways of Avoiding Tension

While watching TOUR players in action, one of the things you may have noticed is that they remain in almost constant motion as they prepare to play a shot. Some examples are the way Mark Calcavecchia wiggles his feet, or Tom Watson's almost incessant waggling of the club and moving of his feet. Some players make a practice swing or two. They are moving their bodies to avoid a buildup of tension before making the full swing. When your body is in motion, your muscles are moving, and they are naturally loose. This allows the swinging motion to happen in a smooth, uninhibited manner that produces the best shots.

Waggling the club and/or making a practice swing also serve other purposes. With a brief waggle of the club you can rehearse your takeaway and the initial few inches of your swing. The waggle also provides you with a transition from the pre-swing into the actual swing without becoming stock still. A practice swing can accomplish the same thing for the entire swing. If you make a practice swing it should truly mirror the swing you would like to make—that is, it should be the same length and at the same tempo with which you would like to strike the ball. If you have seen TOUR player Scott Simpson prepare to play a shot, you have seen the perfect practice swing—an exact preview of the swing he makes a second or two later.

Inside the Ropes

Mark Calcavecchia   *Moving your feet helps overcome inconsistencies in your setup.*

Ranked in the top thirty in driving distance for three consecutive years, 1994–96.

"It's nearly impossible to get your setup perfectly consistent every time without some adjustments to your body as you get set over the ball. You can't just walk up to the ball and plant your feet in the ground and have it feel right. I've always kind of wiggled and juggled my feet around until I felt right about hitting the shot. You don't want to be standing over that ball dead still for six or seven seconds before you start to pull it back. That is just too long and, for me at least, means I've gone into brain lock. That wiggling with my feet is my trigger—my 'go' point."

Waggling the clubhead before the actual swing accomplishes two things: It helps keep tension to a minimum and allows the player to "pre-program" his backswing.

Typically when you think about tension in your swing, you think about tense hands and arms. Certainly this is the most common area of tension, because you are squeezing the club with your hands. Your legs can be too tense as well, however, if you stand too straight-legged and do not flex from your knees. Tension can also result from keeping your feet perpendicular to the target line. Although you make a line between the tips of your shoes parallel to your target line, your feet need not be pointed perfectly straight. In fact, it is almost impossible to keep your balance if you do so. To maintain balance, turn your feet out or fan them open. Typically, the left foot fans out more than the right, but no strict rules apply. The best position is the most comfortable one, which is usually the angle your feet maintain as you walk.

Developing a Personal Pre-shot Routine

A (set-up) routine in my mind is like a switch, a mechanism, to get me to concentrate on that specific shot.

— David Edwards

According to Jack Nicklaus, ninety percent of a good shot derives from two critical factors: how you prepare your mind and the consistency of how you set up to the target.

During the few seconds before you start your swing to execute a shot, you make several crucial decisions in planning of the shot: selecting the club, visualizing the intended flight of the ball—all part of programming your mind with instructions for you to execute.

A shot begins when you start to analyze the requirements of the shot, not when you start your forward press. To achieve optimal performance, you must devise a game plan and use your mind to the best of your ability to prepare and execute a shot. The first element of this plan is a pre-shot routine.

Learn From the Pros

The function of a pre-shot routine is to integrate your mind and body to create the best shot possible. A pre-shot routine has three purposes. First, it help you process information and make decisions to select a club for the shot. Second, it helps you program yourself to make a good swing. Third, it aids in preparing your mind and body to execute a good swing. If you neglect one of these areas, you will fail to fully prepare yourself. Your goal is to train yourself to approach each shot and putt with conviction, confidence and trust in your ability. Anything less is a signal for you to step away from the shot.

Tour professionals have specific pre-shot routines they follow. Greg Norman, like Jack Nicklaus, prefers a very deliberate pre-shot routine. Norman selects the shot he wants to play and visualizes that shot by focusing on the apex of the ball in flight. He walks to the ball, aims his clubhead to the target, aligns his body, and sets his grip. He sets his stance, waggles the clubhead back and forth to loosen up, and gets ready for the shot. To trigger his swing, he slides his clubhead away from his body to align the face with the ball.

Chip Beck also uses a very deliberate, mechanical looking pre-shot routine. He steps into the ball the same way and looks at the target the same number of times on every shot. A player like Lanny Wadkins takes much less time to prepare for a shot. He pulls the club from the bag, sets up to the ball, looks at the target, and goes. He feels more comfortable taking less time. John Daly is also a player who prefers to take less time over the ball. If you have ever watched Daly putt, it look like he is in a hurry to get to his next shot. He simply selects the putt he wants to hit, sets up next to the ball, takes one quick practice swing, sets up over the ball, looks at the hole once and goes.

Each player has a unique style of preparation. The common denominator is that each player has a routine he or she believes in and follows whether they are leading a tournament or in last place. The pace and specific behaviors in a pre-shot routine depend on the individual personality of the player and what feels comfortable. For example, a very aggressive player such as Lanny Wadkins has a very short, quick pre-shot routine. Conservative, calculating players such as Chip Beck or Jack Nicklaus use a slower, deliberate routine.

The pace of your pre-shot routine depends also on how complex or simple you choose to make it. The more elements in your routine, the more complex it will be, and the longer it will take. The simpler your routine, the faster it is, and the easier it is for you to consistently repeat.

How you approach each shot depends on how you prefer to process information. If you are more comfortable learning by way of visual images, your mental rehearsal should comprise visual images of the flight of the ball and pictures of how you will achieve that shot. See yourself swinging with control and good tempo.

If you learn more through sensations you pick up from your body and biophysical feedback, your mental rehearsal should include the feeling of a well-struck ball, such as the feeling a solid hit at impact. Of course, nothing prohibits you from employing both visual and physical sensations.

Ultimately, a pre-shot routine should become automatic.

Keep a Good Rhythm

A pre-shot routine should feel comfortable to you. You shouldn't have to struggle with making yourself do it. When you first change the way you prepare for and approach a shot, it is harder to get into a rhythm and feel comfortable with the new routine. The same thing happens when you make a mechanical swing change. At first the new change doesn't feel right, but with practice you begin to feel comfortable with the change.

If you play better when focused on a target, focusing harder on your routine may hinder your performance because you lose sight of the target or your goal. For some players, focusing more on their routine than the goal has a positive effect. If you have a difficult time eliminating negative thoughts, focusing intensely on your routine helps to take your mind off any negative thoughts.

Ultimately, a pre-shot routine should become automatic, something that you do with without any conscious awareness. At first, when doing your routine you must consciously think about completing the new routine. For it to become ingrained, spend extra time practicing. Do it every time that you address a ball.

A good pre-shot routine should have a steady pace and rhythm from start to finish. Once you pull the club out of the bag and begin to plan the shot, your routine should flow into the swing without interruption. If you become distracted or stop midway, you will interrupt the flow. Inactivity itself breaks the pace of the routine. Golfers often freeze over the ball before they pull back the club—the frozen golfer is waiting for someone to start his backswing for him. This is a significant case of paralysis by overanalysis. The golfer is (1) trying to remember all the mechanical instructions from his or her teacher; (2) paralyzed by the fear of hitting a bad shot; or (3) has not developed a trigger that automatically initiates the swing. The "freeze" or inactivity breeds further indecisiveness and doubt.

Whenever you break the flow of your routine, stop yourself, refocus your mind, and start over from the beginning. Learn from David Edwards: "If I'm lost in the middle of the routine or I realize I haven't gone through my routine, I step back and go through the entire routine because that's as much a part of the stroke."

Mike "Radar" Reid homing in on his target.

Tiger Woods lends a hand to a budding young golfer.

4

Your Full Swing

There is no precise moment when your pre-swing ends and the swing itself begins. As you will see later in this chapter, there is no clear delineation between the end of your backswing and the beginning of the forward swing (downswing). It is not important to know when one portion of the swing begins and ends. It is a package: One thing leads directly into the next. The choice of a target leads into the approach to the ball; your approach to the ball leads to a proper setup; a proper setup leads into the beginning of your backswing; the backswing transitions to the downswing, which leads to impact, which ends in the follow-through. It is all related. The first few inches of the club's movement in your backswing are referred to as the *takeaway*. The first eighteen to twenty-four inches set the tone for the remainder of the swing. The swing itself is a blur, started and finished in the blink of an eye. That is why the pre-shot and early phases of the swing are so important. Once you set the process in motion, there is no time to think and react.

Arguably the greatest ball-striker of all time, Ben Hogan shows his classic form.

Steve Elkington, the owner of one of golf's most mechanically-sound swings. Note how the toe of the club points to the sky in frame two. In frames three and four, Elkington's left arm has extended fully across his chest. In frame seven, notice how the body has turned dramatically toward the target prior to impact. In frame ten, Elkington displays the prototype follow-through position—perfectly balanced, with the hands up to the left of the head.

Your Takeaway

One of the keys to a good swing is to focus on the idea that it is indeed a *swing*. Golfers of all levels sometimes lose sight of this and think about the idea of *hitting* the ball. You should always think of the movement of the club as a *swing* of the clubhead. In other words, your body movements combine to swing the clubhead. No matter how many movements you make or how many things are going on, the goal is to swing the clubhead and (this is important) maintain your sense of connection to the clubhead while swinging it. Always "feel" the clubhead while it is being swung. You never want to feel like you're swinging the shaft—a stiff feeling akin to swinging a baseball bat.

One of the keys to maintaining this feeling of connection to the clubhead can be found in the takeaway, those vital first inches of the clubhead's movement. During the takeaway, the only way to maintain a sense of feeling of the clubhead is to keep tension—particularly in your upper body—to an absolute minimum. To minimize tension, maintain subtle movements of the body from the early phases of your setup right through to the beginning of your swing. In Chapter 3 some TOUR players talked about how they accomplish this.

A second key to maintaining a unified feeling of body and clubhead is to monitor grip pressure so you don't apply an excessive amount (see Chapter 3).

In this view from behind, you can see how Brad Faxon has turned his right hip away from the ball and kept his right elbow tucked close to his torso.

Skip Kendall   *When your swing is "off," quiet yourself internally.*

Tied for twenty-first in greens-in-regulation in 1997, hitting 69.2 percent of the greens he played. In 1998, Kendall was eighth in the All-Around statistical category, which measures a player's total game.

"You have to be crazy to think that you are going to be on your game every single time you tee it up. You have to work through the tough rounds, make what you can of them, and survive to fight another day. This was never more clear to me than in the '92 Q-School, when I shot 79 in the first round. That whole first day I was always in some less than optimal situation—I was behind a tree or I'd short side myself on a green and not be able to get up and down. I felt like I was playing okay but I was scoring very poorly.

"I knew I had five rounds to go and if I could just keep bouncing back, I would have time. When you get off track like that, it can be tough to right yourself. I try not to flood my mind with details; that can make things worse. I try to concentrate on my rhythm and tempo and to quiet myself internally. When I get a little bit jumpy, I feel like there's too much noise inside. I just try to relax, take some deep breaths, and look at the surroundings. We play at some beautiful places. As Walter Hagen used to say, 'Never hurry, never worry, and always take time to smell the flowers.' It works when you feel all jumbled up about your game.

"It worked that week at Q-School: I bounced back to tie for medalist and got my TOUR card."

The final major key to maintaining the feel for your clubhead is to make all the body movements of the swing at the same tempo. Tempo does not refer to how fast you swing the club. Rather, tempo refers to the *consistency* of the pace at which you swing the club. In other words, it doesn't matter how fast or how slow you swing the club, as long as the pace of the swing is *consistent*.

You may wonder why a section dealing with takeaway is discussing tempo. The critical first inches of your swing are the time to make the biggest stride toward ensuring a consistent tempo. If you start moving the club away slowly and smoothly, you have an excellent chance of maintaining the same tempo throughout your swing.

The idea of starting the club away slowly may raise another question: "If I start the club away slowly, how am I ever going to make the club move fast enough to hit the ball far?" The answer is that the club will pick up speed even though your body is moving at the same tempo throughout your swing. This idea is covered more thoroughly below. For the moment, however, you need to know only that it does in fact work out that way. For the time being, however, we should focus on the takeaway.

Why does a slow, smooth takeaway help your tempo? When you start the club away slowly and smoothly, you have started it at a pace that is both manageable and easy to keep free of tension. When you take the club away from the ball quickly you will inevitably squeeze the grip with your hands and increase tension in your arms. Why? Remember that to maintain the feel of the clubhead, you want to have a minimal amount of grip pressure. When you are gripping the club lightly, any sudden jerking of the club requires you to squeeze tighter to prevent the club from flying out of your hands. The more you squeeze, the more tension you create.

Your Takeaway, Part Two

The takeaway is the best opportunity for setting the club in motion at a manageable pace. It is also the best chance to get the club started on the proper path. Here the word *path* refers to the movement of the clubhead throughout your swing. Ideally, the club will travel on the longest possible—or widest—path throughout your swing because the longer the arc of the swing, the more speed it will build up, increasing the distance the ball will travel.

You want the club to remain on a path that will return it to the ball from an angle just inside the target line. (The club does not travel along the target line [a straight line] for very long because you swing the club around your body.) Following this path provides the best chance of the clubhead's being square at impact. To keep the club on this path all the way to impact is a challenge, but it is almost impossible to accomplish if you don't start

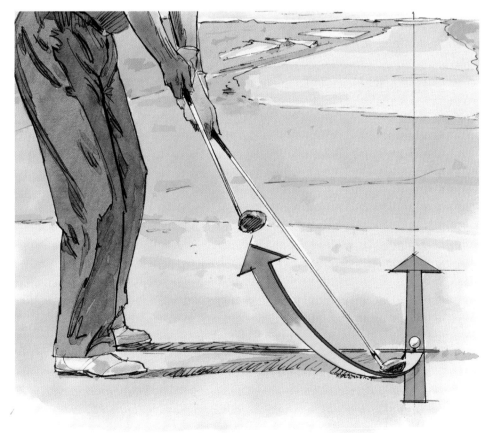

The first 18 inches of the takeaway are the moment when you set the tempo for your swing. Once the club has finished moving straight back, it starts to swing to the inside of the target line.

the club away from the ball on a straight line for as long as possible—that is, until your arms are extended to such a point that they start to swing up rather than back. If you start your swing by immediately moving the club off that initial straight-back path—either to the outside or the inside—you dramatically reduce your chances of hitting a straight shot. Therefore, take the club away from the ball slowly so you can keep it in a straight line for as long as possible. The quicker you jerk the club back, the more likely you are to move it off the path you want—most likely too far to the inside. Taking the club back outside the target line—moving the clubhead away from your body—is not ideal either.

Here are the two basic characteristics of a solid takeaway: It should be slow, and the club should move straight back from the ball for as long as possible. These two characteristics produce a number of desirable results, but how do you go about setting the club in motion to achieve them?

You should slide into the actual movements of the club from some preliminary movement that helps you to stay loose—a waggle, some jiggling of the feet, a forward press of the hands, or perhaps a combination of these things. Once you pull your swing trigger, however, what are the check marks you should be looking for?

One of the most common and effective ways of visualizing the takeaway is what is commonly referred to as the *one-piece takeaway.* Here is how it works: The lines of your arms, from your shoulders to your hands, form a triangle. We'll call it an *upside-down* triangle, meaning that the *base* of the triangle—the bottom part—runs between your shoulders, and the top point of it comes together at your hands. For the initial movements of your swing, that triangle stays intact. The club moves along with it, an extension of the line formed by your left arm. Later in your swing, the triangle breaks down: Your right elbow bends, your body has turned, and the shaft of the club is no longer in a straight line with your left arm. At the outset of your swing, however, the idea of the triangle, along with the club, starting away from the ball all at once and together, is extremely useful.

Another way of visualizing the takeaway is to think of keeping the left arm straight as you move the club back from the ball and as it swings up and across your chest. Remember those great key words "low and slow." They can be helpful when you are struggling with your swing.

A caution: don't take this visual image of a triangle too literally. Don't force your arms to be straight lines, to be absolutely rigid. The visual image of the triangle is meant only to give you a mental snapshot of how the body parts and the club work together. Remember your setup keys: Arms hang relaxed, grip pressure is light. You are not a machine—or even a triangle, for that matter—so don't try to swing like one.

Greg Norman demonstrates full extension of the arms in the takeaway.

As noted, the triangle eventually breaks down. If you are too rigid as you move away from the ball, you will not be able to move successfully into the following phases of the swing.

What Happens as the Club Moves Away from the Ball

Soon after the clubhead begins to move, other things happen. In fact, they happen so soon after the clubhead begins to move that they occur nearly simultaneously. You don't have to *force* them to happen. Many result from a good setup and the takeaway notions described above.

You may be wondering "If that's the case, why bother telling me about them? Why confuse me with a bunch of stuff that will just happen anyway?" The reason is that, at any given time during a round or a part of your season, your sense of what you are doing can vanish, and shots can start flying all over the place. You don't know what to do, you are frustrated. At those times it helps to call on what are referred to as *swing keys,* nuggets of information that can help you get back on track if you focus on only *one of them.* The majority of swing keys lie buried in the reflexive actions of the swing. The things you don't need to think about when things are going well can be your savior in your hours of need. A list of swing keys appears later in this chapter.

During the takeaway, your left shoulder starts to move toward your chin. Eventually your shoulder will feel like it is under your chin, which is why your chin should not droop on your chest at address. Don't turn your head during your backswing to make room for your shoulder. Nothing could be more disorienting, which is why the head position at address is so important. (One of Jack Nicklaus's trademark moves is the cocking of his head—his chin turns slightly to his right—just before he begins to swing. This serves many purposes: It acts as a trigger for his swing, provides room for his huge shoulder turn, and allows him to keep his head steady.)

A split second after the club first moves, your hips and shoulders begin to turn. This movement plays a vital role in the production of clubhead speed, which results in power. A fuller explanation comes later in this chapter.

Finally your weight—which was equally distributed between your feet at address—now shifts so that much of it is on your right leg, more specifically the inside of your right leg and foot. To accommodate this, many players kick the left knee toward the right in the backswing, lifting the left heel slightly off the ground, or rolling the entire left foot onto the instep. If

Nick Price's takeaway is seamless—the definition of one-piece takeaway.

In a fully completed backswing, the left shoulder should be tucked under the chin. Here, Tom Lehman does just that.

this feels good to you, do it. Just remember that the left knee should never jut out toward the target line. Rather, it kicks in toward your right knee.

Being aware that these three things happen early in your swing will inevitably come in handy.

Your Swing, Continued

At a certain point, it becomes impossible for the club to continue straight back from the ball. It does not matter precisely where that point is—it occurs when your hips and

Inside the Ropes

Duffy Waldorf *In your weight shift, don't worry about the percentages.*

Duffy Waldorf. Ranked twentieth in driving distance in 1995 (274.2 yards) and nineteenth in 1997 (279 yards).

"At the start of the swing, when all golfers have to get their weight to the inside of their back foot, I don't really think about how much weight I need to move. What I think about is turning my shoulders. If I make a good shoulder turn, my hips also turn as my weight shifts to my back foot. I make my backswing, and if, in the follow-through, my weight finishes on my front foot, I know I got it shifted correctly in the first place. There are times, of course, when I know my turn isn't right, and I notice when I finish that the weight is still on my back foot. Then I know I didn't get it back enough to begin with—I use where the weight is at my finish position to tell me where my weight was during the swing. The main thing, however, is that I focus on my shoulder turn to shift my weight properly."

---

shoulders begin to turn away from the ball. Because the turning movement of your hips and shoulders is of major importance in your swing, it is important that you understand exactly what *turn* means and exactly how your hips and shoulders turn.

When your arms make that first movement, they are swinging as far back as they can unaided significantly by any additional body movement. You would not be able to hit the ball very far if this were the only movement involved in your swing. Of course, it isn't the only movement.

Most of the turning of your shoulders and hips occurs simultaneously. Your hips may start turning away from the ball just a hair before your shoulders do so, but it does not really matter. The turning of your hips and shoulders is responsible for generating the power in your swing. Think of your swing as the coiling and uncoiling of a spring.

For a spring to coil, at least one end of it must be fixed so that the spring has something to resist against. The same is true of your swing. During the backswing, the inside of your right leg and foot serve as this fixed point, which is where you should feel most of your weight. Your hips and shoulders turn around that fixed point in your right leg. The turning continues until your shoulders have turned approximately twice as much as your hips have. At what is considered the *top* of your swing, your hips should have turned roughly forty-five degrees from the point at which they started and your shoulders should have turned roughly ninety degrees from the point at which they started. These numbers are presented simply to give you an idea of the difference in the turning. It is not important to turn exactly forty-five and ninety degrees. How far you can turn involves many factors: how naturally flexible you are, how old you are, your physical condition, etc.

Eventually your hips reach a point where they cannot turn any farther. At this point the shoulders continue turning away from the ball, tightening and tightening that spring until they have turned as far as they can.

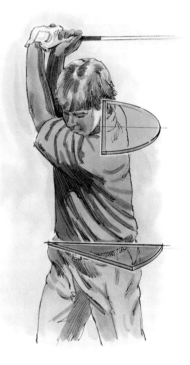

By the time the club has reached the top of the backswing, the shoulders have turned twice as much as the hips, and the back is facing the target.

In this series of illustrations, the first one shows the proper position of the left wrist and clubface at the top of the backswing. In the second illustration, the wrist is cupped and the clubface is closed. In the third illustration, the wrist is bowed, a position sometimes referred to as "laid off," and the clubface is open.

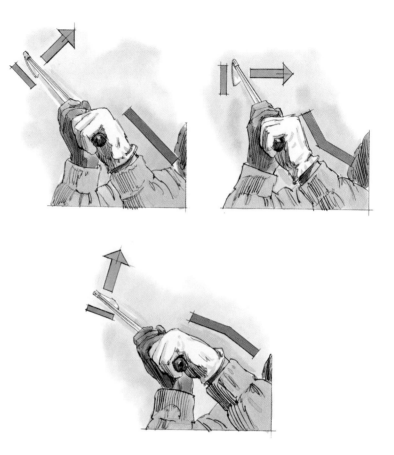

How do you know when your hips and shoulders have reached the point of maximum turn? They just won't move any farther; you have reached your physical limits. There is something quite important to consider, however: The turning of the hips and shoulders must be *parallel with the ground*. In other words, your body must not tilt either to the left (most common in the backswing) or to the right (most common in the downswing). If you maintain and work on this idea of turning level to the ground, your body will let you know when you have made your maximum turn. You *do* want to make your maximum turn, because the farther you turn, the more power you will eventually release on the ball.

The great teacher Percy Boomer best described the turning of the hips as "turning in a barrel." He imagined swinging with a wooden barrel around your legs, rising up to your hips. The image of the barrel does two things: It reminds you to keep your hips level with the top of the barrel, and it inhibits *lateral* motion in favor of the turning action. Ideally you should have very little lateral movement in your swing, which is why you concentrate on keeping your weight on the inside of your right leg and foot. If the weight shifts to the outside of the leg, you will sway laterally away from the ball.

During this turning your arms have continued swinging back along with your shoulders. In fact, your arms are doing a bit of turning of their own, spinning in a clockwise direction. This spinning of your arms happens without conscious effort and is not something you need to think about. Your right elbow has also bent quite a bit by the time you reach the top of your swing. It starts to fold on its own as the club moves behind you. In addition, your wrists have cocked, as they must to lift the weight of the clubhead and support it at the top of your swing. If you keep your grip pressure light throughout your swing you will instinctively cock and uncock your wrists. All of this happens while your hips and shoulders are turning, culminating in the moment known as the top or, more accurately, the *transition phase* of your swing.

The Transition from Backswing to Downswing

When everything falls into place with the right timing, you reach a sweet spot in time—a moment of suspended animation when everything *seems* to hover motionless for just the tiniest of a fraction of a second. This moment, called the *pause at the top*, is incredibly vital to your swing. Here is what happens.

After your hips have finished turning—when they cannot move any farther and still remain level to the ground—your shoulders keep moving. In essence, your hips are ready to be cut loose, but they have to wait for the shoulder turn to finish. More precisely, you must wait for your shoulder turn to finish. When it does, you want to *feel* a pause in the movement of your upper body for just a microsecond. Why? Because this

Jack Nicklaus epitomized power in his heyday. By kicking his left knee in toward his right knee, he increased the amount he was able to turn his hips. This, in turn, allowed him to increase his shoulder turn.

tightly wound spring has already begun to unwind the way you want it to—from the bottom (the fixed point)—up. That split-second pause—which is almost imperceptible if you are swinging with a nice tempo—gives your lower body a chance to get the proper head start on the way down, which is exactly what you want to happen. As you approach that moment when your shoulders shift from turning back to turning through, your hips have already started their forward swing. This brief pause at the top allows a few hugely beneficial things to happen.

First, it allows your upper body to be pulled along by the lower body. Reverting to the spring analogy, the lower body is where the most energy is stored up, so you want the upper body to hang back a fraction of a second until it is whipped forward by the unwinding of the lower body.

Second, the pause at the top allows you to make sure you begin the downswing by keeping your hips and shoulders level, just as they were when they were going back. This helps prevent you from making one of golf's most classic mistakes, swinging *over the top*, or thrusting the right shoulder out toward the target line in an effort that is perceived as powerful (but is in fact a power leak) and that causes all sorts of hideous ball flights.

Third, the pause makes it less likely that you will increase your grip pressure at the top, something that is frequently referred to as *regripping*. This happens most often when the upper body transition is not smooth but is rather a hurried, out-of-control sequence. The sudden shift in tempo causes you to hang on in an effort to control the club.

In this illustration, the club in the middle is considered perfectly parallel at the top of the swing. The club on top is short of parallel, and the club on the bottom is beyond parallel. "Parallel" in this sense is used only as a reference point. Many fine players swing short or beyond parallel.

Fourth, the pause gives you a moment to feel the *planting* of your left foot and the shift to the left leg as the *fixed* point in your swing. As you swing the club back—away from your target—you pivot around your back (right) leg. As you begin the forward swing, you must switch the pivot point to your front (left) leg because you simply cannot swing to and through the ball with all your weight remaining on your right leg—you would probably fall backward. The moment your upper body starts to un-wind, most of your weight switches to your left leg and foot. This weight shift will solidly *plant* your left foot in the ground until well after impact.

Two key yet distinct checkpoints are often used to judge the position of the club at the top of your swing: the position of your club in relation to the ground, and the position of your left wrist. These two things are impor-tant because you cannot see the club (we all wish we could!) and because all will go well in the downswing if you have the club set properly at the top of your swing.

You may have heard that the shaft of the club should be parallel to the ground at the top of the swing. This theory is indeed common, but in real-ity it is not useful. More than anything else, the position of the shaft is a common reference point for marking what is considered a *controlled* swing—that is, to swing past the point where the shaft was parallel to the ground would indicate a swing so excessive that it was impossible to main-tain balance and timing, etc. It is also commonly deemed the point you must reach to have made a backswing sufficiently long enough to generate any power. The first part of the parallel theory—that to go beyond parallel is to be out of control—doesn't hold water. The young Jack Nicklaus, Bobby Jones and many other extremely long, accurate strikers of the ball took the club well beyond parallel. The second part—to come short of parallel indi-cates a deficiency of power—is also a bit flimsy. Some very long hitters of the ball have had very short backswings; TOUR player Dan Pohl comes im-mediately to mind. The crux of the matter is that you can turn as far as your body allows if you can swing with enough strength to control the coil-ing throughout and can *wait* at the top to let things proceed in order.

John Daly is an example of a great player who takes the club well past parallel. Bobby Jones was another. This huge backswing allows Daly to gener-ate tremendous force at impact.

The position of your left wrist, however, is very important. Because the purpose of your swing is to deliver the clubface squarely to the ball, it would be nice if you had some way of knowing the position of the clubface at the top of your swing. Assuming you are using a basically neutral grip, your left wrist should be flat at the top of your swing—that is, it should not bend. If your wrist is flat, you know the clubface is still square. If it is cupped so that the back of your left hand is directly facing you, the club-face is closed. If it is bowed so that the back of your left hand is facing di-rectly toward the sky, the clubface is open.

The idea of an on-plane swing was popularized by Ben Hogan. This illustration shows how that idea is meant to be visualized, with the shaft of the club travelling on the same plane throughout the swing.

Much ado is made of swinging the golf club and the arms *on a plane* throughout the entire golf swing, a notion made popular by Ben Hogan. Although a consistently planed swing is the hallmark of many great players, it is not an event unto itself. It is the result of doing many other things correctly. In other words, don't worry about it. If you turn level, and if you consistently feel like the clubface is square at the top of your swing, you are in good shape. Many terrific golfers have chosen not to focus on Hogan's concept of perfect plane.

The Downswing

Once you have made a smooth transition (think tempo—there's no reason for you to *feel* as if you are quickening your swing) and planted your left foot, your hips move (level!) forward toward your target, and your upper body catches up. You might think of it as a race that finishes in a dead heat. Even though your upper body trails behind at

These two photos of Fred Couples show how once a player is fully coiled in the backswing (left), the wipsaw effect of the downswing begins with an uncoiling of the lower body with the club trailing far behind.

the start of the downswing, it gains speed as it moves without your trying to move any faster. The result is that the club—by extension the farthest point of the spring from the fixed end—receives all the energy and begins to move at ever-increasing speed until impact.

The sequence of events happens so fast on the downswing that, practically speaking, once you have set your weight in your left leg, have planted your left foot, *and* have made it through the transition phase without rushing to "hit at" the ball, you have done all you can to affect what happens next.

Aside from a bit of flex in the knee, your left leg is firm, presenting the strongest possible fixed point against which your coil can unleash. If you have maintained your posture throughout your swing and have turned level away from the ball, the club should be on the desired path for square impact. The club will approach the ball on a curved line that begins slightly inside the target line, runs directly along the target line for a brief flash—impact! —and then extends down the target line before swinging up and around your body.

As you near impact, both arms are fully extended, and at the crucial moment of impact the back of your left hand is directly facing your target. Your arms extend on their own as a result of all the force being generated—it is not a conscious movement as long as you are not standing too close to the ball. (Likewise, the turning of your hands through impact is part and parcel of the release of power. There should not be a conscious turning of the right hand over the left through impact. Such a movement usually leads to a flawed shot.) Once your arms are fully extended, the clubhead makes its final amazing acceleration and catches up to your hands at impact. Your hips have

The notion of weight shift is illustrated clearly in these drawings. At the outset of the swing, the weight is evenly divided between the two legs. In the backswing the weight is shifted to the inside of the right leg. In the downswing, the weight is shifted into the left leg.

turned vigorously so that they are not parallel to the target line but have begun to *face* or turn toward the target, on their way to their final follow-through position.

This may seem like a brief description of the downswing, but the downswing is really a reaction to what you have started with your setup and backswing. The biggest key is patience.

Don't Overlook Your Follow-through

If you have played or watched golf for any length of time, you have probably heard the expressions "He quit on it" or "He didn't finish his swing." What exactly does that mean? It means that to get the full positive effect of everything you have done leading up to impact, you must swing just as vigorously through the ball as you did before striking it. If you quit on your swing—you didn't follow through fully—you gave up on it long before you ever hit the ball. When you slow down through the ball or just slap at it, the chances of the clubface's being square at impact are greatly reduced. If, on the other hand, you are able to complete a full, balanced follow-through, you have done a lot of things correctly.

Like the other parts of your swing, your follow-through blends into the part of the swing preceding it, the downswing and impact. Impact is such a fleeting moment that what you do afterward runs into what you did before.

The first stage of your follow-through is set early in your downswing. Once you have set the weight in your left leg, you have set the pivot point around which the rest of your swing will turn. After you have hit the ball, you will still be turning around your left leg.

The first active stage of your follow-through starts when your arms are fully extended through the impact zone. As you can see in many of the swing sequences in this book or on any slow-motion replay of a TOUR event on television, the complete extension of the arms carries on well into your follow-through. In fact, after impact, you should fully extend your arms for as long as possible. Think about pushing with the right arm and pulling with the left arm, or driving the clubhead toward the target for as long as possible. Because you are making a round swing, you cannot keep the clubhead moving along the target line for very long, but you should feel as if you are moving the clubhead directly for the target for as long as possible. That full, long extension will help you reap the rewards of power you sowed in your backswing and downswing.

Mark O'Meara at impact. Note how his head is well behind the ball, and the manner in which he swings "against" the left leg, which is ramrod straight.

At the same time, you should be forcefully turning—again, *driving* is a good word to describe it—your right hip through toward the target.

After you have reached full extension in your follow-through, your right shoulder will start to turn your head upward so you can watch the flight of the ball. Until this point in your swing, your head should remain steady.

As the club swings toward the conclusion of your swing, you should be thinking about your hands finishing the swing somewhere in the area next to your left ear. That's how far you should swing the club before you think of your swing as finished. When you reach this point your weight should be balanced on your left leg, and your entire body should be facing the target. Have you noticed how the players on the TOUR pose on a shot after striking it? Or perhaps you have caught yourself or a friend doing it after a very fine shot? That's exactly how you should finish every full swing you make.

Lee Trevino a split second after impact. Note how the clubhead "chases" after the ball, a clear signal of full extension at impact and follow through.

Ernie Els at the finish: Perfectly balanced on the left leg, club swung completely around his body.

Inside the Ropes

Jack Nicklaus *Play to your strengths, not someone else's.*

Has won a total of twenty major championships, winning each of the professional majors at least three times. He ranks second among all-time PGA TOUR winners.

"We all know how frustrating the game can be when we're not swinging well. I think one of the problems for everyday players is that they don't really know or understand their own abilities. Sure, it's normal for you to want to model your swing after a pro you admire, but if you don't have the same body build or strength to duplicate that player's swing, you'll be setting yourself up for disappointment and frustration. My advice to any golfer is to define and learn your own best assets and then develop a swing and a game that maximizes them. You'll enjoy the game a lot more, and you will probably play better, too."*

The Keys to the Kingdom of Swing

As you are no doubt aware from your own experience, the entire swing begins and finishes in the blink of an eye. It is not possible, nor is it wise, to attempt to remind yourself to do everything outlined above while attempting to swing the club. The pre-shot phase is different because you can monitor the time and quickly work through a checklist. Once the club starts moving, you simply do not have the time to think. If you try, you will discover that it can have a devastating effect on your game and psyche. In fact, thinking too much during the swing is often referred to as "paralysis by analysis."

Earlier in this chapter the idea of employing *swing keys* was mentioned. The point of a swing key is this: Once you are set to play the shot—your aim is good and your setup feels right—it is best to focus on one thought for your swing. It *is* possible to think of one thing while you swing; in fact, it works quite well. The crucial point of these single thoughts is that they be simple. These thoughts are your swing keys. Swing keys work best when you use them as disposable items—that is, you use one for as long as it seems to work, and when it seems to be losing its effectiveness, you switch to another simple key. Below is a list of great swing keys, which, used one at a time, will help you tremendously. Remember that they are like pills: One at a time is good; the whole bottle at once can be bad for your game's health. Note that these swing keys are presented randomly to show that any one of them can work at any time, independently of other thoughts.

Key: Low and slow. **Meaning:** Take the club away from the ball slowly and low to the ground. This will help you establish the proper tempo for your swing.

Key: Weight back. **Meaning:** Shift your weight back to the inside of your right leg to get your turn started.

Key: Kick the knee. **Meaning:** Kick your left knee toward your right knee to help get your weight back onto your right side. Remember: Kick the knee in, not out toward the target line.

Key: Swing the clubhead. **Meaning:** Keep your grip pressure light, and feel the weight of the clubhead as it moves back away from the ball.

Key: Turn level. **Meaning:** Feel your hips and shoulders making a turn level to the ground.

Key: Trust it. **Meaning:** Have faith in your aim and your setup, and just make a nice smooth swing.

Key: All together. **Meaning:** Make that smooth, one-piece takeaway.

Key: Steady head. **Meaning:** This is the proper way to think about keeping your eye on the ball. Keeping your head still will eliminate all the excess movement that leads to severely missed (topped) shots.

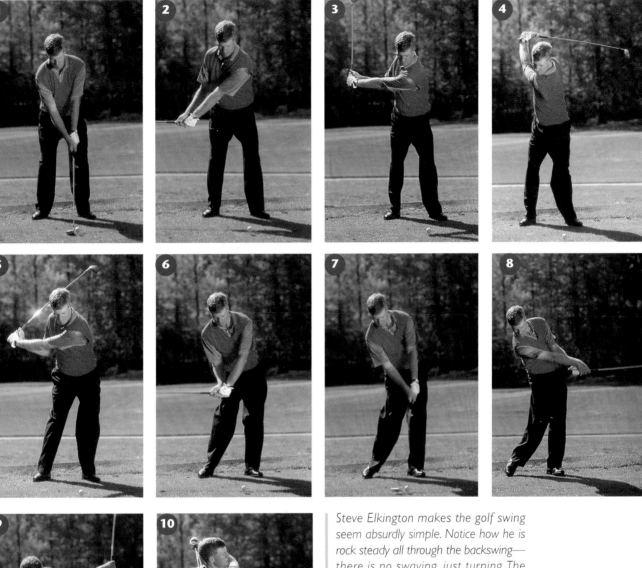

Steve Elkington makes the golf swing seem absurdly simple. Notice how he is rock steady all through the backswing—there is no swaying, just turning. The hands and clubhead arrive at the ball at the same moment.

Key: Start back with the hip. **Meaning:** You feel like you are starting your backswing by turning your right hip away from the ball.

Key: Wait on it. **Meaning:** Be patient at the top of your swing. Don't rush it. Wait for the lower body to lead the way.

Key: Turn to start down. **Meaning:** Feel like you begin your downswing by turning your right hip or front right trouser pocket toward your target. Don't even think about your arms—they're coming.

Key: Back to the target. **Meaning:** At the top of your swing you should feel like you have turned your shoulders enough so your back is facing the target.

Key: Plant it. **Meaning:** To start your downswing, shift your weight into your left leg and plant your left foot solidly on the ground.

Key: Fire them through. **Meaning:** Turn your hips vigorously through the impact zone.

Key: Swing to the finish. **Meaning:** You are going to concentrate solely on swinging through to a full, balanced finish, with your hands by your left ear. If you do this you will have done a lot of things right.

Key: Down and through. **Meaning:** After impact you are going to swing the clubhead down the line toward the target.

Key: Extend. **Meaning:** Extend your arms fully through impact and the beginning of your follow-through.

Key: Chest toward the target. **Meaning:** Turn fully through the target so your chest will be facing the target when you are done.

Key: Right elbow tight. **Meaning:** Keep your right elbow tight to your side at the beginning of and throughout your downswing. This helps prevent you from swinging over the top.

Key: Left arm across chest. **Meaning:** Swing your left arm all the way across your chest in your backswing.

Key: Shoulder under chin. **Meaning:** Extend your shoulder turn so far that your left shoulder feels like it is stretching beneath your chin.

Key: 1, 2, 3, 4 (in tempo, like dancing). **Meaning:** Swing the club at the same tempo throughout your swing, never making a conscious effort to speed things up.

The list above is not complete, but it is unlikely that a complete list could be compiled because each person's swing has its own nuances. Over time you can add your own keys to the list—things you know have worked for you. Above all, distill your thoughts into a few words so you can concentrate on one thing during your swing. You might be surprised at how effective swing keys are, and you can take comfort in the fact that it is not the easy way out—even TOUR players use swing keys.

Common Mistakes

With so much happening during the swing, something will eventually go wrong. Sometimes it will go wrong once every few swings, sometimes every swing. That's the nature of the game.

Listed below are the most common swing faults of the everyday golfer. Remember: A great majority of the problems suffered by the everyday golfer are the result of *mistakes in setup*. You have complete control over your setup no matter how you swing the club. By following the setup procedures outlined in the previous chapter, you will reduce a huge number of errors and lessen the impact of the following errors when they occur:

Swaying off the ball/excessive body movement. In an effort to shift the weight to the left side, some players are overexuberant and make a dramatic weight shift that shifts the weight to the outside of the right leg on the way back. This upsets your swing by knocking you out of balance and leaving no center around which to swing. Make that weight shift a controlled movement, and keep the weight centered around the inside of the right leg.

Leaning out toward the target line. Some players tip toward the ball during the swing, throwing their swing path out of whack. Set your posture at address and then turn level to get the club moving back. If you kick your left knee, kick it toward your right knee, not out toward the ball.

Reverse weight shift (commonly referred to as a "reverse pivot"). When the weight shift is completely flip-flopped (i.e., on the backswing, the weight shifts into the *front* leg, and in the downswing the weight shifts to the *rear* leg), the result is a weak swing with the clubhead way off line. This happens mostly with players who feel they must help the ball into the air by scooping at it through impact. You don't need to help the ball into the air; the club is designed to do it for you.

Inside the Ropes

Tiger Woods *See a PGA professional.*

The 1997 Masters Champion, was second in scoring average in 1996, 1997, and 1998 (69.21).

Almost every golf book addresses the two biggest ball-flight problems of everyday golfers: the slice and the hook, with the slice being predominant. Here is Tiger Woods's advice on fixing your slice (or hook).

"I can't recommend anything for the everday golfer to fix his slice off the tee. Everybody slices the ball for a different, *specific reason. It doesn't even make sense to say something simple like, 'If your slice isn't too bad, just play to the left and allow for it.' That might make things worse, depending on the severity of the slice. The best bet is to see a PGA professional and work together on fixing the problem.*

"There is no clear-cut cure because there are endless causes. Only a qualified eye can determine the specific causes of your slice and work with you to overcome it."

Too much tension. You've already been read the riot act on this one. It can lead to a multitude of swing breakdowns. Keep it loose.

Regripping the club at the top. This happens at the top of your swing when you decide you are going to give the ball a good rip. You quickly loosen and then retighten your grip pressure so you can grab the club more tightly. In so doing, you lose control of the clubface. Make it through that transition under control and this won't happen.

Casting from the top. The word *casting* here is meant to imply a weak fling of the wrists and arms to start the downswing. This prematurely unloads your power. Keep your upper body quiet at the top of your swing.

Over the top. Any time you raise your right shoulder so it is higher than your left, you throw the club dramatically off line. This most often occurs at the top of the swing, when the right shoulder is thrust out toward the target in a move that *feels* powerful. It is not. Your right shoulder should always be slightly lower than your left. You need to place your right hand lower on the club, so you must lower your shoulder slightly to do it. Keep it there.

Slapping at the ball with the arms, rather than turning the body through the ball. The power lies in your body, not in your arms. Let your arms react—they don't initiate the impact. It is like shooting a rifle. When you have done everything else right—aimed and relaxed—the eventual pulling of the trigger should take you by surprise.

Quitting on the swing. Your swing is not over until the ball is well on its way to your target. Do not stop once you have made contact. Remember: Pose on it.

Dramatic changes in tempo. Consciously trying to speed things up in your swing is going to throw off your timing. The sequence of events in your swing must be maintained. If you try to speed things up, something will happen before it is supposed to.

Trying to kill the ball/swinging in anger. It is a frustrating game. The urge to take out your anger at a missed short putt on your subsequent tee shot is one every golfer has felt. It hardly ever works out for the better. It creates tension and harms your tempo and timing. Remember: It is against the law to kill. The ball is your friend—even if you sometimes think, with a friend like that, who needs enemies?

An unsteady head. Keep your head still until your right shoulder drives it up after impact. There's not much to see anyway, and if you move your head, you are not going to like what you see.

BREAKTHROUGH TIPS

According to an old German proverb, "God gives the nuts, but he does not crack them." Here are some tips—"nutcrackers," if you will—that proved critical in player breakthroughs to a higher level of performance.

#1 *Build Clubhead Speed*
Brian Henninger

As a smaller player (five feet, eight inches) I felt the need to increase my distance. I thought that if I could minimize my hip rotation while maximizing my shoulder rotation during my takeaway I could build more torque [coiling tension generated by the difference in turning distances of the shoulders and hips], and thus produce

#2—Control Flying Right Elbow

more hand and clubhead speed during the downswing. I experimented with this idea and got good results. I was able to hit the ball farther. Today I don't even think about it—it's part of my swing.

#2 *Control Flying Right Elbow*
J. C. Snead

I used to have a problem of flying my right elbow. It got too high in my backswing. Everyone who tried to help me correct it focused on ways to control my right arm but Sam [Snead] showed me how to correct it with my left arm. He advised me to raise my left arm no higher than my chest line, that this would keep my right elbow from flying without having to think about it. It worked and I immediately improved control of my ball flight.

#3 *Play Smart Shots*
Dave Rummells

Learning course management has been a big factor in improving my game. I have learned how to distinguish between when I should be aggressive and when I shouldn't. On shorter par 4s, I won't aways hit the driver off the tee. Making bogie on a short par-4 can slow any momentum you're trying to build, and it can deflate your morale. So I think about hitting a club off the tee that will give me the best chance to make a birdie while at the same time help me avoid a shot that can lead to a bogie. On par 5s that are not reachable in two shots, I try to hit my second shot to a spot that will leave me in the best position for my approach shot. Smart shots lead to better scores, it's really that simple.

#4 *Focus on One True Thing*
Chip Beck

On thing I found is that you have to focus on one thought. One cohesive thought can make your entire swing work. The biggest fallacy in golf is that you have to understand the swing in its entirety to perform it. It's simply not true. Golfers are athletes, and the essence of being an athlete is that you can perform an intricate movement with a limited understanding.

#6—Turn Around Axis of Spine
The correct movement is shown at right.

#5 *Maintain Good Balance*
Bruce Summerhays

Any piece of breakthrough advice would have to address a fundamental. For me, maintaining proper balance is most important—it's the best piece of advice I could give anybody. When you swing, stay under control. Even when you're hitting the ball hard, your swing and weight shift should not cause you to lose balance.

#6 *Turn Around Axis of Spine*
Bob Dickson

Taller players like me should make sure that they turn their shoulders around the axis of the spine and avoid tilting them toward the target. Tilting results in taking the club back in an arc that is too upright; this moves the front shoulder forward and down. This move will often cause a "chicken wing" or "flying right elbow" in which the club will be pointed to the right of your target line at the top of the swing. A swing

launched from this position will usually result in a shot that leaks off to the right unless you make compensations in the swing to correct the tilt. All of these gyrations make the swing and game more difficult than necessary.

#7 *Set the Club Properly at the Top*
Jay Haas

Mastering the transition from the backswing to the downswing is very important. If you get the club set properly at the top, it eliminates many of the problems that can occur during the downswing. To get used to what it feels like to set the club properly, try holding the club at the top like a baseball player would waiting for a pitch.

John Daly lets the big dog eat.

The leader of Arnie's Army.

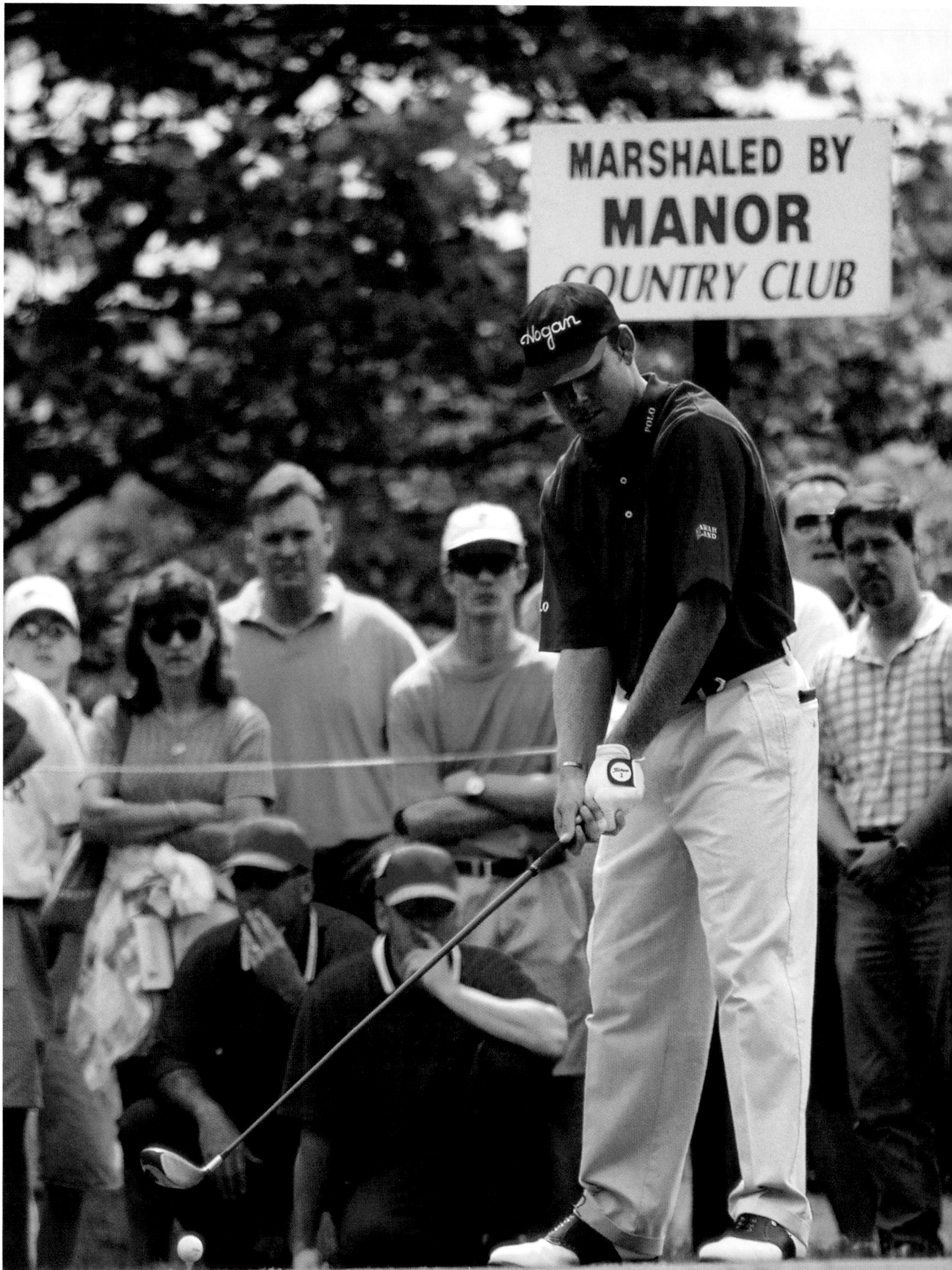
MARSHALED BY
MANOR
COUNTRY CLUB
Hogan
POLO

Playing the Tee Shot

5

This chapter is called "Playing the Tee Shot" and not "Hitting Your Driver" because the driver is not necessarily the club of choice on every par 4 and par 5. The shot you play from the tee sets the tone for the entire hole: Although distance is important, it's not the only consideration. Getting the ball in the fairway is just as important, because a large part of what you can realistically attempt on your second shot will be dictated by the lie of the ball. If you place your tee shot in the fairway, a good lie is almost guaranteed. If you miss the fairway, it's a complete crap shoot: You might get a playable lie, you might not. If you place your ball in the part of the fairway that gives you the most advantageous approach to the green, you will have both a good lie and an easier second shot.

Here's a tip for remembering that a driver may not be the best choice from the tee on every par 4 and par 5: Remove the word "drive" from your golf vocabulary and replace it with "tee shot." Use this as a signal to think through the shot for a second before making your

British Open winner Justin Leonard checks his aim by looking at an intermediate target on the ground a few feet forward of his ball position.

Fred Couples *Create a solid base for your driver.*

Routinely finishes in the top ten in driving distance. He tied for fourth in 1998 (289.1), tenth in 1997, and fourth in 1996. He is a two-time winner of the Players Championship (1984, 1996) and also the 1992 Masters.

"I think one of the main things to playing consistently good drives is to have a nice, solid, balanced base to swing from. To make sure of that, your stance width must be correct. Assuming you are of average build, you want to make sure that your feet are as wide as your shoulders. That is, the distance between your feet—the insides of your feet—should be as wide as or just outside your shoulders. This doesn't have to be precise, of course. You should just feel that's about how wide they are. You should position the ball just off your left heel or toe. This forward position lets you catch the ball slightly on the upswing, which is exactly what you want to do with your driver."*

---

club selection. Here's another tip along the same lines from TOUR player Neal Lancaster, who won the 1994 GTE Byron Nelson Classic.

> Back in the old days, they didn't call it a driver. They referred to it as a "play club." In other words, it was the club you used to put the ball in play—maybe *keep* the ball in play. Most everyday golfers try to hit the ball too hard. To be honest, I tend to do that myself sometimes. It helps to think about getting the ball into play—into position for your next shot—as opposed to driving. If you feel like you're just trying to get the ball into play, it's easier to avoid that urge to swing too hard.

Nevertheless, for the everyday golfer the driver is the club most frequently used to put the ball into play. Therefore, it is worth reviewing some of the fundamental swing thoughts you should be considering when you have the driver in your hand.

The Big Stick: You and Your Driver

When you play a shot with your driver, it is the complete manifestation of what golfers mean when they talk about the "full swing." You play other shots with a full swing as well, but with the driver, everything must come together more precisely than with any other club. Think of the variables in playing the driver: It is the longest club, it has the least amount of loft, and it requires the longest swing if you want to gain the maximum benefit—the longest, straightest tee shot. Because the swing is the longest, there is more movement to it. There is more turning and more weight shifting; there are more challenges to keep your balance and more demands on your timing—the delivery of your body parts and, by extension, the clubhead to the right place at precisely the right moment. These demands on timing are perhaps the most overlooked elements of successful driving, at least in the mind of the everyday player. The urge to crush a tee shot is almost certain to lead to a flaw in timing and tempo—an interruption of the gradual buildup of momentum that leads to powerful shots. All of these difficulties can be overcome, even if you are not a PGA TOUR player.

Once you have elected to play your driver from the tee, you should run through a mental checklist as you prepare to play the shot.

- Have I fully gone through my pre-shot routine? Have I identified a specific target at which to aim? Have I selected an intermediate target—a twig, a leaf, an off-color patch of grass, an old divot—that I can see from my address position and that I can use to align the lead edge of the clubface to my eventual target? Have I stepped into my setup position in the manner most likely to allow me to get my body square to the target line—that is, the right foot first, squaring of the lead edge of the club to the target second and, finally, the final positioning of the left foot and the rest of my body?

- Is my stance wide enough to give me balance, yet not so wide that it will impede my turn? Generally speaking, the insides of your feet should be about a shoulder width apart. Do I have the ball positioned properly in relation to my body? Off your left heel is about right.

Inside the Ropes

Steve Jones *Check your grip pressure for snap hooks.*

Ranked twelfth in driving distance in 1996 (280 yards) and twenty-third in 1997 (278.2 yards). He is the 1996 U.S. Open Champion.

Here he talks about a common malady that occurs almost exclusively with shots played from the tee, the snap hook—a hideous shot that curves hard to the left and then nosedives toward the ground.

"More often than not, when you have a case of the snap

hooks, you should check your grip pressure immediately. If you are holding the club too tightly, you tend to do more with your hands than you should—they have too much influence over what's happening with the clubhead. If your grip pressure is relaxed, what happens to the clubhead will be the result of the arms and body swinging and turning. If you are strangling the club, your hands take over, and those snap hooks aren't far behind."

- Am I free of tension? Am I gripping the club lightly? Is there some flex in my knees? Do I feel loose? Remember that waggling the club and wiggling your feet a little help to keep you loose. Your arms should be hanging straight down and feel limber, like the arms of a swimmer on the starting block.

You're Good to Go

If you have run through that checklist—which probably won't take as long to do as it did to read—you are ready to make the swing. Because you have done everything right so far—chosen the right club, picked a target, and set up properly—you can now focus on the task at hand: striking the ball.

In the chapter on the full swing you read a complete explanation of the buildup of power in your swing. Remember: You do not create power with your arms. Your arms are the transmitters of the power, if you will. The power comes from your body resisting the turn away from the ball (the coiling of a spring) and the subsequent release of that stored energy (you let the spring loose). Your arms—at the far end of this process—benefit by picking up speed in the same manner as a washer tied to a string when it twirls around your finger. Which moves faster, your finger or the washer at the end of the string? The washer.

One of the most frequent errors made by the everyday golfer when he has the driver in his hand is a failure to deliberate, however briefly, on timing and tempo. The two go hand in hand. Timing is the sequence in which the body movements occur, and tempo is the pace at which you are moving. By focusing on tempo, the everyday player dramatically ups the odds that the timing will fall into place. Once you understand the concept of tempo, timing will follow as a result of swing repetitions—playing rounds and hitting balls on the practice tee.

Good or proper tempo is of the utmost importance with the driver. If you think that the proper tempo for your swing is "slow," that's not a bad place to start. Tempo really means moving at the same pace throughout your swing, and starting your swing out slowly gives you the best chance of doing so. You do not have to worry that this will cost you power. In a good swing you will not detect the buildup and release of power. The swing will feel smooth and effortless, as will the impact. (Hence the slang phrase "I hit it pure" derives not from the feeling of a crushing blow, but rather from the odd "nonfeeling" of a dead center hit, which you feel down to your toes in the best possible sense. It is not the jarring feel of an off-center hit, which you feel on the clubhead and in your hands. On the pure shot, the feeling

Inside the Ropes

Duffy Waldorf *Ground your driver—lightly—behind the ball.*

Ranked third in 1998 in total driving, a statistic that combines distance and accuracy.

The everyday golfer is typically most comfortable beginning his swing with the club resting lightly on the ground behind the ball. Some players, notably Jack Nicklaus and Greg Norman, never set the club on the ground behind the ball. This is most noticeable on tee shots because the ball is teed up, and the reasons range from the individual to the logical. (According to the Rules of Golf, if you do not ground the club, you haven't addressed the ball. Therefore, not grounding it prevents complications that arise when the ball moves at address.) What should you do? TOUR veteran and 1995

LaCantera Texas Open Champion Duffy Waldorf has this advice.

"It takes an awful lot of practice to do what those guys [Nicklaus and Norman] do as far as hovering the driver slightly above the ground. What I do, and what I think is easiest for the everyday golfer, is to rest the club very lightly on the ground behind the ball. Don't push down on the club so there is too much weight on it on the ground. The club should touch the ground just slightly. Otherwise you run the risk of it snagging in the grass on your backswing. And that will throw off your timing."

is so fleeting that the ball just seems to vanish from in front of the clubface.) The best thing to keep in mind is that if you start the club back slow, it is easy to keep the same tempo and you allow your body the time to do what it has to do. If you hastily yank the club away from the ball, the timing—the sequence of events—is irrevocably damaged. Your arms and the club get so far ahead of your body that there is no chance for power.

A common flaw in tempo results from the urge to lash at the ball with all your strength. This is a great temptation when the ball is sitting on a tee. (The urge to swing hard is not born of the same urgency felt with fairway woods and long irons played off the ground. As explained in Chapter 6, that urge emanates from the belief that shots played with those clubs are difficult to get airborne. Not so with the teed ball and driver, where the urge to bash the ball is born more of greed than anything else.)

When you watch players on television, you probably notice that they do not all swing slowly. Tom Watson, for instance, seems to swing rather briskly. Scott Simpson, on the other hand, swings slowly. Why? Watson does swing faster, but he swings at the same pace (tempo) throughout. He starts fast and stays fast. If that feels right for you, by all means try it, but by and large the best advice is to start the club back slowly and give things time to develop. Your swing is still going to be over in a split second.

Tiger Woods on the Tee: Pure Power

As the PGA TOUR makes its way toward the next century, no one is more awe-inspiring with the driver in his hands than 1997 Masters Champion and TOUR star Tiger Woods. As seen in frame one of this sequence, Woods is literally a picture of stability at address. His feet are placed wide enough apart to allow him to swing with tremendous force without losing his balance, but not so wide that it would place limitations on his body turn away from the ball.

If you have ever wondered exactly what a "one-piece" takeaway is or what it should look like, look at frame two. Tiger's shoulders and arms have started to move away from the ball, and they do so as a single unit—they form a perfect triangle, the bottom tip of which meets at the hands. The club moves back as an extension of the arms. There is very little movement of the hands up to this point. This puts the club on course to achieve the widest possible arc, which is one element in the mix of maximum power production.

In frame three you can begin to sense the buildup of power. Note that the right foot is planted firmly on the ground—there is no sense that he's leaning away from the target—and that the right leg's role as the rock-solid point around which the body will turn away from the ball is clearly visible. Also visible at this point is the ratio of difference between the hip turn and the shoulder turn. Already the shoulders have turned more than the hips. The clubhead continues along the widest possible arc, and the arms continue to move as one unit with the shoulders. The triangle is still in place. The left shoulder, which will eventually be tucked entirely under the chin, has begun to make its way toward that end.

As Woods continues back in frame four, there are many things from which you can learn. First, note his balance. Although his weight has certainly shifted to his right side, he most certainly hasn't let it get to the outside of his right leg. The sense you should have at this point is that the weight is on the inside of your right leg. Tiger's shoulders have turned to the point where his back is facing the target. His hands are still very quiet; any cocking of the wrists has occurred naturally as a result of the weight of the clubhead. Note that his left arm is ramrod straight but that the right elbow has begun to bend. Nevertheless, the elbow is still tucked very close to his body. This allows him to make the massive upper-body turn and get the club as far behind him as possible without the swing feeling stiff or awkward.

In frame five Tiger has reached the most critical part of the swing for the everyday golfer, for it is here that many players fall prey to the notion of speeding up the swing to hit the ball hard. He knows that the key here is a smooth transition from the backswing to the downswing. The big temptations here for the everyday golfer are (1) to grab the club tighter with the hands, which creates a jerky motion at a point when smoothness is of the essence and (2) to "come over the top," which means you throw your right shoulder out toward the target line (and off plane) in an attempt to deliver a hammer blow, as if you were slamming a huge carnival hammer in an attempt to ring the bell. This over-the-top move might feel powerful, but it is guaranteed to have a hideous effect on the flight of your ball.

At this part in Tiger's swing his hips have already stopped turning back. His shoulders are still turning back; this trailing-behind effect of the upper body allows it to generate tremendous speed as it catches up to the lower body in the downswing. Far from being in a hurry, you should be giving your upper body the time to get set a moment as your hips start their forward move. Tiger generates a tremendous amount of clubhead speed through the ball—in fact, the force he generates is downright violent in the sense that a storm can be violent, and it often seems that he will come right out of his shoes. You can be certain, however, that Tiger is not thinking about hurrying things up.

You can see in frames six, seven, and eight that when Tiger's shoulders finally begin to start back toward the ball, they are on the plane they were on when they moved away from the ball; there is nothing resembling the over-the-top move mentioned above. This is the moment when Tiger's (and your) patience at the top of the swing pays off—here comes the power! As the upper body races to catch up to the lower body so they can reach impact at the same moment, the upper body builds up tremendous speed—so much speed that the clubhead lags behind. When the clubhead begins to catch up is when the afterburners really kick in. Then, bam! Impact. As you can see in frame nine, everything reaches the ball at the same moment—the clubhead, the shoulders and the hips all taut with power, hitting against the left side, which has stiffened to allow the body something to unwind against—in much the same manner that it wound up around the right side.

Finally, notice in frame ten how Tiger's arms and the club extend fully through the ball and how Tiger's right arm folds over the left at the conclusion of full extension. The finish position is one of perfect balance, which is amazing considering the tremendous speed at which the club was moving.

The Driver at the Top: The Critical Transition

From the moment you start the club back until you reach the position referred to as the *top* of your swing, three things happen. You shift your weight, you turn your body, and you swing your arms. Each of these elements of the swing is important, and each is covered fully in Chapter 4. However, after you start the club back slowly, the next big hurdle in hitting a successful drive is the successful transition from backswing to downswing. Another way of thinking about it is the switch from power buildup to power release. This, too, is covered fully in Chapter 4, but because the driver offers the most difficult transition, here are a few key points to remember.

The most common error during the transition phase of the swing occurs when a player attempts to rush the downward motion of the arms. This is simply another aspect of the urge to hit the ball hard and the feeling that you must strike at the ball with your arms. The best way to avoid this is to think of starting your downswing with your lower body. (You might remember from Chapter 4 that you actually *do* start your downswing with your lower body even if you are not aware of it. You should *feel* as if you are starting the downswing with your lower body.) The following are some swing keys that can help you once you feel the club has reached the top of the swing:

- Fire your right hip toward your target;
- Turn your right pocket toward your target;
- Clear your left side—that is, fully turn to your left.

Any of these things will help you to achieve the momentary separation between the upper and the lower body that keeps the timing in order for maximum power. (Don't worry, the upper body catches up in a hurry!)

Inside the Ropes

Scott Hoch   *Getting the driver to parallel is an individual thing.*

Ranked twenty-fourth in All-Around Ranking in 1998.

"I think the idea of getting the club parallel with the ground at the top of the backswing came out of two concerns. One, it was meant to be the point at which you knew you'd made a full enough backswing, and two, it was meant to be the point to help you guard against overswinging. For most everyday golfers, if they overswing it is just going to kill them. It is so difficult to keep your timing on track when you overswing—in fact, when the everyday golfer overswings he can just about guarantee that it is going to throw his timing off.

"A lot of TOUR players go way past parallel. Guys like Fred Couples and John Daly, but that's an individual preference.

They are capable of making a huge shoulder turn and keeping their timing. One of the things I check when my driver is off is the length of my swing. When my rhythm is good, I can swing past parallel a bit and hit very good shots. But when my timing is a little off, I think about shortening my swing a little bit. It is easier to control my swing that way.

"There are other players who do not even reach parallel. That's not necessarily a bad thing, either. Dan Pohl was like that when he played, and he could still hit the ball a long way. Ideally, you want to make the fullest possible turn without reaching for that extra little bit that might throw your tempo out of whack. If you do that, it really doesn't matter if the club is parallel, past parallel, or short of parallel."

Once you have managed the setup, takeaway, and transition phases of the swing with the driver, you are on your way to consistency with that club. These phases do not constitute the entire swing, but they do represent the areas in which you are most likely to make a significant mistake.

Ten Great Driver Swing Keys

Throughout this book you are encouraged to follow a consistent pre-shot routine and checklist. Sometimes, however, the mind can get a bit jumbled with thoughts. If that happens to you on the course, here are ten solid swing keys you can use individually—apart from any other thoughts—to help with your driving:

1. Focus on posture—feel the knee flex.
2. Take it back slowly for the first eighteen inches.
3. Take the club back on a straight line for as long as possible.
4. Keep the clubhead low to the ground.
5. Keep your grip loose enough to feel the clubhead.
6. Keep it smooth at the top.
7. Fire your right hip toward the target to start down.
8. Feel a firmly planted left foot to start down.
9. Get your left shoulder under your chin.
10. Swing to a balanced finish—hands high by your left ear.

Troubleshooting Your Driver

The driver is perhaps the most maddening of all clubs for the everyday player, who has great hopes every time it is in his hands. Then, suddenly, things go awry: A popped-up shot here, a slice there, a wild hook into the duck pond—chaos with your driver, and it is more noticeable than with any other club. Here's a checklist to use when things go crazy with your driver:

- **Popping the ball up in the air.** Popping the ball up in the air most commonly occurs when the clubhead comes into the ball at too steep an angle. The first thing to check is your shoulder turn both back and through the ball. It should feel level to the ground, not like you are tilting toward the target. Another cause of the steep angle is the reverse pivot that occurs when you shift your weight onto your forward leg in the backswing rather than your rear leg. On the backswing you should feel the weight on the inside of your right leg. If you are cognizant of any excess weight at all on the left side (any more than you need to keep your balance), a reverse pivot is occurring. Occasionally the ball pops up simply because you have it teed too high. The rule of thumb for the height you

Ernie Els on the Tee: Smooth, Fluid and Long

Two-time U.S. Open Champion Ernie Els is a tremendously long driver of the ball, but you wouldn't know by watching the smooth, fluid motion he employs. Unlike Tiger Woods, whose swing bespeaks power, Els's languid motion seems almost slow. It is proof that a swing need not look fast or powerful to produce prodigious shots.

This down-the-line view demonstrates one of the solid basic principles that all long hitters achieve at the start of the swing. In frame two, note how the club moves away from the ball on a straight line during the first milliseconds of movement. It isn't yanked hurriedly inside that line, nor is it pushed outside that line.

As the swing progresses in frame three, you get a terrific look at the shoulders turning back, and a clear view of how steady Els's head remains while so much goes on directly around it. This frame also affords a nice view of how the right leg serves as the base around which everything else in the swing turns.

This down-the-line view is the best for observing how the hips start the forward movement while the upper body is still turning away from the ball, as seen if frame five. Notice the difference from the previous frame (frame four) in the position of Els's right hip.

The down-the-line view also gives you a clear look at the plane of the swing. Swinging on the same plane throughout the swing is a goal for all golfers, because doing so ensures a consistent swing, or what TOUR players refer to as a repeating swing. Although some players can deviate from the same plane (Raymond Floyd and Lee Trevino are classic examples), they have phenomenal hand and eye coordination and they have hit hundreds of thousands of golf shots in their life and therefore can consistently get the club to the perfect position at impact. The everyday golfer can benefit greatly from the idea of the shoulders moving away from the ball and back toward it on the same plane. Typically the reference point for the plane of the swing is the angle of the shaft throughout the swing. Just remember that the shaft is a mere extension of what you are doing with your body.

Finally, from this down-the-line view, you can get a full understanding of how the entire right side of your body should "fire" through the shot—there is nothing left in reserve here. Note that the right pocket of Els's trousers goes from being very visible at the top of his swing to being completely out of sight just after impact. This is a concrete indication of how far the hips have turned in both directions. The finish position is also a sweet sight from down the line. The balance is clearly obvious.

tee the ball is that the middle part of the ball should be in line with the top of the driver.

- **Topping the ball.** If you are topping the ball, it could be too far forward in your stance, so make sure the ball is off your left heel. More often than not, however, topping the ball is purely the result of a rushed swing without tempo and timing. Relax, swing slowly, and keep your head still.

- **Hooking the ball from right to left.** Hooking the ball isn't so terrible. Typically you are close to a good swing if you hit a hook. Wild hooks, however, have many causes:

   1. The clubface is closed at address and/or the ball is positioned too far forward,

As a general guideline, with the driver you should tee the ball so that its midpoint is level with the top of the club.

2. Your body is closed to (aimed right of) the target at address, while the club is aimed at the target,

3. Your swing is excessively flat (you come into the ball at a shallow angle),

4. You regripped the club at the top of your swing—that is, you loosened it a bit and then yanked on it in an effort to hit the ball farther,

5. Your grip has gotten a touch strong—maybe you sneaked your left thumb a little too far to the right on the grip,

6. Your tempo and timing are out of whack, with your tempo resembling the start-stop-start-stop depression of a car accelerator.

- **Slicing the ball from left to right.** If you slice the ball, you should check your setup. If you are a slicer and you start aiming your body farther and farther left of the target to compensate, you are probably making matters worse, particularly if you aim your feet left and keep your shoulders turned toward the target. Do you start the downswing with your arms, or cast from the top of your swing with your wrists ("casting" in this case referring to the wrist snap fishermen employ while casting)? Perhaps you are coming into the ball on a line that runs from outside the target line to inside the target line ("outside in" in swing parlance), which most commonly occurs because you took the club away from the ball on that line (rather than straight back), or you came over the top to start your downswing, throwing the club off plane. "Over the top" means that you push your right shoulder out toward the target line (because it feels powerful), rather than turning the shoulders back toward the ball on the same plane as the backswing.

- **Pushing the ball straight right or pulling the ball straight left.** In most cases, pushing or pulling the ball results from one of two things. Your ball position is off a touch, or you "quit" on your swing and shove the clubhead through impact rather than releasing it and turning through the shot.

Troubleshooting note: The effect of almost any swing motion mistake can be limited if your address is correct. In the case of your driver, especially modern ones with deep faces, be certain to get the lead edge of the clubface squared before you step into your setup with your left side. If you wait until your body is set to attempt this, the visual effect of the lack of loft and the deep face will make it difficult to be precise with your aim.

How to Choose the Right Club on the Tee

Here's an axiom that does not hold true: *You drive for show, and you putt for dough.* What it is intended to mean, of course, is that a good driver does not necessarily have an advantage, and that the shots that determine the outcome of a given match or PGA

Tournament are usually putts. The last part is logical, of course, because putts are the shots that finish off a hole. However, for your putts to mean anything, you have to be on the green with a minimal amount of shots expended. Is driving insignificant compared to putting? No; the notion is absurd. That old line should sound something like this: *You drive to show you* can *putt for dough.* If you keep your drives in play you'll get to the green in fewer shots and have more putts that mean something.

(If you are skimming this book, read the parts of Chapter 2 that relate to finding the right driver. The one area where you are most susceptible to making a mistake in choosing a piece of equipment is the driver because it is viewed as a club that, at the expense of all else, should produce the longest possible shots. It is not uncommon to think that a driver should have the least possible amount of loft and the longest possible shaft. Although reading this book indicates a desire to emulate the best golfers in the world, it cannot be stressed enough that the selection of a driver is one area in which you do not want to copy them in the extreme, particularly as it pertains to loft.)

Determining Where You Want to Place the Tee Shot

Keeping your drives in play sometimes means leaving your driver in the bag and opting for another club.

What is the order of thoughts you must consider? Perhaps it would be best to begin your few minutes on the tee by considering what *not* to think. It is always a bad idea to step onto any tee box with the lone thought of hitting the longest possible shot. Granted, there are certain holes where letting it rip is an acceptable plan, but you should never have that branded into your mind as the sole goal of the shot.

The goal of your tee shot is to place the ball in a position that affords you the best prospects for successfully executing the next shot. Anyone who has played the game

Inside the Ropes

Jim Furyk *How to hit a cut shot with your driver.*

Ranked fourteenth in driving accuracy in 1997, and twenty-fifth in 1996. Also ranked sixth in All-Around Ranking in 1998.

"I had a two-shot lead as I came to the final hole of the 1995 Las Vegas Invitational, so I knew I had to keep my drive in play. My natural shot is a cut shot [left to right], and there was a hazard down the left side, so I had to start the ball out over the hazard. I knew I had to hit it perfectly, and I was as nervous as could be. I nailed it, and it cut beautifully and ended up in the fairway. I do not mess with my swing mechanics at all to hit a fade. I take care of it in my setup. I move the ball up farther in my stance and make sure my left foot is open [flared toward the target and drawn back a bit from the target line]. This setup allows me to make sure I clear my left side through the ball and hit the cut. One last thing I do is try not to hit the ball too hard. If you make a nice, smooth swing, it is much easier to cut the ball than if you try to whip the club in there."

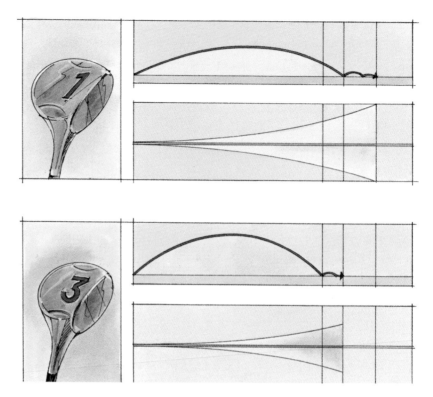

The driver may be the longest club in your bag, but it's not the most accurate. It has the widest range of dispersion on mis-played shots. In certain situations, the 3-wood is a better club to use from the tee because it flies nearly as far as the driver, flies straighter than the driver, and rolls less once it hits the ground.

just a few times knows that even the best-planned shot does not always come off the way you would like it to. Nevertheless, your chances of success increase dramatically if you have a clear idea of what you'd like to accomplish with a given tee shot. Thinking "I want to kill this one" or "I'm just going to swing at this and see what happens" may work occasionally, but not on a consistent basis. Moreover, that type of thought usually increases the chances of a poor shot that will not leave you in position to play the preferred second shot and that will leave you *no chance* of playing a second shot that will help your cause.

Determining where you want to place your tee shot begins by looking down the hole and identifying the trouble spots—water, bunkers, trees, and out of bounds. All of these may cost you strokes and/or impede a clear second shot. What weight you give them in picking the spot you wish to play to depends on their proximity to the tee. Although many different scenarios are given as examples in Chapter 14, which covers course and game management, it is necessary to consider some strategies here.

If you have played a course or a hole before, you should have a good idea of the distances to any potential trouble spots from the tee. If you are playing a course for the first time, you are probably going to have to make your best guess at the distance to any obstacles. When this is the case, you should make some mental notes for future reference by pacing off the yards as you walk toward your ball (if you are walking) or by gauging how well you struck the shot and where the ball landed in relation to where you thought it would.

Once you have identified the trouble spots and know (or have estimated) how far away from you each one is, you have made the first step in determining a target. The next step is to know (or estimate) what sort of stance you would like to have when playing your second shot. As a general rule, it's best to play almost every shot from level ground, because the difficulty of any shot increases when the ball is above or below your feet, or your body is leaning away from or tilting toward the target. It's not always possible to avoid an uneven lie, but it's better if you can.

At this point you have done two things: assessed the distance to any potential obstacles, and made a general assessment of the terrain to determine any flat areas that would be suitable points from which to play your next shot. Ideally, you want to hit your tee shot to the farthest (from the tee) flat spot that leaves a clear avenue of approach for your second shot. What will be required for your tee shot to get there? Can you safely, with an average shot played with your driver (not your all-time best shot), carry any water or bunkers between you and that point? If you can carry them, will the subsequent roll of the ball once it hits the ground put the ball in harm's way—let's say another bunker? (See "Influences on Carry and Roll" below.). Would reaching that farthestmost flat spot require you to flirt with out-of-bounds areas? The possible scenarios are endless. If you cannot carry a given obstacle, you must play so that your ball ends up short of the obstacle. Therefore, you must consider the carry *and* the roll of the shot with any given club. If your driver would fly directly into a hazard, or if the combined carry and roll of your driver would place you in a bad spot, you should rule out the driver for that particular tee.

Perhaps you do not have to consider carrying any hazards because the obstacles— bunkers, trees, etc.—lie off to the side and are avoidable if you hit a good, straight shot. What do you consider in this case? First, remember that the driver is the most difficult club in your bag to hit straight because of its lack of loft. (The more loft a club has, the more likely you are to hit it straight.) Also consider how much room for error you

The 13th hole at Augusta National is a wicked dogleg. In order to have a chance at eagle, players in the Masters must hit a tee shot that turns hard from right to left. The hole defends against "overcooked" hooks with a creek (lower right of photo) that runs down the left side. Trees on the right gobble up straight shots that are played too long.

With water on the left, the target for your tee shot should be the right side of the fairway.

have. If you hit the shot off line (which happens more often than not), will the combined carry and roll get you in trouble? If so, once again you should consider eschewing the driver in favor of a club that is easier to control.

You need to know how far you carry each of your clubs, you must estimate the total yardage the ball will travel (carry plus roll), and you must know your own game and your capabilities. For instance, if a stream cuts across the fairway 210 yards from the tee, you would quickly run through the following list of questions: Can I safely fly the ball over the stream? If I do fly the ball over the stream, is there a suitable spot from which to play my next shot? If so, which club's total distance (carry and roll) will get me to that spot?

If the answer to the first question is "no," select a club that, considering the roll, will leave you safely short of the water. If the answer to the first question is "yes," you still might consider playing short of the stream if the answer to the second question is "no."

Inside the Ropes

Sandy Lyle   *How to hit your drive off the fairway.*

Won the 1985 British Open, the 1987 PLAYERS CHAMPIONSHIP, and the 1988 Masters.

The design of modern drivers makes them easier to play off the ground than the persimmon drivers of a bygone era.

"When we were all using wooden drivers, you would never even consider hitting a driver off the deck. Today fellows like Colin Montgomerie use the driver from the fairway as if it is just another fairway wood. The key is to keep your swing smooth. You want to move the ball slightly more forward in your stance than you would with, say, a 3-wood. Obviously you're concentrating on getting the ball up in the air. To accomplish this you want to think about keeping your weight behind the ball—you do not want to get ahead of it—and hit down on the ball and through to the target. It is best to set up a little open and play a thinnish cut shot. That's the easiest to execute. Always be thinking smooth. Don't snatch at it. In other words, do not be in a hurry to get to the ball once you reach the top of your backswing."

The Rules entitle you to play your ball up to two clublengths behind the tee markers. If you think the club you have may be a little too much, tee your ball back a few feet—it could make a difference.

The point is *not* to discourage you from hitting your driver, but to encourage you to think for a moment before automatically grabbing the driver on every long hole. If, all things considered, you think the driver is the smart choice, then the driver is the club you should select.

Influences on Carry and Roll

Once you have determined where you'd like your ball to go, keep in mind that there is a difference between where the ball *lands* (or first hits the ground) and where it eventually comes to rest. Unlike a well-struck approach that lands on the green, it is difficult to gauge how your tee shot will react once it hits the ground. These are the factors you should consider: the terrain (is it uphill, downhill, sidehill, or flat?), the condition of the ground (is the ground wet, dry, or cement hard?), the direction of the wind (if any), and the angle at which the ball first strikes the ground.

Of these factors, you have control over only one, the angle at which the ball first strikes the ground. First let's discuss the factors over which you have no control.

The terrain. If the ball hits on a downslope in the fairway, it is going to bound forward and, barring an unforeseeable crazy kick, continue rolling forward until the terrain levels out or the ball runs out of steam—whichever happens first. If the ball lands on an upslope in the fairway, the hill will take some zip off the ball. If the ball lands on a right-to-left or left-to-right slope in the fairway, it is going to run in the direction of the hill. The effect of each of these three possibilities is diminished if the ball lands in the rough. The longer grass will slow the ball.

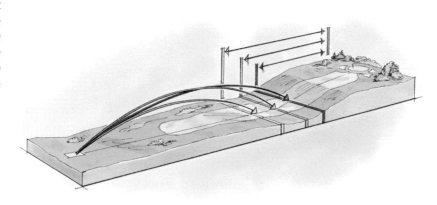

The longest drive may not be the best drive. Since the idea of the drive is to leave you a comfortable approach shot, on a short par four like the one shown here, you may prefer to lay back off the tee in a yardage range that suits you. This also ups the chances of hitting the fairway.

The condition of the ground. If the ground is wet, the amount of roll is diminished or reduced. In fact, if the ground is very wet, you might not get any roll at all. If the ground is about normal (if there's been average rainfall), the amount of roll is what you would use as your standard for "typical." If there has been a bit of a drought and the sun has turned the ground into a runway, the ball is going to run significantly more than is typical.

The direction of the wind. If the wind is behind you, the ball is going to fly farther and roll farther when it hits the ground. The following wind reduces the amount of spin on the ball while it is in flight, which causes it to bounce farther once it hits the ground. If you are hitting into the wind, the ball will fly higher (increasing the angle at which the ball strikes the ground) and have more spin on it. As a result, the amount of roll is diminished in direct proportion to the intensity of the headwind.

When the wind is blowing from the side, there are two possibilities with each type of sidewind (left to right and right to left). If the wind is blowing left to right and you hit a shot with left-to-right spin on it, the ball is going to roll more once it hits the ground. If you hit a shot that curves right to left into a left-to-right wind, the amount of roll will be decreased once the ball hits the ground. If the wind is blowing right to

Inside the Ropes

John Cook   *If your driver is too long, your whole swing changes.*

Ranked fourth in Greens-in-Regulation in 1993 and fifth in 1997. He has won eight PGA TOUR events.

The modern trend toward lighter clubheads and longer shafts in the driver has created a "have your cake and eat it too" dilemma for golfers.

"If your driver is too long—if the length of it isn't part of a consistent lengthening throughout your set, each club being the same amount longer than the preceding one in the set— your whole swing will change with that club that doesn't

match [the driver]. Something that matches the rest of your set would be more advantageous. Unless you are swinging that club and hitting balls with it every single day, there's no way you are going to get your timing down with a forty-eight-inch shaft. I just cannot see it. As far as the size of the head goes, they've gotten so big that unless your fairway woods match your driver in terms of clubhead size, the transition from club to club is jarring to the eye."

left, just reverse the above scenarios: A shot curving from right to left will roll farther, and a shot curving into the wind from left to right will have less roll.

All of these factors—terrain, ground condition, and wind direction— are things you must consider but that you cannot change. Another major factor in the amount of roll you get on your tee shots is the angle of the ball when it first hits terra firma. On a well-struck shot, with little wind to consider, the angle at which the ball strikes the ground is determined by the loft of the club with which you struck the shot. The rule here is simple: Less loft (driver), more roll; more loft (fairway woods and long irons), less roll.

Special Challenges and Demands of Golf

You can hit a great shot and end up ten feet from the hole, or you can hit a lousy shot and have it go in the hole. That's just the nature of golf.

— David Edwards

Golf has unique challenges and demands that players must overcome to play their best. Most sports require the participant to be actively engaged for most of the game. Basketball players must look for a sudden pass from a teammate, baseball players must prepare on every pitch for the ball to be hit to them, tennis players are continuously moving to and from a shot. Golf is different—you have an abundant amount of time to think between shots. The ball stands still until you are ready to propel it. How you choose to spend your downtime can influence your performance. At the very least, you must guard against being too analytical and judgmental between shots.

Golf is the ultimate individual sport. Although you play with others, you are alone. You have no teammates to help you swing the club. When you play well, you take all the credit for your success. When you play poorly, you must take also the blame for your failure. In football, a lineman can miss an assigned block and the team can still move the ball down the field. In soccer, a player can miss a kick at midfield and little harm is done. In golf there are always consequences from a failure to perform correctly, and there is no anonymity. There is no place to hide when you slice a ball out-of-bounds, or when you miss a putt to lose a match. As the ultimate individual sport, golf is the ultimate individual responsibility (every action has its consequences, good or bad) sport.

Golf is inherently paradoxical. Hitting a ball that is two and one-half inches in diameter with a 43-inch long club with a clubhead four inches wide that is traveling at 100 mph into a cup that is four inches in diameter is an imperfect task. Yet, the challenge of this task keeps golfers coming back for more. What is even more astonishing is that the nature of the game breeds perfectionism. To achieve success in golf, you need innate physical talent, willingness to work hard, mental fortitude and a level of commitment and motivation that approaches perfectionism. The irony is that golf is an imperfect game that produces perfectionists. The more you play the better you get, the more you expect to play flawlessly in a game that cannot be played to perfection.

Mastery of the Comfort Zone

When I work with golfers one of my biggest challenges is to help them overcome the "comfort zones" or scoring zones. A comfort zone is an expectation a player has about his ability to shoot a certain score. You leave the "comfort zone" and enter the "discomfort zone" when you score below or above the score you normally expect to total at the end of a round.

Nearly everyone expects to shoot within a certain scoring range on a given day. John, for example, usually shoots in the mid-80s and has a scoring zone of plus or minus six shots from his average score. On a good day he shoots 78, on bad day he shoots 90. In the back of his mind he knows what he can usually shoot. Because of the expectations he holds he always manages to play within his comfort zone. If he shoots 37 on the front nine, he may think, "I've never shot better

124

than 76," and then he proceeds to shoot 43 on the back nine. Conversely, if he shoots 46 on the front nine, he says, "I'm too good a player to shoot 90," and he plays himself back into his comfort zone and shoots 39 on the back nine.

Players at all levels seem to be afflicted with a comfort zone. A professional is out of his comfort zone when he is one or two over par on an easy course. A high handicap golfer who is playing well feels awkward when playing better than he expects. When your expectations don't match your play, you consciously or unconsciously find a way to play back to your comfort zone. A comfort zone is similar to a self-fulfilling prophesy, which occurs when what you believe will happen actually does happen because of your conditioned expectations.

Golf is inherently paradoxical.

Maintain Your Aggressive Style

When you are playing above your expectations early in a round don't sabotage yourself later in the round. Keep the same game plan that got you the low scores. Don't "go negative," that is, don't think that your low score is an anomaly, that "this isn't my normal game." Don't think your low scores as something to protect. Rather, think about building on them.

A common reaction when a player is putting up "uncomfortably" low scores is, "Don't screw it up." Instead of firing at the pin and aggressively rolling putts in or past the hole, you suddenly turn defensive. This style of play seeks to avoid failure, rather than aggressively pursuing the best round of your life. In this state of mind, you notice trouble areas more and begin to worry about the consequences of bad shots. Soon, your defensive style of play causes you to hit the ball fat or leave birdie putts four and five feet short—which you never did while you were

posting the earlier low scores. You have to maintain the same style of play that got you in position to shoot a good score. Think about continuing to play boldly. When you are playing well, what is the only thing that can stop you from continuing to play well? You, and only you.

You Only Get What You Expect.

For any round, learn to discard your expectations. Humans are the only beings that place limits on their potential. If you are a scratch or single-digit handicap player, you must start the day having confidence and believing you have the ability to par or birdie every hole on the golf course. When you start to play above your expectation, assume that you are only playing near your maximum potential. Discard the concept that you are playing above your ability. Rather, you are simply playing closer to your fullest potential.

Stay Focused in the Present

A player who projects his or her final score and then examines whether that score matched his or her expectation is not focused on playing one shot at a time. He or she is thinking ahead about a finishing score and not focusing on the task, which is to get the ball into the hole in the least number of strokes every time you tee the ball in the ground. Throughout the round, keep your mind focused on the process of hitting good shots. If you think about it, that is really all you can do, that is all you can control—concentrate on this and the score will take care of itself. Without a process, present-oriented focus, you are doomed to thinking about a final score and ultimate consequences of each shot before you even hit the ball.

Bill Murray's playing partner, Scott Simpson.

Where all pros aspire to be—the leaderboard.

Playing *the* Fairway Woods *and* Long Irons

6

Fairway woods and long irons are discussed together in this chapter because they cover roughly the same distance in the air and they both are played using a sweeping swing action from a forward ball position. That is where the similarities end, however.

Fairway Woods: The Most Versatile Clubs in Your Bag

The modern fairway wood offers tactical and practical versatility unlike any other club in the history of golf equipment. The modern designs are so easy to hit consistently well that they have made their way into the bags of many players on the PGA TOUR and the SENIOR PGA TOUR.

The continual evolution in the design of fairway woods has made them easier to hit than the modern long iron—which itself is easier to hit than ever before. In this chap-

Jim Furyk in the classic follow-through position, with his chest facing the target.

Steve Stricker prepares to play a fairway wood shot. Note that the ball is slightly farther back in his stance than it would be with the driver.

ter many of the TOUR players give advice about how to take advantage of this fact. Modern metal fairway woods have bigger clubheads, are superbly balanced in feel, and sport sole designs that make them extraordinarily playable clubs from nearly any lie. You sometimes even see them used to play shots around the green!

There are two reasons why the fairway woods are so versatile. The first is the shaft: It is long enough to create a lot of power, but shorter than the driver and therefore easier to control. The second reason is the loft, which is greater than that of the driver. As you move through your fairway woods, they become easier and easier to hit straight because of the increased loft. Obviously, with increased loft, distance is decreased; the question is how much. It's impossible to make a sweeping statement to cover all players, but on average the 3-wood probably carries ten to fifteen yards fewer than the driver and rolls less once it hits the ground. You are, however, more likely to hit it straight, and you have a better sense of how it will react when it hits the ground—it will not run as much—so the 3-wood is often chosen over the driver from the tee, for tactical purposes.

For these very same reasons, clubs such as the 5-wood and even a 7-wood are sometimes intelligent choices from the tee, depending upon the hole you are playing. Each carries a shorter distance, but as the distance of the shot decreases, the odds for accuracy increase. Chapter 12, on course and game management, goes into greater detail on why you might choose one club over another from the tee, and this chapter provides some information on selecting a club for shots played not as tee shots but as approach shots with fairway woods and long irons.

Brett Quigley   *You are better off with more fairway woods and fewer long irons.*

Played his way onto the PGA TOUR by finishing fifth on the 1996 NIKE TOUR money list.

Here he talks about the ideal balance between fairway woods and long irons for the everyday golfer.

"If you are a fourteen- or eighteen-handicapper, in that range or higher, I'd strongly recommend carrying more fairway woods than long irons. I think that realistically a 4-iron is about the lowest iron you need to carry. I wouldn't bother with the 2-iron or 3-iron. Get yourself a 4-wood, a 5-wood and a 7-wood because they are easier to hit, and they are definitely easier to hit out of the rough. If you have a bad lie in the rough, it's impossible to get a 3-iron out of there, but you've got a good chance of getting a 5-wood or a 7-wood out of there. You can carry all these woods if you yank some of those long irons from your bag. And if you need more room to stay within the fourteen-club limit, just stick with two wedges—a pitching wedge and a sand wedge. Not only will these give you more room for fairway woods, but it will cut down on the confusion when you have to decide which wedge to play."

Playing the Fairway Woods: Get Swept Up in the Action

TOUR players and PGA teaching professionals most commonly describe the swing action for fairway woods (and long irons) as *sweeping*. This means that it helps to imagine catching the ball slightly on the upswing. This mental image helps to create several impulses, the most important of which is that sweeping sounds like a slow movement, and it helps when you keep your swing with these clubs slow and under control. The word *sweeping* also conveys the idea that the swing should be wide, that the clubhead should travel on the widest possible arc. And that's exactly what it should do. Two watchwords often paired to describe the swing for hitting fairway woods are *low and slow*. This phrase refers to your takeaway when playing a fairway wood. These two things are important because you are still swinging a club that has a long shaft and requires your maximum control over your swing.

To help promote this imagery, play the ball well forward in your stance, not quite as far forward as you do with your driver, but almost. Typically, with the driver, you would set the ball on a line drawn out from your left heel or your left armpit. With the fairway woods, move the ball back just a bit. The best way to figure out exactly how much, is to go to the practice range and start by moving the ball back toward the center in half-inch increments. Then try various positions—all to the left of the center of your feet—to see which spot is best for you.

Your setup with a fairway wood closely resembles the one you make with the driver. Because the clubs are shorter than your driver, you should stand closer to the ball and flex a little more from your knees to lower yourself toward the ball. Keep your posture at address consistent in relation to the length of the club you are playing.

With shorter clubs, many players hunch their shoulders so the club can reach the ball. This creates many problems, the most obvious of which is a swing path that is dra-

An excellent visualization technique with the fairway woods and long irons is to picture a long "sweeping" swing that picks the ball off the ground.

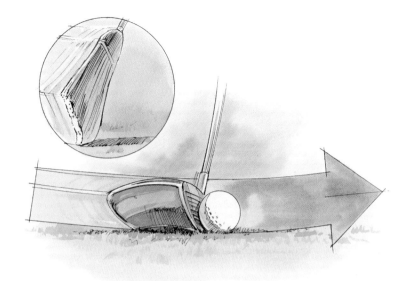

matically too far to the outside on the backswing. For the 3-wood, the width of your stance can remain the same as with your driver—the inside of your heels should be as wide as the outside of your shoulders. With a 4-wood, 5-wood, 7-wood, or any other wood, you should narrow your stance progressively but in very small increments. If you keep your stance too wide, it will hinder your turn in the backswing.

The swing with the fairway woods differs from that with the driver only in terms of its length, but the length of the shaft (shorter) shortens your swing automatically. The critical elements during the swing are once again the takeaway, the transition from backswing to downswing, and the overall tempo and timing of the movements. With fairway woods played off the ground as approach shots or layup shots, the importance of each of these critical elements becomes magnified. This is discussed later in this chapter, because it relates equally to fairway woods and long irons.

Inside the Ropes

Craig Stadler   *With the fairway woods and long irons, take it back low and slow.*

Won twelve events on TOUR, including the 1982 Masters. Ranked thirty-first in scoring average in 1997 (70.29).

The simplicity of Stadler's swing is the reason it has held up for years, and it is also the reason why it's easy to pick things up from him that you can emulate. Here he talks about his thoughts on playing long irons and fairway woods.

"Almost anyone knows one of the big problems with playing these shots is the temptation to get quick with the

swing. The easiest way to avoid that is to think about taking the club back real slow on the first foot of your backswing. Two words are all you need to remember: low and slow. If you take it back low, it stays slow. If you take it back slow, it stays low. If you start out slow, the club will pick up speed gradually. If you start quickly, you get out of whack and you get back to the top before your lower body makes a full turn, and you just never get yourself into a good position. Low and slow will get it done."

Andrew Magee *Even the TOUR players find the fairway woods easier to hit.*

Won four TOUR events and has been a consistent money winner in his nearly fifteen years on the TOUR.

Here he dispels the notion that you need to play and/or carry the long irons to be a good player.

"I played for twelve years out here always having a 1-iron in my bag, but over the past year and a half, I wouldn't dream of putting that 1-iron in my bag in place of my 4-wood. The 4-wood is so much easier to hit, and you can use it in so many more situations. I bend my 3-iron so the loft is somewhere between a standard 2-iron and 3-iron, take the 2-iron out of my bag, and carry a 4-wood. I feel it gives me much more versatility. That 4-wood is much easier to hit off tight lies, and that's the whole deal. We're looking to get the

ball up in the air just like the everyday golfer. The everyday golfer might lack the power to get the ball up in the air, so maybe the 5-wood is a good pick for him. Get yourself a 5-wood with some rails on the bottom, and it's a heck of a lot easier to hit out of the rough than a 3-iron or a 4-iron. If the ball is sitting up in light rough, you can have a go at it with that 4-wood.

"For me, the 4-wood is a substitute for the 1-iron, and a 5-wood covers you wherever you might need a 3-iron. The 3-wood has me covered in the 240-to-250-yard range, so I'm looking at the 4-wood and the 5-wood to cover me from the 210-to-230-yard range."

Raymond Floyd is one of the best fairway wood players of all time. He dominated the 1976 Masters with lethal use of his 5-wood on the par fives, tying the then tournament record of 271. Note how the backswing is slightly shorter than it would be with the driver, and that the ball is moved just slightly back of its position with the driver.

Fairway Woods as Trouble Clubs

Modern fairway woods are tremendously versatile. You can use them to play a tee shot, an approach shot from the fairway, and an approach shot from almost any lie in the rough, or from a divot, or from a fairway bunker. This was not always the case. When woods were actually made of wood, fairway woods were good only for playing from the tee or fairway. In the past when you hit a tee shot into the rough, you almost automatically assumed that the next shot would require an iron unless you caught a perfect lie in the rough that left the ball sitting up.

Today the opposite is true: The automatic assumption is that you can play a wood from the rough if the distance calls for it unless you end up with a particularly hideous lie (e.g., the ball is completely covered with grass). The reasons lie in the design of the clubs. On most persimmon fairway woods the sole was slightly curved, but the shape of the clubs required the entire bulk of the club to move through the grass—and that simply couldn't happen in most cases. Today the designs of the soles on metal fairway woods are such that only the very center of the sole and clubface need slip through the grass to make contact. This has been accomplished by tapering the soles upward toward the toe and the heel of the club. This same design concept makes modern fairway woods the perfect choice to play from old divots and from fairway bunkers, because only a minimal amount of the clubhead—the center of it—comes in contact with the ground.

The sole designs and weight distribution of metal woods (top) make them much easier to hit from the ground than their persimmon predecessors.

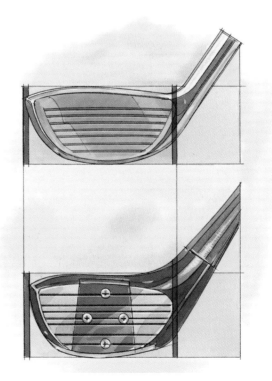

Modern club designs make it possible to play fairway woods from the rough, something that wasn't always the case. Here, Jim Furyk shows how it's done. Notice how he "stays with" the shot—fully extending his arms through impact.

Clubs such as the 5-wood and the 7-wood have come to be referred to as "utility" woods, in much the same way that that word is used to describe an infielder who can play many positions. You can confidently use them in almost any situation where they would provide the required distance. They are easier to hit than long irons in almost every instance, except when the ball is completely covered in long grass or plugged in a fairway bunker (or when the lip you must carry is just too steep). From moderate rough, from an old divot, or from the sand, you can play an excellent recovery shot and keep yourself in the hole by simply moving the ball back to the middle of your stance and allowing for a slight fade. By moving the ball back in your stance you cause the moment of impact to occur slightly earlier and reduce the chances of the club getting tangled in the rough, scraping the ground before you want it to (from a divot), or catching too much sand if your swing is off just a touch.

Another slight adjustment to consider when hitting fairway woods from deep rough is the idea of hovering the club slightly off the ground at

Nick Faldo   *The lie determines your club choice.*

Won three Masters titles and three British Opens, ranked sixth in scoring average in 1995 (69.85) and tenth in 1996 (69.92).

"At the 13th hole in the fourth round of the 1996 Masters, I had 206 yards to carry Rae's Creek and get to the front of the green, and 228 yards to the hole. I had carried a 5-wood all week for just this sort of shot, but when I got to the ball it wasn't sitting so well. That thirteenth fairway is pretty steep—much steeper than it looks on television. So my ball was sitting about six inches above my feet, and it was actually a bit of a downhill lie as well. The hardest thing about that shot is getting your stance comfortable so you can get the club on the ball without first contacting the ground, which is why I selected the iron. I was worried I might hit it a bit low and hot and run it through the green, but I figured that wasn't the worst thing that could happen and I could probably get away with it. I aimed for the left half of the green and tried to fly it into that ridge and hoped it would feed down toward the hole, which is exactly what it did.

"The only adjustment I made, and which I make any time the ball is above my feet, was that I choked down on the club until it felt right. Otherwise I just made my normal swing."

address. The real problem presented by rough is that it impedes the progress of the club. If you set the club down in the grass before playing the shot, you raise the chances of the takeaway being somewhat less than smooth and slow. Any time you do that, you are creating a problem for yourself.

The ease with which the modern fairway woods slide through the rough is something you should consider during the club selection process. For example, if (all things being equal) you had 165 yards to the center of the green from the rough and had only a moderate lie (not a perfect one), and you have a 7-wood that you carry about 175 yards, what could you do? Rather than playing the iron that flies 175 yards under normal conditions from the fairway, or the iron that flies 185 yards and allowing for some interference by the rough, you can alleviate much of the guesswork involved and strike the shot with a greater amount of confidence by selecting your 7-wood and choking down about an inch on the club.

The Flight of Trepidation: Is This Going to Get Airborne?

When playing a fairway wood or long iron from the ground, many everyday golfers have a fear that is singular to lower-lofted clubs played off the ground, perhaps the 3-wood and the 5-wood, and the long irons up through the 4-iron. The fear can be summed up like this: The ball is on the ground and you have a club with a modest amount of loft in your hands. With the ball on a tee and the same club in your hand, you would swing away freely and send the ball on its way.

With the ball on the ground, however, it appears that you will really have to work to get the ball up into the air. Perhaps you might even have to help it get up in the air.

Dale Douglass executes a fairway wood shot. Notice how there is room for the ball to run between the bunkers, making this a smart shot.

The ground appears unforgiving, and you don't see how you'll ever be able to slip the club under the ball. Once you make the decision to help the ball into the air, you've created a problem because most golfers think of an awkward tilt to the right in the downswing and an attempted scoop at the ball to lift it. The result is nearly always a poor shot, because the weight shift to the right is the exact opposite of the proper way to play the shot, and any scooping action with the wrists simply puts the clubhead out

Inside the Ropes

Fred Funk   *Fairway woods are great, but they're not always the best choice.*

Hit 80.1 percent of fairways played in 1994. In 1995 he hit 81.3 percent; in 1996, 78.7 percent; in 1997, 79.8 percent; and in 1998, 78.1 percent, placing him among the most accurate drivers of the PGA TOUR.

A four-time winner on the TOUR, Fred Funk certainly agrees that the modern fairway wood is a good choice over the long irons for the everyday player. However, as Funk points out here, the choice of the wood from the rough should not be automatic.

"If you are in the rough, unless you catch a perfect lie, it's never easy to catch the ball clean with a fairway wood or an iron. If you've got an okay lie—say the top half of the ball is visible above the grass—you have more of a chance with the wood than an iron. At least I do.

"But if you catch such a bad lie that the ball is totally covered with grass, or you are playing a course with just an inch or two of Bermuda rough or real thick rye grass—man,

that stuff is like glue. It those cases you are not going to get any club through there. You've got to use a somewhat lofted iron and just punch it out of there—advance it as far as you can. If you are comfortable with a ninety- or 100-yard wedge, then try to leave yourself a shot in that distance. Sometimes you just have to take your licks, and try to get up and down as best you can."

Funk also points out that any time you have a fairway wood in your hand, you are obviously trying for some extra distance, which is why he suggests the following.

"The swing with the fairway wood is much more of a sweeping action, which is something I have to remind myself of because I'm more of a 'picker.' When I'm playing a fairway wood, I widen my stance for a solid base, which makes me comfortable reaching for the widest possible arc. That feeling of swinging on a wide arc gives you that sweeping motion you want in the swing."

in front of the shaft and almost ensures that you'll hit the shot thin *if* you avoid hitting the ground first (too far behind the ball) because of the reverse weight shift.

How can you overcome this fear? The superb international player and TOUR player Frank Nobilo makes an excellent point in this chapter, and it is one the everyday golfer should always remember when playing a fairway wood or long iron. The point: Although the club in your hands has less loft than some clubs, it does have loft on it. This means that if you strike the ball squarely, it is definitely going to get airborne. In fact, it will fly quite high in the air when struck squarely. You should remember this and forget about "helping" these clubs. The designer of the club made sure you don't have to, and whatever you perceive as a swing adjustment that might help the ball get in the air will almost assuredly have the opposite effect.

You don't have to swing harder with these clubs. The same thoughts that lead to a good tee shot will work here: long, low, and slow on the takeaway; consistent tempo throughout the swing; and a smooth transition from backswing to downswing. Don't rush it! You do not have to slip the club under the ball on the ground. Rather, you should aim to contact the ball directly with the clubface, and let the loft of the club do the work for you.

Long Irons: Still Valuable Tools

It is a bit ironic that we have reached the point where long irons seem to be the odd clubs out in the set makeup and in club selection for certain shots, because the evolution of perimeter weighting made its first impact with the irons. For years, the everyday golfer was faced with the sight of 2-, 3-, and 4-irons with frighteningly small clubheads barely larger than the ball itself. Almost surely this fact led the everyday player to believe that he had to swing these clubs inordinately hard to get the ball airborne.

When perimeter-weighted irons came along, this aesthetic land mine was removed: The clubheads were larger and the flight of the ball was not so dramatically altered if impact was not in the dead center of the clubface. Indeed, when perimeter weighting in irons first hit the scene, it was most noteworthy for one thing: It made the long irons easier to hit.

This remains true today. The long irons are easier to hit than they have ever been. You should know this because in certain situations your long irons are still quite valuable clubs to play.

It is worth taking a moment here to discuss the pride factor in playing the long irons. Many everyday golfers see the TOUR players on television every weekend and frequently learn through the commentators that a player has selected a long iron for a certain shot—a 1-iron from the tee perhaps, or a 2- or 3-iron for a long approach. The urge to emulate the TOUR player causes the everyday player to feel as though, to consider himself a competent golfer, he, too, must be able to select a long iron for any given shot and execute it superbly.

Frank Nobilo   *Make your best swing with the long irons, and trust the club design.*

Joined the TOUR after finishing eighty-first on the 1996 money list. A constant challenger in the big-gest events, Nobilo, a New Zealander, has won numerous tournaments around the globe. In 1997 Nobilo ranked thirty-seventh in scoring average (70.41).

Here he suggests that rather than fearing your swing with the longer clubs, you should concentrate and execute to overcome the challenge.

"Long irons certainly do seem to be the nemesis of the

everyday player. I think one of the reasons for this is that they fail to take into account that the club is designed to make the ball go farther and that they don't have to swing harder just because it's a 3-iron as opposed to, say, a 6-iron or a 7-iron. My best advice with a long iron is to make the best swing possible because the ball is not going to get where you want it to any other way. Too often players try to hit these clubs so hard, when if anything the swing has to be made smoother and more controlled."

This is not true, of course. The PGA TOUR players are master craftsmen, players who devote endless hours to practicing their art. Good golf is about producing consistently good shots. What club you strike the shot with is irrelevant. You can learn a lesson on this from the very same players on TOUR.

The next time you watch them play a short par 4, take note of the club selections. Some players will use a 1-iron, others a 2-iron, and others may even use some type of wood. If the players who chose the 1-iron because they know it's the right club for them were to concern themselves with what the other players were doing, they would be guilty of the same type of misplaced logic.

You must know your own game and think for yourself on the course. Producing consistently better shots with fairway woods doesn't make you any less of a golfer. It is worthwhile, then, to reiterate this point as plainly as possible: All things being equal, when you have a choice between a fairway wood and a long iron for a given shot, the fairway wood is almost always the easier club to hit.

Now you might wonder if your long irons still have a place in your bag and in your game. The answer is yes, because they provide you with certain possibilities that a fairway wood does not. Exactly which long irons you carry and which fairway woods you carry is covered in full in Chapter 2, but assuming you still carry some long irons, it's a good idea to look at how and when you can use them to your greatest benefit.

Your Swing with the Long Irons

The setup and swing when playing a long iron from the fairway is comparable in almost every way to playing a fairway wood. The ball should be forward in your stance—somewhere between the center of your feet and the left heel. The view of the clubhead as you look down the shaft at address is a factor in aiming the club properly. Because the clubhead is smaller than that of a wood, and because it has a minimal amount of

Mark O'Meara   *Know the difference between being aggressive and swinging too hard.*

Won the 1998 Masters and British Open and ranked fifth in scoring average (69.63). He also ranked fourth in scoring in 1996 (69.69).

"Geez, when you think of memorable shots, you like to think of ones you hit under pressure. In the '91 Ryder Cup at Kiawah Island I was playing with Lanny Wadkins against Sam Torrance and David Feherty. Sam gets up there and sticks a 3-iron about two feet from the hole, and I had to respond.

"At the time I was thinking, 'Just get it on the green. Whatever you do, don't hit it in the water.' I figured the best way to do that was to make a good, aggressive move at the ball. I did, and I hit it to about four feet.

"I think the everyday golfer has a tendency to confuse the word aggressive with the notion of killing the ball or swinging as hard as he can. When you hear these guys out on TOUR talking about making an aggressive swing, that's not what they mean. In that situation I was simply thinking about making a full swing and not quitting on it or trying to steer it. Aggressive means just making a good, full, confident swing without backing off."

loft, you might tend to cheat on the alignment of the clubface toward the target and to leave the club slightly open (aimed right of the target). Don't fall into this trap. Make sure the lead edge of the iron is square to your target. Leaving it open at address will make you miss your target to the right. Have confidence that the loft of the club will get the ball airborne.

To overcome the urge to swing too hard with the long irons, be aware of the weight of the clubhead in your hands as you set up to play the shot. Make sure your grip is light enough that you can truly feel that weight, almost as if the shaft weren't there, or as if the clubhead were hanging from a string rather than the rigid shaft. When you make your swing, think about swinging the clubhead—that weight—and not the shaft. This will cause you to swing slowly and smoothly, and especially help you to make a smooth transition from backswing to downswing. Once you make that transition, just think about swinging completely through the ball to a balanced finish. If you jerk the club at the top to start down, you will lose that sense of where the clubhead is. Why this tip here and now and not with the discussion of your fairway woods? Because your irons are heavier and your woods are so lightweight. It's easier to make that connection of feel with the clubhead with the added weight of the irons.

Long Irons as Shot-Making Weapons and Recovery Clubs

What advantages do your long irons offer you over your fairway woods? Not many, but some are useful in certain situations. Remember that, given a long iron and a fairway wood that carry about the same distance, the long iron will be played on a lower trajec-

Ernie Els playing a 1-iron. The key to playing long irons is to make certain the backswing is complete and unhurried. Notice how Els waits for the swing to be completed, the club nearly reaching parallel. Once he starts down, he makes sure to create full extension through the ball.

Justin Leonard   *Have confidence with your aim on the longer shots.*

Won the 1997 British Open and ranked tenth in scoring average on TOUR (69.76) that same year.

"During the final round of the 1997 British Open I needed a birdie at the seventeenth hole. I had 215 yards to the hole, and for me that's a really good, hard 3-iron down low. I wasn't really sure I could get it all the way to the pin, but I actually hit it almost to the back of the green and made the putt. Under the circumstances it was the best shot I could have possibly hit.

"I wasn't thinking about mechanics at all. I concentrated on picking the right spot to hit it to and making sure I was lined up to that spot. That's a good point for the everyday player to consider on the long irons. The farther you are from the hole, the more difficult it is to get aimed properly. If you pay attention to that and then just stick with your normal swing, things will work out. You just have to have confidence that your aim is dead on, then stick with it."

tory because it has less loft, and the ball will run more once it hits the ground. (The reasons why the fairway wood flies as far with more loft is the length of its shaft, which generates more clubhead speed, and the mass of the clubhead, which is significantly larger.) Depending on what a certain shot requires, the lower shot is sometimes preferable to the higher one.

Perhaps a certain approach to a green appears to call for the ball to run onto the green rather than carry onto the green. Or perhaps the risk of carrying it to the green is too great—water or a bunker lies off to the side, for instance, at the depth of the green at which the carry with a wood would place the ball. In this example you may elect to play the long iron and run the ball onto the green. Perhaps the hole is cut at the very front of a green that slopes off sharply to the rear. Again, bouncing or running the ball up onto the green may be a better play, because if you carry the ball too deep into the green you'll end up with a very long putt—if you end up with a putt at all.

The lower loft on long irons is also valuable in two other shot-making situations. Certainly, if you are attempting to keep the ball underneath any overhanging tree limbs, the lower loft will produce a lower initial trajectory. In fact, any time you deem the lowest shot to be the best shot, the long irons get the nod. If a given situation calls for you to curve the ball from left to right, the lower loft is also easier to curve. (Chapter 12 offers a complete explanation of "working the ball." For the moment, it's sufficient to know that the lower the loft on the club, the easier it is to curve it from left to right, and the greater the loft on the club, the easier it is to turn it from right to left.)

Finally, don't forget about your long irons as recovery clubs from the rough. Although fairway woods are easier to hit in most cases, sometimes the lie dictates another course of action, especially if once again you determine that a running shot is better. When the ball is in the rough, the lead edge of the long irons can actually help you cut through the grass and get the ball back in play. If your lie is such that you think you can't get the wood through the grass, by moving the ball back toward the

Jim McGovern *Ball position is a key when playing a long shot from a divot.*

Won two NIKE TOUR events and teamed with Jeff Maggert to win the 1994 Diners Club Matches.

Even the best-planned, best-executed shot does not always turn out as you would like. In fact, it is not at all unusual, especially on a course getting heavy play, to have a drive that ends up in the fairway settle down in an old divot. It's frustrating, but you can recover from it. Here's Jim McGovern's advice on how to handle the situation:

"There are a couple of adjustments you need to make to play the ball out of a divot. The first is to take a little less club, because the loft will help you get the ball up in the air. If the

ball was sitting normally, and you think you should use a 3-iron, you would take a 4-iron if it was sitting down in a divot. The next adjustment is to move the ball back a little in your stance. The reason for this is that it's crucial for you to strike the ball first. To do this, you move it back and hit down on it. You have to go down there after it or it won't go anywhere. Now, since you've moved the ball back a little, you are probably going to catch it a little before the clubface has gotten completely square. That's no big deal—just aim a little to the left of your target and allow for the ball to drift a little to the right."

center of your stance and aiming left of your target to allow for a little fade, you can deliver a powerful blow with a long iron and return the ball back to play. The key here is to have realistic expectations for the outcome. You cannot always make up for a poor tee shot with a single shot. The same shot played from heavier rough with a fairway wood—using the same descending blow you create by moving the ball back to the center of your stance—could make the ball pop straight up in the air. As with any golf shot, use your common sense. If the lie is so miserable that the best you can hope for is to advance the ball a hundred yards or so, then reach for a wedge and make the best of the situation.

Your Target and Club Selection

Just as you must consider the ball's destination when preparing to play your tee shot, you must do likewise when playing a fairway wood or long iron as either an approach shot or a layup shot. Any shot you play with a fairway wood or long iron, with the exception of woods numbered 7 and above, will run enough when it hits the ground that you have to factor this into your plan. With clubs like a 7-wood and a 9-wood, the ball flies extraordinarily high and runs only a short distance upon landing.

Unless you are punching out from trees or in some other special situation, you choose a fairway wood or long iron for one of two reasons: You want to play the ball onto the putting surface, or you want to play a long shot to position the following shot. There are a few things to consider.

If you are playing an approach to the green on a long par 4, the green was designed to receive such a shot (unless the course architect was feeling cranky the day he designed the hole). Generally speaking, this means that the approach to the green is free of hazards that have to be carried, the green is fairly large in surface area and it is

Wayne Grady   *It's okay to hit a fairway wood from the tee.*

Won the 1990 PGA Championship, adding a second PGA TOUR victory to the four tournaments he's won internationally.

He emphasizes getting the ball in play off the tee.

"If you are having trouble with your driver, there's no reason not to go with a shorter club like the 3-wood or even the 5-wood from the tee just to get the ball in the fairway. It's a lot easier to play the ball from the fairway, and it also gives

you a bit of confidence so you can go back to the driver later. I'll never understand why, but a lot of people are very stubborn and they just will not do that. They insist on using the driver and continue making mistakes off the tee, and all of a sudden you've ruined your round and spoiled your day. There's no reason for it. Just hit the 3-wood and put it in the fairway."

flat or has some sort of upslope built into it to act as a backboard to help slow the ball, which is expected to come into the green at a low trajectory. If the shot on a long par 4 isn't toward a green that has these characteristics, you should stop to consider how aggressive you want to be and weigh the potential risks and rewards of the shot. In other words, if the green is very small, is fronted by a hazard of some sort, or slants away from you, you should estimate the risks. If you hit the ball in the water, it costs you two strokes. If you hit it in a fronting bunker, how easy will the up and down be? If the green slants away from you and your ball goes sailing into the green like a missile, where is it going to run after it hits off that downslope? You then weigh these risks against the possible reward: If I hit it perfectly, I have a chance for a birdie or an easy two-putt for a par. Are you going to hit it perfectly? How are you feeling about your game today?

On the same shot, there may be hazards lying off to the sides of the greens. If any of them is particularly nasty—water or perhaps a bunker even Houdini couldn't escape from—remember to figure that into where you play for the ball to land, because the odds of an off-line shot increase with the long clubs.

If you are playing a fairway wood or a long iron in an attempt to reach a par 5 on the second shot, you should consider the same points, especially if you are playing on an older course and the architect was thinking that the approach shot would unquestionably be played with a short iron. This means that the design probably incorporated a small, thoroughly protected green, which *might* be (depending on your level of play) akin to throwing your ball to the lions.

If you are playing a fairway wood or a long iron as a layup shot (you can't reach the green and want to advance and position the ball for the next shot when you can reach the green), don't just grab the 3-wood and let 'er rip. Aside from the hazards and carry-and-roll considerations, there is something else to think about. Let's say you hit the 3-wood and it leaves you seventy yards from the hole. For many golfers, that's a

Ian Woosnam prepares to make his club selection. No doubt the bunkers short and right have had an influence on the shot he's about to play.

tough shot because it's not a full swing with any club, and it requires great touch and feel.

The best plan is to remind yourself of the distance you can hit one of your wedges with a full swing. For example, if you hit your sand wedge 100 yards, then plan your layup shot to leave yourself a shot that is about 100 yards in length. In some cases this may mean you don't play the longest possible layup shot. Maybe you hit a 5-wood instead of a 3-wood. Think about it: You can't reach the green anyway, so why not do everything you can to make the next shot the easiest one possible.

One final note on the layup shots: These are dangerous situations in which even TOUR players make lazy, thoughtless swings, or forget to plan their shots properly. Why? The tendency is to think that because you can't reach the green—your eventual target—the shot is unimportant and simply something that must be gotten out of the way for your round to proceed. As a result, there can be a letdown in picking a target and making a good swing. Don't fall asleep mentally: Any single shot can be the one that makes or breaks the round. Stick to your routine on these shots. Pick a specific target and aim yourself properly toward it. Pick a good swing key and use it. Execute the shot, and you can go play that wedge and make your birdie. Get sloppy and push one into the trees, and suddenly you are struggling for par.

Keys to Entering the Zone

You get so focused on what you're doing that you don't even know what score you're shooting. You have the ability to make your golf club part of your body. You don't feel your golf swing. You don't get confused by thoughts. You don't see water, or the bunker six or eight feet in front of the pin. I can put a ball within a foot or two of where I am aiming from 183 yards (when I'm in the zone).

— Greg Norman

You felt confident, no one could beat you. You could make any shot you wanted. You were so engrossed in playing each shot that you were oblivious to your playing partners. The passage of time transcended normal laws.

Your swing was effortless and easy, the club an extension of yourself. You felt in complete control of your emotions. You encountered no conflicting thoughts. You executed each shot as you envisioned it. You saw the putts going into the hole before you drew back your putter. You never had so much fun in your life. You were in the zone, and only after the round did you realize that you played the best round of your life.

Moments such as these are what golfers live for, but they are rare. You have probably played in the zone at one time or another, perhaps for a stretch of a few holes or for one nine-hole side. Your mind and body worked in harmony to produce optimal performance.

It is impossible to force yourself into the zone. It comes without heraldry and leaves without warning. But you can create a mindset that will help you enter the zone more frequently.

Here are several questions that reveal the elements that bring on the conditions for entering the zone.

Do You Believe?

Believing that you are a good player and that you can hit good shots are conditions to playing well, and precursors to entering the zone. Self-confidence is your belief about how well you can play or how good your skills are. Confidence springs from quality practice, playing well in the past, trusting your mechanics, and knowing you are physically talented.

Can You Totally Focus?

The ability to totally focus on the task at hand is critical to reaching peak performance in sports. Most of us can concentrate well, but do you know what to focus on? Total focus requires that you think exclusively about the shot at-hand, and not let your mind wander to other thoughts, such as a past shot or the putt you will have make on the next green.

Are You Zoomed In?

Your attention can vary from broad to narrow. You need both to play well. During shot-making, keep your attention broad as you assess all the factors that influence club and shot selection. Then narrow it as you engage with a specific target. You play your best when you can narrow your focus on one thought or object during execution, such as your target or swing cue.

Can You Put Your Swing on Auto-Pilot?

An automatic and effortless swing is integral to playing in the zone. To achieve an effortless swing, you must develop a strong memory pattern of the swing. This allows you to put your swing on auto-pilot—you don't think about how to swing—it just happens. Instead, you can focus on the shape of the shot or flight of the ball.

Do You Stay in Control, and Are You Thinking Clearly?

When playing in the zone, golfers feel very much in control of themselves and their performance. They see the shot in their mind's eye, there is no conflict, no doubt, no battle for control of their emotions. They are devoid of anger or frustration, which destroys control, certainty and tranquillity.

A clear and decisive mind allows you to enter and dwell in the zone. How often have you been "stuck" between clubs when selecting a club, and then you couldn't put a decisive swing on the ball? The clearer you are about what you want to do and how you will achieve it, the more decisive you can be. Doubt and indecision send mixed signals to your body. Choose what you want do and commit to the shot.

The Fun of Playing in the Zone

One goal of athletes in all sports is to have a "once in a lifetime" performance. It is an absolute joy to play when everything comes together at once and the mind and the body are working in harmony. On these days, you strike the ball with effortlessness and ease, roll putts in unconsciously from everywhere, and feel in total control of the situation. You always feel great as you shoot your best score.

Part of the joy comes from knowing that you played well, but it may also come from beating a tough opponent, attaining a goal, or feeling like you won the battle with yourself and played to your potential. It is fun to experience the feeling of hitting a perfectly struck shot that happened just as you envisioned it. It is fun to make a difficult forty-foot putt that dropped into the center of the cup. Perhaps your joy also emanates from your appreciation of the outdoors and the surroundings or from the company of your playing partners. You might also feel joy from savoring the exhilaration of the flow and your total immersion in the activity.

One question that is still a mystery: Do you have fun because you are playing well? Or does enjoying your game help you to play better? The answer is yes to both questions. Did you have fun only after starting to play well and achieve your goals or did you make an effort to have fun playing before teeing off? Here is how one professional player summed it up this "chicken-and-the egg" mystery: "Your objective is to play well and win, but if you can do that having fun—that is the ultimate. So one complements the other. When you make a few good putts, you're having fun and if you are having fun you can play well."

> **The best players in the world rarely, if ever, play in the zone for four straight rounds.**

Final Thoughts on Playing in the Zone

Playing in the zone does not occur often. The best players in the world rarely, if ever, play in the zone for four straight rounds. You don't know when playing in the zone will happen, you cannot command it to appear. But you can lay the groundwork, and then you can just let it happen.

Without the desire to play your best, without commitment to working hard, and without the physical and mental preparation to give you confidence, you cannot truly enter the zone.

A healthy Paul Azinger is a beautiful sight.

Contouring the fairways is one method that golf course architects use to make play more interesting.

Playing *the* Middle Irons *and* Short Irons

aturally, golfers expect to move the ball closer to the hole with each shot played. The preceding two chapters have discussed playing clubs—the driver, fairway woods, and long irons—that are played to accomplish two things: to reduce the distance between your ball and the hole, and to put you in the best position to play a shot very close to the hole. Although it is possible to play a fairway wood or long iron close to the hole, it is not the norm, because the longer shafts and lack of loft on these clubs make them prone to stray off line. This chapter covers the clubs that allow a much greater opportunity to get the ball close to the hole with a full swing, namely the middle irons (5-, 6-, and 7-irons) and the short irons (8- and 9-irons and the wedges). From the 5-iron through the wedges, the shaft on each club becomes shorter by a half inch, and the loft of the club becomes greater. This combination offers increased odds for accuracy: straighter shots with more precise control over distance. (The shorter shaft creates a shorter swing, which

No active PGA TOUR golfer has won more events (34) than Tom Watson.

With the middle and short irons, the club starts to move into the ball from a steeper angle because the swing is more "up and down," a result of standing closer to the ball. The steeper swings mean you'll be taking divots, like Nick Faldo does here.

increases the chances of squaring the clubface at impact. More loft means more backspin and less sidespin, which means the ball flies on a straighter line.)

This chapter is limited to shots played with a full swing. Although all of the clubs discussed are used to play a vast variety of shots that do not require a full swing, those types of shots are covered in Chapter 8, "Your Short Game: The Great Equalizer."

Setting Up to Play the Middle and Short Irons

The decreasing club length has a practical impact on three elements of your setup: posture, stance width, and ball position. Each of these must be adjusted before you begin to swing the club.

Posture adjustment is most directly related to the club length. If you were playing a 7-iron and positioned your body as if you were playing a driver, you would probably miss the ball completely and you would certainly strike it poorly if you did make contact. There are two reasons for this: You would be standing too far away from the ball for the shorter club, and you would be standing too erect for the clubhead to reach the ground.

Scott McCarron *The best shots begin with good alignment.*

Was thirty-fifth in birdie average (3.65 per round) in 1996. He won the Freeport-McDermott Classic that year.

"In 1995, with just two events remaining on the TOUR schedule, I needed to finish solo third or better in one of them to keep my TOUR card and avoid a return to Q-School. At the Las Vegas Invitational I found myself in a position to do just that. The $102,000 paycheck for third place moved me from 212th on the money list to 128th on the money list. I made the cut at the Texas Open to keep my TOUR card.

"I had about 195 or 200 yards down the hill to the seventeenth green at Las Vegas, and I needed to stick it tight so I could keep my TOUR card. I hit it in there to about ten feet and everything worked out fine—got to keep my card and won a tournament the following year. Before I played the shot I was thinking that if I just made sure I got my alignment right I could get it close. I work a lot on my alignment. I'm always asking my caddie to check on my alignment. In any pressure situation, that's the first thing that can go wrong. I figure if you can avoid the first thing that can go wrong you are on your way to doing a lot of other things right. On that shot I clearly remember picking a spot a foot in front of the ball and lining my blade up to that and then getting my body set to the target. I guess it worked."

The adjustment to your posture must be made with care, however. The overwhelming tendency of the everyday golfer is to reach for the ball by hunching over from the shoulders in an attempt to extend the arms and, as a result, the clubhead toward the ball. This hunched-over stance causes two problems. First, it creates such a high degree of tension in your arms that you will never be able to swing the club back as far as you need to. Second, if you are hunched over from your shoulders at address you are practically pre-programming a takeaway that is much too far outside to begin your backswing effectively.

The correct way to lower yourself to the ball is to flex your knee and bend from your hips. Neither adjustment is huge. Simply combine the two until the club is low enough to play the shot. Your arms should still hang straight down, just as they should for any shot. Any time you feel like you are reaching for the ball with your arms, take a step back and reset yourself to play the shot.

Besides increasing your knee flex and hip bend, you should move your feet slightly closer to the ball. To determine whether you are standing the proper distance from the ball, assume your address position over the ball. Hold the club with your left hand only, and ground the clubhead directly behind the ball. Take your right hand and turn it palm upward so your first four fingers (excluding your thumb) are pointing toward the target. Then place your right hand (still face up) between your waist and the end of the grip of your club. If you are standing the proper distance from the ball, your right hand fills the space between your waist and the end of the club. If your right hand doesn't fit in that space, you are too close to the ball. If there is excess space (i.e., your hand does not fill the space), you are too far from the ball.

For years, Scott Hoch has been one of the best short iron players in the game. His up-right swing is custom-made for the short clubs. Notice that his head is still stock still even though the ball is well on its way to the target.

Stance Width

With the middle and short irons, the second adjustment in your setup is the width of your stance. When you are setting up to play your woods or long irons your stance is as wide as it should ever be (with the exception of a few specialty short-game shots). Your stance is wide for the long clubs so you can maintan your balance. If your feet were close together with the long clubs, your turn would be restricted so you would feel as if you were going to fall over during your swing. With the middle and short irons the turn is not quite as large as with the longer clubs, and your feet should not be as wide apart. Why is that? These clubs require a shorter swing, and you want the winding action of the backswing to get started much quicker, because (as you read in Chapter 4) the shorter clubs start moving up (as opposed to straight back from the ball) much sooner. Narrowing your stance allows this to happen.

Tom Lehman *Take adrenaline into account when choosing a club.*

Won the 1996 British Open and was the PGA TOUR Player of the Year that same season. He was third in greens-in-regulation that year (71.8).

"I'll never forget the 1995 Ryder Cup at Oak Hill. It was the eighteenth hole and I was paired with Corey [Pavin] in a match against Nick Faldo and Colin Montgomerie. It was an alternate shot, and our drive was sitting in the first cut of rough, and the lie was a little downhill. I had 185 yards to the front edge of the green, 205 to the hole. I hit a perfect, ripping 5-iron onto the front part of the green, and we made the putts to win the match. That was one of those cases where the adrenaline was pumping something fierce and there's no denying it. You have to take that into account—it was a good situation to feel like you could just rip one. Under pressure like that, you want to be decisive and there's no backing off during the swing, so you want to consider that in your club selection. If you think a club is right when you are pumped up, go with it."

How much you narrow your stance is a matter of personal comfort. Start by narrowing it a little bit—say, about an inch—to see how it feels; then adjust accordingly. Because people come in all shapes and sizes, there are no strict rules on this. It is a bit of a cliché, but you have to experiment to learn what is best for you.

Ball Position

The third pre-shot adjustment for middle and short irons is to gradually move the ball back in your stance. This allows you to make clean contact with the increasingly shorter clubs. As the clubs get shorter and you stand closer to the ball, your swing plane becomes more upright, and the bottom of your clubhead's swing arc—that brief moment when it is low enough to the ground to strike the ball—begins later and ends sooner. Moving the ball back a bit as the clubs get shorter places the ball where the clubhead will reach the bottom of its swing.

Use the following guidelines when moving the ball back in your stance: For the middle irons (the 5-, 6-, and 7-irons), start by splitting the distance between your driver ball position (off your left heel) and the middle of your stance (or the middle of your chest, whichever you find easier). From there you can fine-tune it. For full shots with short irons (8- and 9-irons and wedges), start by playing the ball in the middle of your stance—a line straight down from the center of your chest. Unless you are attempting some type of specialty shot, don't move the ball back any farther than the center of your stance. A word of caution: As you move the ball back in your stance there is a tendency to view the club as being closed or hooded when in fact it is aligned squarely. The typical response to this is to open the clubface slightly. Don't fall into this trap! Aim the club squarely, step into your setup, and then trust it.

Sandy Lyle *Out of the fairway bunker with a short iron, the lower body stays quiet.*

From the middle to the late 1980s, Scotsman Sandy Lyle was a consistent factor in the big championships. The long-hitting Lyle was at his peak then, winning the 1985 British Open, the 1987 Players Championship, and the 1988 Masters.

Of all the shots he has hit in more than twenty victories worldwide, the one Lyle and many golf fans remember best was on the final hole of the 1988 Masters, where he birdied the final hole to win.

"I had been leading most of the week on and off and had a two-shot lead heading into Amen Corner on Sunday, where I had a bit of a wobble. I made a bogey at number eleven and then a double bogey at the twelfth and when that was all done with I had lost the lead. I made a nice birdie at the sixteenth, however, to go level with [Mark] Calcavecchia. That's how it stood going into the eighteenth hole. I hit a 1-iron from the tee to avoid the bunkers on the left there, but I hit it very solid and I ended up in the first of the two bunkers there on the left side of the fairway.

"The shot I now faced was a very dangerous one. I was playing from a very steep-faced bunker, and I couldn't see the pin from where I was. There was a very real chance that I might catch the lip and have the ball end up in the bunker right in front of me, and that would have meant a double bogey or worse. The pin was on the front of the green, and there was a bunker short and left of it as well. There were so many things that might go wrong.

"The shot called for a 7-iron, and I had to pick it cleanly or it would surely hit the lip. Under those circumstances, and with your body leaning away from the target, it is necessary to keep the lower body very still and swing mostly with your arms. You move the ball back in the stance a bit to make sure you hit it before you hit the sand. Dig the feet in solidly, and maybe choke down a bit to shorten up the club to make sure you don't catch the sand before the ball.

"If all worked according to plan I thought I could get it somewhere on the green. It did, and I ended up twelve or so feet from the hole. It was a nice bonus to make the putt."

The Accuracy Factor

With middle and short irons, the emphasis is on accuracy. Shots are consistently more accurate because the swing is shorter. A shorter swing means that fewer things can go wrong. Getting the club to parallel, a swing goal frequently discussed in relation to the driver, is not a factor because the shafts on the middle and long irons are not long enough for you to achieve that checkpoint, and to attempt it would cause you to overswing. You still want to make a full swing, however. What is a proper-length swing with the middle and short irons—one that is not too short and not too long? The answer is one of those things you don't have to think about much. Standing closer to the ball and narrowing your stance as described above shortens your swing to the proper length—there is no need to make it more complicated.

Because the shaft of the club is shorter with middle irons and short irons, you will naturally swing it on a more upright plane on the backswing and downswing. Under ordinary conditions you want these shots to fly as high as possible, and the upright swing plane and the adjusted ball position combine to create what is commonly referred to as a *descending* blow. The

In this sequence of Davis Love III hitting a 5-iron, note how the stance has narrowed from previous examples of the setup with longer clubs, when the insides of the feet were as wide as the outsides of the shoulders. Also, the ball is positioned much more toward the center of the stance. Note, too, that the swing is not as long, with the clubhead pointing more toward a one o'clock position at the top as opposed to the three o'clock position it would point to with the longer clubs. At impact, Love's arms have returned to the perfect "triangle" position they were in at address.

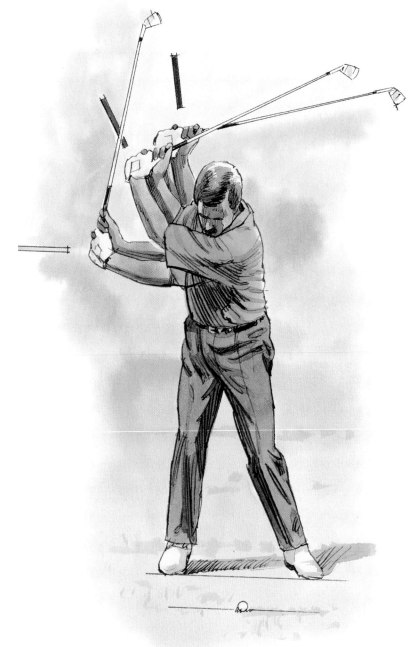

You can change the distance and trajectory of a middle or short iron by changing the length of your backswing. The longer the backswing, the longer and higher the shot will fly. The reason you would shorten the backswing is for more control of the shot, i.e. to hit it straighter and to hold its line.

descending blow is a good image because when you hit down on the ball, it goes up, and you get the maximum benefits of the loft on the club—including backspin, a key ingredient in accurate ball flight. Do not distort this image so that you slam the club into the back of the ball without following through. Shots played with a descending blow are just like any other: You must turn and swing through the ball. Nevertheless, the descending-blow imagery is useful. The idea of sweeping the ball away as with the longer clubs is not nearly as effective.

Inside the Ropes

Stewart Cink *Out of the rough, stay down and be aggressive through the ball.*

Was twentieth in All-Around Ranking in 1998. Also was named the 1997 PGA TOUR Rookie of the Year.

"On the seventeenth hole of the last round of the '97 Hartford Open I was tied for the lead and didn't hit a great drive. I was left of the fairway and in pretty bad rough. There was a pond just in front of the green, and I had to decide whether to lay up short of the green or to go for it. I chose a 9-iron and barely—just barely—carried over the water and the ball rolled up onto the green and I went on to win the tournament.

"I had about 150 yards to the hole—less than that to carry the water, which was the more important thing, because if I hit it in the water I was dead. My thought process was something like this: The most important thing about playing a shot out of the rough was to stay down and through the ball and be aggressive, then rely on the loft of the club to pick the ball out of the rough and take it on. I knew it was going to be a flier, so I knew it would go a bit.

"Now, this ball was buried in the grass, but in the type of grass that we had there in Hartford, it could still be a flier. It wasn't like having the ball buried in Bermuda rough. The ball was below my feet, so I made two adjustments. I moved the ball back in my stance a little bit to make sure I hit the ball with an extremely descending blow, and I stood a little closer to the ball. Because I had to lower myself down to the ball, standing closer to it meant that I could bend from the waist and not lose much power. If you start reaching for the ball from you shoulders, you lose a lot of power."

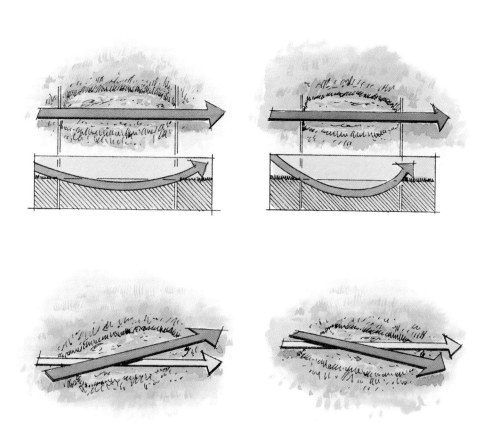

These illustrations offer a quick lesson regarding divots. The first illustration shows a shallow divot, like one you might make with a middle iron. The second one shows a deeper divot, the type produced by the descending blow of the short irons. If these divots get too deep, you might have the ball back too far in your stance. The second set of illustrations shows what you can learn from your divots. The yellow line represents the target line. If your divot crosses your target line from outside to inside, the club is coming into the ball too far from the outside. If the divot crosses the target line from inside to out, then the club is coming at the ball too much from the inside.

Billy Andrade   *When the target is downhill, it calls for less club.*

Ranked thirty-fifth in birdies (3.65 per round) in 1997.

"I was in a play-off at the 1991 Kemper Open with Jeff Sluman at Kemper and we went to a par-3 to start the play-off. I had just played the hole about forty-five minutes earlier and hit a great shot, a 6-iron in there pretty tight. So I picked the '1' out of the hat to see who would go first, and I was up. The hole was downhill and played about 200 yards and the pin was tucked on the right-hand side of the green. It was pretty gutsy to decide to go for it—but this was a play-off, and a par 3, and I was going first, so I had to stick it in there. I didn't realize until I went back the next year what a tough shot it is, because if you go long, there's a tough bunker to deal with, and left is dead. Anyway, I hit it in there about six feet and won the play-off.

"When you get into the middle irons, you are starting to get to the clubs you should be able to get close to the hole, so you have to be more precise with your club selection and yardage. This was 200 yards, which is long for a 6-iron, but it was downhill, which reduces the effective yardage. You have to make sure you consider things like that when you have those scoring clubs in your hand. The scoring clubs are the middle irons and short irons—the ones you feel like you cozy in there pretty good."

Hitting down on the ball with these clubs has a result that does not occur with the driver and the longer fairway woods and long irons: You make more noticeable contact with the ground, often taking a divot out of the turf. Always remember that the divot starts at the ball, not behind it. You are never attempting to hit the ground first. You always want to initiate impact with the clubface striking directly into the back of the ball.

Controlling the Distance on Middle and Short Irons

Playing shots that land close to the hole results from controlling the accuracy and distance of the shot, and the accuracy results almost entirely from proper alignment. Other factors, such as the lie of the ball, your stance, and the wind, are covered in Chapter 11.

There is no scientific method for determining down to the inch how far a shot will fly. If there were, players would always land the ball directly on top of the hole. You also have little control over precisely how far your tee shot will travel before playing a middle or a short iron. You almost never end up with a distance to the hole that is exactly the distance you carry a given club. What do you do when a distance falls between the carry distance of two clubs? In general it is nearly always better to take the longer club and take a little off it rather than trying to hit the shorter club a longer distance. The easiest way to take a few yards off a club is to grip down on it a bit—a half inch or an inch. This shortens the arc of your swing and slightly reduces the clubhead speed. Of course, the position of hazards or trouble spots will affect your decision.

One way to more precisely control the distance of the short irons is to choke down on them, like Lanny Wadkins is doing in this photo.

Of course, there are occasions when the shorter of the two clubs simply feels like the right one for you. If that feeling is overwhelming, just follow Mark Calcavecchia's advice in this chapter.

The middle and short irons are clubs that you intend to use to land on the green. This rules out most—not all, but most—of the complications that arise when considering how the ball is going to react once it hits the ground. Because greens tend to be softer than the rest of the golf course (except at major championship venues) and the ball is coming into the green at a steeper angle than it would with a longer shot, the ball is not likely to run very far after landing. The main consideration is how far you are going to carry the ball. The effect of any humps or mounds on the green must be considered, of course, but those are subtleties that come into play more and more as your level of play is raised.

Mark Calcavecchia *Follow your instincts when you are under pressure.*

In the top twenty-five in birdies four times, between 1994 and 1998.

Here he describes a famous shot not just in his own golf history, but in the history of the game as well.

"In the 1989 British Open I was in a four-hole [aggregate] play-off with Greg Norman and Wayne Grady. At the eighteenth hole at Troon [the final play-off hole], I didn't hit a very good drive and it ended up in the rough. The rough was dry and not super long, so I still had a shot at it. I chose a 5-iron and it came off the club going dead at the flag and never wavered the whole way. I remember looking at the ball in midair and thinking, 'Oh my God, I can't believe I hit such a good shot.'

"The thing about shots under pressure is that people always want to know what you are thinking about just before you play them. I have to be honest and say that at that moment in time at that place I think it was just meant to be—it was my time. On the whole, I think it depends on the situation and how you are playing that week. One week you might be thinking a lot about swing mechanics and it is working so you zone in on some swing key prior to playing the shot. Another week it might be a feel thing, or maybe picturing the shot in your mind before you hit it. It depends on what's working for you at the time. As anyone who has played any length of time knows, different things work for you at different times. A certain swing key may work well for a week or so, and then it stops working and you try something else. That's just the way it is in golf.

"That shot just happened to be the perfect distance for that 5-iron, and I hit it full bore. It is not unusual to find yourself between clubs with the middle and short irons because you are trying to be a little more precise. In that case I usually recommend taking more club and trying to take a little bit off it. Choke down a little bit and make a controlled swing. Sometimes, though, your instincts tell you to go with the shorter club. If you feel like you've got to hit that shorter club, you might move it back an inch or so in your stance and hit it hard."

For these reasons, the middle and short irons are often referred to as the *scoring clubs*. Obviously, any shot with any club affects your score, but these clubs offer you the best opportunities to get the ball close to the hole. If you want to lower your scores, you must be more precise with these clubs, which means knowing exactly how far you can carry each of them. Again, this differs from the thought process with the longer clubs, with which you consider the carry and the roll together. The idea of knowing how far you carry each of your clubs is covered in Chapter 2.

How precise you are with these clubs also depends on how accurately you assess the yardage of the shot you are about to play. The everyday golfer faces much more of a challenge than TOUR players in this instance. The TOUR player's job is to play superb golf, and he has the time to make sure he knows the yardages from various points on every hole at a tournament site. The everyday golfer does not have time to do this, and if you were to start pacing off distances like the players on TOUR, you would run the risk of incurring the wrath of your fellow players and others on the course.

How do you overcome this barrier? It's not much of a barrier at all. Most golf courses are adequately marked for distance, and some even provide yardage books. When a yardage book is not available, you must rely on the markings on the golf course. Some courses give general markings at 200, 150, and 100 yards. At the very least there is usually some type of 150-yard marker. Before you begin play, check with the club professional, one of the assistant professionals, or the starter to find out where

You can clearly see in this photo that Lanny Wadkins aggressively attacks with his short irons. So should you—it offers you the best chance of getting the ball close to the hole.

Inside the Ropes

Tommy Tolles and Larry Nelson

with confidence.

When you know the club is right, swing

Tolles ranked twentieth in scoring average in 1996 (70.30) and thirty-fifth in 1997 (70.36). He played his way onto the TOUR by getting through the 1994 Q-School, and two years later he finished sixteenth on the TOUR money list. Nelson won ten PGA TOUR events, including the 1983 U.S. Open and the 1987 PGA Championship.

As you get closer to the hole, in the middle iron and short iron range, you sometimes come up on a shot where a certain club just matches the yardage and situation perfectly. When that happens, as Tommy Tolles and Larry Nelson describe here, you can settle into a shot with complete confidence, make your normal swing, and hit a great shot. When you think the club is just perfect, take advantage of the situation and fire right at the spot you pick.

Tommy Tolles: "In the '97 Masters on Sunday, it was a calm but overcast day, and I was playing with Fuzzy Zoeller. We got to the sixteenth hole, and the pin was on the back right so that if you hit the ball to the perfect spot on the left side of the green, it catches that hill and curls up and around behind the hole and you can get it real close. I had 178 yards to get it to that spot, and that is exactly how far I hit a 6-iron. Sometimes it just happens that way—you have a club you hit 178 yards, you get up to a hole, it's a par 3, and you have to hit it 178 yards. There's none of that, 'Well, maybe it is a

5-iron or a 6-iron or maybe a 7-iron.' You know the club immediately, and you are very comfortable with it. Well, I hit this low, driving shot, and it was headed right for that spot, and while it was in the air Fuzzy was saying, 'Keep your eye on this one, it could be the longest hole in one in history.' He was talking about how long the ball would roll once it hits the green, because it moves so slowly along that bank. It is like suspended animation as that ball creeps along the green, because you can't really see what's going on and you hear the crowd whooping and you don't know whether it went in or not. I ended up a couple of inches from the hole, and I'll tell you, I was pretty excited back on the tee. It was some scene."

Larry Nelson: "It was the fourteenth hole of the final round of the 1983 Open. I had 119 yards to the hole, which is the perfect distance for a pitching wedge for me. That's a great spot to be in, because you can get very comfortable over the ball and not have to worry about mechanics. If you know you have the yardage right and you know you can hit a club that exact distance, you can make a swing with total confidence. I was one behind Watson at that point, but I felt that if I could make a birdie, I had a really good shot at winning. The reason I remember the shot so well is the amount of confidence I had when standing over the ball. I hit it close and made the putt."

In this sequence, Nick Price shows perfect form with a short iron. The stance is as narrow as it will get for the full swing and the ball is in the dead center of the stance. Most important, notice how he accelerates the club through the ball and completes the follow-through—a key element overlooked by many everyday golfers.

these markers are and what they look like. Often they are some type of colored disk in the fairway or on a sprinkler head. Sometimes they are marked on cart paths, other times they are colored sticks or poles; or they can be a certain type of tree located the same distance from the hole on each hole. Make sure you familiarize yourself with what they are before you begin to play. At the same time you are making this inquiry, ask this very important question: "Are the distances measured to the front of the green or to the center of the green?" Most commonly the answer is the middle of the green.

It is important to know where the distances are measured *to* because greens are typically deep enough that, from any given spot in the fairway, your club selection could vary by as many as three clubs based on where the hole is positioned. As a general rule, you can assume a green is roughly thirty yards deep. Because there is probably a ten-yard gap between how far you hit your irons, you can see the importance of knowing exactly how the distance is measured.

Here's a basic example of how you would go through the process of determining the distance. Suppose your ball is five yards short of the 150-yard marker and you know that the yardage is measured to the center of the green. That means you have 155 yards to the center of the green. If the hole is cut in the front of the green you have fewer than 155 yards to the hole, probably closer to 145 yards. If the hole is cut in the very rear of the green, the shot requires you to carry the ball about 165 yards. All of this is based on a green roughly thirty yards deep. Not all greens fit that mold; some are shallower, some are significantly deeper. You need to make an assessment from your point in the fairway or base it on previous knowledge from playing the course.

GETTING STARTED

#1 *Transfer Your Weight Properly*

Hugh Baiocchi

The proper transfer of weight requires that you move your weight to the back leg and foot in the backswing, not to the front leg. This would be a reverse pivot, a fault that I commonly see among beginners. They move the club away from the ball, shift their weight to the front or left side, and then tilt their shoulders slightly forward and down. When they go into the downswing they transfer their weight to their back leg or foot and then hit a big banana slice, which is all you can do from that position. I believe the reverse pivot results from the beginner misinterpreting the instruction that you must keep your head still and eyes over the ball. It's okay to move your head and eyes slightly off the ball (to the rear) when taking the club back.

Keep your head from moving excessively and keep your eyes focused on the ball. The head should move not more than half an inch.

#1—Transfer Your Weight Properly
This figure shows the improper shift of weight—the reverse pivot.

Hal Sutton

Avoid an arms-only swing. Develop a marriage between your arms *and* your body.

#2 *Transition to the Downswing*

Gary McCord

Do not rush the transition from the end of the backswing and the beginning of the downswing.

You do not have to swing hard in order to get the ball toward the target.

#3 *Develop a Proper Grip*

Lou Graham

The most important thing to learn when beginning is the proper grip. Adult beginners think strength is what propels the ball and their grips

#3—Develop a Proper Grip
This figure shows the incorrect technique
of trying to overpower the ball.

167

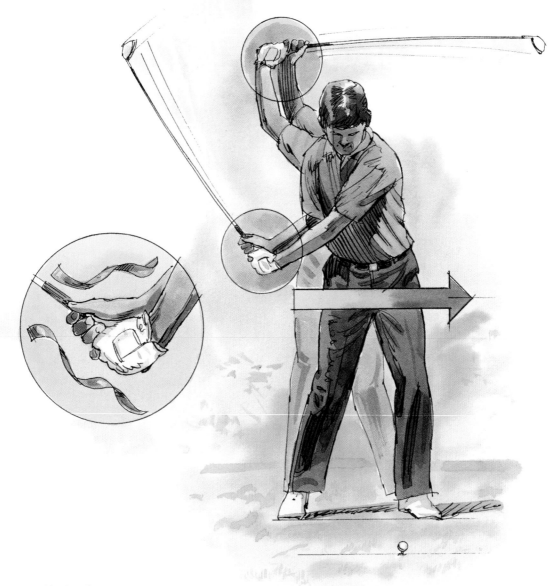

#3—Develop a Proper Grip (continued)
This figure shows the correct technique
of letting the weight of the clubhead do
the work.

show it. They overlap their hands with their right thumb sticking down the shaft, almost like they're picking up an ax. Then they try to overpower the ball. Beginning youngsters are different. They're not so strong that they want to overpower the ball, so they let the weight of the clubhead do the work. They don't take a death grip of the club. They hold it lightly, and when they swing they let the clubhead speed come from moving their legs and rotating their hips, not just from swinging their arms.

Nick Faldo

You need to develop a good grip, so, at the very least, you can return the clubface squarely to the ball.

#4 Use Proper Equipment

Richard Coughlan

Getting the right equipment is a must. You cannot use clubs that are too long or too short. In general women should avoid clubs that have stiff shafts. You don't have to spend a king's ransom to purchase clubs that suit your game.

Bob Estes

Make certain that your clubs are properly fitted—to your body and your swing.

#5 Practice Short Game

Jim Furyk

As a beginner I spent twice as much time practicing my short game as I did beating balls with my driver and fairway woods. This really had positive impact on my overall play. Most of your shots on the course are from 100 yards in, so why wouldn't you want to be good at those things you do most often? If you want to lower your handicap [and what golfer, beginner or otherwise, doesn't], concentrate on your short game.

Bob Dickson

If you want to improve—regardless of whether you're advanced, intermediate, or beginner—work on your game from 100 yards in. For every driver you hit in practice, you should hit five wedges.

Scott Verplank

Work on your short game. Spend time on a practice putting green to develop a consistent putting action. In practicing your putting, work on keeping your head still and stroking the ball as smoothly as possible.

#6 Watch Your Swing on Video

J. C. Snead

Have someone videotape your swing when you're playing well, and then when you're not hitting it well, go back to that videotape and take a look. This can work for anyone, from touring pro to amateur. You will improve and correct your faults much faster.

#7 Improving Your Balance

Tom Lehman

Try to develop balance as early as possible. If you work on maintaining the proper balance throughout your swing, you'll find improvement in almost every other facet of your swing.

Steve Jones

Take the club back slowly. A slow backswing will improve your timing, and better timing leads to better balance.

#8 Limiting Head Movement

Jim McGovern

Keep your head from moving excessively and keep your eyes focused on the ball. The head should move not more than half an inch.

Bob Charles, the patron saint of lefties.

Hats off to Nick Faldo.

Your Short Game: the *Great* Equalizer

It makes no difference what type of game you play—expert or beginner—the part of the game that is easiest to improve and that pays the greatest dividends is the short game, shots you play within 100 yards of the hole. This chapter deals with the phase of your game that consists of *partial* shots, shots that do not require a full swing of the club.

In general, shots played with a partial swing can be the most difficult for the everyday golfer, because the player needs to determine how fast to swing and how big a swing to make. The difficulty is compounded by the fact that most golfers feel as if they must help the ball into the air as they get nearer the green. This chapter outlines the fundamentals of playing the short shots, the strategy behind determining what type of shot to play, and ways to help you overcome the judgment problems that go hand in hand with the partial shots.

Remember, however, that the short game also offers some advantages to go along with the described difficulties. First, because you are playing rather short distances, your

The great Bobby Jones said, "The secret to golf is the ability to turn three shots into two." Here, Phil Mickelson executes a short chip in an attempt to get his ball "up and down."

Bob Estes *Focus on your short game early in your golf life.*

Ranked eighteenth in the All-Around category in 1997. He was also twentieth in scoring average in 1997 (70.09).

"If you are a kid or you have kids and you are reading this, here's some advice: The younger you are, the more you should focus on your short game. It is hard to have a perfect golf swing when you are fourteen or fifteen years old because you are not done growing yet. But that touch you develop by working hard on your short game will stick with you your entire life. When a kid has finished growing, he can start focusing more on building a good golf swing, and the body will be ready for it. And the good news is, he'll already have the great short game to go with it."

brain plays a big part in determining how hard you hit the shots. In most cases you can trust your brain because as you get closer to the hole, your brain receives more reliable visual information. Second, because the swing motions you use to play the short shots are more compact, there is less chance of making a physical error. Fewer moving parts and less overall movement mean less of a chance of a miscue.

When to Do What

The putt figures into your shot selection when you are very near the green, even if you are not on the actual putting surface. Generally speaking, you want to keep the ball on the ground as much as possible. There are certainly exceptions to this, but in general a shot is easier to control when it is on the ground. This is the primary factor in determining what type of shot you are going to play when you get near the green. As a result, this chapter will include shots played with your putter, and the chapter on putting will deal solely with putts played on the actual putting surface.

There are two main reasons for keeping the ball on the ground. First, keeping the ball on the ground with the putter, or getting it on the ground as soon as possible with a low-lofted club, immediately shortens the swing and makes it easier to manage. Second, keeping the ball on the ground almost entirely removes the effects of wind on the ball, which you should never underestimate.

The basic rule of thumb for your short game is: *When you can keep the ball on the ground, do so; when you must put the ball in the air, get it back on the ground as quickly as possible.* This, of course, means you need some criteria to determine when you play which type of shot. To keep things in the proper perspective, the strategy part of playing a shot is presented first. A discussion of *how* to play the shots comes later in this chapter, but for the moment the focus is on *which* shot to play and *why* or *why not* to play it.

The shot selection process in the short game begins with three basic factors: the distance between the player and the hole; the type of terrain between the player and the hole; and the lie of the ball. To keep the information manageable we will start close to the hole and work out to the 100-yard range.

The Putter: Not Only for the Green

The putter is much more versatile than you may realize and can be very effective when you are not on the putting surface. Consider using a putter in the following situations:

- Almost any time your ball is on the fringe of the green, putting makes sense. If the ball happens to be up against the rough, you can still putt, but not if you think the clubhead will get hung up in the grass. In that case you can opt to chip or play a bellied wedge (explained later in this chapter).

- If your ball is in the fairway within ten yards or so of the green, and if the hole is cut in the front of the green, it is often easier to putt than it is to try to judge how far to carry the ball. This assumes that there are no rough patches of grass between you and the ball, or anything like an old divot that might throw the ball dramatically off line.

- If you are just off the green—say, within ten to fifteen yards—and the green includes any severe slopes or tiers, and the hole is cut along or just opposite one of these undulations, it is a good idea to consider putting. This again assumes that you have an unobstructed path to the hole. Putting is wise here because you are more likely to misjudge the distance of the carry to the precise spot you need to land the ball on a pitch or chip shot.

The closer you get to the green, the more your imagination takes over. Here, Scott Simpson uses his putter from off the green.

The Chip Shot

A chip shot is played with the intention of carrying the ball the shortest possible distance over any uncertain terrain and getting the ball on the ground and running as quickly as possible, whereas a pitch shot is a lofted shot played with a lofted club and intended to fly the majority of the distance to the hole.

Aside from a putt, a chip shot is the simplest to execute from the mechanical perspective. It involves a very short swing motion and, as a result, fewer opportunities for error. Therefore, when you cannot play a shot from off the green with your putter, the next option you should consider is a chip shot.

Think about chipping in the following situations:

- Any time you are within twenty yards of the front of the green with no rough to carry, but it is too far to putt, you should chip. When is it too far? It is too far to putt anytime you feel you have to make a stroke so long it will throw your rhythm off, or if the distance is so great it will force you to use more hand action than you typically would for a putt (increasing the odds that you might top the ball).

- When you are on the fringe and there is a pitch mark, an old divot, or an irregular clump of grass that will immediately throw a putt off line, you should chip over it. However, if you are so close to the hole that playing a chip will send the ball well past the hole, you may want to try rolling it.

- When the line of a putt would take it through a fair amount of fringe—enough so that you are uncertain how the ball will react because it is going to slow down when it hits the fringe and pick up speed back on the green—you should consider chipping over the fringe or landing a chip in the fringe so it will take one bounce onto the green.

- If your ball is around (but not on) the green and the hole is on the opposite side of the green, and you have three feet of rough or less to carry, chipping may be the best option. If the hole is near you and you have a significant amount of rough to carry, a chip is probably not the shot.

Inside the Ropes

Lee Janzen   *A good lie is the green light to focus on hitting it to your target.*

Won the 1998 and 1993 U.S. Open Championships. He was ranked sixteenth in the All-Around category in 1998, fourteenth in 1997, and twenty-second in 1993.

"One of the most memorable shots of my career was when I chipped in on the seventeenth hole of the 1993 U.S. Open [sixteenth hole, final round] the first time I won. The thing I remember about it is that I had a great lie, so all I had to

think about was hitting it solid and landing it where I wanted to. When you get a tough lie, you have to grind it out a little more and focus on mechanics, but when you have a good lie, you can start thinking about making it. You can spend your energy picking the right target and the right line for your ball to take."

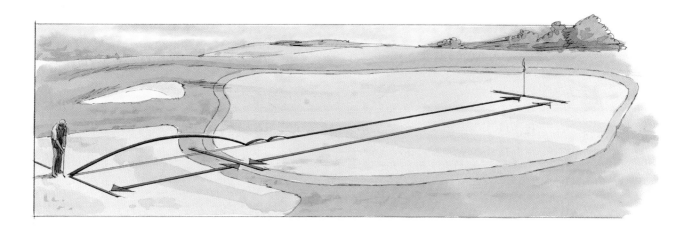

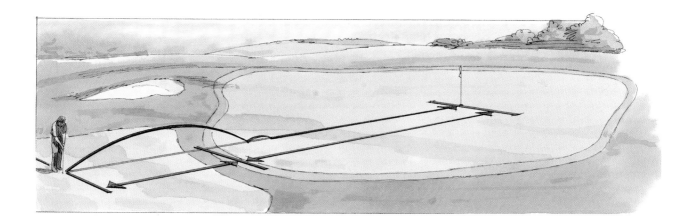

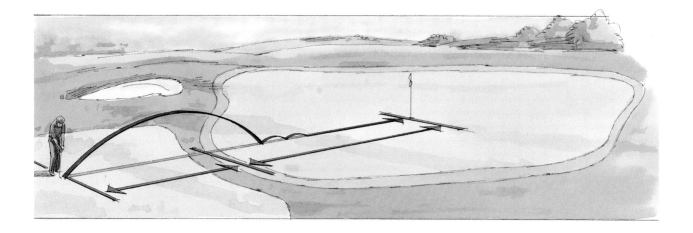

The closer the pin is to you, the higher the pitch shot you need to play. The farther you are from the hole, the lower the trajectory of the shot you want to play. It's easier to predict what the ball is going to do when it's on the ground.

Jay Haas *It is okay to chip with clubs other than your wedges.*

Ranked eighth in the All-Around category in 1994, ninth in 1997 and eleventh in 1995.

"When I'm chipping, I do not like the ball to carry all the way to the flagstick. I want to get the ball on the ground quickly and let it run the whole way to the hole. On longer chips, if that means the best club to play the shot is a 5-iron, then I'll use the 5-iron. On the courses we typically play on TOUR, I frequently use my 7-iron and 6-iron, and in special cases I'll chip with the 5-iron. You shouldn't feel like some clubs are 'chipping' clubs and others aren't. If it feels right or looks right for the shot, go for it."

Chipping is all about the distance between the player and the hole. You need enough room for the ball to land *and* roll without hitting it so hard that it goes beyond the hole.

The Pitch Shot

A pitch shot is played because some factor makes a shot along the ground less than ideal. That factor could be a hazard, rough, the proximity of the hole to your ball (really close but you cannot putt, and a chip would go well past the hole), or a quirk in the layout of the green. Another basic reason for pitching is that the "ball on the ground" theory has a point of diminishing returns, when judging how far to play the ball along the ground is more difficult than judging a shot played through the air. In these situations the ball would typically be fifty to sixty yards out from the green. You also might pitch because the ground is so wet that it is difficult to get enough speed on the ball to move it along the ground.

Pitch shots are always played with some sort of lofted club, whereas you might play a chip shot with a club as low as a 5- or 6-iron. There are various types of pitch shots: Some sit quickly; some run a little; some run a lot. In contrast, all chip shots run, depending on how hard you hit them.

When your ball is around the green, you should run through the following checklist:

- Can I putt the ball? The answer is yes if the ball is sitting cleanly, there is nothing that will impede the progress of the club or the ball, and you are close enough that you do not have to overextend your putting stroke. If these conditions are not in place, go to the next question.

- Can I chip the ball? The answer is yes if there is enough room between you and the hole to land the ball so it will run to the hole but not past it. In other words, if in order to clear an obstacle you must hit the chip so hard that it will run well past the hole, you should not chip the ball. Here you have to make a judgment call.
- Can I pitch the ball? The answer is almost always yes. The real question is whether you *should* pitch the ball. The answer is yes only when you cannot putt or chip, or when you are so far from the green that a shot along the ground makes you uncomfortable.

What's Your Lie?

Deciding the type of shot you are going to play also depends on the lie of the ball. For every shot you play in golf (except from the tee), this is true. If you think you want to putt, closely inspect how the ball is sitting. If the ball is sitting in any sort of depression (an old pitch mark, an old divot, etc.), or if the ball has "semiplugged"—that is, it is in a small indentation it made when it landed—then you should reconsider your choice of shots, because a ball struck with the putter will pop up in the air when you hit it, leaving you well short of your target.

You can play a chip from almost any lie (you should play a chip in the above-described scenario), because in a chip shot the club strikes the back of the ball directly and requires little or no follow-through. A pitch shot, however, requires a lie with enough fluff under the ball to slip the club under. If the ball is buried in deep rough, you will have trouble with the follow-through, which is required for playing a pitch shot. If you can follow through, you might have to swing so hard that the ball will come out "hot" and land past the hole. In any of these cases you will need to use your imagination, play some sort of hybrid chip/pitch shot, and take your lumps. It's part of the game.

Inside the Ropes

Nick Faldo   *Chipping with the club up on its toe gives you options.*

First player to win back-to-back Masters (1989 and 1990) since Jack Nicklaus did it in 1965 and 1966.

"On TOUR, players set the club on its toe for chipping for various reasons. If the ball is sitting down a little, it brings less of the club into contact with the ground. Or sometimes, if you are chipping onto a downslope on a very, very fast green, the ball will come out a little bit 'dead' if you set the club on its toe—it doesn't come out with the full spring of the club. Some guys just like doing it because they get their hands up high and just use a putting stroke, removing any other mechanics from the stroke.

"As far as choking down on the club when you chip, there aren't any rules for it—it is all feel. If you want to put your fingers down to the metal [shaft], that's fine. Whatever you feel you need for that shot."

Playing a Putt from off the Green

A basic putting setup (see Chapter 10) will serve you just fine in most cases. As you get farther from the hole it might be helpful to move the ball back slightly in your stance. The ball should never be to the right of the center of your body, but moving it even a half inch to the right of your normal ball position can have a positive effect on your shot. (When you move the ball back a touch you are moving your hands forward, ensuring that you can be aggressive with your stroke through the ball.)

Whenever you have the putter in your hands, you should be thinking about making an accelerating stroke through the ball. This point is emphasized in the chapter on putting, but it is extremely important when you are playing a putt from off the green and the ball has to travel through grass higher than that on the tightly mown green.

Sometimes, with a long putt from off the green, it is difficult to judge how hard to hit the ball. It helps to visualize how hard you would move your arms if you were to pick the ball up in your hand and roll it to the hole. That amount of arm swing is about what you want when you play the shot. Because you will have to hit the ball a little

Anytime you're having trouble getting a sense of how hard to hit a short shot, just face the target and pretend you're tossing a ball at the hole. That amount of arm swing is about the amount you want to use on the actual shot.

harder than you would if you were on the putting surface (to move it through the higher grass), do this visualization from behind the ball. Take one step away from the ball (and the hole) for every five feet of nonputting surface terrain the ball has to cover. Swing your arms back and forth pretending to toss the ball. This will give you a great feel for how much arm swing to put on the shot.

The Basic Chip Shot

The first step in playing a chip shot is selecting the club. Because you are attempting to move the ball only a few feet (typically speaking), you can select a club based on how far you want the ball to fly in the air. (Remember, the object is to get the ball back on the ground and running as soon as possible.)

The simplest way to decide which club to use for a chip is to limit the number of choices. You can do this by picking a low chip club (such as a 6- or a 7-iron) and a "high" chip club (an 8- or a 9-iron) and choosing between the two depending on how long you want to keep the ball in the air. If you prefer, you can decide from situation to situation and use any club from your pitching wedge down to a 5-iron or so. Which club you choose depends on how far you are from the hole. Typically, the farther away the hole is, the less loft you want to use. With less loft, the ball will fly lower and run farther. The nearer the hole is to you, the more loft you want to use.

The differences in trajectory that each club produces are not that noticeable from club to club, but the variance from one end of the set to the other—for example, the 9-iron to the 5-iron—is. Do not waste time worrying about how long to keep the ball in the air: Get it into the air long enough to clear the obstacles and low enough to produce the desired roll, and you are set.

The following checklist is useful for setting up to play and execute a chip shot:

- First, pick a target where you want the ball to land. The distance to your target depends on the loft of the shot. The lower the loft of the club, the nearer the target should be. The higher the loft of the club, the farther away the target should be. Be specific when picking a target: Pick a very precise spot, and line the lead edge of the club up to it in the same manner you would for a full shot.
- You should be rock solid over the ball—steady head, nothing moving but your arms; no weight shift, no turning, no sliding.
- Assume a slightly open stance. When you open your body to the target, you are aiming it left of the target. To do this, draw your left foot back a little bit and aim your hips and shoulders just a little to the left of the target. Be sure that you keep the club aimed at your target. Opening your stance a little helps you get a good look at the target and helps you feel a little more comfortable over the ball.
- Moving the ball back in your stance accomplishes several goals. First, it will put your hands ahead of the clubhead and help ensure clean contact by promoting a

The length of any chip shot is determined by the length of the backswing. In these photos, Justin Leonard is playing a long, crisp chip shot. Getting the club parallel to the ground is about the longest backswing you'd want to make for any chip shot.

descending blow. With a chip shot you want to contact the ball while the club is still moving down rather than up.

Moving the ball back in your stance also helps you avoid two other nemeses of the everyday golfer: the "chili-dipped" chip shot (when you hit the ground behind the ball instead of the ball itself) and the "skulled" or bladed wedge shot (when you unintentionally contact the ball with the lead edge of the clubface). The chili dip is avoided because moving the ball back makes it almost impossible to hit the ground before the ball. The bladed shot occurs almost exclusively because the everyday player feels it is imperative to help the ball into the air with some sort of wrist flip toward the bottom of the swing. As explained before, this notion is nonsense and ultimately harmful to your score. When the ball is back in your stance you'll feel unnatural and awkward attempting a wrist flip. Trust your equipment to lift the ball.

For nearly all full-swing shots you are advised not to move the ball right of the center of your body at address. For chip shots the opposite is true. Play the ball no farther forward than the middle of your body on a chip shot. You might feel comfortable playing it back as far as your right foot. As you move the ball back, remember two things. First, the farther back you place the ball, the lower the shot (the more run). Second, the farther back you place it, the more difficult it is to keep the clubface square to your target. Therefore, remember to square the clubface from behind the ball and then step into your setup. On the plus side, the farther back you move the ball, the sooner you contact the ball and the less room there is for error. If you feel comfortable playing the ball more toward your right foot than toward the center of your body, go for it. Remember the loss of loft on the club, and adjust accordingly—that is, if the shot calls for a 7-iron loft, use an 8-iron.

- Stand the clubhead up on its toe a little bit. This optional but popular technique can help when the ball is back in your stance. Standing a little closer to the ball creates, in effect, error room for the heel of the club, which is the part that usually snags the ground on a chili-dipped chip shot.

- Lean toward the target. Don't lean so far toward it that you fall over, but you do want to feel as if most of your weight (60 to 70 percent) is on your left side (left leg). The idea is to lean toward the *target* and not the *target line*. Tipping toward the target line will create problems for you, but leaning toward the target will help your body-to-target orientation, especially if you are playing the ball back toward your right foot.

- Check the angle of your right wrist. Because your hands are much farther ahead of the ball than for a typical shot, you need a little more angle in your right wrist at setup and no significant angle at all in your left wrist. The angle in your right

Inside the Ropes

Jeff Maggert   *You have to work at finding the feel for partial shots.*

Was twenty-fourth in scoring average in 1993 (70.24) and twenty-fifth as the 1998 season drew to a close (70.15).

"Everyday golfers aren't the only ones who find shots with less than a full swing difficult to execute. TOUR players constantly work on shots from that distance. When I'm working on it, I'll take maybe a thirty-yard pitch shot and just hit fifteen or so, then I'll move out ten yards farther and hit fifteen more. It is all about 'grooving' your swing for those shots—building some muscle memory. I know that doesn't sound easy for the golfer who only has time to play a few rounds a month, but that's the only way to do it.

"One key I can point out, however, is that because these are partial shots, some people tend to let up on the swing through the ball and decelerate, because they're only trying to hit the ball a short distance. You have to remember that you control the length of the shot with the length of your backswing and follow-through, and that no matter what, you have to accelerate that club through the impact area."

Raymond Floyd demonstrates how to play the low running chip shot. The ball is toward the right foot and the stance is extremely narrow. The movement of the arms is simply a tilting of the triangle—the wrists hinge slightly due to the weight of the club, but are quiet for the most part. His weight is favoring his left side.

wrist, which is determined by how far back in your stance you move the ball, should be maintained throughout the stroke. A nice swing key for your chip shots is: *Hold the angle in the right wrist.*

- Choke down on the club. Use a club at its full length only when you are trying to generate maximum power. Chip shots are about accuracy, not power. The farther down you grip the shaft, the more control you will have over the club (at least until you reach the point of diminishing return, which, in this case, is probably an inch or beyond the end of the bottom of the grip). In general, the shorter the shot you are attempting to play, the farther you will want to choke down. If you feel good putting one or two fingers below the grip, do it. This is something you have to develop a feel for.

- The stroke you use in playing a chip shot is essentially the same one used for putting. Many everyday players mistakenly believe that chipping is mainly a matter of using the wrists to move the club. For a player of exceptional talent and hand-to-eye coordination—such as Isao Aoki—this may be true. For everyday golfers there is no question that keeping the wrists firm is essential to a good chipping stroke.

As with all other shots, make certain your grip pressure is light enough that you have a sense of the clubhead being connected to your hand. If you want to squeeze a little tighter with the pinkie, ring, and middle fingers of your left hand, go right ahead. This will give you the sense that the left hand and wrist should remain firm throughout the stroke.

As far as actually moving the club, you have taken care of all the details in your setup. The motion simply consists of moving your shoulders back to the right and through to the left. Another way of thinking of it is that the stroke is all arms and shoulders and no hands and wrists. How far you hit the ball in the air depends on how far back and through you move the club. The longer the motion you make, the longer the ball will stay in the air. The objective of your stroke is to place the clubface directly on the back of the ball at impact and to follow through the same amount you took the club back. You do not need to attempt to slide the club under the ball. The club will graze the ground on a cleanly struck shot, but it will happen after impact, when the ball is already on its way.

What Type of Pitch Shot and How to Play It

When you cannot putt or chip, it is time to play a pitch shot. The advantage of a pitch shot is that it offers you the widest range of options regarding how the ball will react once it hits the green. You can fly the ball almost to the hole, halfway to the hole, or somewhere in between, depending on what type of pitch you hit. There is no significant downside to these shots other than the fact that the farther you get from the green the bigger the swing required and the more a sense of distance is required—that is, the more capable you have to be of producing shots of varying distances.

As you assess the shot, think about the three types of pitch shot you can play: (1) one that flies very near the hole and bites; (2) one that flies about three-quarters of the way to the hole and runs the rest; and (3) one that flies about halfway to the hole and runs the rest. The three shots have a lot in common in terms of setup and execution. The common factors are:

- The club of choice is always a wedge—sand, pitching, or lob. The closer you are to the green, the less likely you are to use the pitching wedge (unless the lie is bad, as will be explained below).

Inside the Ropes

J. C. Snead *When you are chipping, leave the pin in.*

Won eight times on the PGA TOUR before joining the PGA SENIOR TOUR in 1990.

"I know a lot of golfers wonder whether they should pull the pin when they chip. I say leave it in. Of course, I'm not a very good chipper, and if I could set my bag down behind the hole to stop my ball, I'd put it there. Actually, the pin in hole helps give you better visual perspective. Years ago Jerry Barber taught me that it's a lot better to have the pin in rather than staring at that little black hole in the ground. The farther away you get, the less you see of the hole, so I guess I feel like it gives you a little bit of an edge. Even when I'm putting, if I'm twenty feet or farther away, I have my caddie tend the flag."

There are three common impediments to good chipping. Any one or a combination of them is going to lead to some long days on the course. They are listed here so you can readily recognize and avoid them.

- **The ball is too far forward in your stance.** If you keep the ball to the left of the center of your body, you bring two bad scenarios into play: the chunk shot and the thin shot. If you have the ball just an inch or two left of center, because you are increasing the odds that you will slam the club into the ground before you hit the ball—"chunking" the shot. The closer your ball moves toward your left foot, the more likely you are to start hitting the ball thin—blading it with the lead edge of the club. This is because the club has already started to swing up after bottoming out its arc. In either case the cure is simple: Whether it is chunky or thin, try moving the ball back to the right of center.
- **You use a club with too much loft.** Remember: You are trying to play a running shot here, not a shot that flies to the target. Everything you do in your setup is based on the fact that you are going to play a running shot. If you automatically reach for one of your wedges every time you want to play a chip, you are hurting your chances before you even get started, especially on longer chip shots.

Remember: The longer the shot, the less loft you want on the club. Playing a long chip with a lofted club puts you outside the comfort zone of power production for the chipping stroke.

- **You stand too far away from the ball.** When you stand too far away from the ball, it creates two problems for you. First, it forces you to reach for the ball with your arms (extend them away from your body), and that causes tension. Tension is not desirable in any phase of the game. The second thing that happens when you stand too far away from the ball is that it forces the club to move inside the target line, as if you were going to swing it around your body. The idea of the chipping stroke is that you can move the club straight back and straight through, keeping the lead edge square to the target the entire time. If you move the club inside the target line (when you are standing too far from the ball) you will have to get it back onto the target line while making certain the face returns to a target-square position. You are standing too far away from the ball if you feel any tension at all in your arms, or if you look down and they are extended beyond where they would be if they were hanging straight down—that is, perpendicular to the ground.

- The clubface is always aimed at the target. You will adjust your body lines as you go from shot to shot, but the clubface will always stay aimed at the target.
- Your weight should always favor your left side.
- The butt of the club is aimed at the center of your body. You will be moving the ball around in your stance to play various shots. Keep the butt of the club pointed at the center of your body, and your hands will be in the right place.
- Because this is not a full swing shot, only worry about your arm swing.
- Swing the club along the line of your shoulders. This is a key point for the everyday player—the club**face** is aimed at the target, the club**head** is swung along the shoulder line—that is, outside the target line going back and inside the target line on the follow-through.
- The distance the ball flies is determined by how far you swing the club back and through the ball. No chart can tell you how far the ball is going to fly if you swing the club back three feet and through three feet. Because you cannot watch the club, practicing is the only way you can establish a feel for how far back and through you need to swing to produce a shot of any given distance.

- The trajectory of the ball is determined by the position of the ball in your stance. Because you will be making adjustments in your stance width, think of ball position in relation to your upper body, using the center of your chest as the reference point.

Pitch #1: All Carry

Your best option seems to be a shot that flies all the way to the hole and immediately grabs on the green. You will execute this shot more effectively by playing a soft-cover ball that spins quite a bit. You should use this shot only when you have no room to play another type of pitch.

- Play the ball just an inch or so to the left of the center of your body. This will help you get the maximum loft.
- Set up just *slightly* open to your target. This means that your entire body—feet, knees, hips, and shoulders—is aimed left of parallel with the target line.
- If the pitch is a short pitch, narrow your stance. If the pitch is long (more than forty yards or so), keep your stance a little wider.

The three different types of pitch shots: The highest shot is the "sit" pitch, which stops close to where it lands; the middle trajectory is the "walk" pitch, which carries about three-fourths of the way to the hole and rolls the rest; the lowest trajectory is the "run" pitch, which carries about halfway to the hole and runs the rest of the way.

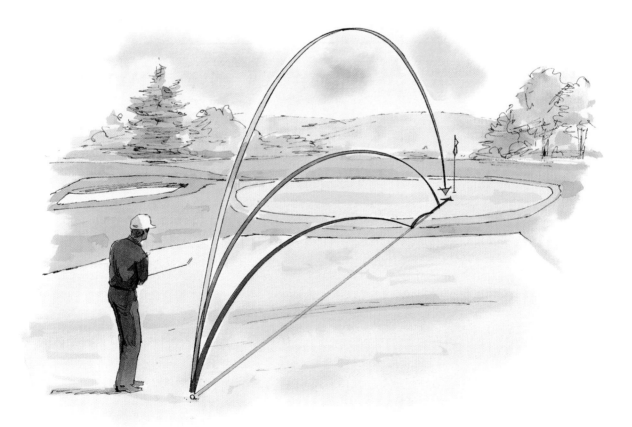

Tom Kite playing a full pitch shot. The key to controlling the distance on a pitch shot lies in making the backswing and the through swing equidistant, as Kite does here.

- Swing the club along your body lines. You are not swinging the clubhead out to the target; rather, you are swinging it to a point left of the target. Swing the club aggressively and at the same tempo throughout.

- Focus on your follow-through. When you finish swinging, the knuckles on your left hand should be facing the sky. Through impact you are not going to lose the angle in your left wrist—that is, your hands are not going to turn over as they would on a full shot. Your mission is to make a conscious effort to avoid that. When you finish this swing you should be staring right at the clubface. The club does not swing all the way around behind your left ear unless the shots are 100 yards or more (the exceptions are some specialty shots described later).

Pitch #2: A Lot of Carry, A Little Roll

Play this pitch in the air to about three-quarters of the distance between the edge of the green and the hole, and let it run the rest of the way to the hole. This is the bread-and-butter pitch shot, the one you will play most often. It gives you more room for error than the shot described above. If you have room on the green to play it, employ the commonalities listed above and the following points:

- Play the ball in the exact center of your body.
- Align dead square to your target, just as you would to play a tee shot or any other full-swing shot you wanted to hit straight.
- The longer the shot, the wider your stance. The shorter the shot, the narrower your stance.

Pitch #3: Half Carry, Half Roll

Play this pitch shot in the air to about halfway between the edge of the green and the hole, and let it run the rest of the way. This shot is best suited for situations when the hole is so far away from you that making a precise judgment of how hard to hit the ball to the hole leaves room for error. If you are playing a pitch from near the green and the hole is cut on the other side of a big green, or if you are still fifty or sixty yards out and you have room to land it, here are the adjustments:

- Move the ball about one inch to two inches to the right of center in your stance. Do not move it back too far because it is a lofted shot.
- Keep the clubface square to the target line, and aim your body just slightly to the right of the target.

Inside the PGA TOUR
Bad Pitching Days

The following list can be helpful when you are having an off day with your pitch shots:

- *Your clubface/body alignment is off. When playing shots with an open or a closed stance, it is sometimes difficult to keep the clubface square to the target. Frequently, when you open your stance (aim left), you instinctively aim the clubface to the right in an attempt to balance things out. This causes you to hit the shot to the right. The same is true when you close your stance (aim right of the target)—that is, the instinct is to aim the clubface to the left. The key to overcoming these tendencies is to aim the clubface at the target from behind the ball and then step into your setup position.*
- *You are swinging the club toward your target when you should be swinging it along your body lines. If you are set up square to the target, this is no problem. However, any time you set your body open or closed to the target and swing the clubhead toward the target, you are not going to get the shot you want. If your body is set open to the target, and if the clubface is square to the target, you must*

swing the club along the body lines. If you swing it straight back and through along the target line, you will push the ball to the right of your target. When your body setup is closed to the target and the club is square to the target, you will miss to the left if you swing the club at the target rather than along your body lines.

- *The butt of the club is pointed somewhere other than the center of your body. If your pitches are flying low or you feel as if you are smothering the ball, check your hands. They are probably well left of the center of your body at address—perhaps near your left hip. If your hands are to the right of the center of your body, nearly every bad shot in golf is a possibility. The two most common shots from this position are the chunked shot and the shot bladed with the lead edge of the club.*
- *Your ball position is off, which forces the bad hand positions described above. Remember, playing the ball up in your stance for a pitch shot means only an inch or two left of center. Playing a ball back in your stance for a pitch means only an inch or two to the right of center.*

- Swing along the lines of your body. This will take the club inside the target line on the way back and outside the target line on your follow-through, producing the lowest-flying, longest-running type of pitch shot.
- The longer the shot, the wider your stance. The shorter the shot, the more narrow your stance.

Coordinating Your Target and Swing

You already know how important it is to have a target for every shot you play. With your short game, as you move closer and closer to the hole, a target becomes even more vital because you have a greater range of options from any given position—different clubs and different shots you can play—and the target is different for every one of those options.

Remember that your target is where you want the ball to land before it starts to roll. If, for example, you are attempting a chip shot that you wish to bump twelve inches or so in the air with an 8-iron, your target is that spot twelve inches away. Likewise, if you are playing a fifty-yard pitch shot and you want to land it halfway onto the green and twenty feet left of the hole, that spot—*not* the hole—is your target. The hole is rarely your immediate target, even though it is your ultimate goal. Aim your body and club in relation to the point where you want the ball to land.

This means you have to do a little reconnaissance work before playing most short game shots: judging the overall terrain, prominent bumps in the green, effect of the wind, etc. While you are making this assessment, start to piece together in your mind what type of shot to play. The basic question is always: Which shot will provide the maximum benefit with the least amount of risk under the circumstances?

Inside the Ropes

Dave Stockton   *Lower is always better than higher.*

SENIOR PGA TOUR superstar, won eleven times on the PGA TOUR, including two PGA Championships (1970 and 1976).

"When it comes to your short game, a lower trajectory is always better than a higher trajectory, unless something forces you to hit it high, something like a lake or a bunker. When you can hit it low, you are not at such a risk as to whether the ball is going to bite or not when it hits the ground. You know it is going to run. When you hit low shots you do not have to worry about trying to help the ball up in the air, either.

"I like to play all of my chips standing very erect and holding the club near the top. I do not choke down on the club at all, and I move the ball to within about a foot of my toes [distance between body and ball, not position in stance] so that I feel very erect, very tall. And I stand the club on its toe so that's the only part that hits the ground; the heel isn't going to be anywhere near the ground. If you do this, and keep your weight on your front foot and make sure your hands lead the clubhead—don't let that left wrist break down!—you are going to hit a solid shot with a slightly downward action."

In this example, the player has two choices of short game shots to play because of the hump in front of the green. If the pin is in the back of the green, the preferred shot is to fly the ball back to the hole. If the pin is in the front of the green, he should consider bumping the ball into the hump and letting it bounce up onto the green. This is because if he attempts to fly it to the hole and comes up short, the ball will roll back down the hill.

Target selection is related to club selection and arm swing as you move farther away from the hole. From a clean lie in the fairway—no matter how far you are from the hole—if you are making less than a full swing, your swing should be an arms-dominated movement that is the same length back as it is going through. Does that mean that you want to make the same length swing from seventy yards no matter what the circumstances are? The answer, of course, is a resounding no. Even from the fairway, you may not always wish to play the same trajectory shot into the green. A lower shot is going to move the target toward you and shorten the overall swing. A higher shot is going to move your target away from you and require a longer overall swing. The numerous factors that determine how long your swing should be from a given distance are covered in the chapter on game management. There is no single "seventy-yard" swing, for example, because the length of your swing on a seventy-yard shot depends on the club you play. A sand wedge is going to require a bigger swing than the lowly pitched 9-iron, for example.

By practicing, you can develop a familiarity with how long your swing should be with a given club from a given distance from both the fairway and the rough. In other words, determine how long a swing you need to hit a pitching wedge seventy yards from the fairway and seventy yards from the rough. The swing from the rough should be slightly longer and more powerful. Then determine how long a swing you need to make with your sand wedge to hit it seventy yards from the fairway and the rough. The swings with the two clubs will be slightly different in length. If you have an L wedge, do the same thing. This will not only help you get the swing down, but also will help you find the maximum range of the L wedge without overswinging.

Once you know how big a swing you need with a given club from a given distance and under certain circumstances, all you need to think about during the swing itself is "back and through" the same distance.

The Short Game Specialty Shots

This chapter has tried to give you some rules for playing garden-variety chips and pitches, and probably 85 percent of the shots you play from 100 yards and in will fall into this category, especially since, week in and week out, you are not likely to face courses set up for championship play. Just the same, the "rub of the green" does not know the difference between you and Greg Norman, so it helps to know what to do when you are faced with an uncommon situation around the greens.

The Flop Shot

The shot usually called a flop shot (sometimes a cut shot) is a short, high shot that lands on the green or the fringe and does not roll very far because of the extremely steep angle at which the ball hits the green. This shot requires practice, and you should not start trying to play it during your rounds without first practicing it. If you do, the results will be unpredictable, to say the least. In essence, this shot goes straight up and straight down. It does not cover much distance—a maximum of fifteen yards or so. You might attempt to play it if you have missed a green and the hole is cut very near you and slopes away from you. You also might play it if you have missed the green and you are very near a bunker (a few feet away) and you need to get the ball tight to a hole cut just the other side of the bunker.

Before you attempt a flop shot, you should realize that it is risky for the everyday player. You should consider whether a simpler shot that has a higher chance of putting your ball on the green (even if it is not close to the hole) is a better choice. If you decide to attempt a flop shot, you should make sure you have the proper lie for attempting the shot. To execute a flop shot you need enough of a grass cushion underneath the ball for the club to slide under. If you do not think that can happen, consider an alternative shot. If there is too much cushion, you will probably slip the club under the ball without ever making contact. In this case you have to play a shot that allows you to pick the ball out of the fluffy grass.

The most difficult thing for the everyday player to grasp is that a flop shot requires a *full* swing even though you are only trying to move the ball a short distance. It is easy to move the ball a short distance, but you wish to combine that element with tremendous height so the ball drops onto the green like a rock dropped out of an airplane. To achieve that result, the club must be moving fairly quickly when it makes contact with the ball. However, altough it is a full swing, it is not necessarily a fast swing—you might think of it as a long, lazy swing.

Once you are ready to play, the first adjustment is to move the ball well forward in your stance, up off your left foot. In addition, do not lean toward the target quite so much as you would to play a standard pitch, and open up you stance (the entire body) significantly—aim fifteen feet or so to the left of your target. (Because your target is so close, aiming your body fifteen feet to the left produces a much more open stance than if you were aiming fifteen feet left of something 200 yards away.) Once your body is set, open the clubface, no matter whether you are using a sand wedge or an L wedge. As you do so, keep two things in mind: Keep the lead edge of the club as square as you can to your target, and make sure the clubface is pointing directly up at the sky.

Inside the Ropes

Kenny Perry *The secret to the flop shot is controlling your arms and clubs together as one.*

Was twenty-second in the All-Around category in 1995 and twenty-seventh in scoring in 1996 (70.44).

"When you are playing a flop shot, the clubhead has to stay even with your hands at all times, right from the setup position. I see a lot of everyday players trying to play this shot and they get their hands way out in front of the ball. I can guarantee you they'll skull it nine times out of ten. Or they'll hit it real low. The key to the shot is that your hands have to arrive at the ball at the same time as the lead edge of the club. That's why I've always worked on tempo for that shot. I work on a nice, smooth backswing and a nice smooth throughswing where everything stays together. Keep the club moving at the same speed from start to finish."

Fred Couples demonstrates the technique for playing a flop shot, a very high, very short shot that sits immediately upon hitting the green. This shot requires a high degree of self-confidence. Of particular note, check his ball position and notice how he swings fully through the ball. Even though this is a short shot, the club is moving very fast. The forward ball position allows him to catch the ball at the beginning of the upswing.

A few more details: First, how far the ball flies is not determined by the *length* of your swing; rather, it is determined by the *speed* of your swing. The faster you swing, the farther the ball will fly. The shot requires subtlety (or finesse) because you are not attempting to hit this shot a long way, and you are not swinging at it like it is a driver. The swing should be long—as if you were playing a full 9-iron—but at about one-third the speed of a full 9-iron. If you hit the shot right, you will barely feel the contact. You are not trying to hit the back of the ball (like every other shot in golf); rather, you are trying to slip the club underneath the ball. Finally, follow through, follow through, follow through. If you stop, the ball won't go anywhere.

The Bellied Wedge

Every few rounds or so you will hit an approach shot that will come to rest on the fringe, right up against the collar of rough that rings the green. If the hole is on the far side of the green from you, this presents no problem. Play a simple, low-running chip and you will be fine. Being close to the hole, however, can present a few problems—for

Posted a scoring average of 68.44 in 1997, his first season on the SENIOR PGA TOUR.

"Like any other TOUR player, I've played my share of bellied-wedge shots. The idea is that the edge of the club slides through the grass easier—like a knife—as opposed to that big, thick clubhead on your putter. The big advantage is that you can control the speed much better. All you have to do is take the lead edge of your wedge and hit the middle of the ball. There aren't any mechanical adjustments—if you normally putt wristy, then use a wristy stroke here. If you are normally a shoulders-and-arms putter, then use your shoulders-and-arms stroke. It is actually pretty simple. Just choke down on the club a little bit and that's about it."

example, you do not want to chip it because you will have to hit it too hard to keep it close to the hole, but your putter might get hung up in the long grass. What do you do?

First, make certain that you cannot play a shot with your putter. Sometimes putting is only a simple matter of not grounding the club behind the ball—that is, hovering it just above the ground at address. This way the club will not get caught going back, and on the through swing it does not have to enter the grass until just before it hits the ball.

Sometimes, though, the type or length of grass just makes it impossible to play a shot with the putter with any amount of confidence. In those cases you have two options, both of which involve keeping the ball on the ground the entire time *and* controlling the speed (because you are close to the hole, remember?).

The first option is described as a "bellied" wedge because you want to contact the ball in its "belly." To play this shot you set up to the ball as if you were going to play a putt and use your putting stroke. Choke down on the wedge (any wedge is fine) enough so that when you make the putting stroke, the lead edge of the club hits the dead center of the ball. You are hitting it "thin" with a putting stroke. Becoming proficient at this shot is not difficult because it involves only the shortest of strokes. The advantage to playing this shot as opposed to using your putter is that only the protruding edge of your wedge, not the entire clubhead, needs to pass through the grass to make contact.

Using Pressure to Your Advantage

I try to make pressure and tension work for me. I want the adrenaline to be flowing. I think sometimes we try so hard to be cool, calm, and collected that we forget what we are doing. There's nothing wrong with being charged up if it's controlled.

— Hale Irwin

Pressure is not always harmful to your performance. Pressure increases your motivation to practice, boosts your concentration to help you hit a difficult shot, and supplies extra energy or adrenaline for a long drive. When I give a presentation, the pressure I feel to do a good job for my colleagues can make me prepare better for the presentation.

Pressure produces excitement and increased arousal, including an adrenaline rush, which can help you to play better, except when it reaches a point where you become overaroused or anxious. This condition inevitably diminishes the quality of your play. For example, the challenge of playing for a club championship, which you may perceive as beyond your skill level and ability to cope, can cause you to experience pressure. Having to execute a difficult shot can challenge you beyond your capabilities and thus cause you to worry, tighten up, chop at the ball and chunk the shot. On the other hand, your performance can suffer when you're not intense enough because you lack concentration and energy to hit the shot.

What Is the Worst Thing That Can Happen?

Many golfers put pressure on themselves by thinking about the worst thing that can happen. Do not allow your fears to escalate into what in

sport psychology is termed "catastrophizing," that is, expecting the worst without any logical foundation and obsessively thinking about how ruinous it would be to mishit the next shot or putt. Rather, you should evaluate the situation rationally. For example, if you do miss a critical putt, "the worst thing" is that you may lose the hole. You may score one stroke higher for the round. But you will live to play the next hole. A fresh dose of reality helps put the situation in perspective. It's just a shot, not the end of the world.

Reinterpret Pressure/Make It Work for You

Successful PGA TOUR players interpret pressure as a positive condition. Here is the thought pattern: "If I don't get in a pressure situation, I'll never have a chance to win. I like the challenge of channeling my emotions when I'm in contention. It is fun to try to win, fun to win the physical game, fun to win the mental game, fun to hold it all together and try to come out on top." The perception is that pressure is but another challenge in mastering how to win. Some players thrive on pressure because it focuses their attention like nothing else. It is a welcomed and familiar friend who helps sharpen their performance.

Breathe the Tension Away

Controlled breathing is a very simple, effective and practical method for relieving the physical tension brought on by pressure. Basketball players take deep breaths prior to shooting free throws, baseball pitchers inhale and exhale deeply before toeing the rubber to deliver the next pitch. These deep breaths drain away the tension. You can learn to do the same when you need it most.

Here is an exercise—rhythmic abdominal breathing—that will help you relieve tension brought on by pressure situations.

1. Sit or lie down in an area where you won't be distracted;
2. Take a slow, complete breath, filing up the lower section of your lungs and then the upper section;
3. Inhale for five seconds, pause, and exhale for five seconds.

Concentrate on the rhythm of your breathing and the air filling the lungs. Place one hand on your abdomen while breathing. If you are breathing correctly, you should feel your hand rise and fall as you inhale and exhale. Slowly and smoothly empty the air completely out of your lungs when exhaling.

Practice this breathing exercise for ten minutes a day for three weeks. After you are comfortable practicing this exercise in a quiet environment, try doing it during your free time in the day, when watching television, riding in a car, waiting in a line and so on. Once you are totally proficient, you can use it on the course, especially during shot preparation. Soon, you'll learn to reduce excess tension by taking no more than two or three deep breaths.

On-Course Coping with Tension and Anxiety

Here are some other methods (in addition to breathing deeply) for reducing anxiety and tension during play.

Slow down. Anxiety and tension cause players to speed up their actions. An anxious player walks faster between shots, rushes his shots, and swings faster. Pressure can also cause you to speed up your preshot routine, "to get the shot over with." Players think that the best way to alleviate the uncomfortable feelings that accompany pressure is to hurry. Unfortunately, the faster you go, the more anxious you become, the more pressure you feel. Don't get caught up in this situation. Pace yourself. Walk to the tee slowly but deliberately. Walk purposely but not hurriedly to your next shot. Slow down and pace your preshot routine. Breathe deeply. Focus on the execution and immediate task at hand.

Tighten and release your muscles. Contracting and releasing a tense muscle (or group of muscles) helps reduce tension. It is often easier to relax a tight muscle when you fully contract it

> **Give yourself some words of encouragement.**

and then release the tension. If you feel tightness in the shoulder and neck region, shrug your shoulder toward your ears and then drop them, arms hanging loosely at your sides. If your arms and hand are tightening up, grip the club tightly and then release your hands and shake them lightly.

Talk to yourself. Give yourself some words of encouragement, such as "You're a good putter, you've made this putt thousands of times before." Create other affirmation statements off the course so you will be prepared the next time you need to give yourself a pep talk.

Take your mind away. Sometimes it helps to make a temporary escape with your mind. Visualize yourself in a tranquil scene, such as on a sunset beach, on a mountain vista, or in a cool forest. Imagine yourself in a familiar setting that is relaxing to you. When you begin to feel more relaxed and mentally refreshed, return your attention to the task at hand.

Lee Westwood displays classic chipping form.

A combination of power and grace equals success for the "Big Easy."

9

Escaping from the Sand

No shot challenges the beginning player more than the sand shot, and it is not necessarily easier for the more experienced everyday golfer. Only when playing a bunker shot do you actually *need to strike the ground with the club before you hit the ball*. The basic sand shot just does not seem to fit in a game where the goal is unfettered contact between club and ball.

Bunkers are scattered all over a typical golf course, especially alongside fairways. Long shots played from fairway bunkers require a different swing and setup than a greenside bunker shot. Indeed, they have an entirely different objective: to pick the ball cleanly off the surface of the sand. As daunting as they can sometimes seem, sand shots pose no more difficulty than any other shot in golf. As with other shots, much of the work is done before you ever move the club—in the setup. Once you determine the proper setup and learn to trust the club, finding your ball in the sand will cease to be the frightening experience it once was.

Paul Anzinger plays from a bunker.

201

Greenside Sand Play: The Proper Club

One of the biggest steps toward successful greenside sand play happens in the store, when you purchase a sand wedge. If you have just recently begun playing golf and are under the impression that you should be able to consistently escape from a greenside bunker with *any* lofted club, you are wrong. You can pick a ball out once in a while with a pitching wedge or a 9-iron, but these clubs will more often cause you to misplay the ball. The bottom of the club on all of the irons up to the pitching wedge is designed so that the club will dig into the ground. If the clubs were not designed that way, upon contact with the ground the club would immediately bounce upward, with the lead edge striking the ball.

Unlike an iron shot struck from turf, a greenside bunker shot requires a club that *bounces* and does not dig into the ground. The bottom of the sand wedge, from the lead edge back, is curved so it will bounce. The curved edge deflects the club upward immediately after it enters the sand, the club displaces a small pile of sand, and the ball rides out of the bunker on that displaced sand. Except for a few special situations, the ball and the club never touch on a properly executed sand shot. If you play this shot with a pitching wedge the club will enter the sand and dig too deeply without displacing any sand, significantly slowing the clubhead.

From left to right, three different types of wedges: the pitching wedge, the sand wedge and the lob (or L) wedge. The sand wedge has a curved bottom that is designed to deflect off the sand. The pitching wedge is flat-bottomed and designed to dig into the turf. The lob wedge has 60 degrees of loft, but is intended mostly for shots played from the turf.

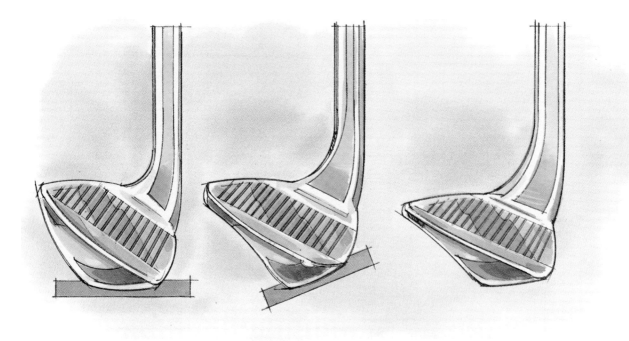

If you carry an L wedge, it, too, is designed with bounce, which makes it playable from the sand. You should not depend on it as your basic sand club, however, because it limits the types of shots you can play. In certain situations, when the hole is cut very near you, the L wedge can be quite valuable. The traditional sand wedge, with fifty-six degrees of loft, is the club you should depend on. It is also the most versatile club in your bag for many short approach shots that are not played from the sand.

The Basic Greenside Bunker Shot

The type of shot you play from a greenside bunker is predicated on three things: the lie of the ball, the severity of the face of the bunker (i.e., the height of the *lip* or the top edge of the bunker), and the distance from your ball to the hole. The typical bunker shot requires you to play from a clean lie, over a moderate lip, to a hole that is far enough away that you can make an aggressive swing. Depending on the circumstances, many adjustments are available to alter a shot, but you must first understand the basic bunker shot so you can use it as a point of reference.

Use the following list of fundamentals to play a basic greenside bunker shot:

- Pick a spot on green where you want the ball to land.
- Aim the lead edge of the clubface at your target. This part never changes.
- Open your body lines so they are aiming slightly left of your target, but keep the clubface square to the target. As you begin to make adjustments, how much you open your body will affect the height and length of the shot.

Note: Dig your feet into the sand about two inches by twisting them back and forth. Dig in enough that you feel rooted. At the very least, your heels and the edges of your soles should be covered with sand. How much you dig in will change depending on the shot you want to play. Digging in stabilizes your stance and lets you lower yourself to make certain the club hits the sand.

- Do not choke down on the club too much, or you will eliminate the effect of digging in with your feet. If you must choke down on the club, limit it to a half inch or so, and make sure your feet are dug in at least two to three inches.

- Position the ball just to the left of center of your body. An inch or two should be plenty.
- Lower yourself down to the ball by flexing your knees. Don't slouch over!
- Plan to strike the sand one inch to two inches behind the ball. For this basic shot the length of your backswing determines the distance of the shot. Swing back and through along your body lines at the same tempo. Generally speaking, however, you do not have to swing very hard.

To play a typical bunker shot, aim the lead edge of the club-face at the target and aim your body to the left of the target. Swing the club along the lines aimed left of the target.

Two keys to any greenside bunker shot are a steep back-swing—very upright—and a complete follow-through. More shots get left in the sand due to a lack of follow through than for every other reason combined.

- Always follow through *completely*! No matter how far you take the club back, follow through as if you have just hit an eighty-yard pitch shot. The failure to follow through completely ruins more sand shots than any other single error. In fact, if you consistently leave the ball in the sand, you can almost be certain that the reason is lack of follow-through.

The nature of greenside bunker play provides you with lots of room for error. Because the basic sand shot is not a surgical strike of the ball (you are actually *trying* to hit it fat), simply following the steps outlined above will get your ball out of the sand and onto the green. And that is always the pri-

Jay Haas *Upslope makes bunker shots a little easier.*

Ranked thirteenth in sand saves in 1997, getting up and down 64.5 percent of the time.

"I'll never forget the bunker shot I holed out on the sixteenth hole of my singles match at the 1995 Ryder Cup at Oak Hill. At the time it seemed like my match was going to be the swing match to decide the entire thing, and the pressure was unbelievable. I was three down with three to go, and I was lying two in the greenside bunker. My opponent was two feet from the hole and lying three.

"The ball was resting on a little bit of an upslope. When you have that lie in the bunker, as long as the ball isn't plugged, you can swing with confidence because you know you are not going to hit it fat and the slope will help lift the ball into the air. It is always a little lucky when you hole out from the bunker, but there's a little skill involved, too. In that case I probably carried it a little farther than I wanted to, but it hopped into the hole on the first bounce. That had a lot to do with the fact that I could make a confident swing because of the lie. Under the circumstances it was a highlight reel shot for me."

mary goal when you are in the sand. At the very least, you want your next shot to be a putt. Once you have become proficient, you can move on to the second goal of greenside bunker play: getting the ball close to the hole.

Getting It Close: The Adjustments

The great advantage that the basic bunker shot has over every other shot in the game is that it requires less than perfect execution to produce acceptable results. Gaining greater control over the greenside bunker shot is not a matter of advanced physics either. Gaining maximum control of the height, distance, and spin on a shot from the sand requires an understanding of the following interrelated points:

- The shorter and higher you want the ball to fly, the more you should open your body in relation to the target. The lower and longer you want the ball to fly, the more squarely you should align your body to the target.
- The shorter and higher you want the ball to fly, the deeper you should dig your feet into the sand. The longer and lower you want the shot to fly, the less you should dig your feet into the sand.
- The shorter and higher you want the ball to fly, the farther you must stand from the ball. The longer and lower you want the ball to fly, the closer you must stand to it.
- The shorter and higher you want the ball to fly, the farther back from the ball the club should enter the sand. The lower and longer you want the ball to fly, the closer to the ball the club should enter the sand.
- The faster you swing, the more velocity the shot will have, which means the effects of your adjustments will be more magnified. The slower you swing, the less velocity the shot will have, which means the effects of your adjustments are lessened.

The key to these adjustments is that they *must be made together.* Playing the shortest, highest possible shot requires the following adjustments:

- Align your body well left of the target—about three feet. Remember: You are very close to your target, and aiming three feet left of it is rather dramatic. Keep the lead edge of the club square to the target.
- Dig your feet in deep—about three inches.
- Stand about three inches farther from the ball than you normally would.
- Plan on hitting about three inches behind the ball.
- Swing back and through along your body lines.

The relationship should be clear: Each adjustment requires corresponding adjustments. For example, hitting a long, low bunker shot to a pin that is far away necessitates the following adjustments:

- Align your body parallel to the target line, and the lead edge square to the target line.
- Dig your feet in one inch.
- Stand about one inch farther from the ball than you would for a pitch shot of the same length.
- Hit one inch behind the ball.
- Swing back and through along your body lines.

    You can vary the speed of your swing independently of these other adjustments. You want to remember three things about the pace of your swing.

1. It should be consistent throughout the swing (tempo).
2. You can use it to modify any shot; that is, you can hit a high shot higher (and shorter) by swinging faster, or hit a high shot lower and longer (relatively speaking) by swinging slower.
3. The finer the sand (the smaller the grains), the slower you want to swing. The heavier the sand (the bigger the grains), the faster you want to swing.

The photo on the left illustrates where the club should enter the sand for a short bunker shot. The photo at right shows the spot where the club should enter the sand for a longer bunker shot. The longer you want to hit the ball, the closer to it you need to hit the sand.

The last point is important: The texture of the sand has no relationship to how far behind the ball you hit. The only adjustment you make for the type of sand is in the speed of your swing. Tip: Ordinarily, the lighter the color of the sand, the finer its texture.

Playing from a Buried Lie

Even though you have the ability to control any bunker shot from a good lie, once in a while the ball burrows into the sand and you can see only the top of the ball—the rest of the ball is in the sand rather than sitting on top of it. This lie, sometimes referred to as a fried egg, can be the result of too much sand in a certain area of the bunker, or a ball that landed in the face of the bunker at a very steep angle. When you are stuck with one of these lies in a greenside bunker (or any bunker), assume that all bets are off regarding the basic sand shot technique. You will need to make the following adjustments:

- The first adjustment is mental. Forget any notions you have about getting the ball close to the hole. Your only focus is getting the ball onto the green.
- Dig in and build a nice base, because you are going to be swinging hard.
- Move the ball back in your stance, almost off your right foot.

In Payne Stewart's setup for a bunker shot, you'll notice that he's dug in slightly with his feet and that he's lowered himself to the ball by flexing his knees more than he would for a regular shot. You can also see that he is leaning toward the target, which helps make his backswing more upright. He completes the swing with a full follow-through.

- Close the lead edge of the club in relation to your target. Your body is going to be aimed right of the target, and your club is going to be aimed left of the target.

- Swing as hard as you can without losing your balance. Don't worry about swinging along your body lines—you want to slam that clubface into the sand like a sledgehammer about one inch behind the ball.

- There is no follow-through. It is impossible because you will have driven the club so far into the sand.

With any luck, the ball will pop out onto the green. If you are playing the ball from a level lie, it will come out low and run quite a bit. Having the ball plugged in the front face of the bunker is a little bit of an advantage. Because you will be leaning away from the target, the ball will come out a little softer and shorter, upping your chances of keeping it on the green. The trade-off is that it is difficult to get comfortable on uneven lies in the sand. Those adjustments are covered in the chapter on special circumstances.

When the ball is buried, like it is here for Corey Pavin, you want to hit down on the back of the ball with a sharply descending blow. The follow-through is negated by this steep approach. The ball will pop out and run quite a bit.

Stuart Appleby *How to play the buried lie: the chopping action.*

Ranked fifteenth in sand saves on the 1997 PGA TOUR, converting 64.2 percent of the time.

"With a ball buried in the bunker, the first thing you hope for is that you have plenty of green to work with. If you do not have much green, it does not matter how good you are; you are really going to struggle with this shot. The best thing to do is to open up your stance, put the ball well back, and keep your hands low during your setup. What you want is that feel of the club almost getting picked up rather than swung—sort of like a chopping action or chopping a log—and try to come down about an inch behind the ball with the neck of the club. The hosel will cut under the sand, and you'll get a powerful little eruption of sand. You won't have any real follow-through. You are just throwing the club down and using the power and steepness of the angle to get under it as quickly as you can."

The Sandy Road from the Tee to the Green

Bunkers come in all shapes and sizes, are designed with varying levels of severity, and can pop up anywhere. On most American courses a typical fairway bunker leaves an opportunity to advance the ball a fair distance toward the green—maybe even to reach the green. (The same cannot be said for the severe "pot bunkers" that dot the fairways of many of the famed courses of the United Kingdom and Ireland. The intent of those bunkers is to penalize you one full shot if you are in one. That means you wedge it out and take your lumps.) The basic rule of thumb for greenside bunker shots holds true for fairway bunker shots as well: Above all else, get it out of the sand.

Out of a greenside bunker, you usually don't need to produce a shot of any substantial distance. From a fairway bunker you want to get out of the bunker *and* get some distance. As a result, these shots require more thought than usual. You should go through the following process while assessing and playing the shot:

- Check your proximity to the green, and assume that you are going to hit every club ten yards less out of a fairway bunker. If you cannot reach the green, decide whether you want to hit the ball as far as you can, or to the place that leaves you the most comfortable shot.

- If you can reach the green, can you clear the lip of the bunker? The closer you are to the lip, the more loft you will need to clear it. Typically, the farther you are from the lip, the better your chances of clearing it. Remember: You will need one club more to produce the same distance out of the sand. However, clearing the lip comes first. If you cannot clear the lip and reach the green, forget about reaching the green and find the best layup spot attainable with the club you must play to clear the lip.

- If you are at all uncertain that a club will clear the lip, take a more lofted club.

- From this point on it is assumed that you are using the club that is going to clear the lip safely and produce the distance to reach your target. If you need a 9-iron to clear the lip, do not take an 8-iron because of the difference in distance! Move your target ten yards closer to you!

- Go through your preshot routine. Select a target, and select an intermediate target.

For a fairway banker shot, the hip turn and leg action on the backswing should be minimal, a condition usually described as a "quiet" lower body. On the through swing, however, the hips get into the act, turning through the ball.

- Dig in with your feet about two inches.
- Aim your body lines left of your target, but keep the face of the club square to your intermediate target.
- Play the ball back in your stance, about halfway between the center of your stance and your right foot.
- This shot is going to curve from left to right or be pushed on a straight line to the right, so be ready for that. (You already made the adjustment when you aimed your body.) In case you hit the ball straight, never aim your body at a point that will put you in more trouble—that is, in another hazard, especially water.
- Choke up on the club about the same amount you dig your feet into the sand. This is one difference between the greenside bunker shot and the fairway bunker

Frank Nobilo   *From the fairway bunker pick the exact spot on the ball you want to hit.*

Ranked twelfth in sand saves in 1997, getting up and in from the sand 64.6 percent of the time.

"On the last day of the 1996 U.S. Open, I was only a shot or so off the lead at the tenth hole when I hit my drive into the fairway bunker. I remember talking about the shot quite a bit with my caddie, because I was so close to the lead, and I didn't want to blow it. We decided a perfectly struck 5-iron would just barely clear the lip. If I caught it heavy it wouldn't get out. I got the ball clean and hit it to about eight feet. I didn't make the putt, but under the circumstances, a par was great. I couldn't have made it to the green with any more loft, and couldn't have cleared the lip with any less.

"The key to shots like that is you have to stay really still on it. I try to think of getting the ball early [before the sand], and that gets the ball up quicker. I really focus on the exact spot on the ball I want to hit. If I'm close to the lip, I don't necessarily move the ball back in my stance.

"Because your feet are on the sand and it is looser than the grass, you can be sure that your feet are going to move if you do not concentrate on keeping your legs still. When you wear spikes, you do not realize how much your feet move out on the grass. Well, those spikes do not help you much in the sand."

shot. Near the green you dig in because you want to hit the sand. From the fairway bunker you dig in because you want a solid base. You do not want to hit the sand with the club, so you have to adjust and even out the length of the club by choking up.

- Take a firm grip, but do not squeeze it to death. You will need to be a little firm because you are hovering the club over the sand while you are making all the adjustments in your setup, and because you are going to be making a swing that requires a less active lower body.

- Swing the club along your body lines. Keep your lower body movement to a minimum. Shift and turn slightly but keep your feet firmly planted.

- Position your feet so the ball is back in your stance. This allows you to pick up the ball clean before the club strikes the sand.

- The club may strike the sand after hitting the ball, but at that point it does not matter. The ball is away.

- Swing through to a good finish. Swing your arms around to a balanced finish.

Teaching Pros' Q & A

Hank Haney, PGA Professional, Proprietor, The Hank Haney Golf Ranch, McKinney, Texas

Q: What's the advantage of taking a playing lesson?

A: Most golfers could substantially reduce their score with better course management, and that's what you can learn from a playing lesson. You can get insight on what side of the tee to tee off from, what shots to play, places to avoid and how to avoid them. Without a doubt, most amateurs would save quite a few shots if they had someone coach them around the golf course and give them swing advice.

Q: I've got two hours a week to practice. How should I use it?

A: First you need to identify your strengths and weaknesses and then divide your time accordingly focusing on your real problems. *As a general rule, you want to spend half the time on your full swing and half the time on your short game.* Then divide that time between your strengths and weaknesses in each part of the game. If you want to shoot lower scores, it would be better to spend more time on your short game. But I think that most people play golf and practice for fun. They enjoy hitting the ball more than they enjoy putting. Because of that, I don't try to persuade people to practice their short game more because I want them to have more fun. If fun for them is just hitting balls then they should hit some balls.

Q: Is it better to work on your game on the course or on the practice tee? In other words, should you play to learn or practice to learn?

A: You should definitely practice to learn. It will come much more quickly. On the golf course, you hit one shot every five or six minutes and it's hard to get much done in terms of increasing your potential. If you try to learn to play on the course, you are going to learn to play the best you can with what you have but you won't improve your skills. On the practice tee, you will hit more shots than you will during a four-hour round of golf.

Gary Smith, PGA Professional, Proprietor, Gary Smith Learning Center, White Columns Golf Club, Atlanta, Georgia

Q: If I'm pulling all of my short irons, what should I be checking for?

A: First check the lie of your irons to make sure they are not too upright. Second check your swing plane. Chances are you are taking the club back too far inside and then releasing out over the top.

Q: I hate to say it, but how about a few cures for the shanks?

A: One cure is to eliminate sliding forward with your body through the impact area. One drill is to turn your left foot in away from the target and imagine you have a stake going up through your left leg so that you can't slide. A shank can also occur when players get the clubhead too far inside of their hands going back and then their hips slide through. That's what puts the ball in the socket—the hosel. In the beginning the problem is caused by a swing fault: Players sort of lock up through the ball. Then it becomes mental. It's really a weird thing.

Q: At what point with the irons should a player stop thinking "get it somewhere on the green" and start thinking "get it close?" 7-iron? 8-iron?

A: It depends on your skill level. Recreational golfers should start getting more flag-oriented with the 8-iron, 9-iron, or pitching wedge if they haven't played a lot of golf. The type of golf ball you play with also makes a big difference because you can put more spin on some balls than on others, depending on what sort of cover the ball has. Also take into account the pin position. You don't want to go for a pin that is surrounded by too much trouble. Also to be considered is the firmness of the green and how much green you have to work with.

Michael Hebron, PGA Professional, Head Professional and Director of Instruction, Smithtown Country Club, Smithtown, New York

Q: What type of player might consider using a long putter?

A: Any player who's not happy with the way he's putting should try something different. One problem would be that the putting style that a golfer has used for years would have to change because of the change in posture, but it is better to try it rather than to continue to putt poorly.

Q: When should you consider using a cross-handed grip, and how do you implement it? What are the things to watch out for?

A: A cross-handed grip should be considered if, during your stroke, the putterhead is passing your hands. Good putters keep the putterhead behind their hands. Cross-handed putting is a sure-fire way to keep the left wrist flat during the putting stroke. Be careful that your stroke does not go outside as opposed to the proper straight back-straight through stroke. The grip is implemented by placing your left hand below your right and resting the shaft of the putter against your left forearm. All you are doing is taking your hands out of the stroke.

Q: What is your all-time best advice for nailing every three-footer?

A: Make sure that your clubface is aiming where you want the ball to go. The stroke at three feet is less important than where the clubface is aimed. A lot of funky strokes make three footers because the player has the clubface aligned correctly.

**Mike Adams, PGA Professional, Director of Instruction,
PGA National, Palm Beach Gardens, Florida**

Q: We have all seen Tiger Woods putt with a wood from the rough. What the heck is he doing? How does he do it?

A: The funny thing is, we originated that shot and I showed it to Butch Harmon at a junior school, and he passed it along to Tiger. The 3-wood has the right amount of loft, a deep enough face and it is long enough that you cannot choke it. The reason people have trouble with their wedge from that position is that they try to scoop the ball out. You cannot do that with the wood. You lay the shaft up against your left arm and stroke through like a putt. Play the ball back in your stance and open your lower half slightly to the target. That wood will get through the rough more easily than a putter.

Q: What is the maximum range the everyday guy should be thinking for his L-wedge? Forty yards? Thirty yards?

A: In general it depends on the strength of the individual. We recommend that beginners not try to hit their L-wedge full. We would rather see them use it around the green for chipping only. For the thirty- to forty-yard shot, we recommend they use a sand wedge and choke down on it. The L-wedge has zero bounce and it is easy for the beginner to mis-hit. Bounce is a correction factor that allows you to hit the ball a little fat or a little thin and still pop it up in the air.

Q: Can you describe how to play the pitch-and-run British style—that forty or fifty yarder? When should you play it?

A: You play it when you have a lot of green to work with. Our philosophy is this: putt everything you can putt within reason. If you can't putt it, then chip it. If you can't chip it then pitch-and-run it. If you can't pitch-and-run it then pitch it. And if you can't pitch it then flop it. The pitch-and-run is the third in our chain of alternatives. Basically the technique is to open your stance, move the ball back, square the clubface back to the target—because when you move the ball back it has a tendency to open the face up—use a one-piece takeaway, and turn the body through it. The club will always travel along the shoulder line and because the ball is back the shoulders are closed, which will create a releasing or running action. Depending on how much green you have to work with, we prefer anything from a 9-iron through a sand wedge. If you hit anything longer than that it tends to run over the green.

Tom Patri, PGA Professional, Director of Instruction,

Westchester Country Club, Rye, New York

Q: Can you fully describe the reverse pivot, what occurs and how to avoid it?

A: The reverse pivot is a movement of the upper body torso to the left which is incorrect—it should be to the right. It is usually a hip slide to the right versus a rotation of the right hip. This move usually gets the club somewhat beyond parallel at the top, a very difficult position to recover from. This move contributes to a severe power loss and a change of path on the downswing. For the average player, this will also result in a ball that starts left of the path and crosses over to the right of the target line. The more talented player may be able to release the club with their hands that will result in a severe pull. The first step in avoiding the reverse pivot is to work on stabilizing your lower body. A reverse pivot is often caused by an overactive lower body. After you remedy that, you can work on making occasional or parallel upper body movements right of center.

Q: The word "release" confuses people. You don't make a conscious effort to roll your wrists over at impact, do you? What does it mean then?

A: The term "release" has a double meaning today. The old school teaching professional would talk about a release of the hands or a release of the arms or releasing the wrists. So many teachers today have gone to big-muscle teaching and could be talking about the release of the body. Who you are and what your style of teaching is may affect what the term "release" means today. I feel like I'm a combination teacher: I have a lot of old school in me and I certainly aware of the nuances of what teaching is today. Depending on who is standing in front of me, "release" could mean something very different. Releasing your hands and the golf club via the arm swing or the hands and wrists could be one explanation. Releasing your body and posting up and pivoting to your left side could be another explanation.

Jim McLean, PGA Professional, Proprietor, Jim McLean Golf School, Doral Resort & Spa, Miami, Florida

Q: If you had to guess, how often would you say the average player should leave the driver in the bag and hit a 3-wood instead?

A: I'd say reasonably that 50 percent of the time the average player would do better to leave the driver in the bag and hit the 3-wood. The shorter club with more loft allows them to do two things: (1) not slice the ball as much and, (2) hit the center of the clubface more often. If you took the average distance of ten shots played with a driver and ten shots played with a 3-wood, you would probably find the 3-woods go as far or farther and definitely hit the fairway more often. You would hit a few longer with the driver, but you would also hit some drives off the charts. If you put the whole average together, the 3-woods might even go further.

Q: Would the game be unplayable for someone who had never used a driver?

A: Absolutely not. Tour players have won tournaments having never used a driver. I have seen a lot of good players use their 2-wood or 3-wood exclusively.

Q: Is there some strategy involved to which side of the tee you should hit from?

A: Absolutely. Most amateurs have no idea how important that is. What we try to do is maximize your angles and give you the widest possible shot at hitting the fairway. If you are fading the ball, you should almost always go to the right side of the tee. If you are drawing the ball you almost always want to go to the left side of the tee. Sometimes there are certain holes where you can't, because there are trees off the tee or wind or other situations arise. Because of how your eyes visualize things from the different sides of the tee, your position will affect your golf swing. It will give you a better chance to hit the curve that you play into the fairway.

David Glenz, PGA Professional, Proprietor, David Glenz Golf Academy, Great Gorge Golf Reserve, Franklin, New Jersey

Q: What makes the ball check up out of the sand? How can I do it?

A: First, it must be a shallow swing that nips the sand. The clubhead must have a fair amount of velocity to spin the ball. If you get a deep cut of sand you won't get spin. It has to be a brisk and aggressive swing that sort of spanks the sand. The stance should stay square to slightly open and the ball should be position slightly ahead of center. Make sure that the handle of the club is not ahead of the clubhead. The clubshaft needs to be straight up and down with the clubface slightly open. You need to aim slightly left. You are going to hit about two inches behind the ball, and you are going to come out about two inches ahead of the ball. You will undercut it in a shallow fashion.

Q: When would you use a pitching wedge out of the sand?

A: It is appropriate to use a pitching wedge in wet, hard sand. The other time I would use a pitching wedge out of the sand is to blast the ball a longer distance. You can use a pitching wedge, 9-iron, 8-iron even a 7-iron to play a longer blast shot. It depends on the swing speed generated by the golfer, but say that my normal bunker shot might go forty feet. If I try to stretch that, I'm getting too thin as far as a shallow cut of sand. I hit the same shot with a pitching wedge, and it will go forty-five to fifty feet. A 9-iron would probably go about twenty feet farther and on down.

Q: Would you ever chip out of the sand as opposed to playing a basic sand shot? Why and when?

A: It depends on how good a bunker player you are. If you had an uphill lie and it was easy to chip the ball (without a huge lip), and the pin was some distance away, it would probably be a situation where you would chip out of the bunker. Chipping gives you the opportunity to hit the ball farther. Especially with the uphill lie, if you try to explode it you have a heck of a time getting the ball to go forward. It will go up in the air more. The other situation would be if you had a real good lie in packed sand and a very long bunker shot. In this situation, if you try to blast it and you make a mistake, you might airmail the green. If you chip it, even if you hit a little behind the ball, it still ends up on the green. Chipping is a less risky shot.

T. J. Tomasi, PGA Professional, Director of The Players School at The Academy of Golf, PGA National, Palm Beach Gardens, Florida

Q: What can you tell from the marks on your equipment? Worn spots on grips, tee marks on the bottom of the clubhead, wear spots on the clubface?

A: You can tell a lot. When I give a lesson I always look at the student's clubs when I'm giving the interview to see whether I can tell anything by the markings on them. It's almost like an archeologist studying artifacts. They tell you about things that are unseen and went before. Certainly the marks on the clubface can tell you where on the clubface you are striking the golf ball. I use impact tape a lot which can record over a series of ten to twenty swings the pattern of impact. This pattern indicates a lot to me about the path of the club and how the club is being released to the golf ball. For example, if you are hitting the ball on the toe you come up and over the shot in terms of the path of the club, so that the club moves dramatically across and inside the golf ball and catches it on the toe.

The marks on the bottom of the club often are indicative of the path of the club. You can see the marks left by the tee and get the same kind of information. Probably the most telling marks are what we call "idiot" marks. Those are the marks on the top of the driver or 3-wood that indicates such a steep descent that the individual actually has gone underneath the golf ball and scratched up his beautiful club.

Always check the grips for wear because they get slippery from being used day in and day out. The more slippery they become the more you increase grip pressure. You wouldn't think that it was that important to have grips that are tacky enough to be able to be held lightly but it is hugely important, maybe the most important part of the whole golf club because the grip is the only contact you have with the club. A lot of people let their grips go and don't realize that it's a hidden cause of their problems.

Q: Name the three most common equipment errors you see with the average player?

A: In my estimation, the most common problem is that their lies are not correct. The lie of the golf club is an important specification because it will not be in the same position at impact as when it sits on the ground on account of the droop or the bowing effect of the forces exerted upon it through impact. The shaft actually bows so that the toe drops down during a strike and that's a much different position than the static position. In the static position, the toe will always be slightly up in the air at address. How much up in the air depends on the player's build. Therefore you want to match the player's physique to the equipment. If a player is incorrectly matched, and the toe drops down too much during impact, the shot will go markedly to the right. Normally, they are too flat. If the toe is too much in the air, then the ball will go to the left. It can go left far enough to make you miss a green with the short irons. This does not happen as much with long irons.

An everyday player should get rid of the 2-, 3-, and maybe even 4-irons and substitute some of the new clubs like the 7-wood and maybe even the 9-wood. Liselotte Neumann does not carry any iron lower than a 5 on the LPGA Tour. There are many players on the SENIOR TOUR who carry a 7-wood. The problem is that you have to have such good acceleration for the longer irons to get them in the air and to go different distances. Many amateurs hit their 2-, 3-, and 4-irons the same distance because the transfer of energy is not sufficient to produce the ten-yard increments built into the clubs. They look like they have three clubs in their bags but they really only have one.

The third mistake I see is with the ball. Because of advance spin rates, many amateurs could get away from the hard two-piece ball that they use for distance and go to some of the softer balls that much more control around the greens.

Mike McGetrick, PGA Professional, Proprietor, Mike McGetrick Golf School, Meridian Golf Learning Center, Englewood, Colorado

Q: In your estimation, which TOUR player has the most easily imitated address position? What do you like about it?

A: For the average-sized guys I would say David Frost. Shorter players might look at Ian Woosnam and tall players might look at Tiger Woods. You need to match your setup to your build. Woosnam is very balanced and aligned very well. His upper body is positioned on top of his lower body and he lets his arms hang. They all have a very balanced and simple setup Their setups are fundamentally correct.

Q: Do you have any thoughts on avoiding pre-swing brain clutter?

A: You can avoid it by doing your preparation either beside the ball or behind the golf ball. There is nothing wrong with thinking. When you program your shot in; mentally think about it or visualize it, and then rehearse it with a practice swing. Doing that prepares your mind and body for the shot because you have experienced it. Therefore, you are more prepared by the time you get up over the golf ball. If you do have a swing thought, it could be more of a soft focus once you get over the ball. I like to see golfers do their preparation before they address the ball. That's the reason golfers always hit their second ball better than their first ball. This way, your first ball is your practice swing.

Q: A waggle is one way to stay loose before the swing starts. What are some others?

A: You can take some deep breaths and exhale to release all the tension. The waggle could be the waggle of the club or the waggle of the body. Keep an athletic motion over the ball meaning that you always keep your body moving, you never come to a standstill. You are not starting from a static position but from a dynamic position. The second you get into a static position, it is time to swing the golf club.

What's a day on the course without a little sand?

PGA TOUR players are fan friendly.

10

Putting: the *Game Within* the *Game*

Golf is often daunting to the everyday player because of the abundance of fundamentals that seem to be nonnegotiable. Golfers read books and magazines, watch videos and golf telecasts, and are besieged with suggestions on how to improve. As a result, golfers often feel as if they cannot do *anything* the way that feels best to them—that they have to play it by the book to improve their scores. Putting offers a welcome relief from the "must-dos" of golf. The mechanics are simpler, the potential mistakes fewer, and the fundamentals are almost all determined according to what feels best to the player. More than any other phase of the game, putting allows you to personalize the process and still be successful. Think of the various machinations you have watched TOUR players use over the years: Jack Nicklaus hunched over the ball as if observing it through a microscope; Arnold Palmer with his knees pinched together; Raymond Floyd and Tiger Woods standing as upright as palace guards; Dave Stockton with his feet spread so very wide, and Corey Pavin with his feet

Brad Faxon is a magician with a putter.

225

so very close together; Billy Casper's wristy-looking pop stroke, and Ben Crenshaw's majestic sweep—a veritable kaleidoscope of styles.

All good putting strokes share a few basic tenets. Beyond those, putting is primarily a mental process that includes an assessment of the numerous factors that will influence the roll, the direction, and the speed at which the ball moves. It is highly unlikely that these factors will all come into play at the same time, but once you know them all, you will be able to size up any putt in seconds, using a mental checklist. In discussing the speed and the line of a putt, it is assumed that your ball rests on a recently mown green—that is, that there are no interfering factors such as a bad lie or high grass.

Loren Roberts   *Arms should hang free.*

Ranked sixth in putting in 1994 and eighth in 1997.

"One of the things I key on when I'm looking at a putt is standing as tall as I can so my arms can swing free during the stroke. Another important thing—I never lift my head to look at the line of the putt. I turn my head to the side so I can see the whole line of the putt and I visualize the whole putt. I do not spot putt. I'm not even concerned about the break when I get set to play. I've seen the putt in its entirety, and I'm simply focusing on the speed. Before I start the putter back, I'm set on the speed I want. Then it is just a free arm swing—elbows in close to the body and forearms on the same plane."

You and Your Putter

No matter what style your putter is, it will be dramatically different from every other club in your bag. The shaft does not necessarily connect with the rear of the clubhead; the face has a minimal amount of loft on it; and, because the clubhead can be shaped in countless ways, the weight of the clubhead can be distributed in just as many ways. Taken together, this means that there are more types of putters to choose from than any other club.

Putters have two basic types of clubheads. One is perimeter-weighted, and the other is basically just a solid head. A perimeter-weighted type has a distinctive scooped-out area behind the center of the clubhead, with mass and weight placed toward the ends of the clubhead, (i.e., the heel and the toe). This type of putter is popular for much the same reason perimeter-weighted irons are: You can strike the ball almost anywhere on the clubface and get a result you can live with.

The solid putterhead can take many forms: a mallet (shaped roughly like a half circle or half oval), a blade (a classic design typically sporting a small flange in the rear), or

Various styles of putters, from left to right: A face-insert; two rear-shafted blade styles; a heel-shafted perimeter-weighted model; a mallet; a center-shafted blade.

Inside the Ropes

Blaine McCallister   *If you are thinking about switching sides, start with two putters.*

Won five times on the PGA TOUR. He plays right-handed but putts left-handed. Ranked thirteenth in putting in 1994.

"I hit my full shots right-handed, but I putt left-handed. It is something that I found worked for me a long time ago. I'm a natural lefty. If you are too, it might work for you. If you are going to try it, I would recommend using two putters at first—one lefty and one righty—until you get used to the

distance factor. The nice thing about switching is that you are focused on stroking the ball and not hung up on mechanics. Everyone I've ever met say that they feel the stroke is freer. The reason is simple—they are not thinking about it. All you have to do is make sure you are aimed right and you are ready to go.

"If you are serious about switching, try a Bullseye™ putter so that you can putt from both sides with the same club."

All good putters have their eyes either just inside or directly over the ball.

When you practice putting, use several balls at a time. It saves time and helps you get into a groove.

a hybrid of the two. The solid putter typically feels heavier than a perimeter-weighted putter and offers a purer feel on impact. The downside is that if the ball is struck slightly off center, it will deaden the effect of impact and adversely affect the speed, and possibly the line of the putt.

You should use whichever type of putterhead looks and feels best to you. Because you move the club such a small distance, the odds are that you will make contact on or near the center of the clubface.

Pay special attention to two things when you select a putter: the point at which the shaft joins with the clubhead, and the length of the shaft. On most putters, the shaft joins with the clubhead in the heel or the center. The type you choose depends on how you like to putt.

A center-shafted putter is most suitable for a golfer with the following characteristics:

- You like to stand close to the ball.
- You like to feel as if your eyes are directly over the ball as you putt.
- The dominant image of your stroke is that you "push" the club through the ball with your right hand.
- You like to crouch or hunch down to get that feeling of being close to the ball.
- You like to play the ball closer to the middle of your stance than it is to your left foot.

By contrast, a heel-shafted putter is more suitable for a player with different characteristics:

- You like to stand far enough away from the ball so your eyes are slightly inside the ball, rather than being over the ball.
- You like to feel as if you make a long, fluid arm stroke, à la Ben Crenshaw.
- You feel like the clubface opens and closes a little bit as you swing the club, like a tiny gate.
- You like to play the ball closer to your left heel than to the center of your stance.

Length is the second factor to consider in the putter shaft. The shaft is the proper length when your arms can hang freely when you hold the club at the very end of the grip. If you have to choke down on the club for your arms to feel as if they are hanging freely (and without tension), then the club is too long. You want to feel the butt of the club against your left hand because it increases your feel for the clubhead. The only time you would choke up on your putter is when you are putting out of the rough.

Aside from the above two points regarding the shaft, everything else regarding your putter is a matter of personal preference. Some putters are very heavy in the head, and some are very light. Is there a marked difference in performance? No. Some putters are cast (molten steel poured into a mold) and others are milled (hewn from a solid block of steel). Is one better than the other? No. Many modern putters have face inserts while others do not. The list goes on and on. The best putter is the one that feels like it will put the best roll on the ball.

The Essence of Your Putting Stroke

No golfer should view the putting stroke as complicated. Granted, putting itself can be maddening—putts lip out, take weird bounces, stop one turn short of the hole—but that is just part of the game you have to learn to accept. The quirkiness that surrounds putting means that all golfers experience hot streaks and cold streaks with the putter. When you are on a hot streak, don't change a thing. When you are on a cold streak,

The putter should always maintain speed through the ball. In order to keep it from slowing down, pretend you're driving a tack into the back of the ball.

don't feel as if you must make enormous changes to your stroke. In fact, when you are battling through one of those streaks, it probably helps to focus on keeping your stroke simple.

The success of your putting stroke relies heavily on the selection of a target and the alignment of the clubface to the target. Various factors, covered later in this chapter, influence target selection. Basically speaking, your target is the apex of the line you visualize your putt taking—that is, the highest point on the curve. For a straight putt, your target is the hole. The odds of a putt's being straight decrease as you move farther from the hole.

On putts that do break, *it is vital that you mentally acknowledge that your target is the highest point along the break line. The hole is not your target.* This cannot be overstated because you have to do things when you putt. First, you have to aim the clubface squarely at your target. Second, you must follow through on a putt with the club moving squarely along the target line, not toward the hole. The single biggest mistake in

Inside the Ropes

Steve Elkington   *Take care in aiming.*

Ranked third in scoring average in 1995 (69.59). Won the 1995 PGA Championship and the 1997 Players Championship.

"*One of the things I see in pro-ams is that my partners do not bother to aim their putts. They say they are going to hit it* a foot left of the hole and putt it in that general direction. Most of the players out here on TOUR work on exactly where the putter is aligned and where that ball is going. Most amateurs I've played with putt pretty well if they aim their putts well. If they don't aim well, the odds aren't good.*"

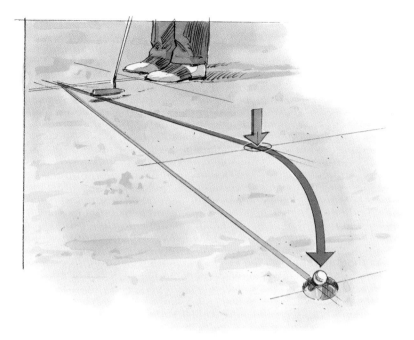

putting is to take the club back and then try to steer the club toward the hole at impact and follow through. The result is always a missed putt.

It is tremendously helpful to relate your putting to your long game to overcome the tendency to become hole-oriented with your stroke. The following process will help you aim yourself properly on the green:

- Cover all the speed and line factors. Determine how hard you want to stroke the ball and along what line you want it to start.

- When you "see" the line of the putt, determine the high point (apex) of that line. That is your target, the spot toward which you want to move the club. *Do not fall into the lazy habit of picking a spot a few inches left or right of the hole on long putts*. This will make it more likely that you will steer the club toward the hole.

- As you would on a full shot, pick an intermediate target to use for aiming the club. It should be just a few inches ahead of your ball on the line toward your main target. Use a blade of grass, a discolored patch, or anything else you can spot. No matter which way your putt breaks, it should be treated as a straight putt until it reaches your intermediate target.

- The stroke is simple: Using your shoulders and arms, move the club straight back from your intermediate target and follow through with the lead edge of your putter square to your intermediate target. *Do not steer the clubhead toward the hole.* You will find this especially difficult to avoid on sharply breaking left-to-right putts. On those putts, focus intently on following through squarely to your target.

All golfers feel different things as they prepare to pull the trigger on a putt. The following tips are helpful no matter what type of putter you are:

- Some golfers find it comfortable to set up open to the target line (it gives them a better view of the target), whereas others like to set up square to it. Either way is correct as long as you *start with the club square to the target and keep it square to the target until the stroke is finished.* Because you are not swinging the club around your body as you would on a full swing, the effect of setting up open is not so dramatic.

- Whether you stand tall at the ball or hunch over, always have your hands ahead of the ball and the clubhead. The design of most putters makes this a natural occurrence. At no time during your setup or stroke should the clubhead get ahead of your hands. In other words, do not move the club with your wrists. Your wrists stay solid during your stroke.

- No matter what type of stroke you use, your arms and shoulders form a triangle at address. Keep that triangle intact throughout your stroke.

- Play the ball somewhere between just left of the middle of your stance and just right of your left heel. Anywhere in that zone is okay, and you can make adjustments based on the way you like to stand.

- Grip pressure is important. Typically speaking, the lighter your grip pressure the better, especially because the tension that results from tightly squeezing the club makes it more difficult to keep the club on line.

On long putts like this one by Lee Janzen, the speed and the break of the putt work in concert to create the line.

Inside the Ropes

Brian Barnes   *The best putting grip is the one that works for you.*

Finished fifteenth in scoring (71.06) on the SENIOR PGA TOUR in 1996.

"When I grip the putter I do not use the reverse overlap grip. I simply use the same type of overlap grip I use on the full swing with one small change—I put the small finger and the ring finger of my right hand on top of the fingers on the left hand. I've always felt like my left hand was the dominant hand in my stroke, so I want to feel like it is stronger on the club. The fewer fingers from the right hand on the shaft, the better. On fast greens, I use a three-finger overlap so that the only fingers on my right hand touching the club are my thumb and index finger. I just try to concentrate on the back of my left hand going straight toward the target."

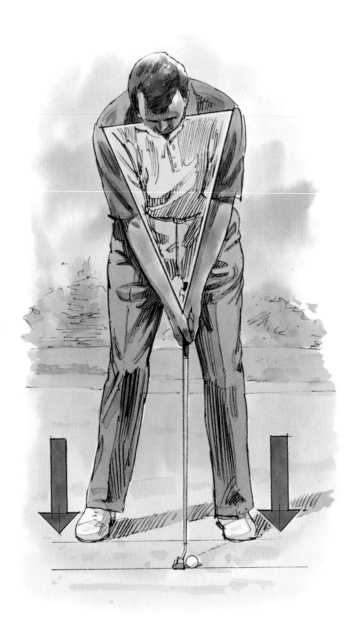

A textbook putting setup. To move the club, simply rock the triangle back and forth. The wrists don't move at all.

- The grip is up to you, but the general feeling is that some version of the reverse overlap grip (index and middle finger of the left hand over the top three fingers on the right hand) works best to immobilize the wrists.
- Keep both thumbs on top of the shaft.
- You should not feel like you are lifting the clubhead away from the ground on the backswing. It should feel like you are slowly sliding it away.
- Once you start the club moving, do not move your feet, turn your hips, or make any weight shift.
- Once you are satisfied with the alignment of your club, do not move your head until completing a slow count of "1 . . . 2" after impact. Peak early, and you will hit a weak, off-line putt. *Keep the club moving at the same pace through the ball—do not slow down.*
- Always follow through. If it is the scariest downhiller you have ever seen, hit the ball out on the toe of the face to deaden the initial roll, *but still follow through.*
- One word: *smooth.* Think it, do it. It works.

Inside the Ropes

Jim Furyk   *Your putting routine is like your full-swing routine.*

Ranked ninth in putting in 1998, and was fourth in 1995.

"*The ritual I go through before hitting a putt is based on my full-swing pre-shot routine. I take some practice strokes first to get a feel for the distance of the putt. Then I get behind the ball and read it to get an idea of the break and the speed I'm going to need to get that break. Then I approach the ball with my eye on the target, just like I would on a full* swing. When I step into the ball, I'm ready to go. The only difference is I do not grip the putter until I'm over the ball. On the full swing, I have the club gripped throughout the pre-shot routine. But you do not do much squatting and stuff during your pre-shot routine with a full shot, so the club does not get in the way. When I do grip the putter, I grip it with both hands at the same time. Once I'm sure my alignment is good, I forget about everything else and just hit it.*"

Accelerate or Exaggerate?

The reason for most missed putts is that the pace—the tempo—of the stroke did not stay consistent throughout. This is typically attributed to decelerating through the impact area—that is, the player slowed the pace at which the club was moving. This is exactly what happens whenever Johnny Miller (or any other knowledgeable TV analyst) says of a poor putt, "He looked up early on that one." The player looks up early because he decelerated, hit a weak putt, and knew he hit a weak putt. (Actually, he does not look up early, he just jerks his head up quickly because he knows he hit it poorly. Combined with the fact that the putt goes shorter than anticipated, the effect is an "early" look.)

Interestingly, you can cure this by "accelerating through the ball"—that is, speeding up the pace of the swing through the ball. Is this an effective cure? Not at all—at least not if you follow it literally, which many golfers often do. People use the word accelerate because it is the opposite of decelerate, but accelerating through the ball results in a putt struck more firmly than you would like. If you focus too much on accelerating, you end up hitting a putt that Johnny Miller might describe as one that "goes off in your hand"—that is, goes way past the hole.

The goal for the pace of your stroke is neither to decelerate nor to accelerate; rather, it is to maintain the same pace back and through the ball. Any gain in clubhead speed occurs naturally if you keep the pace of your stroke the same. If you try to speed the club up, you will hit the ball too hard.

Is this the best putting stroke of all time? Quite possibly, and the owner is Ben Crenshaw. Since Crenshaw favors a rear-shafted putter, the tendency is for the club to swing slightly inside the line on the way back. In this case, Crenshaw is hitting a very long putt, which is why the club comes back so far off the ground. Even on long putts like this, the length of the follow-through should equal that of the backswing.

Focusing on Speed

Because successful putting depends so much on accurately factoring in various elements, it is helpful to outline the main goals before delving into the subtleties. Although the list of things that affect a putt is lengthy, the main thing to remember is that every putt consists of two elements: how hard you hit it and where you aim it. Your goal is to combine these two things—speed and line—so that the ball ends up in or very near the hole. That last statement may strike you as rather obvious, but everyday golfers who struggle with putting frequently *do not focus on getting the ball in the hole* but simply play a putt in the general direction of the hole and hope it falls in. The cause for almost every three-putt in history has been a lousy first putt, and the first putt is typically lackluster because the player plays a "poke and hope" putt.

Of the two elements, speed and line, speed is arguably the more vital of the two. Think about it: If you hit the putt at the right speed and misread the putt by a few inches—even a foot—you will still be left with a tap-in putt. If you err on the speed, you will not only pay in terms of distance but in direction as well, because the ball will break more (if you hit it too slow) or less (if you hit it too fast) than you anticipated.

As you analyze a putt, focus first on the speed. The following factors determine the speed at which you should attempt to play a putt and, in turn, affect your stroke:

- The general pace of the greens (fast, average, slow), which you should always consider in terms of a flat putt. This is based on the firmness of the green and the height at which the grass is cut. Firm greens are faster than soft greens. The lower the grass is cut, the quicker the putt. If greens are wet from rain or early morning dew, they will run slower.
- The general terrain of the surrounding area or, on a smaller scale, the positioning of the green. If a green is situated on or near a dominant geographic feature, that feature usually affects the putt more than the comparatively tiny terrain changes on the surface of the green. For example, if a green is built into the side of a hill, putts toward the hill will move slower and putts away from the hill will move faster. This is true even if the surface of the green itself appears flat.
- The contours of the green. A putt moving uphill will move slower than a flat putt. A putt rolling downhill will move quicker than a flat putt.
- The length of the putt. The longer it is, the faster the initial pace of the ball must be.

Jack Nicklaus at the '75 Masters. Notice how the putter follows the ball straight down the target line.

- The grass type. Any number of grass types are used on greens, typically depending on the geographic location of the course. The key to grass types is this: Some grasses, such as bent, consist of such fine blades that they do not affect the roll of the ball. Some grasses—Bermuda grass is an example—have thicker blades, and they have a definite "lean" to them. It is easy to make the distinction. If the grass appears to be growing straight up, it will not affect the speed of the putt. If the grass appears to be leaning, then it is a factor you must consider. This lean is referred to as *grain*. If a putt runs with the grain—that is, if it runs in the same direction as the grass—it will move faster. If it runs against the grain, it will move more slowly.

- The wind. This is rather unusual. However, if the wind is blowing sternly (think final round, 1992 U.S. Open at Pebble Beach), it can affect a putt exactly as you might imagine: Into the wind would be slower, with the wind would be faster.

- The time of day. Typically speaking, the later in the day you play, the firmer the green is going to be. This can be mitigated somewhat on greens with a lot of grain, because the grass grows longer as the day wears on. Typically grass grows toward the setting sun.

Of all these factors, the most important one is the distance from your ball to the hole. All the other speed factors revolve around this one.

Tips for Getting the Speed Just Right

If you routinely struggle with getting the speed of a putt just right, don't feel alone. Because the ability to achieve the correct speed on a putt is largely a matter of feel, recreational players are often inconsistent in this area. You may even know the feeling: You get two or three putts in a row fairly close to the hole, and the next one seems in-

On short putts, you can reduce the amount of break by increasing the pace of the putt. The danger: If you miss, you may have a tester coming back.

explicably long or short. The good news is that, unlike the full swing, for which you have to develop a feel, a feel for putting is something you probably already possess. It is simply a matter of learning how to tap it.

At its most basic, the distance a putt rolls is established by the distance you move your arms back and forth. As pointed out before, having a stroke that goes back and through the ball the same amount is the key to predicting the distance you will get on a given putt. Moving your arms back and forth the same distance to accomplish a task is something everyone does successfully every day without thinking about it. You have a great feel for it. Think about it: If you are sweeping with a broom, you make strokes that go back and through the same amount. (Think about an umpire using his little broom to clean off home plate.) If you are doodling with a pencil on a notepad, you move the pencil around in a series of equidistant, back-and-forth strokes. Raking leaves, painting a fence, it is all the same: equal-length strokes back and forth.

The best way to groove your stroke before a round of golf is to spend some time on the putting green practicing putts of various lengths. This works best if you work on flat putts. Hit enough putts from five, ten, fifteen, twenty, twenty-five, thirty, thirty-five, and forty feet so you get a feel for the back-and-through strokes for each distance. Most of your putts during a round will fall somewhere in that range, and if you have a feel for the five-foot stroke and the ten-foot stroke, the adjustment for an eight-foot putt is fairly simple. It is important not to skip the longer putts. One reason golfers have trouble judging the distance on long putts is that they never practice them.

The important thing to realize here is that your sense of feel can be transported beyond a fifteen- or a twenty-foot putt, as long as you stay focused. Follow these tips when faced with a putt of unfamiliar distance:

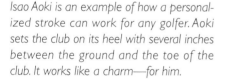

Isao Aoki is an example of how a personalized stroke can work for any golfer. Aoki sets the club on its heel with several inches between the ground and the toe of the club. It works like a charm—for him.

Gene Littler   *Don't decelerate, but do not accelerate either.*

Won eight times on the SENIOR PGA TOUR, continuing a fine career that saw him win twenty-nine times on the PGA TOUR.

"Most golfers are aware that you should not decelerate the clubhead through the ball when you are putting. But you do not want to accelerate it either, as is commonly suggested. You are better off keeping it at the same pace all the way. I think the ball comes off the putter better this way. If you accelerate, the ball can come off the face too fast in any direction. It is better to think about being steady with the pace. This is true even on downhill putts. Clearly you want to hit the ball softer, but you want to keep the same pace. Just caress it off the clubface. The key to an evenly paced stroke is in the grip pressure. You cannot make the type of stroke I'm talking about if you are holding the club too tightly. It causes tension in your forearms and will ruin your shot. The grip should be a firm, light grip. It is the same in both hands—one is not squeezing harder than the other."

- Stand next to the ball, just as if you were going to putt. Rest your putter against your leg—you do not even need it in your hands at this point.

- With your eyes fixed on the hole, start to swing your dominant putting arm back and forth, visualizing yourself rolling the ball from your hand toward the hole on a low trajectory, rolling it most of the way like a bowling ball rather than tossing it. Your dominant arm is the one you use to move the club. If you like to "push" the club through with your right hand (i.e., you should use a center-shafted putter), your right arm is probably dominant. If you feel like you "pull" the club through with your left hand (i.e., you should use a heel-shafted putter), do the rolling drill with your left hand.

- After you move your arm back and forth a few times, you will have an excellent feel for how long the stroke should be to get the ball to the hole.

Do not think of this method purely as an on-course drill. You can use it while practicing, and it also has applications in your chipping game (as described in Chapter 9).

If the distance from your ball to the hole is the biggest factor in determining the length of your stroke, the second-biggest factor is any slope the ball will encounter. The nice part about the "rolling" distance visualization technique described above is that it can be adjusted for use with downhill as well as uphill putts.

When you have an uphill putt, do the visualization technique from behind the ball. If the hill is slight, move one or two steps farther away from the hole. The steeper the hill, the farther you should move from your ball and the hole. When you are swinging your arm, visualize making a flat putt from the spot where you have positioned yourself. When you play the putt

One drill to improve your putting is to set groups of balls at different intervals and not quit until you make them all in succession.

Lagging Is Good, But You Still Should Try to Make It

A popular tip for very long putts is to try to get the ball inside a three-foot circle that surrounds the hole. The tip implies that you are incapable of getting the ball closer to the hole. If you are good enough to get within three feet of the hole, why can't you get within one foot of the hole, or even closer?

In big-time competition, there are often very compelling reasons to "cozy" a putt close to the hole. Indeed, in your weekend match, you may feel from time to time that it behooves you to hit a lag putt—one that does not risk running too far past the hole.

Focusing on getting the ball only inside that three-foot circle on every long putt you face accomplishes only two things: It makes you lazy, and it makes you tentative. You should try to get every long putt as close to the hole as you can. Forget three feet—try to get it within three inches or even make it! There is no such thing as an automatic three-foot putt. Suppose you aim for that three-foot circle and miss it. What's your state of mind then? The point: Get used to getting the ball as close to the hole as you can on long putts. Why would you settle for anything less?

from the actual distance with this elongated stroke, you will be in business. For a downhill putt do the opposite and move closer to the hole to take your practice strokes.

Once you have an idea of the stroke you would need to account for the actual distance and any slopes, you can make any adjustments necessary based on the remainder of the list of things that affect the speed of a putt.

What's Your Line?

The line of your putt is influenced by various factors, including the speed at which the ball is moving at any given point. It is important to settle on a line and to start the ball rolling along that line toward the highest point of the break. That high point along the line to the hole is your target in putting. The alignment of your putter and your stroke depends entirely on determining the line. There are no mathematical formulas for figuring out the break of a putt. It is all up to your eyes and your brain. Here is a list of things your brain should be factoring as you assess the line:

- The terrain of the green between your ball and the hole. The ball will move in any direction the ground takes it.
- The general speed of the greens. The faster the greens are rolling, the more the ball will break. If the greens are wet from rain or early morning dew (running slower), the less the ball will break.
- The speed the ball is moving at any given time. The faster the ball is moving, the less it is affected by the terrain. The slower the ball is moving, the more it is affected by the ground. Because the ball is moving fastest just as it leaves the clubface, it is less susceptible to

Inside the Ropes

Vijay Singh

How aggressive depends on the putt.

Won the 1998 PGA Championship.

"I use two simple keys to determine how aggressive to be with a putt. When it is a downhill slider, I hit it nice and easy and try to die the ball into the hole. If it is uphill and I'm not sure about the break, I just rip it right at the hole."

Russ Cochran *On long putts, stand tall and move the ball back in your stance.*

His victory at the 1991 Centel Western Open made him only the fifth left-handed winner in PGA TOUR history.

"On longer putts, I begin by doing the same thing I do on any putt. I analyze the speed—check things like uphill and downhill—and then I work on the break. I like to keep the ball above the hole and work it toward the hole. Once it crosses over below the hole and starts breaking away, you are losing distance fast. When it is breaking toward the hole it is always working for you. When I'm assessing the line and the speed on a long putt, I stand up a little bit straighter so I have a better look at the entire distance between me and the hole, and it allows for a freer arm swing, which you need on the longer stroke. As far as the stroke goes, I move it back a little in my stance. On long putts I move the ball back toward the center of my stance because I know I'll catch the ball early enough that the club will still be moving at a pretty good clip. I do not want to hit at the ball like I would if the ball was way up in my stance. I want to keep the club moving through."

break at that time. The closer the ball gets to the hole, the slower it is moving and the more susceptible it is to break.

- Uphill putts break less than flat putts; downhill putts break more than flat putts.
- Putts breaking into the grain break less than putts with no grain. Putts breaking with the grain break more than putts with no grain.
- The ball will break away from any significant hills or mountains that surround a hole or the entire course. Typically, the best way to notice this is to look at the green—and the surroundings—from the fairway as you make your approach. You have to balance this against the terrain of the green itself, but nature usually wins. The ball will usually break toward any valleys, rivers, or oceans.

Many players like to get as low to the ground as possible to read the line of the putt. Here, Brad Faxon checks things out from behind the ball.

Any time you miss a putt long, watch it closely as it goes by the hole. This will show you the break on the return putt.

When You Hit a Poor Putt, Pay Attention

When you hit a poor putt, whether it is long or short of the hole, do not turn your head away in disgust. As long as the ball is within five feet of the hole, pay attention to what it does as it runs by (or comes up short of the hole). Why? You have a shortish putt remaining to be played—a putt that will not require much speed. When the ball is moving slowly, it is more susceptible to break. In fact, it is showing you the exact amount of break the ball is going to take on the next putt. Stay focused! A putt that barely misses the hole and rolls by is a preview of the putt returning.

A round of golf is an acquired-knowledge experience. You can learn from every shot—even your bad ones.

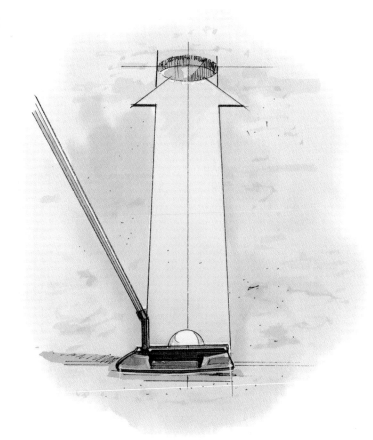

- If a green looks flat, look for the lowest point around the edges. Because greens need some place for water to run off, they usually have a low point, and the green tilts slightly in that direction.
- If a putt looks flat, look at the hole. If a cup liner has the same amount of earth showing all around the top of it, the putt is probably flat. If one side has more dirt showing, the putt will break from that direction as it nears the hole.
- On double breakers, remember that the ball will be moving quicker at the first break and will be less affected. At the second break, it will be moving slower and will be more affected by the break.

BREAKTHROUGH TIPS

Putting accounts for approximately forty-three percent of the modern players' score. It is a facet of the game often underestimated by golfers at all skill levels. Improved putting will result in lower scoring.

Some advice can help you make dramatic improvements in your game. At times, the best advice comes from those who have struggled through problems of their own. Here are some thoughts on putting that these PGA TOUR players reported as having significantly raised their ability to roll it into the cup.

#1 *Align Ball Logo Perpendicular to Line of Putt*

Kenny Perry

After I've determined the line of my putt, I pick a spot about six to twelve inches in front of the ball that is on the line over which I want to roll the ball. Then I position the logo of my ball so it lines up perpendicular to the line of the putt. Now all I have to do is align the face of my putter parallel to the logo and I know I'm lined up correctly. Now I can concentrate on the pace and not worry about direction.

#3—Vary Length of Practice Putts

#2 Keep Left Wrist Firm
Hugh Baiocchi

David Stockton showed me how to avoid "breaking" my left wrist during the putting stroke. He repositioned the grip of my putter along the lifeline of my left hand. This put the putter more across my palm (and not so far down in my fingers), which kept me from hinging and unhinging my wrist. This also helped me keep the putter blade moving straight down the putting line.

#3 Vary Length of Practice Putts
Hugh Baiocchi

I had a problem with pace— I was hitting too many putts either too short or too long. So I practiced hitting putts of varying lengths. I found that this also helped improve my stroke. When you hit long putts you don't expect to make them, just get them close. You concentrate mostly on making a proper stroke, not knocking it dead center in the hole. But hitting hundreds of properly paced putts builds overall confidence in your stroke, and you end up making a lot more of those five- and six-footers. So practicing long putts can help you make shorter putts.

#4 Maintain Tempo in Stroke
Skip Kendall

I recently found myself in a putting slump. Though I had good mechanics, I wasn't getting good results. When I went for a lesson, the instructor observed that during my stroke I was taking the putter back a very short distance and then accelerating through the ball very quickly. I had what is termed a "pop stroke." He recommended that I practice with a metronome (a clockwork device with an inverted pendulum

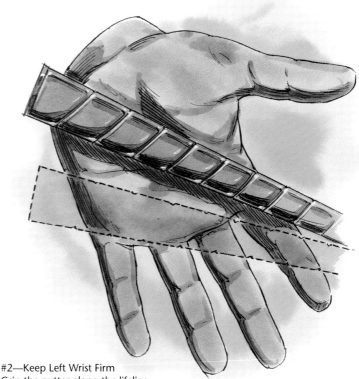

#2—Keep Left Wrist Firm
Grip the putter along the lifeline
of your hand.

that rhythmically beats time or tempo). I experimented and soon found a comfortable rhythm (empirical analysis and modeling have shown that correctly struck putts, regardless of length, are completed at an optimum elapsed time that is just under one second). Without any adjustment to my mechanics and setup, I was able to maintain an even tempo. When I hit a four-footer, my stroke is slower because I don't have to bring the putter back so far. If the putt is longer, the stroke is a little faster because I move the putter a little farther back and come through a little farther. I carry the metro-nome in my bag and use it all the time. Practicing with it has helped me move into the top twenty-five putters [on TOUR].

Keys to Accessing Your Putting Potential

Most makeable putts are missed because of fear or negative attitude, not because of faulty technique per se.

— Jack Nicklaus

Every player knows that putting is more than just a physical skill. The mechanics of putting must work in combination with a player's visual skills, powers of imagination and level of confidence. The mental aspect of putting is challenging; it tests a player's emotional stability and patience.

Our emotions, feelings, and thoughts bring a new dimension to the simple physical task of putting. Just a bit of tension or fear can throw off the best of strokes. A flicker of doubt can cause a golfer to be tentative or steer the stroke. Trying too hard to make a putt can cause a player to tense up and leave a putt three feet short of the hole. And when not putting well, players search for the secret to making putts. These players switch to a new putter, change their techniques, or alter their putting routines. What they don't understand is that the secret to making putts is inside them. Here are the most important keys to accessing your putting potential.

A Positive Attitude

According to the dictionary, attitude is defined as "a mental position or feeling in regard to something." What is your definition of great putting attitude? Does your present attitude *help* or *hurt your performance on the green?*

If your putting attitude is supportive and helpful, then you are on your way to better putting. If it's filled with negative thoughts, start choosing a healthier attitude.

Many players can start a round with a positive attitude, but then as the round progresses, they adopt a negative mindset. These players often make the mistake of letting others choose an attitude for them. How often has your playing partner or opponent said to you: "Geez, you're putting terribly today." Or, "You just can't buy a putt today, can you?" Absent your own positive attitude, you start to believe what others are telling you. And soon you find yourself playing *down* to the lower expectations that follow poor attitudes.

In sport psychology, we call this "psyching yourself out." It's a challenge to stay positive and remind yourself that good things are yet to happen. Choose your own positive attitude about your putting game, and stick with it. Remind yourself that you "are rolling your putts well" or that you're "seeing the line" and that eventually the putts will drop. Ultimately, you will win the inner battle and thus build a great putting attitude.

Further, work toward adopting what I call "The Golden Attitude." With each putt, fill yourself with enthusiasm, hope(positive expectation), belief in your ability to properly execute the sequence of mechanical putting tasks, conviction that you can sink it, and an acceptance of the result. This mindset allows you to totally focus on "the now and the new' as opposed to "the old and the bad." It also helps you focus on the process of making putts instead of derailing yourself with thoughts of missed putts and lip-outs. If you felt that the ball was going in every time you putted, how much better would you putt? Much better, I assure you. Remember, putting is not just a physical skill.

High Putting Confidence

Confidence means believing in your skills, and in putting you must have conviction that you can make putts. Confidence comes from practice, making putts on the course, developing your touch, and believing in your ability. Confidence is a mindset that says, "I can do this."

Mindset for Making Short Putts. Do you find it harder to make a three-footer than a ten-foot putt? Many players who can putt well from longer distances think they are poor putters from short range.

If you suffer from the three-footer blues, there is help. The problems starts when you label your putts or identify a length of putt that you "should" make—that dreaded three-footer. Most golfers can handle a ten-to-fifteen foot putt because they are not always expected to make them. It's okay if you miss, no one is perfect. That makes it easier to relax and focus on the task. But when it comes to the shorter putts, you are expected to make those because "only bad putters miss short putts."

This expectation in part is what causes you to change your approach. The tension begins to mount as you get closer to the hole. Thinking about a putt as a "must make" or a "should make" causes you to focus on the result, which increases anxiety and makes short putts more difficult than they really are. Here are some ideas for instilling a better mindset for making short putts:

- Don't label your putts. Don't think about the putt as a par-putt ("I need this to make par."), birdie putt or bogey putt. Look at every putt as just another putt in the long, succession of putts that you want to make. A putt is a putt and you are trying to make

Work toward what I call "The Golden Attitude."

each and every one. Simplify your putting by approaching it as another simple task to perform. The task does not change—you are required to roll the ball into the hole the best way you know how. The only thing that changes is how you perceive the task.

- Forget about the result. Don't let your mind slip ahead and think about missing or three-putting. Worry about the result brings on tension and fear. Stick to the requirements of the task—getting a good read, picking your line, and feeling the speed. These tasks are manageable and under your control. Focus on them and you will make more putts

- Don't deviate from your normal routine. Do what you normally do with a ten-foot putt.

- Create a positive picture in your mind of the ball rolling on your line into the hole. See or feel the ball going into the hole as you prepare to hit it. Your final thought: "Hit it solidly." A solidly struck ball rolls truer.

Strong Sense of Touch

One of the most important skills is touch, the ability to control your speed, and thus, the distance the putt travels. Most three-putts are caused by poor distance control. Your touch also influences the line you select. When you select a line for a breaking putt, you must dial in the right speed or the putt won't hold its line.

An Execution Focus

The goal is to make putts. All golfers know this but you can't focus on making or missing. You have to focus on the elements of the task that will help you make putts. Read the green, select a line aiming to a target, believe that if the ball travels over the line you've chosen it will fall into the hole, and then strike the putt solidly along your line. Understand that once you contact the ball, there is nothing more that you can do. To repeat: Concentrate on what you can control. Read the green, pick a good line, and hit the ball on your line with the right speed. The outcome is out of your control so live with the results and move on. Don't berate yourself if you miss. That only reinforces that you are a bad short-length putter, which makes matters worse.

Concentrate on what you can control.

Strong Imagination and Good Vision

Putting is a visual task that requires strong imagination. You must be able to read greens and also see or feel your line. Your imagination allows you to predict the line of your putt, given a certain pace, that your ball must travel on to go in the hole. The better you can see the breaks and see the line, the more putts you will make.

The Ability to Trust Your Stroke

Once you have a consistent stroke, putting becomes a visual and mental task. Long hours of practice will enable you to groove your stroke so that you can focus on the line and speed when you play. If you become "stroke bound" or overly mechanical on the course, you will most likely steer your putts and not be able to focus on speed or line.

Everybody has experienced a great putting round or a stretch of holes in which they putted well. Think back to when you had a great putting round. What was your attitude like that day? How did you feel when you stood over a putt? What was your focus? What thoughts and feeling helped you to putt your best? This is the mindset you need to replicate to putt your best. The secret to great putting is within you. Tap into it and access your putting genius.

Warm Up With Your Putter

Before playing a round warm up with your putter. A warm up has three important purposes: to focus the mind, instill confidence, and get a feel for the speed of the greens. Once you start playing you don't want any doubts about your stroke cluttering your mind, and you don't want to divert your focus to the mechanics of your stroke. Warm up is the time to find your stroke, tune your touch and focus the mind. Here are five elements to incorporate into your putting warm up.

Hit the Ball Solidly

Hit the ball solidly on the sweet spot of the putter. Solid putts stay on line better, and they improve distance control because the ball rolls truer, giving you when it comes to rest the distance you imagined in your mind's eye. Hit a few balls solidly across the green without a target and carefully watch the ball roll.

Control Your Pace

Get a feel for the speed of the greens. Controlling your pace and the ability to lag the ball close from long range is critical to good putting. Hit some long putts to the fringe of the green and pay attention to how the ball rolls and how fast it stops.

Instill Success Pictures

Before you tee off you should see, feel and hear the ball go in the cup. This will plant some good images in your mind and when you get on the first green, it will give you a feeling of comfort.

Click in Your Focus

The putting warm up is an excellent time to get your game face on. It helps you focus on the cues that are important for performance. Focus on reading the green, visualizing a line, and seeing the ball roll into the center of the cup.

Practice Your Routine

This is the time to get comfortable with your preputt routine. Make sure you hit three or four putts using your full preputt routine. That's what you will do on the course, so you should start warming up your routine on the practice green. This will also help your concentration on the first few putts you hit.

Beating the Yips

The yips are one of golf's most perplexing challenges. They usually start with missing short putts. The player then begins to fear missing putts of longer lengths and finally, fears the act of putting in its entirety. Yip sufferers suspect it is a physical ailment or mechanical flaw, which leads them to believe that the problem can be corrected with a change in technique or practice habits.

But the yips come from the golfer's inability to gain neuromuscular control, often brought on by anxiety. Intense anxiety interferes with the golfer's control of his muscles, literally locking them in place. The player cannot draw the putter back from the ball and initiate the putting stroke. The players wants to move the club back, but his or her hands and arms act as if they're in a vise. Like a deer in the middle of the road frozen by the headlights on an oncoming car, the player freezes. Another disastrous form of the yips occurs when the player makes a smooth takeaway but then tenses up at impact and stabs at the ball.

Forget about what might happen, good or bad.

The yips are beatable. First, stop labeling yourself as victim of an incurable physical ailment. Next, understand that the physical symptoms of the yips spring from a faulty, conditioned way of thinking about putting. Here are some new and better ways of thinking for you to consider.

Throw away the fear of missing putts. Fear and anxiety come from what you think might happen in the immediate future. Don't let you mind wander to outcome of the putt or missing. Stay focused on the execution of the putt and how you are going to hit a good putt. Forget about what might happen, good or bad.

Forget about the past. You can't change the fact that you missed several short putts during your last round. Every round is different and every putt you have is different. Look at each putt as a new opportunity for success.

Simplify your approach. Prepare for your putt with only one focus—to hit the target that you have selected. Compare it to throwing darts in which you focus on the bullseye and let your body do the rest. Look at your target and as your eyes return to the ball pull the trigger. Continuous motion helps prevent you from freezing over the ball.

See the ball going in the hole, over and over. When you read the putt and select the line, imagine the ball rolling along the line and going into the hole. As you walk up to the ball, see the ball going in the hole. Stay focused on that image. Over the ball, again imagine the ball rolling toward the hole and disappearing, making the wonderful sound of a holed putt.

Putting mechanics do play a significant role to your success on the greens, but confidence and proper focus can help a good putter become a great one.

Jesper Parnevik demonstrates his secret of tanning while playing—turning up the bill of his cap.

Because a hot putter generally determines who wins, the practice green is a very popular place.

11

Trouble Shots *and* *Shotmaking*

Golf is a game of thinking on your feet and knowing how to play any shot you might encounter during a round. The ability to face adversity without losing faith in yourself often separates a successful round from one that spirals out of control. You do not have to be a PGA TOUR player to realize that the easiest way to overcome adversity is to be prepared for it.

Very few problems in golf are insurmountable. This chapter will explain how to deal with nearly every bad bounce you get. It will show you how to make the ball curve, fly low, sit, run, or do whatever else may be called for. No matter what, it pays to be a shotmaker.

Good players understand that the key to scoring is the ability to turn three shots into two. They turn trouble into opportunity and break their opponent's heart in the process. Even PGA TOUR players miss fairways and greens, so it pays to devote some of your practice time to learning how to play from difficult lies.

Raymond Floyd takes it over the trees to his target.

How to Curve the Ball from Left to Right

There are two reasons why you would want to curve the ball from left to right. First, a certain tee shot or hole position may call for a shot that curves gently from left to right. This controlled movement from left to right is known as a *fade*. A fade is also useful if you want to try banking a shot against a right-to-left wind, effectively negating the influence of the wind on the ball.

Second, you might want to curve the ball around something—most likely a tree. This situation might call for a more dramatic degree of curve, a shot that is more accurately described as a *slice*.

Whether you want to hit a subtle, controlled fade or a dramatic slice, here are a few things to keep in mind about such a shot:

- It will typically fly higher than a straight shot or a hook struck with the same club.
- Once it hits the ground, it will run less than a straight shot or a hook.
- The less loft on the club you're using, the easier it is to curve the ball from left to right. Once you get up into the lofted irons, it becomes more and more difficult.
- It is most effective from a clean lie, moderately effective from light rough, and will not work in deep rough.
- A left-to-right wind will make the curving action more pronounced.
- It does not require you to make any adjustment to your grip.
- You always aim the lead edge of the clubface at your target.

The point regarding the grip is important, because many everyday players are under the mistaken impression that weakening their grip (turning both hands toward the left) is the way to play a left-to-right shot. They think this because a weak grip is often blamed as the cause of a slice. Although this may be true, intentionally weakening your

Inside the Ropes

Hale Irwin   *When you can, work the ball into a breeze.*

Three-time U.S. Open Champion, has led the SENIOR PGA TOUR in virtually every statistical category while dominating the over-fifty circuit.

"A lot of everyday players hear TOUR players talk about 'holding' a shot into the wind. That means they curve the ball 'into' a crosswind. For example, in a left-to-right wind you would hit a draw. You can't always do that. There's a point where you can hold it, and a point where you can't. In a very strong wind, there's no way you can curve the ball enough to hold it. When it's just a typical breeze you can hold it, and what it allows you to do is to bring the ball down softer on the green. If a shot is riding the wind [curving in the same direction the wind is blowing] when it hits the green, then you start losing control of the shot because it's going to roll when it lands. That's particularly true on firm greens, and you never really know how far it's going to roll. The primary function of holding the ball into the wind is to control the ball once it gets on the ground."

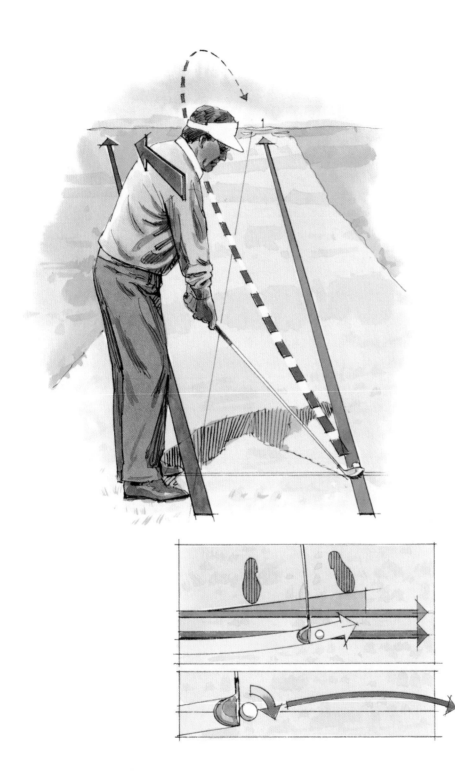

grip is a bad idea, because you will not be able to hit the shot with any force, and you will not have much control over the shot.

The process begins with aiming the club. Just as you would on any other shot, aim the lead edge at your target. (Remember: The target is where you want the ball to hit the ground, not where you want it to run to.) Once you have selected the target, approached the ball from behind, and aimed the club, set the clubhead on the ground and hold the clubhead lightly with one hand. You do this because you are going to be moving your body and do not want to change the aim of the club.

Once the club is aimed, you want to open your body to the target. (Remember that "open" has two meanings: You "open" your body by aiming it left of your target; you "open" the clubface by aiming it right of the target. In this case you do not want to open the clubface.) Make sure this adjustment is complete. Aim your feet, knees, hips, and shoulders all along the same line, which will be pointing left of your target line. The farther left you aim, the greater the amount of curve on the ball. *Aim the club where you want the ball to land. Aim your body along the line where you would like the ball to start curving back toward your target—that is, the point on the curve where the ball is farthest from the target line.*

When you swing the club, swing it along your body lines. On the backswing, the club does *not* swing straight back from the target; rather, it moves outside the target line. Through impact, it crosses over from outside the target line to inside the target line. On a gentle fade, this feeling of the club moving outside the target line is very, very subtle—the less you open your stance, the more subtle it is. At various points in this book you are encouraged to extend the clubhead down the target line toward the target. In this case you are not swinging the club toward the target. You want to extend the club, but you want to extend it down the line to the left of the target line, the line along which your body is aimed.

How to Curve the Ball from Right to Left

The reasons for curving a shot from right to left are similar to those for curving it from left to right—it is either the optimal ball flight for a certain tee shot, hole position, or wind condition, or you want to curve the ball around something. When the ball curves slightly from right to left, it is called a *draw*. When it curves significantly from right to left, it is a *hook*. No matter what it is called, here are a few things you should know before you play a right-to-left shot:

- It will typically fly lower than a straight shot or fade with the same club.
- Once it hits the ground, it will run more than a straight shot or a fade.
- The less loft on the club you are using, the easier it is to curve the ball from right to left. The more loft on the club, the more difficult it is to hit a draw.
- Like the left-to-right shots, it is most effective from a clean lie, moderately effective from light rough, and will not work in deep rough.
- A right-to-left wind will exaggerate the curving action.
- It does not require you to make any adjustment to your grip.

To curve the ball from right to left, aim your body lines (shoulders, hips, knees) to the right of the target while leaving the clubface aimed at the target. Swing the club along your body lines.

- You always aim the lead edge of the clubface at your target.

Just as with the left-to-right shots, you do not want to make a grip adjustment to hit a fade or a hook. A strong grip (both hands turned toward the right) feels very powerful because it places your right hand underneath the shaft. In this position it feels as if you can quite easily close the clubface through impact. You *can* close the clubface dramatically through impact with your hands in this position—so much so that once you make the following adjustments, you will smother any shot you attempt to play with such a grip. Why not make the grip change and not bother with the other adjustments? It is too unpredictable and too difficult to control.

Play draws and hooks with the alignment of your body. In this case, aim your body lines to the right of your target line so your feet, knees, hips and shoulders all run along the same line. Before you do that, however, make sure the clubface is aimed squarely at the target. The more you aim your body to the right, the bigger the hook. The point where you aim your body will be the highest point on the curve of the shot. When you swing, swing the club along the lines of your body. Don't worry about swinging it toward the target.

A Punch Shot out of the Trees

When a wayward shot finds a home amid trees, take the wisest course of action. Play the ball back out onto the fairway and take your lumps. However, don't take the shot lightly, simply because the goal is to advance it only thirty or forty yards. Two key points to consider regarding the trees through which your ball must travel: Your ball will get to the height of overhanging limbs quicker than you think, and the farther you are from the gap in the trees you are attempting to play through, the harder it is to thread the ball through that gap. If your shot starts out off line, it is going to be more off line by the time it reaches the gap.

Remember the following points when playing a low punch shot:

- Keep it low by selecting a less lofted club. Remember that the ball climbs quickly with lofted clubs. If you think an 8-iron may brush overhanging limbs, use a 6-iron. Very seldom should you play these shots with a wedge. A 9-iron should be the most lofted club you ever use, but the 5-, 6-, and 7-irons are probably the safest. In selecting a less lofted club, however, remember the effect it will have

Inside the Ropes

Billy Casper *You can hit "impossible" shots if you focus on the task at hand.*

Won 51 PGA TOUR events and three major championships, which includes a pair of U.S. Open titles.

"In the playoff for the 1970 Masters, I was up against Gene Littler, and on the second hole I hit a terrible drive that bounced off a pine tree and rolled down into what was normally a water hazard. The good news was there wasn't any water in the hazard. The ball was sitting on heavy grass that had been walked on by the gallery, and about two inches behind there was a branch. The branch was blocking the club's approach to the ball. My only chance was to take a

9-iron, try to avoid the branch, hit on the back of the ball, and pop it over some trees that were between me and the fairway. I moved the ball back in my stance so I could hit down on it. When you have something blocking the club's way to the ball you have to pick the club up rather than swing it back. Moving the ball back in your stance allows you to get the club cleanly to the ball. Anyway, that shot in the Masters turned out just perfectly—it was the best shot I ever hit, I think. I ended up parring the hole and Littler made a bogey."

When punching out from the trees, do what Ben Crenshaw does in this photo: choke up on the club for added control, place the ball back in your stance, and shorten your follow-through for a lower ball flight.

on the roll of the ball, so you can effectively plan where to land the shot in the fairway.

- Aim for the widest gap in the trees, one you know you cannot miss. If that means playing out sideways or even slightly away from the green, do it. One safe shot does not put you out of a hole. Three or four rattling around in the trees can ruin a hole and a round.

- Open your body very slightly to your target to get a good look at it, and play the ball slightly right of the middle of your stance to make sure you contact it first.

To play a low punch shot, play the ball back in your stance, keep your hands well ahead of the ball through impact, and stop the follow-through at about waist level.

- Tighten the grip pressure in your left hand. You want to pull the club through with the left hand to avoid any scooping action near the ball.
- Choke down on the club for more control.
- There is no turn or weight shift involved; this is a very short swing. Set up with your weight favoring your left side and swing the club with your arms. Your wrists should cock—it is not a stiff-armed chip shot—but the weight of the club will help your wrists do what they need to do.
- Do not worry about the follow-through. How far the ball travels is based on how far you take the club back.

If you are unsure of the initial trajectory that a certain club will produce, lay the club on the ground with the face pointing up and the grip pointing toward your target. Step on the clubface until the back of the club is flat on the ground. The angle of the shaft while you are stepping on the club is the approximate trajectory of the ball.

Advanced players (or those who like to attempt fun shots) can combine the punch shot techniques with the fade/slice and draw/hook setups to produce curving punch shots. You simply have to exaggerate the stance adjustments (opened or closed) because there is no follow-through. Remember: It's difficult to curve the ball with more lofted clubs.

Shots from Hilly Lies

There are four basic types of hilly lies: (1) ball lower than your feet; (2) ball higher than your feet; (3) a downhill lie, when your body is leaning toward your target (your right foot is higher than your left foot); and (4) an uphill lie, when your body is leaning away from the target (your left foot is higher than your right foot).

The Ball Is Below Your Feet

When the ball is below your feet, swing on a more upright plane. Because the ball is below your feet, you must get the club "lower" to play the shot. Do this by simultaneously increasing your knee flex and bend from the hips. If you *only* lean more from the hips, you will only swing the club more upright, and you will lose your balance. So get your knees involved. Move the ball back slightly in your stance so that you catch the ball cleanly.

Typically, the ball will curve from left to right. You should assume that the ball is going to move that way and aim at a spot left of where you want the ball to actually land. This is different from playing a fade. In this case you *are* going to aim the lead edge of the club at a point left of your target and allow for the ball to work slightly from left to right. Because there is always a chance that you might hit it straight, do not aim at anything that will get you in trouble, especially water. How far left you aim depends on how far below your feet the ball is. The less severe the slope, the less you should aim to the left.

The Ball Is Above Your Feet

Whenever the ball is above your feet, swing on a flatter plane. A flat swing is a hook swing, so you can assume that this shot is going to curve from right to left. The first adjustment to make is to stand more upright to the ball—less knee flex and less bend from the waist. Choke up on the club to shorten it and to prevent hitting the ground

---

Inside the Ropes

Al Geiberger   *Think baseball swing when the ball is way above your feet.*

One of only two players (the other being Chip Beck) to shoot a score of 59 during a PGA TOUR event.

"Sometimes the ball will get stuck on the side of a hill, especially on a lot of modern courses with mounding. When the ball is way above your feet—knee-high or so—the first thing you have to do is choke down on the club, because the hill is bringing the ball closer to you. There's not as much room in there [between your body and the ball]. You have to make a conscious effort to shorten the club to the proper length for the shot. You want to think of it as a more horizontal swing, like a baseball swing. That can be a good thing, because a baseball swing probably feels more natural than a golf swing. Moving the ball back in your stance will help with two things: It'll help you catch the ball clean and lessen the hooking effect of the lie. If it's a good lie, you might hook it, and if it's a heavy rough lie you'll probably pull it. You might want to take a little more club because you're choking down on it and you might not hit it as far."

Brad Faxon shows how to handle uneven lies: 1. When the ball is sitting on an uphill lie, play the ball forward and lean with the hill. Expect the ball to fly high and to the left. 2. When the ball is on a downhill lie, play the ball back in your stance, lean with the hill, and expect the ball to come out low and right. 3. When the ball is above your feet, stand up taller and expect the ball to curve from right to left. 4. When the ball is below your feet, lower yourself to it with your knees, and expect it to curve from left to right.

before you hit the ball. You can play the ball in the middle of your stance. Aim everything—body and clubface—at a point right of where you would like the ball to land and allow for it to work from right to left. Apply the same caveat about aiming at trouble. Remember: There is always a chance that you might hit it straight. How far to the right you aim depends on how far above your feet the ball is; the less severe the hill, the less you need to aim to the right.

A Downhill Lie, When Your Rear Foot Is Higher Than Your Front Foot

When the ground forces you to lean toward the target, you should not fight it. Let your body lean at the same angle as the ground. This shot will typically fly straight but be pushed to the right. Play the ball back in your stance so you catch it clean, and aim your body and the club to the left of where you would like the ball to land—how far left depends on the severity of the slope. This shot is going to fly low on you, so you might want to take one less club because the ball is going to run once it hits the ground. The added loft will also help get the ball up in the air, which is one of the main challenges from a downhill lie. However, don't alter your swing in an attempt to lift the ball into the air. It will still get airborne if you strike it cleanly. If you bring a scooping action into play, you have no chance for a clean strike.

An Uphill Lie, When Your Front Foot Is Higher Than Your Rear Foot

If you feel as if the ground is forcing you to lean away from the target, go ahead and do just that—lean with the ground, positioning your shoulders level to the slope. This shot is going to fly straight but be pulled left of your target, so aim your body and the clubface to the right of where you would like the ball to land. Playing the ball up in your stance (left of center) will help you to catch it cleanly. The slope is going to add some loft to the shot, so take one more club than normal and allow for the ball to stop quickly once it hits the ground.

A Knockdown Shot

While watching a PGA TOUR event on television, you might hear something such as, "He's going to knock down a little 8-iron here." The *knockdown* is a shot that flies lower, slightly shorter, and, when properly struck, more accurately than a typical iron shot. There are three basic reasons for playing a knockdown shot: (1) It can be more accurate, so you can hit the ball closer to the hole; (2) If you are in between clubs, you can take the longer of the two and take a little bit off of it; and (3) Because it holds a low and true (straight) trajectory, it can be a good choice into the wind.

The knockdown shot is accurate because you use a shorter swing, basically a backswing that is three-quarters of the length you would normally make with a given iron, and a follow-through that is also abbreviated. You also choke down on the club a little, making it shorter and easier to control. All this adds up to less room for mistakes, which is why many players use this shot when they feel they have a good chance to hit it close to the hole.

Here's how to play a knockdown shot:
- Select one club more than the distance would call for with a full swing. If you are in between clubs, go with the lower loft.
- Play the ball in the center of your stance. While keeping the clubface square to your target, open your body lines (feet, knees, hips, and shoulders) just slightly to the left of the target.
- Choke down about an inch on the club.

Knowing which way the wind blows is a key element to properly executing your shots. Here, Tiger Woods and his caddie check the trees for any signs of the wind up above the ground—where the ball spends most of its time.

- Make a three-quarter backswing, and through impact "hang on" a little tighter with your left hand. Do not let your right hand "roll over" your left. An image that will help is that of your left elbow moving away from your body like a chicken wing. On the follow-through your hands stay out in front of your face (after you've looked up to follow the shot)—they do not swing around by your left ear, as they would on a full shot.
- The ball should fly straight to the target or cut (move left to right) ever so slightly. If it lands on the green it will roll a little or not at all.

Shots from the Rough

If your ball lands in the rough, you are at the mercy of the lie you get. If the grass is deep (you see only the top of the ball), your options are severely limited. From moder-

Al Geiberger   *Check the grass and the lie before you play the shot.*

Winner of 11 PGA TOUR events including the 1966 PGA Championship.

"One big mistake golfers of all levels make is that they don't pay attention to the direction the grass is growing. If the grass is growing at or toward your ball, it makes a big difference. When the grass is leaning toward your target, the club slides right through, and you can make clean contact. When the grass is growing against you, the grass just climbs all over the face and grabs the club as it gets near the ball. I don't try to do anything fancy in that case. I just try to swing a littler harder, be a little more aggressive, get a little more acceleration going through there. It's really a mistake to try to get cute with these shots. It's a shot a lot of people try to get clever with, and it just doesn't work. I've seen that happen in Florida, where that Bermuda grass is all growing toward the west and it doesn't even look very deep—doesn't really even look like a bad lie—and a guy will just sort of slap at it thinking he can slide the club under there and hit a little soft shot. Well, he can't and—bloop—he plops it about halfway to the hole. I just use the same club I normally would, keep the lead edge square, hit down on the ball, and hit it hard. I might move it back in my stance a little bit, but not if I had to get the ball up in the air quickly."

---

ate rough, you have some chance of playing a useful shot, and from light rough you can do nearly anything except be certain you can hold the ball on the green.

If the rough is so deep that the top of the ball is an inch or more below the top of the grass, you really do not have much chance to play a clean shot. In a case like this, take your pitching wedge (its sharper lead edge will slice the grass better than your sand wedge), move the ball back in your stance and play the ball out to the fairway.

If the grass comes just to the top of the ball or slightly above it, you have a chance to play one of two shots. First, you can attempt to play a fairway wood if the distance allows and you think the club will get through the grass and to the ball. Most modern fairway woods are up to the task. If the fairway wood is too much club, or if the rough is just too thick, you can play an iron shot by doing the following:

- Select one less club than usual. If it is a 6-iron distance, take the 7-iron.
- Select a target that is going to allow for quite a bit of run once the ball hits the ground.
- Move the ball back in your stance. Aim the club slightly left of your target and set your body open (left) in relation to the club. This shot is going to squirt to the right on you, but if you make these adjustments you will be ready for that.
- Do not ground the club. Hold it over the grass as you prepare to take your stroke to ensure a clean takeaway.
- The swing should feel very powerful. You should feel as if you are taking the club back on an outside line—that is, outside the target line. Another way of thinking of this is that you want to swing very upright.
- Again, this is a powerful swing. Hit the ball hard. Hang on tight with your hands. The follow-through is whatever you can make of it. It is not going to feel fluid, as it does on a tee shot. It will feel as if you just ripped through the ground.

When you catch a fluffy lie like this one, accept your punishment and try to get the ball back in play.

• The ball will come out lower than normal, and it will run farther once it lands.

If the ball is sitting in light rough (the grass comes up to about the middle of the ball), you can play a normal shot. Whether the ball sits on the green will depend on the club you play. A lofted shot played with a fairway wood or a short iron probably will. A middle iron or a 3- or 4-wood probably won't. You may want to move the ball toward the center of your stance

A "flier lie." The grass between the ball and the clubface will reduce spin, producing a shot that will fly farther and roll farther once it lands.

In his prime, no one could get out of trouble more deftly than Tom Watson.

to make sure you strike it with a descending blow. Not grounding the club will eliminate the risk of getting it snagged in the grass during the takeaway.

A note on club selection: If you have played golf for any length of time, you are probably familiar with the term *flier lie*. A flier lie occurs only in the rough, and it typi-

Inside the Ropes

Steve Stricker   *How to handle a flier lie.*

Ranked in the top thirty in scoring three times between 1995 and 1998. Also was tied for seventh in sand saves in 1998.

"You can tell a ball is a flier because there's grass behind the ball. Usually it's sitting up a little bit with some grass behind the ball. If the ball is sitting down, it's not going to fly as much, even if there is some grass behind it. If the grass is leaning toward your target, then the ball is really going to jump out of there. The adjustments I make are that I take less club and I try to deaden the club through impact. I try to hold on to it a little more and not release the club real strong, because then it's really going to fly on you."

cally occurs from light rough. Two things have to happen for you to have a flier: The grass must get between the ball and the clubface, and you must be able to make what feels like full contact and swing to a follow-through. In other words, if your ball is in four-inch rough, you do not have a flier. Typically speaking, a flier looks as if it is sitting up in the rough. A flier results in two things. The ball carries a little farther because there is no spin on it—the grass gets between the ball and the grooves on the clubface. Because there is no spin, the ball also runs when it hits the ground, no matter what club you hit. If you think you have a flier lie, take one less club and play for the ball to run.

One final point on playing shots from the rough: If the grass is growing in the direction of the shot you are playing and you catch it clean, it will fly a bit farther. If you hit it heavy, it will not make a difference. If the grass is growing against the direction in which you wish to play the shot—that is, away from the target and toward the ball—

Nick Faldo tosses a few blades of grass in the air to gauge the general direction of the wind.

the ball will not fly as far as it normally would with that club, no matter how cleanly you hit it. When the grass is growing against you, take an extra club.

How the Wind Affects Your Ball

Assuming your swing is fundamentally sound or close to it, the two biggest influences on the flight of a ball are the lie and the wind. The ways in which the lie of the ball affects your shot have already been noted. Here's a list of things to consider regarding how the wind affects the flight of your ball:

- When you hit a shot into the wind, it will fly higher and shorter than normal. Generally speaking, it will not roll much when it hits the ground. Any curve on the ball will be exaggerated: A hook played into the wind will hook more severely.

- When you play a ball downwind, it will fly farther than normal and run farther than normal, because the wind takes the spin off the ball. It is quite difficult to hold the green with a shot played downwind from the fairway and nearly impossible to do so on a shot played from even the lightest rough. When you are playing downwind, allow for some run. If the wind is strong enough for you to consistently feel it (i.e., it is not softly gusting now and again), you should consider taking one club less than normal for the distance.

- When playing a shot with a crosswind, the curving action on any shot will be exaggerated if it curves with the wind. In other words, a left-to-right shot played with a left-to-right wind will curve even more to the right.

A frequently debated point on playing in the wind is that of playing directly into a strong wind. More specifically, should you change the type of shot you play because you are hitting into a strong wind? It is up to you. You have two options: You can simply take one or two or three more clubs than the distance calls for (depending on the wind) and make a normal swing, or you can take one more club and try to hit the ball low by moving it back in your stance or playing a knockdown shot. For the everyday golfer, the best chance of success is the first choice, hitting a less lofted club. When you play a knockdown shot or move the ball back in your stance to keep it open, you increase the chances that the ball may start to curve off line. When the ball starts to curve off line while flying into the wind, it will continue to curve off line. Much of your decision lies in the severity of the wind. The stronger the wind, the more you might want to consider playing the knockdown shot, simply because the shorter swing may feel more controlled in the wind. If the wind does not feel like it is going to blow your hat off, just take an extra club or two.

The Effect of Differences in Elevation

When your target is significantly higher or lower than where your ball lies, your shot must account for the difference. Remember that there must be a difference in elevation between the point you are playing from and your target. In other words, if you play from a point that is level with the green, a valley between you and the green will not alter the effective carry of the shot. You should be concerned with the *actual* relationship between where you stand and your target. Typically speaking, a change of thirty feet in either direction calls for a change of one club. If the point where the green sits is thirty feet higher than where you are playing the shot, you should use one club more. If the green sits thirty feet lower than where your ball lies, you should use one club less. What if it is fifteen feet? That is a half-club difference.

A few other things affect the flight of your ball:
- If it is very hot out but not humid, the ball will fly a little farther.
- If it is humid—humid enough for you to feel it—the ball will also carry farther. If it is very cold outside, the ball will fly shorter.
- If you are playing at a very high altitude, the ball will fly farther.
- If you are playing off wet fairways (this includes morning dew), the ball will fly farther. From wet rough, the ball will fly shorter.

The Pitch-and-Run, a.k.a. the Bump-and-Run

If you have ever watched the British Open or if you have played golf in the United Kingdom on links courses, you may be familiar with what is called the *pitch-and-run* or the *bump-and-run* shot. It is not included in the short-game section because it really is a specialty shot. Play this shot into the wind or downwind when the green is very firm and when you have determined that no lofted shot will hold. It is possible to play the shot effectively from as far away as 100 yards from the green, as long as nothing between you and the hole (such as a bunker) will stop the ball's motion. The basic mechanics are:

- Slightly open stance, weight forward.
- Ball in center of stance.
- Choke up on club for control.
- Firm left-hand grip.
- The ball is punched (as described in the punch shot above), and the right hand never rolls over the left.

The key to the shot is having a feel for which club to play, which is based on how far you want to carry the ball toward your target before you let it run the rest of the way in. The farther you are from the green, the farther you will have to carry it—that is, you will need a more lofted club. This shot is all about feel and practice. You should be familiar with it before you start playing it. You will probably use such a shot only a few times in a given season, but it is nice to have it in your bag when the need arises.

Odd Lies: Divots, Leaves, Pine Needles, Hardpan

If your ball is sitting in an old divot hole:

- Open your stance but leave the club square to the target.
- Play the ball back in your stance.
- Take the club back more upright. Hit "down" on the back of the ball.
- Allow for the ball to move right in flight.

If your ball is sitting on leaves or pine needles:

- Do not ground the club; hover it just over the ball.
- Open your stance; leave the club square to the target.
- Hold on a little tighter with your left hand.
- Allow for the ball to squirt right, because the face will "skid" open when it contacts the leaves or pine needles.

When the ball is in a divot, play it back in your stance so you can strike it with a descending blow.

Bob Murphy   *From hardpan, try to bump the ball.*

Finished second in the Senior PGA TOUR All-Around category (which statistically measures a golfer's total game) in 1996.

"All sorts of things can go wrong when your ball is on hardpan because you can no longer slide the club underneath the ball. You can eliminate any type of flop shot or high shot. Normally you'd want to attempt some sort of bump-and-run shot and take less club. You never want to use your sand wedge—that bounce will kill you off hardpan. You have to hit the ball first, so play it back in your stance. A good word to think of is pinch—you want to pick the ball cleanly. If you play a bump-and-run, the shorter swing will help you control the club and get the cleaner hit. If you don't have room to run the ball to your target, you're in trouble and I can't help you!"

If your ball is sitting on hardpan:

- Open your stance and move the ball back in your stance.
- Try to "pinch" the ball—hit down on it with soft hands.
- If you can play a shot with a three-quarter swing, do so.
- If you are trying to pitch the ball, do not use your sand wedge. The club will bounce off the ground, and the lead edge will blade the ball.

How to Play a Ball from the Water

A ball in the water is usually a ball out of play and incurs a penalty stroke. Once in a while, however, that ball teases you: It sits right on the edge of a pond, a mere inch or two from the bank. You have probably thought about trying to play such a shot, or even seen a TOUR player do it on television. Under the right circumstances you *can* play the ball from the edge of the water. When considering such a shot, think it through—weigh the possible advantages of pulling the shot off versus taking the penalty and a clean lie in the grass. If you decide to play the shot from the water, here are a few things to keep in mind:

- At least half of the ball should be above the water. If the ball is completely submerged, forget about trying to play it.
- If you feel as though you must put your foot/feet in the water to play the shot, *do not* remove your shoe or shoes. You have no idea what you might be stepping into or on, and you really don't want a gash in your foot from a sharp stone or a broken bottle. If you decide to play this shot, accept that you are going to have wet feet for the rest of the round. Carrying an extra pair of socks in your bag might help. If you have a rain suit or jacket, put it on. It will help keep you dry and clean.
- The club of choice is your pitching wedge. The sharp lead edge will cut through the surface of the water. If you use your sand wedge, the bounce on it could create problems for you.

Sometimes you just have to improvise, like Lanny Wadkins does here. Any time your stance is on a hill, lean in the direction the hill takes you. For an uphill chip like this one, shorten up on the club.

- Lean toward the target because you want to hit the ball with a descending blow.
- Turn the lead edge of the clubface in so it appears "shut" to you.
- Pick the club straight up and slam it into the water about an inch behind the ball, just as if you were playing a sand shot from a buried lie. You do not need to hit the ball itself.
- Don't worry about the follow-through—there isn't one. With any luck, the ball will ride a wave of water up onto dry ground.

THE SCIENCE OF GOLF

Two questions inevitably enter the minds of golfing newcomers. Why is a golf ball dimpled? Why does a golfer carry so many clubs? Both are attempts to control that pesky ball's flight and to move the ball from tee to hole in as few strokes as possible.

How far and in what direction a ball travels primarily depend on the club selected and on the force and spin imparted to the ball on impact. How well a player manages these three variables is the difference among a birdie, par, and a bogie.

Dimples on a golf ball increase its flight time, and hence its distance, by affecting the pattern of air flow surrounding the ball as it sails through the air. The layer of air closest to the ball is the boundary layer. If this layer experiences laminar flow (which typically happens on a smooth ball), the air layer tends to separate and break away from the ball easily. Because this separation can happen early—sometimes before the air gets even half the distance to the back of the ball—it causes a large wake of low pressure to form behind the ball, resulting in a high drag force. By contrast, if the air layer is turbulent (as it will be with a rough ball), the turbulent boundary layer mixes rapidly with the air next to it. Under this condition the boundary layer does not get a chance to slow down (it is getting constant momentum from the outside layer of air) and thus tends to hug the ball, resulting in a smaller wake of low pressure and so less drag.

The dimples on an airborne golf ball, therefore, reduce drag forces considerably—by about half—and the ball travels up to 70 percent farther than if it were smooth. Unfortunately, the dimples also amplify the forces that cause hooks and slices.

Advantages of the Metal Wood

When struck by a metal wood, a ball becomes a "fully charged ball." To a physicist, this means a complete transfer of kinetic energy from the club to the ball. Wood, claims John Zebelean, who designed the first steel wood, produces a poor transfer of kinetic energy. Steel, he says, "transfers a tremendous impulse of energy to the ball and charges it at a faster rate, so you have less loss of energy." He also believes that metal woods increase a player's accuracy, because they shorten the time the ball is in contact with the clubface, thereby lessening the ball's susceptibility to bad hits caused by the shaft flexing or the ball being hit off center.

The face of each club is inclined at a different angle so that each gives a different loft to the ball. Loft is the angle between a line perpendicular to the face of the clubhead and the horizontal. The degree of loft determines in large part the ensuing trajectory of the ball.

These distances are calculated assuming a calm day at the course. The lightest club is the driver; the heaviest is the putter. Although a driver is lighter than the other clubs,

Loft Angle and Range per Club

	Most Typical Angle of Lift (Degrees)	Average Range of Distance (Yards) Traveled by the Ball		PGA TOUR Professional
		Men	Women	
Woods				
No. 1 (driver)	11	200–300	160–180	250–260
No. 2 (brassie)	13	210–250	155–170	—
No. 3 (spoon)	16	200–230	150–170	230
No. 4	19	190–220	145–165	—
Irons				
No. 1	17	190–220	145–165	220
No. 2	20	180–210	140–155	210
No. 3	23	170–190	135–150	200
No. 4	27	155–175	125–140	190
No. 5	31	140–155	115–130	180
No. 6	35	125–145	110–120	165–175
No. 7	39	120–140	100–110	155–160
No. 8	43	110–125	90–100	143–150
No. 9	47	90–120	70–80	135–140
Wedges				
Pitching	51–54	70–100	50–85	125–130
Sand	58	—	—	100
Putter	0–4	—	—	—

it imparts more momentum to the ball than the irons because it is longer and its weight is concentrated in the clubhead.

Graphite is a popular shaft material for clubs, especially those used to hit long distances (driver, 3-wood). A manufacturer heats this carbon material to almost five thousand degrees Fahrenheit, usually combining it with an epoxy resin to form a composite. Boron is sometimes used; boron is twice as stiff as steel but only a third as heavy. Studies have shown that a ball hit by a graphite driver will travel approximately three yards farther than one hit by a steel driver.

The velocity imparted to a ball on impact certainly affects how far it will travel. Although a golf ball's maximum initial speed is about 171 miles per hour (mph) (the official Rules allow no more than 174 mph), 125 mph is closer to what an average golfer achieves. Most pros, however, obtain 150 mph with their drivers and 120 with their irons. It takes a force of 660 pounds to make the ball leave the tee at 150 mph— no small accomplishment.

Linear and Rotational Energy

When a club comes in contact with a golf ball, it transfers two types of energy: linear (for distance) and rotational (for spin). Each hit generates a limited amount of energy, so if more energy goes to rotation, less is available for distance. Because it counteracts the ball's tendency to fall, however, backspin enables a ball to fly on a flatter trajectory, and once the ball hits the ground, it will roll farther.

Players successful at golf have undoubtedly learned to make spin work for them. The first step in acquiring this skill is to understand how spin influences the flight of the ball; then a player can plan how to impart the appropriate spin.

When a ball is hit dead on, pure backspin is imparted. Up to 8,000 revolutions per minute (rpm) can be generated. The angled face of the club pinches against the ball and makes it rotate backward toward the club. For just a millisecond, the ball actually climbs up the face of the club. The grooves on the clubface help generate backspin because they increase the amount of friction between the ball and the club. Conversely, wet conditions decrease friction and thus reduce backspin. A headwind increases backspin; a tailwind decreases it. Balata-wound balls stay on the clubface microseconds longer than two-piece balls and hence have a faster spin rate.

Rotational forces generated by backspin increase the amount of lift experienced by a golf ball; therefore, if a ball with backspin has the same trajectory as one without backspin, it will stay in the air longer. For example, if both trajectories have a height of sixty-five feet, a ball with backspin will stay in the air for six seconds; one without backspin for only four seconds. These two seconds can equate to as many as thirty yards on the course.

A ball's rate of spin is partially dependent on its coefficient of spin, which is determined by the relationship between the ball's core and its cover. A ball having a harder core relative to its cover will spin faster. Traditional Surlyn-covered, two-piece balls spin more slowly than balata-covered balls. Softer covers spin faster. This factor is particularly significant on the green because a two-piece ball will roll farther than a wound ball.

The Effects of Shaft Flexibility

As previously noted, a ball hit squarely by the face of the club experiences pure backspin, but if a player angles the face of the club at all, sidespin is also generated. A counterclockwise spin will cause the ball to veer left (hook); a clockwise spin will cause it to veer right (slice).

The flexibility of a club's shaft also affects the distance a ball travels. Just as a rubber band pulled tight stores elastic energy, so a club stores energy as it flexes. When the club andthe ball collide, this energy is released, giving the ball a higher initial speed and more loft.

Club manufacturers rate shaft flex as ladies (L), flexible (A), regular (R), stiff (s), extra stiff (X), and double extra stiff (XX). The stiffer the flex, the more speed and strength a player needs to make the shaft straighten out on impact. More flexible shafts enable players who have weaker arms and wrists to generate increase clubhead speed through the club's whipping action.

The Weather Factor

Sole weighting endows a club with more backspin capabilities. By concentrating the club's weight below the center of the ball, more lift is generated on impact. This is another improvement that, unless players are quite consistent in their play, can actually be a detriment. (Sometimes backspin is not desired—for example, when hitting the ball against a prevailing breeze.)

Golfers generally prefer sunny days on the course. Experience has probably shown them that the weather influences the way a ball plays; on a cold day wound balls are harder and do not fly as far. Players in Alaska take note: Two-piece balls are less susceptible to weather changes.

Warm-blooded human beings are not the only species that enjoy golf courses. At the Jinga course in Uganda, Africa, a special rule states that "if a ball comes to rest in the dangerous proximity of a crocodile, another ball may be dropped." (One wonders what the interpretation of "dangerous" is.) Closer to home, at the Glen Canyon course in Page, Arizona, the rules state that "if your ball lands within a club's length of a rattlesnake, you're allowed to move the ball." (How about dropping a new one instead, please?) It may be that these critters are drawn to the cooler temperatures found on a golf course, which in a desert can be as much as eight to nine degrees less than the temperature of the surrounding area.

Excuses for lousy scores run riot in the clubhouse. Stephen Leacock, in a critical essay, "Mathematics for Golfers," calculated the odds that his friend Jones, a habitual excuse-giver, would have a day without difficulties at the golf course. Leacock used these assumptions: (1) Jones was subject to fifty different difficulties, each of which was likely to happen once every ten days, and (2) Jones plays four games of golf a week. Using applications of permutations and probabilities, Leacock calculated how often Jones should not have a good excuse for blowing his game. The answer: once every 2,930,000 years. Leacock adds, "From watching Jones play, I thing this is about right."

Putting

Many a golfer meets his nemesis on the green. Percentage wise, putting makes up a large part of the game. Pros use their putters an average of thirty times a round, so this play makes up about 43 percent of their games.

Some golfers, even pros, become irate when they miss a putt. A recent study should console them, however. It found that TOUR players make only 54.8 percent of the putts attempted from six feet; they make only 33.5 percent of those from ten feet; and at fifteen feet, it gets quite abysmal—only 16.8 percent are made. Perhaps even more interesting, the study found that pros tend to do better when the shot is for par, compared to for a birdie. Apparently, being at par exerts an effective mental pressure on the player that pays off.

Other research that may help a duffer on the green was done by Brian W. Holmes, of the Department of Physics at San Jose State University, who developed a computer model to determine how a golf ball and a hole interact. His findings:

- If a ball is rolling without slipping, it must be moving at 5.34 feet per second (ft/sec) or less to be captured. Otherwise it has enough velocity to sustain a straight-line path across the top of the hole.
- If the velocity is less than 4.31 ft/sec, the ball will be captured before it reaches the opposite rim of the cup.
- Between 4.31 and 5.34 ft/sec, the ball will hit the opposite rim. Its action then depends on how much the ball bounces and on how much friction is generated from the ball's rotation against the rim.
- If a ball is bouncing or skidding (a propensity for which varies from green to green), it will be captured at greater speeds. This is because a skidding ball has less angular momentum, which can provide "kick" to bounce the ball out of the hole.
- It is a little easier to sink a wound ball than a two-piece ball.

The above analysis holds for balls directed straight at the hole. Off-center collisions are more complex, and although Holmes has developed equations that show different reactions from different angles of attack, it is (perhaps fortunately for the reader) beyond the scope of this book to go into them.

Put a Little Extra On Your Putt

Short-game guru Dave Pelz has also studied putting. He says that after rolling thousands of balls at different speeds, "I determined that the ball should be traveling fast enough that if the hole were covered, the putt would roll seventeen inches past." This speed enables the ball to hold its line through what Pelz calls the "lumpy doughnut." As he describes it, most of the green is marked up and stamped down from footprints, except for the last foot before the cup, which is smooth because golfers make it a point to keep off that area. Thus, as a ball makes its way toward the cup, it must contend with depressions as deep as one-eighth inch (or 7½ percent of the ball's total height) until it is about a foot from the cup. Then the ball actually has to run up a little ramp, when it is going slow and least prepared to do so. This effect explains why so many putts veer off or stop short at the last second.

Pelz says that depressions made from footprints last at least two and a half hours, so unless you are the first one on the green for the day, you will have to confront and compensate for lumpy doughnuts accordingly.

Pelz offers the following additional pointers for fine putting.

Square to the Target Line

The putter face must be square to the target line at the moment of impact. Otherwise, 90 percent of the deviation is imparted to the ball; that is, for a twenty-foot putt, the ball will miss the hole by about three feet if the face is ten degrees off.

Hit the ball with the sweet spot of the club. If you miss this spot by a quarter of an inch, 98 percent of your error will translate to the ball. For any putt longer than eight feet, this error will make you miss the cup.

To find the sweet spot on your club, hold the putter by the top of its grip, between your index finger and thumb, like a plumb line. Take a golf tee and tap the face of the putter, beginning with the toe end, then the heel, and gradually zero in on the point at which the putter head swings straight back, twisting neither inward nor outward. This area is the sweet spot. (Although some clubs have a directional line on top of the putter, these marks do not always coincide with the sweet spot, so checking it can be worthwhile.) Years ago this spot was the size of a dime, but today it can be as large as a half dollar.

Also important for accurate putts is proper club length. Some professionals say that a club is the right length if, when you take your normal stance, only an inch or less of space is between your top hand and the top of the club.

Theories on learning are certainly pertinent to the game of golf. Otherwise, why bother practicing driving or putting? It was formerly believed that the repetitive practice of a motor function would cut a deeper groove in the brain, making recall more spontaneous and accurate. This theory was discarded when it was discovered that memories in the brain are not stored in one central bank, but are dispersed throughout the gray matter. The spinal cord may even store some memories (possibly explaining why a chicken runs around with its head cut off).

Of course, a player can avoid the green altogether by shooting a hole-in-one. The key to this strategy, however, is getting the ball in the right hole. Rick Syme, of Macon, Georgia, was recently teeing off on the par-4, 328-yard seventeenth at Macon's Oak Haven Golf and Country Club. He used a 3-wood to cut a corner over the trees, but wind conditions took his fade much farther than planned—clear over to the sixteenth hole, in fact. Jim Grigsby, who was putting on the sixteenth with his son, had the flagstick out when he heard "Fore!" Syme's ball swished through the trees, landed about seven feet from the hole, and rolled in. For this less-than-accurate shot, Syme assessed himself a two-stroke penalty and took a drop off the sixteenth green. His next shot landed on the seventeenth green and he one-putted for a bogie 5. Not a bad recovery, Rick.

Excerpted from WHAT MAKES A BOOMERANG COME BACK: The Science of Sports *by Sharon L. Blanding and John J. Monteleone.*

The "Walrus," Craig Stadler.

Water is the bane of every golfer, professional
and amateur alike.

12

Managing *your* *Game*

Of all the great champions who have played on the PGA TOUR, some come to mind because of majestic tee shots, others because they are great putters, and still others because they are great scramblers. The elite players—those who compete and win for decades, who play well on tough courses, who are always a threat in the major championships—all share one thing: They are great golf strategists. They manage the course and their games. They do not often play foolish shots. That is the huge difference between the greatest champions who have ever played and most everyday players. The great player plans his shots for the entire hole and executes them in order. The not-so-great player plays shot after shot without considering the consequences. As Arnold Palmer once said, "One of my favorite things my father always said when I was a boy was, 'Golf is played 90 percent from your shoulders to the top of your head.' He used to love to say that. And he was right." This chapter will help you establish a true purpose for every shot you play.

Jack Nicklaus is a master strategist and tactician.

285

It Starts on the Tee

Many words have been written describing the difference between the hole and your target. The hole, of course, is the place where you would like your ball to eventually end up, but if you are thinking your way through a round, the hole is your true target only a handful of times when viewed in the context of all the strokes you play. (Remember: On any shot that is not a putt, your target is the point on the ground where you would like the ball to land. On a putt, your target is the highest point of the break, the point at which you aim the clubface.)

A fundamental component of managing your game is dismissing the idea that the hole is your target from the moment you step on the tee, and realizing that you have *multiple options* on every tee. A golf course architect designs a hole using two visual plays so the player will view the hole in a certain way. First, you almost always have a view of the flagstick from the tee. This tempts you to become "holecentric" in your thoughts and to see a straight line or the shortest line to the hole. Second, the hole is designed to lead you visually to the flagstick in a certain way. Sometimes that path is the best path and sometimes not. Frequently the tee box on a hole is pointed in the direction (along the line) that the architect would like you to take or that entices the expert player to attempt the perfect shot. Bends in the fairway as well as trees, water, bunkers, and the like are placed in the area toward which the architect would like you to drive the ball. How far are those obstacles from the tee? Normally they are placed at a point that will put them in play if you try to hit the ball the maximum distance or along a direct line from the tee to the hole, or both. Sad to say, the majority of golfers allow the architectural camouflage to lead them into trouble.

The ideal tee shot was discussed in Chapter 5. The target for your tee shot is the farthest (from the tee) flat spot you can reach that still leaves a clear avenue of approach for your second shot. Chapter 5 also outlines how you should select the target for your tee shot and includes the influences on the carry and roll of your tee shot. A golf hole can have any number of additional factors that figure into selecting a target for your tee shot. The basic goal of managing your game is picking the right target for each shot, and because the tee shot sets the tone for the hole, it might be the most important phase of managing your game.

Inside the Ropes

Jeff Sluman   *Playing golf is about making the adjustments.*

Won the 1988 PGA Championship and the 1997 Tucson Chrysler Classic.

"When you are in a groove, every pin seems accessible to you—it seems like you can get to every one of them. You leave yourself better angles off the tee. When you are really, really on you can pinpoint your shots. Most of the time, though, you are not on at all. That's when it becomes a game of how good your bad shots are. It is a matter of adjustment. You should try to recognize early in the day what your tendencies are going to be for the day and just play with them."

Calvin Peete *When things go sour on you, try hitting the opposite of the bad shots.*

Led the PGA TOUR in scoring in 1984, in greens-in-regulation three times, and in driving accuracy for ten consecutive years (1981–90).

"When I'm not producing the type of ball flight I expect to, I try something rather simple. If I am hooking the ball and I do not want to, I try to play intentional fades. If I'm fading the ball and I do not want to, I set up to play a draw. There are lots of things you can do—shorten up your backswing for more control, or sometimes even just choking down on the club a little bit. Everyone has their own little things they do."

Consider the following points when selecting your target before playing a tee shot on a driving (non-par-3) hole. One thought before you continue: *Your target should always be in the fairway.*

If the fairway is bordered on one side by very heavy trees and if there are no other obvious obstacles, think about playing away from the trees. However, you have some room for error, so you should not entirely rule out the driver.

If the fairway is bordered by trees on both sides, with no other hazards or obstacles, realize that the margin for error is now reduced. Straight begins to be more important than long, which means that the demands on your driver are greater. Perhaps it is time to start thinking about a 3-wood. A lot has to do with the distance between the two tree lines—that is, the width of the hole.

Trees are the first obstacle to consider because they can affect your ball at any point during its flight and obstruct the path of your next shot. Aside from your swing and the wind, which affect your ball while it is in the air, trees are the only thing that will affect the flight of your ball.

If your predominant ball flight is from right to left, you should favor the left side of the tee box.

If the wind is blowing across your target line on a given shot, the problems (trees, water, bunkers) on the side the wind is blowing toward are now magnified. What will fly straighter in the wind, a ball struck with minimal loft or more loft? A ball struck with minimum loft (your driver) will stay in the air longer, but will be more susceptible to being struck off line. A ball struck with less loft (a 3-wood or a 5-wood perhaps) will fly higher, exposing it to more wind, but it is also more likely to be hit straight, without sidespin.

The next question is: Is the wind blowing in the same direction as your predominant ball flight? If so, the curve of that ball flight will be exaggerated. Therefore, if your typical ball flight with your driver is left to right, and if the wind is blowing left to right, your fade could very easily become an out-of-control slice. Under such conditions, especially if trouble lurks on the right side of the hole, consider reducing the curve you put on the shot by hitting a more lofted club and sacrificing some distance. The straighter the ball is flying, the less the wind will affect the ball's direction.

If the wind is blowing the opposite of your typical ball flight (e.g., it is blowing from left to right and you typically curve the ball from right to left), the scenario has changed. The wind will diminish the effects of your typical curve, making a straight shot more likely with the driver. Therefore, your chances of hitting a straight shot are improved.

As far as the wind is concerned, you might not have a crosswind, but rather a headwind (you are playing into it) or a tailwind (the wind is blowing toward your target). The scenarios are rather simple. Because it helps the ball fly farther and roll farther once it hits the ground, a tail wind brings hazards into play that you would consider unreachable under normal con-

Bruce Devlin *Out on the course is no place to start making changes.*

Won eight times on the PGA TOUR and has won once on the SENIOR PGA TOUR.

"Part of managing your game properly is to realize that the golf course is no place to start making changes to your grip or overhauling your setup. If you feel like you have to make an adjustment, think of something simple like making a bigger shoulder turn or double-checking your alignment. Making big changes is what practice ranges are for. Trying to make big changes during a round is just going to get you into more trouble."

ditions. If there are no hazards to consider, there is nothing to worry about. If the wind makes some hazards suddenly seem reachable with your driver, the solution is simple: Use a more lofted club. The ball will fly shorter and run less once it hits the ground.

If you are playing into the wind with your driver, the ball will not carry as far. Realize that a headwind also can bring hazards into play that are not typically in play. When the wind is blowing in your face, do not assume that you can fly a bunker you always carry under ordinary conditions.

Any time you combine a predominant ball flight, wind direction, and a code red (described below), you are looking at big trouble. Only the bravest (or most foolhardy) pull the driver out of the bag under such conditions.

Other Influences in Selecting a Target for Your Tee Shot

Assuming that you play the majority of your golf in the United States, trees and wind are the two most common obstacles to overcome on your tee shots—they are seemingly everywhere. Tee shots often present other familiar hazards as well, such as water, bunker, desert or waste areas, sharp terrain changes (which might block your view of the green), out of bounds, canyons, curves in the layout of the hole, etc.

For the everyday golfer there is a logical sequence to run through when assessing these elements and deciding on a target and what club to use.

Anything that will take the ball completely out of play—water, out of bounds, a ravine from which the ball is obviously not recoverable (lost)—is basically a code-red situation on the tee. If these things are on the side of the hole that your ball naturally curves toward, the potential for disaster is increased. If the wind is blowing that way as well, the potential for a blowup is increased twofold. The trouble is gravest with out-of-bounds and potential lost-ball situations, which basically penalize you two strokes and gain you nothing in terms of distance. At least when you hit the ball into the water, you have picked up some distance.

Other problem areas—rough, bunkers, waste areas (assuming you can find your ball), etc.—are still cause for concern, but are problems from which you can recover.

Whenever you are faced with a tee shot that has a code red in the vicinity, your first thought should be, "How can I take that out of play?" The answer is always the same: by taking a line that runs away from the trouble (but will still put you in the fairway) and by playing a club that increases your chances of hitting the ball straight (i.e., a club with more loft than your driver). If you are uncertain about what you are going to do once you get over the ball, or if you are unsure about your target, you probably will not like the outcome of the shot. If you have to sacrifice thirty yards off the tee to avoid a code red, do it!

How much and how often you decide to play away from hazards depend on two things: your ability as a player, and how honest you are with yourself about your capabilities. The wise golfer knows his limits *and* knows that testing them or trying to stretch them is seldom a good choice. However, does that mean you should never choose to play along a daring line that runs close to a code red? It depends on your reason for playing. If you like to challenge yourself and would rather go for it, then have at it, and have fun. Sometimes the brave attempts work out. Remember: Most attempts at miracle shots fail.

Any time you feel extra pressure to hit the ball straight, always remember that the more loft a club has, the better your chances of hitting it straight. Playing a longer club for your second shot beats reloading from the tee, which will be your third stroke.

Bob Estes *Learn from previous rounds on the same course.*

Led the PGA TOUR in sand save percentage (70.3) in 1997.

"In 1994 I won the Texas Open at Oak Hills in San Antonio. The fifteenth hole has a tree right in the middle of the fairway that you have to carry to get your ball on the green. The first three rounds of the tournament, I hit that tree. On the last day, I was finally able to clear it on my second *shot and two-putt for a birdie. The problem the first three days was that I hit my drive too far, and the 2-iron I was hitting couldn't clear the tree. In the last round, I laid back off the tee so I could hit a 3-wood on the second shot and clear the tree. That's what I did, and I won the tournament. As you can see, the longest shot isn't always the best shot."*

Here are a few more points to consider when playing from the tee:

- If, on a hole that doglegs, you think you can hit the ball through the fairway with your driver, do not hit with your driver. For the most part, doglegs require only two straight shots: one to the point where the bend is, and the next one to the green. Few doglegs are so abrupt or so gradual that it helps to curve the ball around the bend. Just play it straight.

- Except for expert players, it is seldom a good idea to choose a line that requires you to carry a tree or trees to bite off some of a dogleg. Remember: The closer the tree is, the less likely you are to carry it.

- If you are faced with a forced carry off the tee, think carefully. Very seldom does a forced carry over water require you to carry the entire body of water. Unless a course is poorly designed, there is usually a target area in the fairway that allows shorter hitters to play the hole. Always remember: When you play a brave line, the ball is more likely to be off line as its distance from you increases. That last little bit you try to bite off is at the same point where your ball is running out of steam and curving most dramatically.

- Typically, teeing up on the side of the tee box opposite the side of the fairway your target is on gives you a better view of the hole. If your target is on the left side of the fairway, consider teeing up on the right side of the tee. If your target is on the right side of the fairway, consider teeing up on the left side of the tee box. This assumes a straight or slightly bending ball flight. If you are prone to big hooks and slices, stick to the middle of the tee or try teeing up on the same side as your target and allowing for your typical ball flight.

Payne Stewart

In between clubs, look for the trouble.

Won the 1989 PGA Championship and the 1991 U.S. Open.

"When you are in between clubs, focus on any trouble that is long or short of the hole. If there's trouble short, take the longer club. If there's trouble long, take the shorter club."

Layup Shots, Approach Shots, and Tee Shots on Par 3s

Your strategy for approach shots depends primarily on the length of the shot. When it comes to distance, there are two types of shots: the Yes ("Yes, I can hit it that far") and the No ("No, I cannot hit it that far"). The distance in question is the distance between your ball and the green—more specifically, the spot on the green where you would like your ball to end up.

First consider the No. An approach shot is a No when you cannot comfortably fly a hazard between you and the green, or when the combined carry and roll of your longest shot will not reach the green. There should be no doubt in your mind that you can fly a given hazard with an ordinary (not extraordinary) shot if you decide to try to carry a hazard between you and the green. If you are not 100 percent sure you can make the distance, you should lay up.

If you are going to lay up short of a hazard, first make sure that you do, in fact, lay up. Do not try to hit the ball as close as you possibly can to the hazard. An unexpectedly long bounce will put you *in* the hazard.

When you are laying up short of a hazard, you need to know two distances: the distance between you and the hazard, and the distance between you and the hole. The distance between you and the hazard is important, because you will probably want to play so your ball will land at least fifteen yards short of the hazard. Note that this is where you want the ball to end up. You must consider carry and roll when laying up. You need to know the distance to the hole so you leave yourself a shot of a length you are very confident in playing. For example, if you hate playing seventy-yard wedge shots, but feel great about 100-yard wedge shots, take that into consideration when laying up. As a result, you may want to lay back farther from the hazard than fifteen yards if a shorter layup shot will leave you with an approach of the distance you like.

The same is true for No approaches that do not involve a hazard and are a simple matter of distance. You should play them to a distance you are comfortable with for the subsequent shot. If you decide to hit the longest shot you can, remember that the longer the shot you attempt, the more likely you are to have trouble. The purpose of hitting a layup shot is to set up the next shot, one where you have a wedge in your hand and a clean fairway lie that allows you to control the ball. The longer the layup shot, the more likely you are to hit it into the rough, reducing your control over the short shot that remains.

Yes approaches also are largely controlled by the distance of the shot you face. A Yes is a shot you feel you can bounce onto the green or fly to the green. Because the goal is to get the ball close to the hole, the question facing you on any Yes approach shot is how aggressive you should be in making the hole your target. Consider this question first from the perspective of distance. The farther you are from the hole, the less you can depend on making a completely accurate shot. Focus on a specific target

Bernhard Langer prepares to hit his approach shot from the fairway. An accurate layup shot left Langer just short of the bunker.

Inside the Ropes

Skip Kendall   *Recognize the slope of the green before hitting your approach shot.*

Won twice on the NIKE TOUR and finished fourteenth in greens-in-regulation on the PGA TOUR in 1997.

"When you are playing an approach shot from the fairway it is important to try to judge the general slope of the green so you know which way the ball is going to roll after it lands. If the hole is cut on the left and the green looks like it slopes to the left, then I'm not going to play the ball so it lands on a straight line to the hole. Instead, I'm going to land it right of the hole so it works toward the hole once it is on the ground. I think almost any player can look at a hole and see that sort of thing."

on the green, as several TOUR players recommended in Chapter 6, and give yourself the widest margin of error either way. As a general rule, the farther you get from the green, the wiser it is to play to the middle of the green and ignore the position of the hole. Do not be lazy. Pick the exact spot where you would like the ball to land and then go through your routine. Do not confuse playing for the middle of the green with playing an easy shot, because it is not.

The closer you get to the hole, the more likely it is that the flagstick will be your target. The shorter the iron, the truer the line of flight and the more predictable the roll of the ball once it hits the green. As you move into the middle irons, you can think about playing directly toward the flag, but there are always factors to consider. Remember: The farther you are from the hole, the more likely that these variables will affect your shot selection. Do not forget to factor in your ball-flight tendencies.

With water on the left and the pin in the same proximity, Tom Kite takes the pond out of play by playing for the right side of the green. He will be unconcerned if the ball misses the green, as long as it's dry.

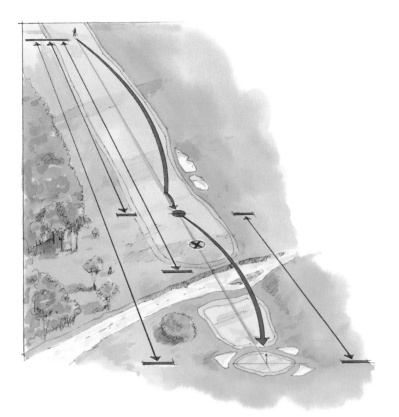

When you lay up short of a hazard, keep two things in mind: Lay up short enough so that there's no chance the ball will bounce in, and lay up to a distance that will leave you your favorite shot.

- The first factor is the lie. If you are in the rough or if your ball is sitting poorly in the fairway, the flag is only an option if you are hitting a wedge shot of some sort. Otherwise, play for the middle of the green. Obviously, this is not a factor if you are playing from the tee on a par-3.

- If there is a hazard just short of the green and if the hole is cut in front of the green, playing directly at the hole should be a consideration only with a wedge or a 9-iron from the fairway. No matter what club you play, consider playing it long, beyond the flag.

- If there is a hazard on one side of the green and if the hole is cut on the same side of the green, play for the middle of the green no matter what club you use. If the hole is cut in the center and if you are playing from a clean lie, and if there is no wind or if the wind is blowing away from the hazard, you can fire at the flag with any short iron. If the wind is blowing toward the hazard, play for the opposite side of the green.

- If there is water or sand behind the green and if the hole is cut deep, your target should be the center of the green with short irons, the front of the green with middle irons.

- If the hole is cut on either side of the green and if there is no hazard on that side and no real downside to missing the green on that side

Inside the Ropes
Scott Hoch
Under the gun, focus on the fundamentals.

Won eight PGA TOUR events, and since 1982 has finished in the top forty on the money list every year except one.

"One of the best shots I ever played was a chip-in for an eagle to win the Greater Milwaukee Open in 1997. When you are under pressure like that, everyone always wants to know if you should make big adjustments. If that's the way you think, then there must be something wrong with the way you set up for every other shot. You cannot bring anything different under pressure. You should be thinking about the same points you always do because they should be your best points, and it allows you to focus."

Bob Murphy   *When you are in between clubs, the decision depends on your tendencies.*

Finished second among Senor PGA TOUR players in the All-Around category in 1996.

"If I'm stuck between clubs, a lot of my decision depends on the situation and where the hole is cut. If it is Sunday afternoon and I'm pumped up and in the hunt, I can assure you I'm going to hit that 8-iron based simply on adrenaline. Any other time, it depends on the pin placement. If it is back

right, I'll probably go with the 7-iron because I typically hit a soft fade. If the hole is cut on the left, I do not want to hit a fade, so I'll take the 8-iron and hit it hard. That's because when I press hard on that 8-iron, I'm going to be more likely to hit it straight or maybe even with a little draw. You have to make the decision based on the scenario at any given time."

(remember that heavy rough is tough to chip out of!), you can be more aggressive at playing to the flag with middle and short irons.

- Any time the flag is in the center of the green, you should fire right at it with a middle or a short iron. If you are playing a longer approach you may want to allow for some roll—that is, pick a target on the green short of the hole.

Managing the Rest of Your Game

The game is not over once you reach the green or the area around it. Lose focus at that point and the shots will add up in a hurry. The following points will help you finish off each hole strongly:

- If you are in a bunker, do not assume that you should play toward the hole. If you have a difficult stance or lie, play toward the part of the green that offers the

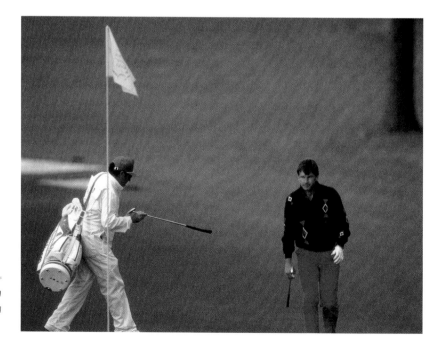

Nick Faldo is a modern-day Ben Hogan in his methodical approach to attacking a course.

Starting in 1958, Arnold Palmer won the Masters every other year for seven years—1958, 1960, 1962, and 1964. Ranks fourth, winning 60 times on the PGA TOUR.

"I remember one time when I was about fourteen or fifteen years old, and I was hitting some balls. Well, it is not like it is out here on TOUR with all of these finely manicured courses. I was hitting balls from rough that was a few inches deep or deeper. My father came along while I was hitting those balls and I said, 'Geez, I wish I could get someplace better than this to hit balls.' Well, he got madder than a hornet and said, 'Boy, every shot you hit isn't going to be from a perfect lie.' I got the message."

surest escape from the sand. If you cannot play toward the green, play to a spot that will leave you an easy chip.

- If you have a bad lie in the greenside rough, your first goal is to get the ball on the green. Do not try shots that combine bad lies and unfavorable hole positions (i.e., the hole is close to you). It is more important to get the ball on the green than it is to try to get it close, because once you are on the green, your lie will be good. If you leave an attempted "cute" shot in the rough, you will be faced with the same shot you just had.

- Focus, focus, focus on seemingly simple chip shots. Give yourself a cue such as "Keep your head still" to avoid chili-dipping the easy ones.

- Observe what is going on around you if you think it will teach you something about a shot you have to play next. If you can learn something about the speed or the line of a putt by watching someone else's ball, pay attention. If you are playing a chip or a pitch from the same area where someone else is and if that player is going first, watch where the ball lands, the height of the shot, and the roll.

- When chipping or putting, avoid leaving yourself downhill putts of more than a few inches. Leaving the ball below the hole is almost always a good idea because uphill putts break less, and you can be more aggressive with your speed.

- Almost any shot you play with a partial swing from the rough is going to run a fair amount. A chip or a pitch from the fairway or fringe can be controlled a bit. From the rough, play for the run.

Playing Your Best When You're Outmatched

I got to a point where hard work didn't seem to accomplish a whole lot. I was spinning my wheels. So I focused more on the mental part.

— David Edwards

Are you intimidated when faced with playing a superior opponent in match play? As you stand on the first tee do you think, "How am I going to beat this guy? He's a better player than me."

You imagine how awful it would be if you embarrassed yourself by not playing the 15th hole because the match was already over. Your palms start to sweat, you feel a queasiness in your stomach, your mouth feels dry, and you worry about topping your first shot of the day.

Here are some mental strategies that will help you overcome fear, intimidation—and pressure you may be feeling—when playing a superior opponent.

Believe in Your Ability to Win

Confidence is the best antidote to pressure, fear and intimidation. Focus on your ability to win holes, and that if you win enough of them, you can win the match. When Steve Scott played in the championship match of the 1996 U.S. Amateur championship, he faced Tiger Woods, a formidable foe and defending champion. But he gave Tiger all he could handle before being nipped at the very end of the 36-hole match. Don't talk yourself into losing before you tee it up.

Don't Focus on Your Opponent

The more you watch your opponent's game, the more you get caught up in thinking, "How am I going to beat this player? His or her game looks so solid." This is where intimidation begins-

when you fixate on your opponent's reputation or superior abilities. This only hurts your confidence. Rather, focus on what you need to do to prepare and play your best. Quietly find your game and play it to the hilt.

Play Your Game, Not Your Opponent's

Steve Scott got to the final match by playing his own game and his own style of golf. He didn't change his strategy because he was playing a superior player. Follow his example: Decide how you are going to attack the course and stick to your game plan. For example, if your opponent pulls out a driver on a hole and you have already decided to hit a three wood, don't let your opponent's choice change your mind on how you planned to play the hole.

Play Conservative, But Aggressive

This advice may appear contradictory, but it isn't. You always want to give yourself a chance—of making par or birdie, or even bogie, if that will win the hole. Keep your ball in play. Select a tee shot that gives you the best chance to find the fairway. When you have a short iron into the green take dead aim; fire at the pin and try to get it very close. Be aggressive when a scoring opportunity presents itself. But if you have a long iron into the green, aim at the middle of the green and rely on your putter to give you the score you need to win the hole.

Choose and Keep a Positive Attitude

Stay positive. Many players start with a positive attitude, but as the round progresses their attitudes become negative when they make mistakes. This only causes more mistakes. A poor shot on one hole represents a very small percentage of the hundreds of thousands of shots you will make. One bad hole is finitesimal, simply too small a sample to judge yourself harshly, that is, as a poor player. Do not give poor play on a single hole the power to change your mindset from positive to negative. Think to yourself, "I'm a good player, I just made a bad shot." Ben Hogan once said, "The most important shot in golf is your next one." Good advice: You can't get back the last shot, so concentrate on the next one. Play on and stay positive.

Increasing Your Motivation

Golfers who lack motivation either do not apply themselves with the needed effort or do not have a clear vision of their goals. In an extreme case, a person who lacks motivation has learned early in life that he or she doesn't need to work as hard as others to be successful.

Undermotivated golfers often feel that his or her success is a result of natural talent, and that practice won't have an influence on the quality of his play or outcome of his match. His confidence in his innate ability helps him perform well in competition, but his lack of work ethic keeps him from being the best he can be.

The player who lacks motivation needs to understand that he can improve his game with increased effort and better work habits. An undermotivated player has to start thinking about doing some things he has not done in the past.

Talent and hard work equal success. Physical talent without hard work and dedication is a waste. Success is achieved when a player with physical abilities applies a strong work ethic to improve his or her skills. Ability is inborn but

Think to yourself, I'm a good player, I just made a bad shot.

skills are learned, modified and improved through practice.

Focus more on your goals. Undermotivated players often lack direction. Begin to set goals. Goals give you a sense of purpose and direction in practice and increase effort and persistence in a task. Set both practice and competitive goals, such as number of putts, number of fairways hit, greens in regulation in a round.

Increase pride and joy in practice. Players who lack motivation often think that practice is boring and lacks a challenge. Find ways to make practice more challenging, such as playing mind games. Test yourself by seeing how many balls you can hit to an imagined fairway on the range, or how many greens you can hit in a row. Challenge yourself by hitting different types of shots to the same target, and recovery shots. Practice with a buddy and compete against him or her. Play "Call Your Shot," in which you and your buddy take turns selecting a certain type of shot (fade, draw, punch, etc.) that each has to hit. Select ten balls and see who can get the most balls closest the pin or in the fairway. Play eighteen holes on the practice green hitting putts with your eyes closed. Put a small wager on the game.

Work on weaknesses. Assess the areas of your game that are strong and weak and dedicate yourself to working on the weaker areas. This will give you a reason to keep coming back to the practice range—to bring all parts of your game up to parity with your strengths.

Work on your mental game. To reach your full potential you must work on the mental side of your game. You have all that it takes to play your best: ability, skill, motivation, but you need effective attitudes and beliefs to become a mentally tough and complete player.

Berhnard Langer, the finest German
golfer ever.

Crossing a hazard the easy way.

13

Practicing *to* Improve

P ractice means different things to different golfers. The image of the TOUR player practicing is one of mountains of balls piled up on the practice tee, being pounded until the last bit of sunlight has faded. It is the stuff of legend: Ben Hogan muttering that he dug his game out of the ground; players hitting balls in the twilight until their hands bled, players becoming known as the last one off the practice tee each day. This image is not entirely true to life. Although TOUR players do spend a lot of time hitting full shots, they spend just as much time working on their short games. And they practice with a purpose; they always have a clear goal when they head to the practice tee.

It is a given that you do not have a fraction of the time to practice your game that a TOUR player does. After all, it is his job to practice. In all probability, the best you can do is squeeze in a few hours a month working on your game. This chapter will help you make sure every minute you can devote to practicing will be a minute well spent. Remember, perfect practice is the key to improvement.

The world's most recognizable player, Tiger Woods, on the practice range.

Giving Purpose to Your Practice

You have probably read this before, but it bears repeating: You will gain nothing by grabbing your driver and a bucket of balls and firing them off in jackhammer fashion. In fact, it will hurt you more than it helps you, because the lack of focus simply means you will be ingraining poor habits deeper into your game. You should always practice with a clear purpose in mind, even if you only have ten minutes to do so.

To establish a purpose for any practice session, it helps to understand the three basic goals of practicing. One goal is to warm up before a round; another goal is to work on ball flight—that is, hitting shots on target; and a third is to work on fundamentals and pay less attention to ball flight. The first type, warm-up practice, should occur before any round you play. The other two types depend on how you feel about your game at any given time. The second type, which helps you connect your setup, tempo, alignment, and timing, is probably more practical for most players with limited time—think of it as game maintenance. The third type of practice is more likely to make sense to you at the start of each season, or if you plan to overhaul your game completely. If you are planning a complete overhaul, however, you are going to need considerably more time than you will with the maintenance-type practice, and it will help considerably if you do this under the watchful eye of a PGA professional.

Warm-up Practice

Your objective just before playing a round of golf is to prepare your body to play. You know you cannot just grab your clubs and head to the first tee without giving your

No one in the history of the game has practiced with more diligence than Tom Kite. It paid off in an historic career.

Ben Crenshaw *The pre-round warm-up should help you find your rhythm for the day.*

Won the 1984 and the 1995 Masters, and has long been regarded as one of golf's best putters.

"When I begin my pre-round warm-up routine, I'm usually looking to establish my rhythm and tempo for the day. I'm trying to get those muscles loose and get a feel for my motion that day and how fast or slow things are moving and maybe get a grip on my timing. That's all I do for the first twenty-five balls or so I hit because, as all golfers know, you feel different every day, and your hands do not always feel right on the club. When you feel like that, you've got to spend a little time finding your grip pressure. I pay attention to ball contact and where it's going, but I'm focused more on tempo and balance.

"I find it's helpful to start out with my short irons, my wedges. The shorter swing motion is less complicated and a little easier to get a feel for. Because you're trying to get your feel for the day, you like to keep things simple. Some days that feel comes more quickly than it does on other days, and when it comes more quickly, you can speed up your warm-up if you want. Some days, though, it just takes a good while to find that feel.

"When I move to the putting green, I'm doing the same thing. I'm looking for distance control on almost every day I putt, and you only do that by touch and how far you see the ball going and making adjustments accordingly. The key when you are on the putting green is making that motion feel smooth. I try to make both halves of my putting stroke feel equally smooth. If I feel a hit, then I back off and say, 'I've got to swing this putter more.'"

body a chance to rev up. A lot of people would never dream of using a machine or driving a car without giving it a chance to warm up, but they expect their bodies to perform at the drop of a hat. Warm-up practice might not guarantee that you will play the greatest round of your life, but it does guarantee that you will play the first couple of holes much better than if you did not warm up. It will also force you to stop using the excuse "I'm not loose yet." In addition to preparing your body, warm-up practice lets you gradually shift your mental focus away from the details of everyday life and toward the idea that you are about to play golf.

Consider this caveat regarding pre-round practice: On the practice tee before a round of golf is *not* the place to be attempting to fix or to change your swing. The potential for negative results is too great, and the resulting impact on your psyche will not help your game. It is better to approach the first tee feeling loose and prepared for anything than it is to approach it worrying that your swing is not working.

The following elements are the keys to a pre-round warm-up session:

Follow the stretching program outlined in Chapter 15. It will take you five or ten minutes, and it is invaluable in protecting yourself against injury.

Swing the club back and forth without the ball. Take any club, and starting from your address position, swing the club back as far as it feels comfortable—do not reach for any backswing position—then swing the club through to the finish. When you reach your finish position, start the

Chris Perry *Change your practice routine so you do not get bored.*

Was the 1994 NIKE TOUR Player of the Year.

"I try not to practice the same every time I'm on the range. When I'm warming up in the morning before I play, I'm just trying to get a sense of rhythm for the day. When I'm practicing to work on my game, like in the beginning of the week before Thursday [the first tournament day], then I work on mechanics. Things like staying on my right side or keeping my head still. Once the tournament starts, I do not like to work on stuff like that.

"Even when you are warming up, though, you should hit enough balls to get loose. A lot of everyday players do not take enough time to get loose; they don't hit enough balls. They hit a few wedges and a couple of 7-irons, and they're ready to go. It would really help if they hit more. It doesn't have to be intense; it just helps to get loose.

"Now, if I'm playing well, I don't bother to practice much after the round. I might hit a few bunker shots if I wasn't doing well out of the sand that day. But once the tournament starts, I'm not out here beating balls for two hours after the round. That'll just wear you out. Once the tournament starts, it's about focusing on the mental part. It's not about the quantity of the practice I get, it's about the quality of it."

club right back to your position at the top. Eventually you will feel your range of motion begin to increase.

Start to hit balls, but do so initially with the sole purpose of getting a feel for your clubs for the day. Work from the shorter clubs up to the longer ones. Beginning with your sand wedge, hit a few flip wedges about twenty yards or so. Every three or four balls, move your range out about ten yards. After you get out to seventy or eighty yards, hit a few full wedge shots. Do not get too caught up in the idea of hitting these shots perfectly. If it helps, tee them up to ensure clean contact and allow you to focus solely on swinging the club.

Sandy Lyle stretches and gets loose before his pre-round warm-up session. All players, no matter the skill level, should do the same.

Greg Norman practices putting aided by the experienced eye of his caddie. The caddie is positioned where he can toss the balls back to Norman and keep an eye on his stroke.

After you feel good and loose, work your way through the set, hitting just a few balls with every other club in the bag. Do not hit too many with any one club, especially your driver. The idea is not to hit forty drivers on the practice tee. You only need a couple to give you a feel for the club that day. Hit more than that, and you are increasing the chances that you will develop a bad feeling about that club for the day.

Move over to the practice green and try to get a feel for long putts and the speed of the greens. Trying to get a range of feel for long putts is probably more beneficial than hitting thirty putts from inside ten feet, which you have a better feel for naturally. Hit a handful of chip shots if you feel like it.

Once you are loose, keep moving until you start the round. Do not sit down and give yourself a chance to tighten up.

Target Practice

Think of target practice as the way to keep your game in tune. The key to making this type of practice successful is not to burden yourself with excessive swing thoughts. One simple swing key is more than sufficient. Target practice is good if you can sneak away to hit balls for a half hour at lunchtime or after work. This is really ball-flight practice, and ball flight is the basis for most of the adjustments you make in your game.

Before you begin target practice, make sure you stretch and have your full range of motion available to you.

Start with targets close to you. If the practice area has flags or "greens" you can use them as your targets. If it does not, pick out an area where you want to land the ball.

Make sure you stop after each ball and go through your pre-shot routine, selecting your target and intermediate target, getting the clubface lined up properly, and stepping into the shot properly. (If you need a refresher in this, see Chapter 3.)

One way to keep your interest level up is to change targets for every shot you hit. This will help prevent your practice outing from turning into a slugfest, because it more closely resembles what happens during a round of golf (when you very seldom hit any club other than the putter two times in succession).

An excellent way to target practice, and another way of keeping things interesting, is to "play" a round of golf right there on the practice tee. Place your bag nearby, and mentally place yourself on the first tee of a course you are very familiar with. After clearly seeing the hole and establishing a target for the tee shot, pull the club you would use to play the shot, and play a teed ball just as you would if you were actually on the course. Because you know the course well, you will be able to determine the outcome of your tee shot. If you think it would be in the fairway, then play the type of shot you would play from the fairway. If you think it would have ended up in the rough, play the type of shot you would play from the rough. If you think you hit it in

Billy Ray Brown   *When your time is limited, practice your alignment.*

Won three PGA TOUR events. Ranked tenth in eagles in 1997.

"I know a lot of everyday golfers do not have any time at all to practice—people have so much going on in their lives. If you can only sneak a little time each week to practice, my advice is to work on your alignment. Lay some clubs on the ground to use as a guide; that way your swing can develop around a solid setup position. It seems like whenever I happen to walk by a practice range on pro-am days, I see people whacking balls out and not caring about their alignment. They're just practicing their swing, but you can't practice your swing without a target. You need to be target-oriented when you're on the practice tee. Laying down those clubs helps you do that."

the trees, punch out of the trees. You can and should make this more fun by deliberating over each shot just as you would on the course—that is, consider the lie and the wind and the club selection. Go through your pre-shot routine before each shot, and put the club back in the bag after each shot. If you hit the middle of the green, give yourself two putts, and if you think you hit it tight, give yourself a one-putt birdie.

It is worth repeating: When you are doing target practice, do not worry too much about your swing. Focus on your routine and the flight of the ball.

You should have a target for every single practice shot you hit. Mindlessly flailing away at a bucket of balls will accomplish nothing other than ingraining poor habits into your game.

Lee Janzen   *Try Hogan's technique to prepare for pressure.*

Won the U.S. Open two times (1993 and 1998).

"You hear a lot about grip pressure when a player is under the gun. I know Ben Hogan practiced trying to grip the club as tight as he possibly could so that when he got nervous and tense he wouldn't be able to grip it any tighter than he had already practiced. Hogan worked a lot on his grip. He spent the first five minutes of every practice session making sure his grip was right, and then he didn't worry about it after that. That's really good advice. If you work on the proper grip for the first five minutes every time you practice, then you shouldn't have a problem with your grip. You should have a consistent grip and at least have the club in the right spot. "

Swing Practice

Swing practice is a little more heavy-duty than the other two, but it accomplishes something very important. Swing practice allows you to revisit your swing fundamentals in a mind-set devoted entirely to those fundamentals without concerns regarding

The quickest way to improve your game is to work closely with a teacher in whom you have great confidence.

Jimmy Powell   *Use video to check your swing.*

Won four times on the SENIOR PGA TOUR.

"No one should know your golf swing better than you do. The golf swing needs to be such a finely tuned movement, but it all happens so fast that the naked eye cannot catch it in motion. It's one thing to have a good feel for your swing, but to see it can be even more helpful. That's why I've been *working with a camera on my swing since 1960. When people ask me who my teacher is, I say, "Sony," because the camera does not lie. I like to check for little things starting to creep into my swing so I can catch them before they cause me big problems. I call them "gradualisms," and I check for them every two or three weeks on camera."*

the flight of your ball. Because fundamental errors are responsible for nearly every error a golfer can make, it makes great sense to work hard on these things at the beginning of each season and to devote time to it now and again, especially if you hit a spot where the game has become a struggle.

An important thing to remember about swing practice is that you should do it only on the practice tee. If you try this type of thought process while you are playing, you will drive yourself crazy and almost certainly foul up your game. Even if you are attempting a swing overhaul, leave your swing thoughts on the practice tee; while you are on the course, use your playing thoughts.

In swing practice you will be aided greatly by the knowing eye of a PGA professional, because you cannot see what is happening while you are swinging the club. When you are working on things in a piecemeal fashion—isolating various elements of your swing—it is important not to be overly concerned about the flight of the ball. Judge whether the practice session is successful by seeing how persistent you are at remembering to check each element of your fundamentals and by how aware you are of the specific element you are thinking about during any given swing.

The fundamentals you will be working on during this type of practice are explained in Chapters 3 and 4. The biggest thing you can do to make your swing practice focused and productive is to create a little "swing station" on the ground, using your clubs. Lay one club on the ground just outside the ball and parallel to your target line. Lay another club along your toes, to use as a reference in positioning your feet, hips, and shoulders. The two clubs should be parallel. Then take a third club and use it to mark ball position for whatever club you are swinging. You can position this third club perpendicular to the other two, and you can put it either between your legs or outside the club you are using to mark the target line. If you hit every shot off a tee it will prevent you from tearing up the ground and having to move frequently. It will also help you make clean contact every time, so that you will not lose focus worrying about hitting shots heavy or thin.

Short-Game Practice

The practice techniques above focus almost exclusively on hitting long shots. You should never forget that you play slightly more than half your shots from within 100 yards of the hole. You should not neglect to practice chipping and pitching and bunker play. In fact, if you feel like practicing and you only have fifteen minutes to spare, focus solely on some element of your short game. For instance, practice only bunker shots for fifteen minutes. It will help.

Figure out how much total time you have to practice per month or per week, and devote almost half your time to short-game practice, including putting. You can work on any of the things outlined in the chapters on the short game and putting.

Here are a few suggestions for putting practice:

Gary Player always said that right before heading for the first tee he would make a series of two-foot putts, just to imprint in his memory the image of the ball going into the hole.

Stuart Appleby *Use a striped ball and string to practice your putting.*

Was thirty-sixth in scoring average in 1997 (70.37).

"When you are standing sideways and looking at the hole, it is not natural. It is more natural for you to look straight ahead. As a result, it is tough to get yourself to look properly at the hole. Because of how we stand next to the ball, we have a straight putt but we do not see it as straight. What I do is I find a straight putt, and I have a string about two inches off the ground running from my ball to the hole. The string is tied to two thin metal sticks I can poke in the green.

Then, I can get a feel for what my setup is like on a dead straight putt. It gives me a reference to aim at. So that I can see how well the ball is rolling on that line, I use a marker to make a stripe around the center of the ball. Then I put the line under the string, aimed right at the hole. If I am mis-hitting the putt, the ball wobbles, and it tells me I'm coming across it or pulling it. It helps me find my takeaway, but more important, it helps show what's wrong with my follow-through."

Many TOUR players do a drill on the putting green where they start by holing a certain number of putts from one foot (say five putts), and then move back to two feet, three feet, etc., all the way back to ten feet. Any time they miss, they go back to the beginning. Another version of this is to surround the hole with balls at the same distance and hole them all, then move back a few feet. If you miss, you start over.

One thing to remember about practicing your putting is that it is hard on your back. Remember to take periodic breaks in the action, or you will be hurting later in the day and maybe even the following day.

Practicing the Unexpected

Because every golfer is familiar with the feeling of ending up in a place he never dreamed he could, it pays to be prepared. You are more likely to pull off an awkward shot if you are familiar with what it feels like. If the place where you practice has some little hills, practice hitting shots from all sorts of awkward lies. You do not need a steady diet of it—just do it once in a while so that you know the feeling.

Bonus tip: If you are a slicer, try hitting practice shots with the ball above your feet. It will familiarize you with the feeling of a draw swing. If you hook the ball, try hitting practice shots with the ball below your feet. It will teach you what a fade swing feels like.

Practicing the unexpected is good for your short game as well. When you are practicing your chipping, give yourself some bad lies and try to play to close-in hole positions. Give yourself awkward lies from all sorts of slopes. It is the only way you will be ready for them when it is time to play.

Kenny Perry *You have to practice the feel for speed.*

Won three times on the PGA TOUR and finished eighteenth on the money list in 1996. Ranked third in eagles in 1998.

"The speed of putts is the most important thing. You can make a lot of putts if the ball is rolling soft around the hole— you have got four and a quarter inches that the ball can fall into. If you get it moving too quickly, it will lip out unless it is dead center, and even then, it might hit the back of the hole and bounce out. Maybe you are born with a sense of how much pace to put on a putt, but I do not think so. It is something you have got to learn and work at. I spend a lot of time on the practice green hitting thirty- and forty-foot putts so I can develop a sense of feel for the speed. I see guys come up and drop three balls six feet from the hole on the practice green, then they head to the first tee. How in the world are you going to get a feel for speed from three-foot and six-foot putts? Anyone can figure out how hard to hit them. It is the long ones you have got to practice to build a feel for speed."

Practicing with a Pro

If you seek out a PGA professional and say you would like him to be your swing coach or that you would like to work with him to improve your game, it will pay you huge dividends. Nearly every TOUR player has a swing coach. If the world's best players can learn something from a teacher, you can, too. Working with a PGA professional also gives you a partner— someone to tell you that you are doing well, someone to cajole you into working a little harder or at least to keep to a schedule, someone to watch you and see what you cannot. It could be the smartest thing you ever do for your golf game. If you have time, ask to take some playing lessons. You will be amazed at how the on-course thought process is different from the practice-range thought process. You will learn to think like a professional out on the course.

The busiest place at any PGA TOUR event is the practice tee. Before a round, players are typically just trying to warm up. After the round, they work to correct swing flaws they encountered during the round.

Russ Cochran   *A drill for practicing long putts.*

Finished tenth on the PGA TOUR money list in 1991. Tied for fourteenth in Greens-in-Regulation in 1997.

"When I'm practicing long putts on the practice green, I use a little drill that helps me get a feel for the speed of putts. After I hit a putt, before I look up, I say to myself, 'That's a foot short,' or 'it's just right,' or however it felt to me. Then I look up at the ball. If it felt a foot short but was actually three feet short, then I get a feel for the difference between my feel and the reality, and I make whatever adjustments I need to make for the week."

Practicing alone at the driving range or in your backyard can get monotonous. To spice things up, set specific goals to challenge yourself and reshape tedious drills into engaging exercises. Here are some guidelines for setting your practice goals:

1. *Set realistic goals to improve your game.* Do not pull out your driver and say you're going to pound balls until you hit one over 300 yards. Instead, create lateral boundaries and strive to hit nine out ten balls within that designated area.

2. *Focus on daily mini-goals that will help you achieve a long-term objectives.* For example, your goal for the day might be to make three of ten putts from twelve feet, but by the end of the month, you want to be able to make six putts from twelve feet.

3. *Allot yourself a limited amount of time to attain a goal.* If you are chipping from twenty feet, give yourself ten minutes to sink one. The next time out, allow only eight minutes.

4. *Use specific measurable goals to evaluate your progression.* Instead of saying, "My goal is to make as many putts as I can today," say, "My goals is to make three twenty-five foot putts in a row before I leave today."

5. *Focus on the positive instead of the negative.* Instead of saying, "My goal is not to shank any balls today," say, "My goal is to hit these practice balls on the center of the clubface."

6. *Revise and reset your goals with regularity.*

Improving the Quality of Practice

All my life I've tried to hit practice shots with great care. I try to have a clear-cut purpose in mind on every swing. I always practice as I intend to play.

— Jack Nicklaus

The time you spend on the practice tee and green is proportional to the improvement you make in your game, but only if it is quality practice. Many amateur golfers think that mindlessly hitting driver after drive as far as they can is good practice. Good exercise, maybe, effective practice, no. Getting the most out of your practice means giving complete attention to each shot. Practice with the intention of improving an area of your game and maximizing transfer of what you've learned to the course, rather than just smashing balls as far as possible.

If you are to transfer what you learn on the practice tee to on-course situations you must hit shots in a variety of conditions similar to those you encounter on the golf course. Healthy practice also involves switching clubs often and practicing different types of shots in a variety of situations. The best practice relates to your play on the golf course and accelerates learning. It also combines your mental skills training with your physical practice so you can readily use your mental skills to achieve optimal performance on the golf course.

Quality Practice Makes Perfect Practice

Each time you hit a ball, you should focus on accomplishing something specific, and be totally immersed in that purpose. Your goal can be as simple as checking your ball position or as complicated as working on a major mechanical change, such as grooving a one-piece takeaway.

Professional golfers have already mastered the fundamentals of the swing. When they practice, they work on fine tuning the swing and making minor adjustments. Golf is their livelihood, so they practice nearly every day. Recreational golfers usually practice the fundamentals of the swing (stance, posture, grip, backswing, downswing, and so on). Other commitments at home, work or school make it impossible for the recreational golfer to spend two or more hours per day practicing. This makes quality practice time even more important for the recreational player. Thus, the level of skill and the amount of time you have to practice dictate the purpose and scope of your practice.

When you practice you should have a specific idea of what you are trying to improve. Know what the correct move feels like and how it looks, and what the wrong move feel like and how it looks. Use a video camera, step in front of a mirror, or ask an instructor or friend to give you some feedback.

One Step at a Time

Your mind can only hold one thought at a time. It is impossible to think about grip pressure, posture, and the plane of your swing at the same time. Develop good practice habits and limit your work to making one specific change in your swing at a time. After you have mastered a particular change move to the next area you want to improve. Each part of the golf swing influences another part: the swing is a chain reaction. Later you can put the pieces together into a complete whole for an improved overall swing.

Practice versus preround preparation

How you practice depends on the purpose of your practice. A player who is practicing to improve his game has different goals than a player who is preparing to play a round. The former may want to improve mechanics while the latter is really warming up.

Preround practice is not only to loosen up your muscles but also to find your rhythm and tempo for play that day. It is also to find a shot pattern that you can trust for the day. A shot pattern is the consistency of ball flight from shot to shot. For example, if you normally fade the ball from left to right, can you be confident that flight patter will happen on the course from what you experience in warm-up?

Preround practice is not the time to make a mechanical change in your swing. You won't correct the problem in the limited time you have, and you certainly won't be able to ingrain the change in your memory. The best you can do at this point is to find a swing key that helps you produce a consistent pattern with your shots for that day. If you have a good idea of the pattern of your shots, you can play that shot for the day and later work on making a swing change.

Developing Practice Goals

There are two types of practice goals. The first is physical goals, which are goals you set for improving the quality of your putting stroke and/or swing technique. Making a mechanical swing change, working on your swing tempo, or generally focusing on the movement pattern of your swing are examples of areas that can be used to formulate physical performance goals.

The second type is outcome goals, which relate to the result of your performance. Examples

Pre-round practice is not the time to make a mechanical change in your swing.

include how many consecutive putts you can make from three feet, hitting seven of ten nine-irons within thirty feet of the target, or hitting four of five drivers into a specified target area. It is easier to evaluate whether you have achieved an outcome goal than a performance goal.

Physical performance goals are difficult to evaluate because you don't receive clear-cut feedback about how well you are doing unless you have an instructor continuously watching you. When you set goals to improve your swing technique, set your goals based on the amount of time you want to devote to working on each one.

For example, if you are working on keeping your wrists firm in your putting stroke, devise a goal that helps you to achieve your objective. Your goal might be to spend ten minutes a day at home putting on the carpet keeping your wrists firm. The goal is not to make the putt, it is to focus on keeping your wrist fixed when you stroke the ball. If you spend ten minutes a day working on your stroke you have achieved your goal. To get clear feedback on how your are progressing, ask for assistance or use a video camera. When you can consistently keep your wrists firm without thinking about it, the change is ingrained in your memory and you have achieved your objective.

Outcome goals are much easier to evaluate. For example, let's assume that your putting mechanics are sound and you want to groove your putting stroke. Instead of working on the mechanics of the stroke your goal is to make five or ten putts from ten feet away. You know exactly what the task is and you get instant and clear feedback about how well you are doing.

Weapon in hand, Brad Faxon takes aim for his attack on the cup.

The pride of New Zealand, Frank Nobilo.

14

Etiquette and the *Rules of Golf*

Of all the traditions the game of golf has established, the civility with which it is played may be the best known. All true golfers observe proper etiquette and the Rules of Golf voluntarily, with no one to police their actions except themselves. Players of all levels routinely call penalty strokes on themselves, the only game where that happens. In other sports, players feel no remorse at "getting away with one." Not in golf. Any top-level player would gladly call a penalty on himself rather than gain an unfair advantage. It is a matter of respect, respect for the game, for your fellow competitors and, most of all, for yourself.

Any player who has ever picked up a club is well aware of how frustrating the game of golf can be. It's not uncommon to see an experienced golfer lose composure and breech one of the game's most elementary rules. As you'll read in this chapter, even TOUR professionals like Tom Kite, Nick Faldo, Curtis Strange, and Paul Azinger have committed fouls during the heat of competition.

By taking a drop, Greg Norman is exercising an option afforded him by the Rules of Golf.

Etiquette and Common Courtesies

Respectable behavior on the golf course is mostly a matter of common sense. In some cases it overlaps with the Rules of Golf. Keep in mind the points in the following list when you are out on the golf course, even during the most friendly round:

- Stay quiet when any player is preparing to play a shot and when the shot is actually played—roughly speaking, from the moment he assumes his address position until he completes his follow-through. Along with not speaking during this time, you should not be making any noise with your clubs, things in your pockets, etc.
- Never stand close to a player preparing to play a shot. First, you might get hurt. Second, he may be distracted if he sees you out of the corner of his eye.
- When a player is playing a shot or putting, never stand along the line of play. That line extends from the hole, back to the ball, and continues past the ball. Do not stand on the line of play to try to get a line on a putt unless your partner is putting and you have his permission. Whenever a player is setting up to play a shot, you should be behind the player's back or standing a good distance away, opposite the ball. You should never be in his peripheral vision.

When a fellow competitor is preparing to play a shot, etiquette dictates that you stay clear of his peripheral vision.

A red stake signifies a lateral hazard. If your ball ends up in one, you have a number of options regarding how to proceed.

- On the putting green, never tread on the expected line of putt for any player. Be aware of where all balls are on and immediately around the green so that you can avoid stepping or standing on someone's line.
- If you do not have a caddie, be prepared to tend the flagstick when it is not your turn to play. When tending the pin, hold the flag portion with your hands so it does not flap in the breeze. Loosen the stick so it can be easily removed, but do not move it from the center of the hole (it can throw off perception). Try to avoid casting a shadow with your body across the line of the putt. When you lay down the flag, make sure it is out of the line of play.
- Always repair any marks your shots leave in the greens. For good measure, fix one or two others nearby as well. If you accidentally drag your cleats and leave marks in the green, fix them.
- Fill in your divots, whether with the turf your club tore loose or a mixture of sand and seed provided by the course.
- When you have finished playing from a bunker, use a rake to smooth over any marks you have made. It is courteous to make sure no one is playing a shot while you rake.
- Do not throw clubs. Ever. You could hurt someone, including yourself, and it is the most juvenile behavior a golfer could possibly display.

If you're using a golf cart, be aware of where you leave it when you get out to play. Around the greens, always park the cart at the back or to the side of the green, in a path toward the next tee. Don't park it in front of the green.

- If you are riding in a cart, keep track of it. Do not park it wherever you feel like it. Near the green, always park the cart on a line between you and the next tee, so you can quickly vacate the area for the following group.
- This book encourages you to go through a routine before every shot, but you should do so at a reasonable pace. Be prepared when it is your turn to play.
- The last one to hole out should not have to replace the flag. If you are already in the hole, get the flag and be prepared to replace it as soon as the final ball is holed on each hole.
- If you are using a caddie who is carrying two bags, be prepared to pull a few clubs in the event that the two players are on opposite sides of the hole. All that walking back and forth not only is tough on the caddie, but it also delays the pace of play.
- Unless the course is empty, which is rare, do not play more than one ball, and do not linger on the green rehitting putts you just missed. If the course is empty, it is acceptable to play a few balls from a given position.
- Always watch the ball of everyone in your group, and be prepared to lend a hand in looking for a lost ball. It will keep play moving along,

and people will be more willing to help you when you are looking for one of your own.

- A mulligan (a second shot taken after a poorly hit initial one) is not a divine right for all golfers. Play one ball from the first tee and get on with it, particularly if you are on a busy golf course.

- Always be aware of the group behind you. If you are going to be looking for a ball for a while, let them pass through. If they are simply playing more quickly than you, let them play through. If you are in a foursome, you should invite any threesomes or twosomes to play through if they are behind you and waiting.

- Always stay alert to the surrounding weather conditions. Get off the course if there is even a hint of lightning. If someone in your group wishes to stop play because of the weather, you should let him know that it is entirely up to him, and he need not be concerned with what the others in the group think.

The Rules of Golf

The Rules of Golf are maintained by two governing bodies in golf: the United States Golf Association (USGA) and the Royal and Ancient Golf Club of St. Andrews, Scotland (R&A). The Rules set forth by these two parties are, for the most part, very similar, and they work closely together to ensure that this is the case. The most important piece of advice you can get on the Rules is to get a Rules book and carry it in your bag. Being familiar with the Rules will save you shots over the long haul. You can get a copy of the Rules of Golf by contacting the United States Golf Association at P.O. Box 708, Far

Paul Goydos discusses his options with a Rules official. The everyday golfer doesn't have this available to him, so it's best to carry a Rules book in the bag.

Hills, NJ 07931; by phoning (908) 234-2300; or by visiting the USGA website at www.usga.org.

Even though the USGA and the R&A go to great lengths to make sure all golfers are familiar with the Rules, many golfers are not. The following Rules situations are the ones you are most likely to encounter in your weekend matches.

The Order of Play

Whether you are playing match play or stroke play, the facts surrounding the order of play remain the same. On each subsequent tee, the winner of the previous hole has the honor of playing first from the tee. While the balls are in play on a given hole, the player farthest from the hole always plays first. If this Rule is violated in match play, you can force the violator to replay the shot, in the correct order, from as near as possible to the original spot. If this Rule is violated in stroke play, it does not matter unless two players agree to do it to somehow gain an advantage. In that case, they are disqualified. One final note on this subject: "Away" means just what it says:

The teeing area is two club lengths deep from the tee markers.

If one ball is on the green sixty feet from the hole, and another is in a bunker thirty feet from the hole, the ball on the green is away.

Playing a Provisional Ball

When you think your ball may be lost or out of bounds, you can play a provisional ball from the spot of the original ball. This allows you to avoid going back to the original spot if you cannot find the original ball or if it is out of bounds. You can play a provisional ball without penalty as long as you declare that it is a provisional ball ("I'm going to hit a provisional ball in case that one is lost.") and you wait to play it until after everyone else has played. If you find your original ball inbounds, you must play it, and you can pick up the provisional as if nothing had happened.

The Teeing Ground

The area from which you must play is rectangular in shape. The outer edges of the two tee markers define the front and the side of this rectangle. The back line is two club lengths from the front line. You may *stand* outside this box, but the ball must be inside it. In match play, if someone plays from outside the box you can make him replay the shot without penalty. In stroke play it is a two-stroke penalty, and the ball must be replayed from the tee box. In case you have ever wondered whether it *really* is a stroke when you accidentally nudge the ball off the tee, the answer is no.

The Hazards of Hazards

Perhaps the most confusing Rules situations commonly encountered by the average player involve hazards. A hazard is any bunker or water hazard. With a bunker, the hazard is only the part where the turf has been removed and replaced with sand. Any turf facings surrounding the bunker are not part of the hazard. A regular water hazard is defined by a yellow line painted on the ground or yellow stakes. If your ball is inside that marking, it is in the hazard whether it is in the water or not. The second type of water hazard is a lateral hazard, which is marked with a red line painted on the ground or red stakes. The term *lateral* means that you cannot, practically speaking, drop a ball behind the hazard if you hit your ball into it. Again, all ground within the markings is part of the hazard, whether it is underwater or not.

When the subject is a regular water hazard, there are many things to keep in mind. First, you have to have a reason to believe that the ball went into the water—that is, you or someone else saw it go in. If no one saw the ball go into the water and you cannot find it in the water, you must treat it as a lost ball. If you know it went into the water, you have two options, both of which cost you one penalty stroke *plus* the stroke originally played: (1) you may play a ball from as near as possible to where you played the original ball; (2) drop a ball behind the water hazard, keeping the point at which the original ball last crossed the hazard line directly between the hole and the point you drop (there is no limit on how far you may drop behind the water hazard).

When the ball rests inside the
lines of a hazard, it is illegal to
ground the club before striking
the shot.

If you are dealing with a lateral hazard, you have an additional option. You can drop within two club lengths, no nearer the hole, of the spot where the ball last crossed the hazard line, or drop within two club lengths of a point on the opposite margin of the hazard that is equidistant from the hole.

Whenever you are in a hazard, bear two things in mind. First, you cannot ground your club at address—that is, you cannot touch the sand or water (or any turf within the markings of a water hazard) until you are actually striking the ball. If you violate this Rule in match play, you lose the hole. If you do it in stroke play, it is a two-stroke penalty. Second, there is no penalty for playing a wrong ball from a hazard, so you do not need to worry about identifying your ball if it is plugged in the sand, for example.

Moving Loose Impediments

First, loose impediments are almost anything natural that is not growing out of the ground. This includes stones, twigs, leaves, branches that have broken loose from trees, and so on. You can move any loose impediment as long as it is not growing or firmly stuck in the ground, or is not stuck to the ball. If a piece of grass is stuck to your ball and you are not on the green, do not touch it. If you move your ball while removing a loose impediment from around it, the penalty is one stroke, and you must replace your ball. Sand and loose dirt are considered loose impediments only on the green. If your ball is in a hazard, you cannot move any loose impediments.

Declaring Your Ball Unplayable

What golfer hasn't hit shots into places from which no mere mortal could ever hope to extricate himself? When you do so, it is wise to consider declaring the ball unplayable and taking a drop for the relatively benign penalty of one stroke. There are three options:

- Play a ball from as near as possible to the spot you originally played from—that is, the spot from which you hit the shot that got you into all this trouble in the first place.
- Drop a ball within two club lengths of the spot where the ball lay. Do not drop the ball any closer to the hole.
- Drop a ball behind the point where the ball lay, keeping that point directly between the hole and the spot where you are going to drop the ball. There is no limit to how far back you may go before dropping.

There are two exceptions under this Rule. (1) You cannot declare a ball in a water hazard unplayable. (You simply take relief using the water-hazard Rule.) (2) If you decide to declare your ball unplayable in a bunker and use either of the last two options, you still have to drop the ball in the bunker. One last bit of good news: You can clean the ball after you lift it.

Playing the Wrong Ball

Before you play, you should use an indelible marking pen to put some distinctive marking on your ball so you know it is yours at all times. If you are in a match-play situation and you play a wrong ball, you lose the hole. (Remember, if you do this from a hazard, it does not count.) If the wrong ball played belongs to another player in your group, the owner shall place a ball on the spot from which the wrong ball was first played and continue playing. In match play, if both players play the wrong ball by inadvertently hitting each other's ball, then the first one to hit the wrong ball loses the hole (unless it was from a hazard). If the players cannot determine when the switch occurred, the hole is played out with each playing the ball he is currently playing (i.e., the wrong ball). In stroke play, violation of this rule is a two-shot penalty. As soon as you realize you are playing the wrong ball in stroke play, you must start playing the correct ball. If you do not do so by the time you hit your next tee shot, you are disqualified.

Remember that unless your ball is in a hazard, you can always lift the ball to identify it. You can even clean it just enough so you can identify it. Before you lift the ball, you must inform your opponent that you are going to lift the ball to identify it, and

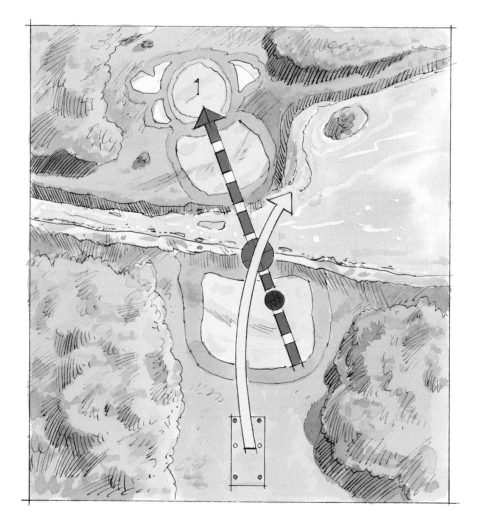

When the ball enters a water hazard, the key thing to watch is the point at which the ball crosses the line of the hazard. You can drop your ball any-where keeping that point be-tween you and the hole.

give the other player a chance to watch you do it. You also must mark the ball's position with a coin, a tee, or something else. If you do not do all of these things (mark it, announce, let your opponent observe) or you clean the ball more than you need to for identification, the penalty is one stroke. If you do all these things, and it is your ball, just replace the ball and play on.

Declaring Your Ball Unfit for Play

Some players think that if their ball is damaged, they must wait until they hole out to replace it. Not so. Anytime you notice that your ball is visibly cut, cracked, or out of round, you can take it out of play without penalty if you follow the following guidelines:

- A ball is not unfit for play only because it has dirt or mud on it, the paint has chipped, or it has a scratch on it. You must be reasonably able to assume that whatever is wrong with the ball will adversely af-fect its flight.

- You must announce your intentions to your opponent or fellow competitor.
- You must mark the spot of the ball, because you are going to replace it with the ball you are playing or a new ball.
- You cannot clean the ball.
- You have to give your opponent a chance to look at the ball.

If you violate any of the above, the penalty is one stroke. If the ball is deemed by all to be unfit for playing out the hole, you may replace it with another ball on the spot where the original ball was. Otherwise, put the original ball back and play away.

The Rules in Action

Understandably, from time to time a Rule situation arises that might cause confusion. The following rulings handed down by tournament officials in TOUR events and other major events will help you the next time you encounter a similar predicament.

Rule 18: Ball Moved, Deflected, or Stopped

In 1995 Tom Kite, always considered a Rules expert, endured two violations of the same Rule on the last hole of the U.S. Open's third round. As Kite addressed his bogey putt (a player has addressed the ball, taken his stance, and grounded the club), his ball moved slightly. A player is considered to have moved his own ball if he has already addressed it and incurs a one-stroke penalty. Kite let the ball settle and then made the putt. He did not replace the ball after it had moved, however, and was assessed another penalty stroke to finish the hole with a triple-bogey 7.

Rule 10: Order of Play

Everyone knows that the player farthest from the hole putts first. It is common, however, for a player who rolls a long putt close to tap in and then let the others finish. In match play, an opponent can actually concede a putt he considers a "gimme." Technically, the player who is away can force the tap in to be marked and played in order. In their singles match in the 1995 Ryder Cup, Seve Ballesteros and Tom Lehman had an awkward moment after Lehman had rolled his birdie putt to tap-in range. Expecting—but not getting—a concession, Lehman tapped in for par as Ballesteros said "No." Lehman had to retrieve his ball from the cup, mark where it had been, and let Seve putt. It was an unpopular gesture with the American fans, but it followed the Rules. Lehman ended up winning the match, 4 and 3.

Rule 15: Whose Ball Is It, Anyway?

Golfers are required to finish a hole with the same ball they hit from the tee (unless there is significant damage to the ball during the hole, and a change is agreed to by an opponent). Therefore, if a player hits the wrong ball during the hole, it is a violation of

Check with your fellow com-petitors before "putting out."

Rule 15 and results in a two-stroke penalty. During the 1994 British Open Championship Nick Faldo's ball was in the fairway on the seventeenth hole, but so was the ball of fellow competitor Jim McGovern. Faldo did not check closely enough to identify his ball and hit McGovern's down the fairway. Upon discovering the error, Faldo was forced then to play his ball with what was now his fourth shot. Even if Faldo had finished the hole with the wrong ball, he would have incurred only the two strokes and had to play from the spot where his tee shot had landed. Incidentally, if Faldo had played the wrong ball from a hazard, there would have been no penalty, only a replay from the hazard.

Rule 18: Tread Lightly

There is no penalty for inadvertently moving a ball while a player is searching for it. For example, if a player accidentally kicks his ball while trudging through the brush, he must simply replace the ball in its original spot. If the ball is visible and the player causes it to move, the penalty is one stroke. Jumbo Ozaki ran afoul of this rule at the 1994 Masters. His ball ended up in the pine needles just off the eighteenth fairway. As Ozaki walked within a club length of his ball, the needles pushed upward and dislodged his ball. Ozaki took the penalty stroke and then hit his shot. He had to accept a second penalty stroke because he did not place his ball back in its original position. Had the ball rolled before Ozaki moved within a club length of it, there would have been no penalty.

Rule 13: The Big Brush-off

This ruling is as famous for the way it was called as for the infraction itself. Paul Azinger's drive on the eighteenth hole at the 1991 Doral Ryder Open landed in a lateral water hazard just under the surface of the water. He took his setup with his right foot in the water and his left foot on a rock. He was having trouble securing his left foot because of some pebbles on the rock and brushed them into the water with the bottom of his shoe. Azinger went on to make par on the hole after a brilliant recovery and signed for a 4 on the hole. A television viewer called in to claim Azinger had violated the Rule against moving loose impediments in a hazard and should have incurred a two-stroke penalty. PGA TOUR Rules officials consulted with officials at the USGA, who agreed with the viewer. Azinger was disqualified from the tournament because he had already signed an incorrect scorecard.

Rule 10: Thou Shalt Not Touch the Green

A player's caddie commonly gives him advice as to the intended line of his putts. Rule 10, however, states that a caddie may not touch the green surface when pointing out the line or give advice once the stroke has begun. "Squeeky" Medlin, John Daly's caddie at the 1991 PGA Championship, had helped him read a putt and was standing behind the hole, holding the flagstick. The problem was that the bottom of the flagstick was resting on the green. Some television viewers claimed Squeeky was indicating to Daly where to hit the putt.

As a matter of courtesy to other players on the course, fix any pitch marks your ball makes on the green.

Tournament officials reviewed the tape and decided there was no violation, and Daly went on to win the PGA Championship.

Rule 5: Fitness Check

As stated earlier, a player must finish the hole with the same ball he hit from the tee. One exception to this rule involves a ball that is unfit for play. If a player feels his ball is too damaged or out of round, he must ask his opponent to confirm the problem before replacing the ball. In the 1989 Ryder Cup, Paul Azinger was matched against Seve Ballesteros. Ballesteros checked a ball he had just landed on the green and decided it was unfit for play. He did not check with Azinger on his intention to put a new ball in play, so Azinger asked to see the damaged ball. Although there was some damage, the ball was not visibly cut, and Azinger would not allow Ballesteros to replace it. Seve had to wait until the next hole to use the new ball.

When on the green, always walk around or step over the line of a fellow competitor. Your footprints could adversely affect his putt.

Rule 13: If You Build It . . .

This may be the most infamous ruling in golf. Craig Stadler was near the lead in the third round of the 1987 Shearson Lehman Brothers Andy Williams Open when his ball landed under a low-hanging tree. The only way to play the shot was to kneel in the grass and root it out. Because Stadler did not want to get his knees dirty, he put a towel on the ground and knelt on it while playing the shot. Stadler finished the round, and highlights of the shot were played before the final-round coverage. Television viewers called in to complain that Stadler had violated Rule 13 which prevents a golfer from building a stance. Tournament officials agreed, and Stadler was disqualified because he had signed for an incorrect score. If the violation had been noticed before the end of his third round, it would have been a two-stroke penalty.

Rule 4: Irreparable Harm

Golf can be frustrating. Golfers react in different ways to frustration, and Curtis Strange's reaction put him in a bad spot. After three-putting a hole at the 1996 Houston Open, Strange banged his putter against a bridge on his way to the next tee, and the putter snapped. He had to putt with his wedge for the rest of the round. Had his club broken during the normal course of play, he would have been allowed to re-place it. As it turns out, Strange won the tournament.

Rule 14: Double Displeasure

This is not an easy rule to break. T. C. Chen was leading the 1985 U.S. Open when he missed the green on the fifth hole and set up for a short chip. The thick Championship rough around the green snagged Chen's wedge as it struck the ball. When the grass let loose a split second later, Chen's club accelerated and hit the ball again. The Rules state that a player may strike the ball only once during a stroke. The penalty is one stroke. Chen ended up with an 8 on the hole. He eventually lost the tournament by a stroke to Andy North.

Loren Roberts surveys his path to the hole.

Justin Leonard posing.

15

Getting Your Body Ready to Play Golf

Golf may not be the most physically demanding game, but it is not a good idea to roll out of bed and start swinging a golf club. Not only will a laissez-faire attitude toward your body hurt your score, it also might hurt you. The golf swing is an awkward motion for your body to make. If you make it when your body is not ready, you will eventually pay the price in terms of pain or injury. By contrast, if your body is ready when it is time to play, you will see immediate benefits. A huge bonus in following the strength and stretching program described in this chapter is that it will improve the quality of your life as well as the quality of your golf game. Stretching before you play not only benefits your game on the course, it helps pervent injuries that could keep you off the course.

The following program is recommended by Frank W. Jobe, M.D., medical director of Centinela Hospital Medical Center's biomechanics laboratory, and fitness consultant to the PGA TOUR.

Looking not unlike an on-deck hitter awaiting his turn at bat, Fred Funk loosens up by swinging two clubs.

Pre-Round Stretching

If you struggle through the first few holes of every round because you feel tight, you can remedy the situation. By spending five minutes doing the following six stretches before you tee off, you will be able to gain an edge over your competitors and shave a few strokes off that early-round "get loose" period. In addition, stretching will help you avoid injuring yourself. "Because of all the hyper rotation and side-to-side bending golfers do, the spine is the number one area of injury," says Jobe. "These stretches emphasize building a good range of motion and building flexibility, especially in the spine. The increased flexibility this program will provide you with allows you to make a more fluid and less restricted swing."

Jobe recommends walking for five minutes before you do these pre-round stretches. Walking is helpful because it raises your body temperature slightly and, according to Jobe, "stretching cold muscles isn't as productive."

Neck Rotation

Turn your head to the right, looking as far over your shoulder as possible. Take your left hand and gently push against the left side of your face. Hold for ten to fifteen seconds, then repeat the process on the other side. *How this helps you:* This stretch simulates the actual neck movements in your swing: left shoulder to chin in your backswing, and right shoulder to chin in your follow-through. (See Figure 15-1.)

Figure 15-1

Figure 15-2

Figure 15-8   Figure 15-9

hand. Hold for ten to fifteen seconds, then repeat to the other side. *How this helps you:* This simulates the swing by working the sides of the abdomen and the trunk-rotator muscles. (See Figure 15-10.)

Calf and Achilles Tendon Stretch

To stretch your calf, stand a little ways from a golf cart and grasp the cart, arms outstretched. Bend one leg and place your foot on the ground in front of you, with the other leg straight behind. To stretch your calf and Achilles tendon, lower your hips downward and slightly bend your knee. Keep your back flat and rear heel down. Hold stretch ten seconds. (See Figure 15-11.)

Back Stretch

Put a club across the lower back and through the crook of the elbows. Make body turns as in your swing, utilizing normal foot work. Next, hold the club across the shoulders behind the neck and repeat. Finally, drop the club behind your back and, with arms extended, elevate the club and arms and continue to swing gently. This last exercise loosens the upper back and shoulder region. (See Figure 15-12.)

No-Ball Warm-Up

Start by swinging two wedges, beginning with small swings and building to full swings with good tempo. (See Figures 15-13 and 15-14.)

Letting Go with the Right Hand

Make practice swings, letting go with the right hand near impact. This will remind your body to utilize its left side and not let go with the last three fingers of the left

Figure 15-10

Figure 15-11

hand. Allow the left elbow to fold past impact. Do not keep the arm straight. (See Figures 15-15 and 15-16.)

Full Follow-Through

Make practice swings with both hands on the grip, focusing on tempo and finishing on the left side with the right heel in the air. (See Figure 15-17.)

Strength Training

In a study conducted by Wayne Wescott, Ph.D., strength consultant for the YMCA, golfers who followed an eight-week strengthening and stretching program improved their clubhead speed by five miles per hour. Not only will a strength program help you feel strong and burn fat (muscle burns fat more efficiently), it will help you hit the ball farther, too!

The following program builds strength in the lower body, develops the all-important trunk and lower back muscles, and creates powerful shoulders and forearms, which all contribute to a more powerful swing and longer shots. More important, it will not bulk up your biceps and chest muscles, the ones that can make your swing feel stiff or inflexible.

You should do ten to twelve repetitions of each exercise every other day. Some of these exercises require using dumbbells. You should use a weight you feel comfortable with; the idea is not to build huge muscles or place undue stress on your body.

Calf Raise

Stand facing a wall, with your toes about twelve inches away from it. Put one hand on the wall for support. Place your right ankle against the back of your left calf, and rise up on the toes of your left foot. Lower and repeat, then switch legs. Hold a weight in your free hand for greater resistance.

Half Squat

Standing with your feet shoulder-width apart and a dumbbell in each hand (or a barbell across your back), slowly squat without arching your back. A full squat ends with your thighs parallel to the floor. A half squat takes you half as far.

Side Lunge

With a dumbbell in each hand, step to the side as far as possible with your left leg until the thigh is almost parallel to the floor. Looking down this leg, make sure your knee is not farther forward than your toes. Return to the starting position and repeat for the other leg.

Curl-Up

Lie on your back, arms folded across your chest, with knees bent and feet flat on the floor. Raise your left shoulder, crossing it toward your right side. Hold for five seconds, then lie back, and repeat on the other side. Hold a weight plate on your chest for extra resistance.

Trunk Raise

Lie on our stomach, legs extended, and your fingers laced behind your head. Raise your upper body as much as possible. Hold for three seconds, relax, then repeat.

Lying Leg Crossover

Lying on your back with your legs extended, raise one leg to a vertical position. By rotating your hips, swing that leg across your body and try to touch it to the floor. Try to keep both shoulders grounded while doing this. Hold for a few seconds; repeat the exercise using the other leg.

Wrist and Forearm Combo

While seated, take a dumbbell in one hand and rest that forearm atop your thigh so your hand extends beyond the knee, palm up. Repeatedly curl the wrist toward your forearm. From the same position, slowly twist the wrist

Figure 15-12

Figure 15-13

Figure 15-14

Getting Your Body Ready to Play Golf   345

Figure 15-15

from side to side. Next, reverse the hand so the palm faces down and repeatedly curl it up and back. Finally, rest the side of your forearm on the same leg and cock your wrist upward. Lift the dumbbell by bending your elbow toward your shoulder. Once there, flex your wrist forward. Repeat all these exercises for the other wrist and arm.

Arm Raises

Holding dumbbells at your side, simultaneously raise the weights laterally until your hands reach shoulder height. This exercise may also be done by extending the arms straight in front of you (do not lock your elbows).

Triceps Push-Up

Sitting on the edge of a sturdy chair or bench, place your hands behind you on the sides of the seat and extend your legs. Slowly lower your buttocks until your upper arms are almost parallel to the chair seat, then return to the starting position and repeat.

Figure 15-16

Building a Stronger Grip

So much is happening during your swing that you sometimes can lose track of the fact that your hands are the only part of your body connected to the club. The other thing that is often overlooked is that your hands take a beating when you play golf, absorbing the blow of every shot you play. It pays to keep your hands strong in terms of both performance and injury prevention. One way to do this is to keep a tennis ball or a rubber ball in your car or near the phone and squeeze it during otherwise idle time. Another way to build hand strength is to fill a bucket with sand or rice and plunge your hand, clenched in a fist, into the bucket. Once the hand is completely in the sand or rice, slowly open and close it fifteen to twenty times. Switch hands.

Take Care of Your Back

Of all the parts of your body, your back is probably the most prone to golf-related injuries. An interesting fact regarding back injuries is that most of them are *not* purely the result of poor swing mechanics. Back problems are frequently aggravated by improper body mechanics when teeing the ball up, taking it out of the hole, or lugging your golf bag around. Here are some tips to help you avoid back problems.

- Always take care when you pick up your golf bag, whether you are loading it in the car, taking it out of the trunk, or picking it up after every shot if you are walking while you play. A fully loaded bag with clubs is heavy, and bending from the waist without using your knees imposes tremendous strain on your back. Use your knees when you lift or lower your bag. Be especially careful if you are leaving for the course early in the morning or arriving after a lengthy drive, because your body is still stiff and even more vulnerable to injury.

- When you bend over to tee the ball up, pick it out of the hole, mark the ball or fix a ball mark, and always bend your knees. In addition to bending your knees, try to lean on your club for support.

- When you are practicing on the putting green, take frequent breaks to stand erect and arch your back. If you do not take frequent breaks, cramping muscle pains may occur when you hold a rigid, bent-over body position for an extended period hitting putt after putt. A good preventive exercise is to stop periodically and do a standing back bend to counter all the forward bending you do as you putt. Place both hands shoulder-width apart on the edge of a golf cart and let your upper body drop down as you keep your knees slightly bent (Figure 15-18). Hold ten seconds.

Figure 15-17

Be Smart About Being Fit

If you have any medical problems, such as high blood pressure or heart ailments, consult your physician before undertaking the program outlined here or any other program. Listen to your body, and be careful not to overstrain. If you experience any unexpected pain, discomfort, or exhaustion, stop and seek advice from your physician. If you find your program difficult or if it causes discomfort, you may need to modify it. This is particularly true if you have any restrictive conditions, such as arthritis or lower back pain.

Figure 15-18

Fred Funk was once the golf coach at the University of Maryland.

KEMPER
OPEN

Chris

KEMPER
OPEN

1

AXON 1

STRICKER 3

MORSE

The spirit of volunteerism is alive at all PGA TOUR events.

Appendix

THE PLAYERS CHAMPIONSHIP

Tournament History

Tournament Players Championship

Year	Winner	Score	Runner-up	Score	Location
1974	Jack Nicklaus	272	J.C. Snead	274	Atlanta CC, Atlanta, GA
1975	Al Geiberger	270	Dave Stockton	273	Colonial CC, Fort Worth, TX
1976	Jack Nicklaus	269	J.C. Snead	272	Inverrary G&CC, Lauderhill, FL
1977	Mark Hayes	289	Mike McCullough	291	Sawgrass CC, Ponte Vedra Beach, FL
1978	Jack Nicklaus	289	Lou Graham	290	Sawgrass CC, Ponte Vedra Beach, FL
1979	Lanny Wadkins	283	Tom Watson	288	Sawgrass CC, Ponte Vedra Beach, FL
1980	Lee Trevino	278	Ben Crenshaw	279	Sawgrass CC, Ponte Vedra Beach, FL
1981	*Raymond Floyd	285	Barry Jaeckel	285	Sawgrass CC, Ponte Vedra Beach, FL
			Curtis Strange		
	(Won playoff with par on first extra hole)				
1982	Jerry Pate	280	Brad Bryant	282	TPC at Sawgrass, Ponte Vedra Beach, FL
			Scott Simpson		
1983	Hal Sutton	283	Bob Eastwood	284	TPC at Sawgrass, Ponte Vedra Beach, FL
1984	Fred Couples	277	Lee Trevino	278	TPC at Sawgrass, Ponte Vedra Beach, FL
1985	Calvin Peete	274	D.A. Weibring	277	TPC at Sawgrass, Ponte Vedra Beach, FL
1986	John Mahaffey	275	Larry Mize	276	TPC at Sawgrass, Ponte Vedra Beach, FL
1987	*Sandy Lyle	274	Jeff Sluman	274	TPC at Sawgrass, Ponte Vedra Beach, FL
	(Won playoff with par on third extra hole)				

THE PLAYERS CHAMPIONSHIP

Year	Winner	Score	Runner-up	Score	Location
1988	Mark McCumber	273	Mike Reid	277	TPC at Sawgrass, Ponte Vedra Beach, FL
1989	Tom Kite	279	Chip Beck	280	TPC at Sawgrass, Ponte Vedra Beach, FL
1990	Jodie Mudd	278	Mark Calcavecchia	279	TPC at Sawgrass, Ponte Vedra Beach, FL
1991	Steve Elkington	276	Fuzzy Zoeller	277	TPC at Sawgrass, Ponte Vedra Beach, FL
1992	Davis Love III	273	Ian Baker-Finch	277	TPC at Sawgrass, Ponte Vedra Beach, FL
			Phil Blackmar		
			Nick Faldo		
			Tom Watson		
1993	Nick Price	270	Berhard Langer	275	TPC at Sawgrass, Ponte Vedra Beach, FL
1994	Greg Norman	264	Fuzzy Zoeller	268	TPC at Sawgrass, Ponte Vedra Beach, FL
1995	Lee Janzen	283	Bernhard Langer	284	TPC at Sawgrass, Ponte Vedra Beach, FL
1996	Fred Couples	270	Colin Montgomerie	274	TPC at Sawgrass, Ponte Vedra Beach, FL
			Tommy Tolles		
1997	Steve Elkington	272	Scott Hoch	279	TPC at Sawgrass, Ponte Vedra Beach, FL
1998	Justin Leonard	278	Glen Day	280	TPC at Sawgrass, Ponte Vedra Beach, FL

Tournament Record: 264—Greg Norman, 1994

Current Course Record: 63—Fred Couples, 1992; Greg Norman, 1994

KEY: * = Playoff

Masters Tournament

Tournament History

Year	Winner	Score	Runner-up	Score
1934	Horton Smith	284	Craig Wood	285
1935	*Gene Sarazen (144)	282	Craig Wood (149)	282
1936	Horton Smith	285	Harry Cooper	286
1937	Byron Nelson	283	Ralph Guldahl	285
1938	Henry Picard	285	Ralph Guldahl	287
			Harry Cooper	
1939	Ralph Guldahl	279	Sam Snead	280
1940	Jimmy Demaret	280	Lloyd Mangrum	284
1941	Craig Wood	280	Byron Nelson	283
1942	*Byron Nelson (69)	280	Ben Hogan (70)	280
1943–1945: No Tournaments—World War II				
1946	Herman Keiser	282	Ben Hogan	283
1947	Jimmy Demaret	281	Byron Nelson	283
			Frank Stranahan	
1948	Claude Harmon	279	Cary Middlecoff	284
1949	Sam Snead	282	Johnny Bulla	285
			Lloyd Mangrum	
1950	Jimmy Demaret	283	Jim Ferrier	285
1951	Ben Hogan	280	Skee Riegel	282
1952	Sam Snead	286	Jack Burke, Jr.	290
1953	Ben Hogan	274	Ed Oliver, Jr.	279
1954	*Sam Snead (70)	289	Ben Hogan (71)	289
1955	Cary Middlecoff	279	Ben Hogan	286
1956	Jack Burke, Jr.	289	Ken Venturi	290
1957	Doug Ford	282	Sam Senead	286
1958	Arnold Palmer	284	Doug Ford	285
			Fred Hawkins	
1959	Art Wall, Jr.	284	Cary Middlecoff	285
1960	Arnold Palmer	282	Ken Venturi	283
1961	Gary Player	280	Charles R. Coe	281
			Arnold Palmer	
1962	*Arnold Palmer (68)	280	Gary Player (71)	280
			Dow Finsterwald (77)	
1963	Jack Nicklaus	286	Tony Lema	287
1964	Arnold Palmer	276	Dave Marr	282
			Jack Nicklaus	
1965	Jack Nicklaus	271	Arnold Palmer	280
			Gary Player	
1966	*Jack Nicklaus (70)	288	Tommy Jacobs (72)	288
			Gay Brewer, Jr. (78)	
1967	Gay Brewer, Jr.	280	Bobby Nichols	281

Masters Tournament *(continued)*

Tournament History

Year	Winner	Score	Runner-up	Score
1968	Bob Goalby	277	Roberto De Vicenzo	278
1969	George Archer	281	Billy Casper	282
			George Knudson	
			Tom Weiskopf	
1970	*Billy Casper (69)	279	Gene Littler (74)	279
1971	Charles Coody	279	Johnny Miller	281
			Jack Nicklaus	
1972	Jack Nicklaus	286	Bruce Crampton	289
			Bobby Mitchell	
			Tom Weiskopf	
1973	Tommy Aaron	283	J.C. Snead	284
1974	Gary Player	278	Tom Weiskopf	280
			Dave Stockton	
1975	Jack Nicklaus	276	Johnny Miller	277
			Tom Weiskopf	
1976	Ray Floyd	271	Ben Crenshaw	279
1977	Tom Watson	276	Jack Nicklaus	278
1978	Gary Player	277	Hubert Green	278
			Rod Funseth	
			Tom Watson	
1979	*Fuzzy Zoeller	280	Ed Sneed	280
			Tom Watson	
1980	Seve Ballesteros	275	Gibbby Gilbert	279
			Jack Newton	
1981	Tom Watson	280	Johnny Miller	282
			Jack Nicklaus	
1982	*Craig Stadler	284	Dan Pohl	284
1983	Seve Ballesteros	280	Ben Crenshaw	284
			Tom Kite	
1984	Ben Crenshaw	277	Tom Watson	279
1985	Bernhard Langer	282	Curtis Strange	284
			Seve Ballesteros	
			Raymond Floyd	
1986	Jack Nicklaus	279	Greg Norman	280
			Tom Kite	
1987	*Larry Mize	285	Seve Ballesteros	285
			Greg Norman	
1988	Sandy Lyle	281	Mark Calcavecchia	282
1989	*Nick Faldo	283	Scott Hoch	283
1990	*Nick Faldo	278	Raymond Floyd	278
1991	Ian Woosnam	277	Jose Maria Olazabal	278

Masters Tournament (continued)

Tournament History

Year	Winner	Score	Runner-up	Score
1992	Fred Couples	275	Raymond Floyd	277
1993	Bernhard Langer	277	Chip Beck	281
1994	Jose Maria Olazabal	279	Tom Lehman	281
1995	Ben Crenshaw	274	Davis Love III	275
1996	Nick Faldo	276	Greg Norman	281
1997	Tiger Woods	270	Tom Kite	282
1998	Mark O'Meara	279	David Duval	280
			Fred Couples	

Tournament Record: 270—Tiger Woods, 1997

Course Record: 63—Nick Price, 1986; Gren Norman, 1996

KEY: * = Playoff   *Figures in parentheses indicate playoff scores.*

Note: Tiger Woods shot a Master Tournament record 70-66-65-69-270. Woods's 18-under-par total was one stroke better than previous record-holders Jack Nicklaus (1965) and Raymond Floyd (1976). He also became the youngest Masters champion at 21 years, 3 months, 15 days. Woods's 12-stroke margin of victory was the largest in tournament history.

U.S. Open

Tournament History

Year	Winner	Score	Runner-up	Score	Location
1895	Horace Rawlins	173	Willie Dunn	175	Newport GC, Newport RI
1896	James Foulis	152	Horace Rawlins	155	Shinnecock Hills GC, Southhampton, NY
1897	Joe Lloyd	162	Willie Anderson	163	Chicago GC, Wheaton, IL
	(Competition extended from 36 to 72 holes after 1897)				
1898	Fred Herd	328	Alex Smith	335	Myopia Hunt Club, Hamilton, MA
1899	Willie Smith	315	George Low	326	Baltimore CC, Baltimore, MD
			Val Fitzjohn		
			W. H. Way		
1900	Harry Vardon	313	J. H. Taylor	315	Chicago GC, Wheaton, IL
1901	*Willie Anderson (85)	331	Alex Smith	(86)	Myopia Hunt Club, Hamilton, MA
1902	Laurie Auchterlonie	307	Stewart Gardner	313	Garden City GC, Garden City, LI, NY
1903	*Willie Anderson (82)	307	David Brown (84)		Baltusrol GC, Short Hills, NJ
1904	Willie Anderson	303	Gil Nicholls	308	Glen View Club, Golf, IL
1905	Willie Anderson	314	Alex Smith	316	Myopia Hunt Club, Hamilton, MA
1906	Alex Smith	295	Willie Smith	302	Onwentsia Club, Lake Forest, IL
1907	Alex Ross	302	Gil Nicholls	304	Phila. Cricket Club, Chestnut Hill, PA
1908	*Fred McLeod (77)	322	Willie Smith	(83)	Myopia Hunt Club, Hamilton, MA
1909	George Sargent	290	Tom McNamara	294	Englewood GC, Englewood, NJ
1910	*Alex Smith (71)	298	John McDermott	(75)	Philadelphia Cricket Club, Chestnut Hill, PA
			Macdonald Smith	(77)	
1911	*John McDermott (80)	307	Mike Brady	(82)	Chicago GC, Wheaton, IL
			George Simpson	(85)	
1912	John McDermott	294	Tom McNamara	296	CC of Buffalo, Buffalo, NY
1913	#*Francis Ouimet (72)	304	Harry Vardon	(77)	The Country Club, Brookline, MA
			Edward Ray	(78)	
1914	Walter Hagen	290	#Charles Evans, Jr.	291	Midlothian CC, Blue Island, IL
1915	#Jerome Travers	297	Tom McNamara	298	Baltusrol GC. Short Hilsl, Nj
1916	#Charles Evans, Jr.	286	Jock Hutchison	288	Minikahda Club, Minneapolis, MN
1917–1918: No Championships—World War I					
1919	*Walter Hagen (77)	301	Mike Brady	(78)	Brae Burn CC, West Newton, MA
1920	Edward Ray	295	Harry Vardon	296	Inverness, CC, Toledo, OH
			Jack Burke		
			Leo Diegel		
			Jock Hutchison		
1921	James M. Barnes	289	Walter Hagen	298	Columbia CC, Chevy Chase, MD
			Fred McLeod		
1922	Gene Sarazen	288	John L. Black	289	Skokie CC, Glencor, IL
			#Robert T. Jones, Jr.		
1923	#*Robert T. Jones, Jr.(76)	296	Bobby Cruickshank	(78)	Inwood CC, Inwood, LI, NY
1924	Cyril Walker	297	#Robert T. Jones, Jr.	300	Oakland Hills CC, Birmingham, MI
1925	*Willie Macfarlane (147)	291	#Robert T. Jones, Jr.	(148)	Worcester CC, Worcester, MA

U.S. Open (continued)

Tournament History

Year	Winner	Score	Runner-up	Score	Location
1926	#Robert T. Jones, Jr.	293	Joe Turnesa	294	Scioto CC, Columbus, OH
1927	*Tommy Armour (76)	301	Harry Cooper	(79)	Oakmont CC, Oakmont, PA
1928	*Johnny Farrell (143)	294	#Robert T. Jones, Jr.	(144)	Olympia Fields CC, Matteson, IL
1929	#*Robert T. Jones, Jr. (141)	294	Al Espinosa	(164)	Winged Foot GC, Mamaroneck, NY
1930	#Robert T. Jones, Jr.	287	Macdonald Smith	289	Interlachen CC, Hopkins, MN
1931	*Billy Burke (149-148)	292	George Von Elm	(149-149)	Inverness Club, Toledo, OH
1932	Gene Sarazen	286	Phil Perkins	289	Fresh Meadows CC, Flushing, NY
			Bobby Cruickshank		
1933	#Johnny Goodman	287	Ralph Guldahl	288	North Shore CC, Glenview, IL
1934	Olin Dutra	293	Gene Sarazen	294	Merion Cricket Club, Ardmore, PA
1935	Sam Parks, Jr.	299	Jimmy Thomson	301	Oakmont CC, Oakmont, PA
1936	Tony Manero	282	Harry Cooper	284	Baltusrol GC, Springfield, NJ
1937	Ralph Guldahl	281	Sam Snead	283	Oakland Hills CC, Birmingham, MI
1938	Ralph Guldahl	284	Dick Metz	290	Cherry Hills CC, Denver, Co
1939	*Byron Nelson (68-70)	284	Craig Wood	(68-73)	Philadelphia CC, Philadelphia, PA
			Denny Shute	(76)	
1940	*Lawson Little (70)	287	Gene Sarazen	(73)	Canterbury GC, Cleveland, Oh
1941	Craig Wood	284	Denny Shute	287	Colonial Club, Fort Worth, TX
1942–1945: No Championships—World War II					
1946	*Lloyd Mangrum (72-72)	284	Vic Ghezzi	(72-73)	Canterbury GC, Cleveland, OH
			Byron Nelson	(72-73)	
1947	*Lew Worsham (69)	282	Sam Snead	(70)	St. Louis CC, Clayton, MO
1948	Ben Hogan	276	Jimmy Demaret	278	Riviera CC, Los Angeles, CA
1949	Cary Middlecoff	286	Sam Snead	287	Medinah CC, Medinah, IL
			Clayton Heafner		
1950	*Ben Hogan (69)	287	Lloyd Mangrum	(73)	Merion Golf Club, Ardmore, PA
			George Fazio	(75)	
1951	Ben Hogan	287	Clayton Heafner	289	Oakland Hills CC, Birmingham, MI
1952	Julius Boros	281	Ed Oliver	285	Northwood CC, Dallas, TX
1953	Ben Hogan	283	Sam Snead	289	Oakmont CC, Oakmont, PA
1954	Ed Furgol	284	Gene Littler	285	Baltusrol GC, Springfield, NJ
1955	*Jack Fleck (69)	287	Ben Hogan	(72)	Olympic Club, San Francisco, CA
1956	Cary Middlecoff	281	Ben Hogan	282	Oak Hill CC, Rochester, NY
			Julius Boros		
1957	*Dick Mayer (72)	282	Cary Middlecoff	(79)	Inverness Club, Toledo, OH
1958	Tommy Bolt	283	Gary Player	287	Southern Hills, CC, Tulsa, OK
1959	Billy Casper	282	Bob Rosburg	283	Winged Foot GC, Mamaroneck, NY
1960	Arnold Palmer	280	#Jack Nicklaus	282	Cherry Hills CC, Denver, CO
1961	Gene Littler	281	Bob Goalby	282	Oakland Hills CC, Birmingham, MI
			Doug Sanders		
1962	*Jack Nicklaus (71)	283	Arnold Palmer	(74)	Oakmont CC, Oakmont, PA

U.S. Open *(continued)*

Tournament History

Year	Winner	Score	Runner-up	Score	Location
1963	*Julius Boros (70)	293	Jack Cupit	(73)	The Country Club, Brookline, MA
			Arnold Palmer	(76)	
1964	Ken Venturi	278	Tommy Jacobs	282	Congressional CC, Washington, DC
1965	*Gary Player (71)	282	Kel Nagle	(74)	Bellerive CC, St. Louis, MO
1966	*Billy Casper (69)	278	Arnold Palmer	(73)	Olympic Club, San Francisco, CA
1967	Jack Nicklaus	275	Arnold Palmer	279	Baltusrol GC, Springfield, NJ
1968	Lee Trevino	275	Jack Nicklaus	279	Oak Hill CC, Rochester, NY
1969	Orville Moody	281	Deane Beman	282	Champions GC, Houston, TX
			Al Geiberger		
			Bob Rosburg		
1970	Tony Jacklin	281	Dave Hill	288	Hazeltine GC, Chaska, MN
1971	*Lee Trevino (68)	280	Jack Nicklaus	(71)	Merion Golf Club, Ardmore, PA
1972	Jack Nicklaus	290	Bruce Crampton	293	Pebble Beach GL, Pebble Beach, CA
1973	Johnny Miller	279	John Schlee	280	Oakmont CC, Oakmont, PA
1974	Hale Irwin	287	Forrest Fezler	289	Winged Foot GC, Mamaroneck, NY
1975	*Lou Graham (71)	287	John Mahaffey	(73)	Medinah CC. Medinah, Il
1976	Jerry Pate	277	Tom Weiskopf	279	Atlanta Athletic Club, Duluth, GA
			Al Geiberger		
1977	Hubert Green	278	Lou Graham	279	Southern Hills, CC, Tulsa, OK
1978	Andy North	285	Dave Stockton	286	Cherry Hills CC, Denver, CO
			J.C. Snead		
1979	Hale Irwin	284	Gary Player	286	Inverness Club, Toledo, OH
			Jerry Pate		
1980	Jack Nicklaus	272	Isao Aoki	274	Baltusrol GC, Springfield, NJ
1981	David Graham	273	George Burns	276	Merion GC, Ardmore, PA
			Bill Rogers		
1982	Tom Watson	282	Jack Nicklaus	284	Pebble Beach GL, Pebble Beach, CA
1983	Larry Nelson	280	Tom Watson	281	Oakmont CC, Oakmont, PA
1984	*Fuzzy Zoeller (67)	276	Greg Norman	(75)	Winged Foot GC, Mamaroneck, NY
1985	Andy North	279	Dave Barr	280	Oakland Hills CC, Brimingham, MI
			T.C. Chen		
			Denis Watson		
1986	Raymond Floyd	279	Lanny Wadkins	281	Shinnecock Hills GC, Southampton, NY
			Chip Beck		
1987	Scott Simpson	277	Tom Watson	278	Olympic Club Lake Course, San Francisco, CA
1988	*Curtis Strange (71)	278	Nick Faldo	(75)	The Country Club, Brookline, MA
1989	Curtis Strange	278	Chip Beck	279	Oak Hill CC, Rochester, NY
			Mark McCumber		
			Ian Woosnam		
1990	*Hale Irwin (74-3)	280	Mike Donald	(74-4)	Medinah CC, Medinah, IL
1991	*Payne Stewart (75)	282	Scott Simpson	(77)	Hazeltine National GC, Chaska, MN
1992	Tom Kite	285	Jeff Sluman	287	Pebble Beach GL, Pebble Beach, CA

358 The PGA TOUR Complete Book of Golf

U.S. Open (continued)

Tournament History

Year	Winner	Score	Runner-up	Score	Location
1993	Lee Janzen	272	Payne Stewart	274	Baltusrol GC, Springfield, NJ
1994	*Ernie Els (74-4-4)	279	Loren Roberts	(74-4-5)	Oakmont CC, Oakmont, PA
			Colin Montgomerie	(78)	
1995	Corey Pavin	280	Greg Norman	282	Shinnecock Hills GC, Southhampton, NY
1996	Steve Jones	278	Tom Lehman	279	Oakland Hills CC, Bloomfield Hills, MI
			Davis Love III		
1997	Ernie Els	276	Colin Montgomerie	277	Congressional CC (Blue Course), Bethseda, MD
1998	Lee Janzen	280	Payne Stewart	281	Olympic Club, San Francisco, CA

Tournament Record: 272—Jack Nicklaus, 1980; Lee Janzen, 1993 (both Baltusrol GC)

18-Hole Record: 63—Johnny Miller, 1973 (Oakmont CC); Tom Weiskopf, 1980 (Baltusrol GC); Jack Nicklaus, 1980 (Baltusrol GC)

KEY: * = Playoff   # = Amateur   *Figures in parentheses indicate playoff scores*

Notes: With his two U. S. Open victories (1994, 1997), Ernie Els became the first foreign-born golfer to win two U.S. Opens since Alex Smith of Scotland won the title in 1906 and 1910.

In the first ninety-four U.S. Opens, no one shot less than thirty for nine holes. In the next two U.S. Opens, Neal Lancaster did it twice-the second nine of the fourth round at Shinnecock Hills GC in 1995 and the following year, the second nine of the second round at Oakland Hills CC.

British Open

Tournament History

Year	Winner	Score	Runner-up	Score	Location
1860	Willie Park	174	Tom Morris, Sr.	176	Prestwick, Scotland
	(The first event was open only to professional golfers)				
1861	Tom Morris, Sr.	163	Willie Park	167	Prestwick, Scotland
	(The Second Open was open to amateurs also)				
1862	Tom Morris, Sr.	163	Willie Park	176	Prestwick, Scotland
1863	Willie Park	168	Tom Morris, Sr.	170	Prestwick, Scotland
1864	Tom Morris, Sr.	167	Andrew Strath	169	Prestwick, Scotland
1865	Andrew Strath	162	Willie Park	172	Prestwick, Scotland
1866	Willlie Park	169	David Park	171	Prestwick, Scotland
1867	Tom Morris, Sr.	170	Willie Park	172	Prestwick, Scotland
1868	Tom Morris, Jr.	157	Robert Andrew	159	Prestwick, Scotland
1869	Tom Morris, Jr.	154	Tom Morris, Sr.	157	Prestwick, Scotland
1870	Tom Morris, Jr.	149	David Strath	161	Prestwick, Scotland
			Bob Kirk		
1871	No Championship				
1872	Tom Morris, Jr.	166	David Strath	169	Prestwick, Scotland
1873	Tom Kidd	179	Jamie Anderson	180	St. Andrews, Scotland
1874	Mungo Park	159	Tom Morris, Jr.	161	Musselburgh, Scotland
1875	Willie Park	166	Bob Martin	168	Prestwick, Scotland
1876	Bob Martin	176	David Strath	176	St. Andrews, Scotland
			(Tied, but refused playoff)		
1877	Jamie Anderson	160	Robert Pringle	162	Musselburgh, Scotland
1878	Jamie Anderson	157	Bob Kirk	159	Prestwick, Scotland
1879	Jamie Anderson	169	Andrew Kirkaldy	172	St. Andrews, Scotland
			James Allan		
1880	Robert Ferguson	162	Peter Paxton	167	Musselburgh, Scotland
1881	Robert Ferguson	170	Jamie Anderson	173	Prestwick, Scotland
1882	Robert Ferguson	171	Willie Fernie	174	St. Andrews, Scotland
1883	*Willie Fernie	159 (158)	Robert Ferguson	159 (159)	Musselburgh, Scotland
1884	Jack Simpson	160	Douglas Rolland	164	Prestwick, Scotland
			Willie Fernie		
1885	Bob Martin	171	Archie Simpson	172	St. Andrews, Scotland
1886	David Brown	157	Willie Campbell	159	Musselburgh, Scotland
1887	Willie Park, Jr.	161	Bob Martin	162	Prestwick, Scotland
1888	Jack Burns	171	Ben Sayers	172	St. Andrews, Scotland
			David Anderson		
1889	*Willie Park, Jr.	155 (158)	Andres Kirkaldy	155 (163)	Musselburgh, Scotland
1890	John Ball, Jr.	164	Willie Fernie	167	Prestwick, Scotland
			Archie Simpson		
1891	Hugh Kirkaldy	166	Andrew Kirkaldy	168	St. Andrews, Scotland
			Willie Fernie		

Championship extended from 36 to 72 holes)

British Open (continued)

Tournament History

Year	Winner	Score	Runner-up	Score	Location
1892	Harold H. Hilton	305	John Ball, Jr.	308	Muirfield, Scotland
			Hugh Kirkaldy		
			Alexander Herd		
1893	William Auchterlonie	322	John E. Laiday	324	Prestwick, Scotland
1894	John H. Taylor	326	Douglas Rolland	331	Royal St. George's, England
1895	John H. Taylor	322	Alexander Herd	326	St. Andrews, Scotland
1896	*Harry Vardon	316 (157)	John H. Taylor	316 (161)	Muirfield, Scotland
1897	Harold H. Hilton	314	James Braid	315	Hoylake, England
1898	Harry Vardon	307	Willie Park, Jr.	308	Prestwick, Scotland
1899	Harry Vardon	310	Jack White	315	Royal St. George's, England
1900	John H. Taylor	309	Harry Vardon	317	St. Andrews, Scotland
1901	James Braid	309	Harry Vardon	312	Muirfield, Scotland
1902	Alexander Herd	307	Harry Vardon	308	Hoylake, England
			James Braid		
1903	Harry Vardon	300	Tom Vardon	306	Prestwick, Scotland
1904	Jack White	296	John H. Taylor	297	Royal St. George's, England
			James Braid		
1905	James Braid	318	John H. Taylor	323	St. Andrews, Scotland
			Rowland Jones		
1906	James Braid	300	John H. Taylor	304	Muirfield, Scotland
1907	Arnaud Massy	312	John H. Taylor	314	Hoylake, England
1908	James Braid	291	Tom Ball	299	Prestwick, Scotland
1909	John H. Taylor	295	James Braid	301	Deal, England
			Tom Ball		
1910	James Braid	299	Alexander Herd	303	St. Andrews, Scotland
1911	*Harry Vardon	303	Arnaud Massy	303	Royal St. George's, England
		(143 for 35 holes)		(148 for 34 holes)	
1912	Edward (Ted) Ray	295	Harry Vardon	299	Muirfield, Scotland
1913	John H. Taylor	304	Edward (Ted) Ray	312	Hoylake, England
1914	Harry Vardon	306	John H. Taylor	309	Prestwick, Scotland
1915–1919: No Championships—World War I					
1920	George Duncan	303	Alexander Herd	305	Deal, England
1921	*Jock Hutchison	296 (150)	Roger Wethered	296 (159)	St. Andrews, Scotland
1922	Walter Hagen	300	George Duncan	301	Royal St. George's, England
			James M. Barnes		
1923	Arthur G. Havers	295	Walter Hagen	296	Troon, Scotland
1924	Walter Hagen	301	Ernest Whitcombe	302	Hoylake, England
1925	James M. Barnes	300	Archie Compston	301	Prestwick, Scotland
			Edward (Ted) Ray		
1926	Robert T. Jones, Jr.	291	Al Watrous	293	Royal Lytham, England
1927	Robert T. Jones, Jr.	285	Aubrey Boomer	291	St. Andrews, Scotland
			Fred Robson		

British Open (continued)

Tournament History

Year	Winner	Score	Runner-up	Score	Location
1928	Walter Hagen	292	Gene Sarazen	294	Royal St. George's, England
1929	Walter Hagen	292	Johnny Farrell	298	Muirfield, Scotland
1930	Robert T. Jones, Jr.	291	Macdonald Smith	293	Hoylake, England
			Leo Diegel		
1931	Tommy D. Armour	296	Jose Jurado	297	Carnoustie, Scotland
1932	Gene Sarazen	183	Macdonald Smith	288	Prince's, England
1933	*Denny Shute	292 (149)	Craig Wood	292 (154)	St. Andrews, Scotland
1934	Hanry Cotton	283	Sidney F. Brews	288	Royal St. George's, England
1935	Alfred Perry	283	Alfred Padgham	287	Muirfield, Scotland
1936	Alfred Padgham	287	James Adams	288	Hoylake, England
1937	Henry Cotton	290	R. A. Whitcombe	292	Carnoustie, Scotland
1938	R. A. Whitcombe	295	James Adams	297	Royal St. George's, England
1939	Richard Burton	290	Johnny Bulla	292	St. Andrews, Scotland
1940–1945: No Championships—World War II					
1946	Sam Snead	290	Bobby Locke	294	St. Andrews, Scotland
			Johnny Bulla		
1947	Fred Daly	293	R. W. Horne	294	Hoylake, England
			Frank Stranahan		
1948	Henry Cotton	284	Fred Daly	289	Muirfield, Scotland
1949	*Bobby Locke	283 (135)	Harry Bradshaw	283 (147)	Royal St. George's, England
1950	Bobby Locke	279	Roberto De Vicenzo	281	Troon, Scotland
1951	Max Faulkner	285	Antonio Cerda	287	Portush, Ireland
1952	Bobby Locke	287	Peter Thomson	288	Royal Lytham, England
1953	Ben Hogan	282	Frank Stranahan	286	Carnoustie, Scotland
			Dai Rees		
			Peter Thomson		
			Antonio Cerda		
1954	Peter Thomson	283	Sidney S. Scott	284	Royal Birkdale, England
			Dai Rees		
			Bobby Locke		
1955	Peter Thomson	281	John Fallon	283	St. Andrews, Scotland
1956	Peter Thomson	286	Flory Van Donck	289	Hoylake, England
1957	Bobby Locke	279	Peter Thomson	282	St. Andrews, Scotland
1958	*Peter Thomson	278 (139)	Dave Thomas	278 (143)	Royal Lytham, England
1959	Gary Player	284	Fred Bullock	286	Muirfield, Scotland
			Flory Van Donck		
1960	Kel Nagle	278	Arnold Palmer	279	St. Andrews, Scotland
1961	Arnold Palmer	284	Dai Rees	285	Royal Birkdale, England
1962	Arnold Palmer	276	Kel Nagle	282	Troon, Scotland
1963	*Bob Charles	277 (140)	Phil Rodgers	277 (148)	Royal Lytham, England
1964	Tony Lema	279	Jack Nicklaus	284	St. Andrews, Scotland

British Open *(continued)*

Tournament History

Year	Winner	Score	Runner-up	Score	Location
1965	Peter Thomson	285	Brian Huggett	287	Southport, England
			Christy O'Connor		
1966	Jack Nicklaus	282	Doug Sanders	283	Muirfield, Scotland
			Dave Thomas		
1967	Robert De Vicenzo	278	Jack Nicklaus	280	Hoylake, England
1968	Gary Player	289	Jack Nicklaus	291	Carnoustie, Scotland
			Bob Charles		
1969	Tony Jacklin	280	Bob Charles	282	Royal Lytham, England
1970	*Jack Nicklaus	283 (72)	Doug Sanders	283 (73)	St. Andrews, Scotland
1971	Lee Trevino	278	Lu Liang Huan	279	Royal Birkdale, England
1972	Lee Trevino	278	Jack Nicklaus	279	Muirfield, Scotland
1973	Tom Weiskopf	276	Johnny Miller	279	Troon, Scotland
			Neil Coles		
1974	Gary Player	282	Peter Oosterhuis	286	Royal Lytham, England
1975	*Tom Watson	279 (71)	Jack Newton	279 (72)	Carenoustie, Scotland
1976	Johnny Miller	279	Jack Nicklaus	285	Royal Birkdale, England
			Seve Ballesteros		
1977	Tom Watson	268	Jack Nicklaus	269	Turnberry, Scotland
1978	Jack Nicklaus	281	Ben Crenshaw	283	St. Andrews, Scotland
			Simon Owen		
			Tom Kite		
			Raymond Floyd		
1979	Seve Ballesteros	283	Ben Crenshaw	286	Royal Lytham, England
			Jack Nicklaus		
1980	Tom Watson	271	Lee Trevino	275	Muirfield, Scotland
1981	Bill Rogers	276	Bernhard Langer	280	Royal St. George's, England
1982	Tom Watson	284	Nick Price	285	Royal Troon, Scotland
			Peter Oosterhuis		
1983	Tom Watson	275	Andy Bean	276	Royal Birkdale, England
			Hale Irwin		
1984	Seve Ballesteros	276	Tom Watson	278	St. Andrews, Scotland
			Bernhard Langer		
1985	Sandy Lyle	282	Payne Stewart	283	Royal St. George's, England
1986	Greg Norman	280	Gordon Brand	285	Turnberry GL, Scotland
1987	Nick Faldo	279	Paul Azinger	280	Muirfield, Gullane, Scotland
			Rodger Davis		
1988	Seve Ballesteros	273	Nick Price	275	Royal Lytham and St. Annes, England
1989	*Mark Calcavecchia	275 (13)	Wayne Grady (16)	275	Royal Troon GC, Scotland
			Greg Norman (no final total)		
1990	Nick Faldo	270	Payne Stewart	275	St. Andrews, Scotland
			Mark McNulty		

British Open *(continued)*

Tournament History

Year	Winner	Score	Runner-up	Score	Location
1991	Ian Baker-Finch	272	Mike Harwood	274	Royal Birkdale, England
1992	Nick Faldo	272	John Cook	273	Muirfield, Gullane, Scotland
1993	Greg Norman	267	Nick Faldo	269	Royal St. George's, England
1994	Nick Price	268	Jesper Parnevik	269	Turnberry GL, Scotland
1995	*John Daly	282 (15)	Costantino Rocca	282 (19)	St. Andrews, Scotland
1996	Tom Lehman	271	Ernie Els	273	Royal Lytham & St. Annes, England
			Mark McCumber		
1997	Justin Leonard	272	Darren Clarke	275	Royal Troon GC, Troon, Scotland
			Jesper Parnevik		
1998	Mark O'Meara	280 (17)	Brian Watts	280 (19)	Royal Birkdale, England

Tournament Record: 267—Greg Norman, 1993 (Royal St. George's)

18-Hole Record: 63—Mark Hayes, 1977 (Turnberry); Isao Aoki, 1980 (Muirfield; Greg Norman, 1986 (Turnberry); Paul Broadhurst, 1990 (St. Andrews); Jodie Mudd, 1991 (Royal Birkdale), Nick Faldo, 1993 (Royal St. George's); Payne Stewart, 1993 (Royal St. George's)

KEY: * = Playoff   *Figures in parentheses indicate playoff scores.*

Notes: In 1997's British Open, Justin Leonard made up five strokes to Jesper Parnevik in the final round, matching the championship record for best comeback by a champion after fifty-four holes, set by Jim Barnes in 1925.

The only player to post a nine-hole score of 28 in British Open history was Denis Durnian, who accomplished the feat in 1983 on the front nine at Royal Birkdale.

Harry Vardon (1896, 1903, 1911), J.H. Taylor (1894, 1900, 1913) and Gary Player (1959, 1968, 1974) are the only players to win British Open titles in three different decades.

Jack Nicklaus and Nick Faldo share the record for most rounds in the British Open in the 60s with 33.

Henry Cotton set the record for the largest fifty-four-hole lead in British Open history when he took a 10-stroke lead into the final round at Sandwich in 1934. He shot a closing 79, but still defeated Sidney Brews by five.

PGA Championship

Tournament History

Year	Winner	Score	Runner-up	Score	Location
1916	James M. Barnes	1 up	Jock Hutchison		Siwanoy CC, Bronxville, NY
1917–1918: No Championships Played—World War I					
1919	James M. Barnes	6 & 5	Fred McLeod		Engineers CC, Roslyn, LI, NY
1920	Jock Hutchison	1 up	J. Douglas Edgar		Flossmoor CC, Flossmoor, IL
1921	Walter Hagen	3 & 2	James M. Barnes		Inwood CC, Far Rockaway, NY
1922	Gene Sarazen	4 & 3	Emmet French		Oakmont CC, Oakmont, PA
1923	*Gene Sarazen	1 up (38)	Walter Hagen		Pelham CC, Pelham, NY
1924	Walter Hagen	2 up	James M. Barnes		French Lick CC, French Lick, IN
1925	Walter Hagen	6 & 5	Williaim Mehlhorn		Olympia Fields, Olympia Fields, IL
1926	Walter Hagen	5 & 3	Leo Diegel		Salisbury GC, Westbury, LI, NY
1927	Walter Hagen	1 up	Joe Turnesa		Cedar Crest CC, Dallas, TX
1928	Leo Diegel	6 & 5	Al Espinosa		Five Farms CC, Baltimore, MD
1929	Leo Diegel	6 & 4	Johnny Farrell		Hillcrest CC, Los Angeles, CA
1930	Tommy Armour	1 up	Gene Sarazen		Fresh Meadow CC, Flushing, NY
1931	Tom Creavy	2 & 1	Denny Shute		Wannamoisett CC, Rumford, RI
1932	Olin Dutra	4 & 3	Frank Walsh		Keller GC, St. Paul, MN
1933	Gene Sarazen	5 & 4	Willie Goggin		Blue Mound CC, Milwaukee, WI
1934	*Paul Runyan	1 up (38)	Craig Wood		Park CC, Williamsville, NY
1935	Johnny Revolta	5 & 4	Tommy Armour		Twin Hills CC, Oklahoma City, OK
1936	Denny Shute	3 & 2	Jimmy Thomson		Pinehurst CC, Pinehurst, NC
1937	*Denny Shute	1 up (37)	Harold McSpaden		Pittsburgh Field Club, Aspinwall, PA
1938	Paul Runyan	8 & 7	Sam Snead		Shawnee CC, Shawnee-on-Delaware, PA
1939	*Henry Picard	1 up (37)	Byron Nelson		Pomonok CC, Flushing, LI, NY
1940	Byron Nelson	1 up	Sam Snead		Hershey CC, Hershey, PA
1941	*Vic Ghezzi	1 up (38)	Byron Nelson		Cherry Hills CC, Denver, CO
1942	Sam Snead	2 & 1	Jim Turnesa		Seaview CC, Atlantic City, NJ
1943: No Championship Played—World War II					
1944	Bob Hamilton	1 up	Byron Nelson		Manito G & CC, Spokane, WA
1945	Byron Nelson	4 & 3	Sam Byrd		Moraine CC, Dayton, OH
1946	Ben Hogan	6 & 4	Ed Oliver		Portland GC, Portland, OR
1947	Jim Ferrier	2 & 1	Chick Harbert		Plum Hollow CC, Detroit, MI
1948	Ben Hogan	7 & 6	Mike Turnesa		Norwood Hils CC, St. Louis, MO
1949	Sam Snead	3 & 2	Johnny Palmer		Hermitage CC, Richmond, VA
1950	Chandler Harper	4 & 3	Henry Willliams, Jr.		Sciotto CC, Columbus, OH
1951	Sam Snead	7 & 6	Walter Burkemo		Oakmont CC, Oakmont, PA
1952	Jim Turnesa	1 up	Chick Harbert		Big Spring CC, Louisville, KY
1953	Walter Burkemo	2 & 1	Felice Torza		Birmingham CC, Birmingham, MI
1954	Chick Harbert	4 & 3	Walter Burkemo		Keller GC, St. Paul, MN
1955	Doug Ford	4 & 3	Cary Middlecoff		Meadowbrook CC, Detroit, MI
1956	Jack Burke	3 & 2	Ted Kroll		Blue Hill CC, Boston, MA
1957	Lionel Hebert	2 & 1	Dow Finsterwald		Miami Valley CC, Dayton, OH

PGA Championship (continued)

Tournament History

Year	Winner	Score	Runner-up	Score	Location
1958	Dow Finsterwald	276	Billy Casper	278	Llanerch CC, Havertown, PA
1959	Bob Rosburg	277	Jerry Barber	278	Minneapolis GC, St. Louis Park, MN
			Doug Sanders		
1960	Jay Hebert	281	Jim Ferrier	282	Firestone CC, Akron, OH
1961	*Jerry Barber (67)	277	Don January (68)	277	Olympia Fields CC, Olympia Fields, IL
1962	Gary Player	278	Bob Goalby	279	Aronomink GC, Newtown Square, PA
1963	Jack Nicklaus	279	Dave Ragan, Jr.	281	Dallas Athletic Club, Dallas, TX
1964	Bobby Nichols	271	Jack Nicklaus	274	Columbus CC, Columbus, OH
			Arnold Palmer		
1965	Dave Marr	280	Billy Casper	282	Laurel Valley CC, Ligonier, PA
			Jack Nicklaus		
1966	Al Geiberger	280	Dudley Wysong	284	Firestone CC, Akron, OH
1967	*Don January (69)	281	Don Massengale (71)	281	Columbine CC, Littleton, CO
1968	Julius Boros	281	Bob Charles	282	Pecan Valley CC, San Antonio, TX
			Arnold Palmer		
1969	Raymond Floyd	276	Gary Player	277	NCR CC, Dayton, OH
1970	Dave Stockton	279	Arnold Palmer	281	Southern Hills CC, Tulsa, OK
			Bob Murphy		
1971	Jack Nicklaus	281	Billy Casper	283	PGA National GC, Palm Beach Gardens, FL
1972	Gary Player	281	Tommy Aaron	283	Oakland Hills CC, Birmingham, MI
			Jim Jamieson		
1973	Jack Nicklaus	277	Bruce Crampton	281	Canterbury GC, Cleveland, OH
1974	Lee Trevino	276	Jack Nicklaus	277	Tanglewood GC, Winston-Salem, NC
1975	Jack Nicklaus	276	Bruce Crampton	278	Firestone CC, Akron, OH
1976	Dave Stockton	281	Raymond Floyd	282	Congressional CC, Bethesda, MD
			Don January		
1977	*Lanny Wadkins	282	Gene Littler	282	Pebble Beach GL, Pebble Beach, CA
1978	*John Mahaffey	276	Jerry Pate	276	Oakmont CC, Oakmont, PA
			Tom Watson		
1979	*David Graham	272	Ben Crenshaw	272	Oakland Hills CC, Brimingham, MI
1980	Jack Nicklaus	274	Andy Bean	281	Oak Hill CC, Rochester, NY
1981	Larry Nelson	273	Fuzzy Zoeller	277	Atlanta Athletic Club, Duluth, GA
1982	Raymond Floyd	272	Lanny Wadkins	275	Southern Hills CC, Tulsa, Ok
1983	Hal Sutton	274	Jack Nicklaus	275	Riviera CC, Pacific Palisades, CA
1984	Lee Trevino	273	Gary Player	277	Shoal Creek, Brimingham, Al
			Lanny Wadkins		
1985	Hubert Green	278	Lee Trevino	280	Cherry Hills CC, Denver, CO
1986	Bob Tway	276	Greg Norman	278	Inverness Club, Toledo, OH
1987	*Larry Nelson	287	Lanny Wadkins	287	PGA National Palm Beach Gardens, FL
1988	Jeff Sluman	272	Paul Azinger	275	Oak Tree GC, Edmond, OK

PGA Championship (continued)

Tournament History

Year	Winner	Score	Runner-up	Score	Location
1989	Payne Stewart	276	Andy Bean	277	Kemper Lakes GC, Hawthorn Woods, IL
			Mike Reid		
			Curtis Strange		
1990	Wayne Grady	282	Fred Couples	285	Shoal Creek, Birmingham, AL
1991	John Daly	276	Bruce Lietzke	279	Crooked Stick GC, Carmel, IN
1992	Nick Price	278	John Cook	281	Bellerive CC, St. Louis, MO
			Jim Gallagher, Jr.		
			Gene Sauers		
			Nick Faldo		
1993	*Paul Azinger	272	Greg Norman	272	Inverness Club, Toledo, OH
1994	Nick Price	269	Corey Pavin	275	Southern Hills CC, Tulsa, OK
1995	*Steve Elkington	267	Colin Montgomerie	267	Riviera CC, Pacific Palisades, CA
1996	*Mark Brooks	277	Kenny Perry	277	Valhalla GC, Louisville, KY
1997	Davis Love III	269	Justin Leonard	274	Winged Foot CC, Mamaroneck, NY
1998	Vijay Singh	271	Steve Stricker	273	Sahalee CC, Redmond, WA

Tournament Record: 267—Steve Elkington/Colin Montgomerie, 1995 (Riviera CC)

18-Hole Record: 63—Bruce Crampton, 1975 (Firestone CC); Raymond Floyd, 1982 (Southern Hills CC); Gary Player, 1984 (Shoal Creek); Vijay Singh, 1993 (Inverness)

KEY * = Playoff *Figures in parentheses indicate playoff scores.*

Statistical Leaders—Year-by-Year

Scoring Average

1980	Lee Trevino	69.73
1981	Tom Kite	69.80
1982	Tom Kite	70.21
1983	Raymond Floyd	70.61
1984	Calvin Peete	70.56
1985	Don Pooley	70.36
1986	Scott Hoch	70.08
1987	David Frost	70.09
1988	Greg Norman	69.38
1989	Payne Stewart	*69.485
1990	Greg Norman	69.10
1991	Fred Couples	69.59
1992	Fred Couples	69.38
1993	Greg Norman	68.90
1994	Greg Norman	68.81
1995	Greg Norman	69.06
1996	Tom Lehman	69.32
1997	Nick Price	68.98
1998	David Duval	69.13

Driving Distance

1980	Dan Pohl	274.3
1981	Dan Pohl	280.1
1982	Bill Caffee	275.3
1983	John McComish	277.4
1984	Bill Glasson	276.5
1985	Andy Bean	278.2
1986	Davis Love III	285.7
1987	John McComish	283.9
1988	Steve Thomas	284.6
1989	Ed Humenik	280.9
1990	Tom Purtzer	279.6
1991	John Daly	288.9
1992	John Daly	283.4
1993	John Daly	288.9
1994	Davis Love III	283.8
1995	John Daly	289.0
1996	John Daly	288.8
1997	John Daly	302.0
1998	John Daly	299.4

Driving Accuracy—Pct.

1980	Mike Reid	79.5%
1981	Calvin Peete	81.9
1982	Calvin Peete	84.6
1983	Calvin Peete	81.3
1984	Calvin Peete	77.5
1985	Calvin Peete	80.6
1986	Calvin Peete	81.7
1987	Calvin Peete	83.0
1988	Calvin Peete	82.5
1989	Calvin Peete	82.6
1990	Calvin Peete	83.7
1991	Hale Irwin	78.3
1992	Doug Tewell	82.3
1993	Doug Tewell	82.5
1994	David Edwards	81.6
1995	Fred Funk	81.3
1996	Fred Funk	78.7
1997	Allen Doyle	80.8
1998	Bruce Fleisher	81.4

Greens-In-Regulation—-Pct.

1980	Jack Nicklaus	72.1%
1981	Calvin Peete	73.1
1982	Calvin Peete	72.4
1983	Calvin Peete	71.4
1984	Andy Bean	72.1
1985	John Mahaffey	71.9
1986	John Mahaffey	72.0
1987	Gil Morgan	73.3
1988	John Adams	73.9
1989	Bruce Lietzke	72.6
1990	Doug Tewell	70.9
1991	Bruce Lietzke	73.3
1992	Tim Simpson	74.0
1993	Fuzzy Zoeller	73.6
1994	Bill Glasson	73.0
1995	Lennie Clements	72.3
1996	Mark O'Meara	*71.783
1997	Tom Lehman	72.7
1998	Hal Sutton	71.3

Putting

1980	Jerry Pate	28.81
1981	Alan Tapie	28.70
1982	Ben Crenshaw	28.65
1983	Morris Hatalsky	27.96
1984	Gary McCord	28.57
1985	Craig Stadler	*28.627
1986	Greg Norman	1.736
1987	Ben Crenshaw	1.743
1988	Don Pooley	1.729
1989	Steve Jones	1.734
1990	Larry Rinker	*1.7467
1991	Jay Don Blake	*1.7326
1992	Mark O'Meara	1.731
1993	David Frost	1.739
1994	Loren Roberts	1.737
1995	Jim Furyk	1.708
1996	Brad Faxon	1.709
1997	Don Pooley	1.718
1998	Rick Fehr	1.722

All-Around

1987	Dan Pohl	170
1988	Payne Stewart	170
1989	Paul Azinger	250
1990	Paul Azinger	162
1991	Scott Hoch	283
1992	Fred Couples	256
1993	Gil Morgan	252
1994	Bob Estes	227
1995	Justin Leonard	323
1996	Fred Couples	215
1997	Bill Galsson	282
1998	John Huston	151

Sand Save Pct.

1980	Bob Eastwood	65.4%
1981	Tom Watson	60.1
1982	Isao Aoki	60.2
1983	Isao Aoki	62.3
1984	Peter Oosterhuis	64.7
1985	Tom Purtzer	60.8
1986	Paul Azinger	63.8
1987	Paul Azinger	63.2
1988	Greg Powers	63.5
1989	Mike Sullivan	66.0
1990	Paul Azinger	67.2
1991	Ben Crenshaw	64.9
1992	Mitch Adcock	66.9
1993	Ken Green	64.4
1994	Corey Pavin	65.4

1995	Billy Mayfair	68.6
1996	Gary Rusnak	64.0
1997	Bob Estes	70.3
1998	Keith Fergus	71.0

Total Driving

1991	Bruce Lietzke	42
1992	Bruce Lietzke	50
1993	Greg Norman	41
1994	Nick Price	43
1995	Nick Price	40
1996	David Duval	47
1997	Joe Durant	67
1998	Hal Sutton	62

Eagles

1980	Dave Eichelberger	16
1981	Bruce Lietzke	12
1982	Tom Weiskopf	10
	J.C. Snead	10
	Andy Bean	10
1983	Chip Beck	15

1984	Bary Hallberg	15
1985	Larry Rinker	14
1986	Joey Sindelar	16
1987	Phil Blackmar	20
1988	Ken Green	21
1989	Lon Hinkle	14
	Duffy Waldorf	14
1990	Paul Azinger	14
1991	Andy Bean	15
	John Huston	15
1992	Dan Forsman	18
1993	Davis Love III	15
1994	Davis Love III	18
1995	Kelly Gibson	16
1996	Tom Watson	#97.2
1997	Tiger Woods	104.1
1998	Davis Love III	83.3

Birdies

1980	Andy Bean	388
1981	Vance Heafner	388
1982	Andy Bean	392

1983	Hal Sutton	399
1984	Mark O'Meara	419
1985	Joey Sindelar	411
1986	Joey Sindelar	415
1987	Dan Forsman	409
1988	Dan Forsman	465
1989	Ted Schulz	415
1990	Mike Donald	401
1991	Scott Hoch	446
1992	Jeff Sluman	417
1993	John Huston	426
1994	Brad Bryant	397
1995	Steve Lowery	410
1996	Fred Couples	+4.20
1997	Tiger Woods	4.25
1998	David Duval	4.29

* carried to farther decimal to determine winner
\# changed to frequency
+ changed to average per round

All-Time Tour Winners

1.	Sam Snead	81
2.	Jack Nicklaus	70
3.	Ben Hogan	63
4.	Arnold Palmer	60
5.	Byron Nelson	52
6.	Billy Casper	51
T7.	Walter Hagen	40
	Cary Middlecoff	40
9.	Gene Sarazen	38
10.	Lloyd Mangrum	36
11.	Tom Watson	34
12.	Horton Smith	32
T13.	Harry Cooper	31
	Jimmy Demaret	31
15.	Leo Diegel	30
T16.	Gene Littler	29
	Paul Runyan	29
18.	Lee Trevino	27

19.	Henry Picard	26
T20.	Tommy Armour	24
	Johnny Miller	24
	Macdonald Smith	24
T23.	Johnny Farrell	22
	Raymond Floyd	22
T25.	Willie Macfarlane	21
	Gary Player	21
	Lanny Wadkins	21
	Craig Wood	21
T29.	James Barnes	20
	Hale Irwin	20
	Bill Mehlhorn	20
	Doug Sanders	20
T33.	Ben Crenshaw	19
	Doug Ford	19
	Hubert Green	19
	Tom Kite	19

T37.	Julius Boros	18
	Jim Ferrier	18
	E.J. Harrison	18
	Greg Norman	18
	Johnny Revolta	18
T42.	Jack Burke	17
	Bobby Cruickshank	17
	Harld McSpaden	17
	Curtis Strange	17
46.	Ralph Guldahl	16
T47.	Tommy Bolt	15
	Ed Dudley	15
	Nick Price	15
	Denny Shute	15
	Mike Souchak	15
	Tom Weiskopf	15

Tournament Players Clubs

Club	Architect	Club	Architect
TPC at Sawgrass Ponte, Vedra Beach, FL	Pete Dye	TPC at Sugarloaf Atlanta, GA	Greg Norman
TPC at Eagle Trace Coral Springs, FL	Arthur Hills	TPC at The Canyons Las Vegas, NV	*DSI
TPC at River Highlands Cromwell, CT	Pete Dye/*DSI	TPC at Jasna Polana Princeton, NJ	Gary Player
TPC at Prestancia Sarasota, FL	Ron Garl	TPC at Myrtle Beach Myrtle Beach, SC	Tom Fazio
TPC at Avenel Potomac, MD	Ault, Clark & Associates	TPC of Virgina Beach Virginia Beach, VA	Pete Dye
TPC of Scottsdale Scottsdale, AZ	Jay Morrish Tom Weiskopf	TPC at Deere Run Group Moline, IL	*DSI/Golf Resources
TPC at Piper Glen Charlotte, NC	Arnold Palmer	TPC at Wakefield Plantation Raleigh, NC	Irwin Design
TPC at Southwind Memphis, TN	Ron Prichard	TPC at Valencia (2000) Valencia, CA	**DSI
TPC of Michigan Dearborn, MI	Jack Nicklaus	TPC of Twin Cities (2000) Minneapolis, MN	Arnold Palmer
TPC of Tampa Bay Tampa, FL	*DSI	TPC at Lake Nona Orlando, FL	Pete Dye, Arnold Palmer, Tom Fazio
TPC of Summerlin Las Vegas, NV	*DSI	TPC at Fairfield Plantation New Orleans, LA	no architect listed
TPC at Heron Bay Coral Springs, FL	Mark McCumber		

*PGA TOUR Design Services, Inc., Bobby Weed, Chief
Designer
**PGA TOUR Design Services, Inc., Chris Gray, Chief Designer

Tournament Players Courses

Club	Architect	Club	Architect
TPC at The Woodlands The Woodlands, TX	Bob Von Hagge	TPC at PGA West La Quinta, CA	Pete Dye
TPC at Las Colinas Irving, TX	Jay Morrish	TPC at Snoqualmie Seattle, WA	Jack Nicklaus

Glossary

"A" game—When you're playing at the highest level possible for you.

ace—A hole-in-one.

address—The position a player takes while preparing to play a shot. The address position is the foundation of the golf swing because it is at this moment during the pre-swing preparation process that the player finalizes his aim at the target and sets his body in position to begin the swinging motion. The term also refers to the act of assuming this position.

albatross—A score of three under par on a given hole. A double eagle. The most famous albatross in the history of the game was recorded by Gene Sarazen in the second Masters Tournament (1935), when he holed out his second shot at Augusta National's fifteenth hole on his way to winning the event.

alignment—The aiming of your body, (your feet, knees, hips and shoulders) and the clubface at *address* (see address).

all square—Even in *match play*.

amateur side—The low side of the hole (low side dependent on the direction of the break). The term refers to the fact that professional golfers supposedly miss most putts on the high side of the hole.

Amen Corner—Collectively, the eleventh, twelfth and thirteenth holes at Augusta National Golf Club. So named by the writer Herbert Warren Wind for the fact that a player who survived this stretch of holes without calamity should be thankful.

approach shot—Any shot played in an attempt to reach the green. If you hit a good drive on a par 4 and are playing your second shot with the intention of reaching the green, you are playing your approach shot.

apron—The closely cropped grass that separates the putting green from the rough and/or fairway. The grass is cut lower than on the fairway but not as low as on the putting green. Also known as the *fringe*.

architecture—The practice of golf course design. To play the game at a high level it is vital to understand how the design of a course impacts on the way it should be played.

Arnie's Army—The fans who swarmed golf courses in pursuit of Arnold Palmer during the time when he became known as golf's "King."

attest—When you vouch for a fellow competitor's score by signing his scorecard.

automatic press—A wager that players agree on prior to a round, an automatic press is typically started when a team finds itself two down.

away—The ball farthest from the hole and therefore the next to be played.

back nine—The last nine holes of a golf course, assuming it's an eighteen-hole course.

backswing—The initial part of the swing that begins when the clubhead and the body start to move and turn away from the ball.

baffing-spoon—A wooden club that was the most lofted of a set of wooden clubs called spoons.

ball flight—The action of your ball in the air.

ballmaker—Back in the early days of golf a ballmaker was a craftsman along the lines of a clubmaker. Obviously, he made golf balls—one at a time.

ball mark—A small impression in the green made by a ball landing there. You can and should fix it, which you can do with a tee or a small metal tool designed for this purpose.

ball marker—An object—usually a small coin—used to mark the position of the ball on the green so you can lift and clean the ball and remove it from another golfer's line of putt.

ball retriever—A telescopic device outfitted with a small device on the end so that golf balls can be "fished" out of the water.

ball washer—A device, typically located near the tee box, into which a ball is placed and scrubbed clean in soapy water by tiny brushes located in side the unit. Some ball washers are operated by pumping a handle on the top, up and down, while others work by turning a crank on the side. Ordinarily a towel is attached to the side of the unit so the player can dry the ball.

banana ball—A left-to-right shot that ends up well right of the intended target. A major-league slice.

bare lie—There is no grass under the ball.

baseball grip—Similar to the way a baseball bat is gripped, the hands touch, but no fingers interlock or overlap. Sometimes referred to as the "ten-finger grip."

beach—Slang for sand bunkers.

bellied wedge—This shot is most often used after the ball comes to rest against the edge of the rough surrounding the green, and the ideal shot would be played along the ground. However, it's difficult to get the head of the putter smoothly through the rough. The solution is a bellied wedge, a shot played with a sand wedge using a putting stroke in which the ball is contacted in its belly (center) with the lead edge of the club.

bend—To intentionally cause the ball to curve either from right to left or left to right.

bentgrass—Durable, thin-bladed grass used on many championship golf courses, particularly in the northern parts of the United States.

Bermuda (grass)—Course, thick-bladed grass used in warm climates because of its ability to withstand oppressive heat.

bingle bangle bongle—A betting game with three points available on each hole. The first point is awarded to the person who hits the green in the fewest strokes, the second point to the closest to the hole once all are on the green, and the third to the first person to hole out. Also known as bingo bango bongo.

bird's nest—A lie in the rough where the ball sits down and is surrounded by grass on all sides.

bisque—A floating handicap stroke that may be taken at any point in the match by the recipient.

blade—To contact the ball at its equator with the lead edge of an iron, resulting in a low shot that often travels too far.

blind shot—A shot in which the target is not clearly visible.

block—The failure to release the right side of the body through the ball, resulting in an open clubface at impact and a shot that starts and stays to the right of the target.

blue tees—Traditionally, the tee block markers for championship or other professional tees were painted blue.

bogey—A score of one over par on a hole.

borrow—The amount of break you play on a putt to account for any slope of the green.

bounce—The curvature on the bottom or sole of a *sand wedge* (see sand wedge) that helps prevent the club from sticking in.

brassie—A wooden club, fitted with a brass soleplate, that has more loft than a spoon (three-wood) and less loft than a *driver*.

bump-and-run—A shot played around the green that is intended to hit into a slope, bounce onto the green, and then roll toward the hole.

bunker—A hollow depression often filled with sand and defined as a hazard.

buried lie—When the ball is partially or entirely covered by sand or grass.

bye holes—In match play, the holes still to be played on the course when a match is decided before the eighteenth hole.

cabbage—Slang for exceedingly long grass, or a particularly nasty lie in the rough.

caddie—A person who carries a golfer's bag during a round, often providing course information (yardages), suggestions (which club to hit, which way a putt breaks), and service (e.g., raking bunkers, replacing divots). Also, the act of working as a caddie.

Calamity Jane—Nickname for the hickory-shafted blade putter used by Bobby Jones.

carry—The distance a ball flies in the air, or the act of a ball safely clearing a hazard or an obstacle.

carryover—In betting games, the value of a hole that is tied is added to (carried over) the value of the subsequent hole or holes. The carryover is an important element of betting matches because it makes every hole matter.

cartpath—A paved, loose gravel, or dirt path designed for motorized golf carts to drive upon from tee to green. The cartpath interjects itself into the game in a variety of ways, not the least of which is creating problems for the golfer as he takes his stance. A paved cartpath is an immovable obstruction, and you can take relief if your ball is on one, or if you have to stand on one while addressing the ball. If the path has rails or sides or whatever, they are considered part of the path. If the path is just a well-worn dirt path, it's up to local rules to determine if you get relief.

casual water—Any water on a course that isn't part of a hazard, and you're entitled to relief from it.

chip—A short shot played near the green, the idea being to get the ball very near the hole. A chip is a played with the intention of the ball running quite a bit once it lands on the green. Because of this, a chip is differentiated from a "pitch" by these characteristics: The clubhead moves very little back and through on a chip, and it moves almost halfway back and through on a "pitch." A chip has a low or medium trajectory but would never be described as a lofted shot. A chip doesn't usually bite; when it does, it's an accident or the result of an expert player's attempt to do so.

closed—Your stance is *closed* if your left foot is closer to the target line than your right foot. Your clubface is *closed* if it is aimed left of the target at either address or impact.

clubhead speed—The speed, in miles per hour, that the clubhead is moving at impact is known as clubhead speed. It is the major determining factor in creating distance.

collar—An alternative term for *fringe* or *apron*, it describes the closely mown grass that directly surrounds a green. The grass is approximately fairway height and separates the green from the rough.

collection area—Some greens are designed in a manner so that from certain portions of that green, all shots that roll off the green funnel to a common area known as a collection area. The collection area is meant to test the player's skill as a chipper or a pitcher, since they will have to negotiate the slope their ball just rolled downto get close to the hole.

concede—In match play, when you "give" someone a putt—that is to say, when you allow him to pick the ball up without holing out. You may also concede a hole by picking up your own ball when it appears that your opponent is clearly going to win the hole.

course management—A player's ability to play a golf course in a manner that utilizes the his strengths and downplays his weaknesses.

course setup—The overall characteristics that influence the playability of a course, other than its design. In other words, the length of the rough, the width at which the fairways are cut, the speed of the greens, etc., are all part of the course setup.

cross-handed—A style of gripping the club that puts the hands in a position opposite that which is considered conventional. So a right-handed player, who typically places the right hand underneath the left hand, would place the right hand on top of the left.

Curtis Cup—A biennial team competition between women players representing the United States and Great Britain and Ireland.

dead-wristed—A stroke that utilizes a stiff-armed stroke without cocking the wrists.

delayed hit—When the wrists stay fully cocked until very late in the downswing.

digger—A player who takes a substantial divot with his iron shots.

dimple—The little depressions on your golf ball that help lift the ball into the air.

divot—The piece of turf you rip out of the ground on iron shots, or the hole you make in the ground. The word is derived from a Scottish word for the pieces of sod they used to make roofs with or, when dried out, as fuel for their fires.

dogleg—A hole that plays straight away from the tee and then veers sharply in one direction or another. A hole that bends to the right is called a dogleg right, and a hole that bends to the left is called a dogleg left.

dormie—In match play, when you're ahead by as many as there are holes remaining to be played, you have your opponent dormie.

double breaker—A putt that curves in two different directions.

downhill lie—A ball in a position that forces you to stand with your body leaning toward the target.

downswing—The part of your golf swing that begins at the end of your backswing at ends at impact with the ball.

draw—A controlled shot that moves from right to left in the air.

driver—Theoretically, the longest club with the least amount of loft in your set, designed for playing the ball from the tee.

drop—Something you sometimes do when you incur a penalty or when you are entitled to relief. Any time the Rules dictate that you drop (when you declare a ball unplayable, hit one in the water, or take relief), you do so by extending your arm directly in front of you and letting go of the ball. Where you drop the ball depends on the circumstances, but you must never drop it nearer to the hole.

eagle—A score of two under par on a hole.

etiquette—Collectively refers to acts that result in a player being aware of and courteous to other players, and being certain to do his best not to destroy the golf course.

face—The part of the clubhead designed to contact the ball.

fade—An intentional shot which curves from left to right. The difference between a fade and a *slice*, which also curves from left to right, is that a slice curves significantly more and typically beyond a predictable amount. The word fade refers to both the shot in flight and the act of hitting the shot. The *fade* is generally regarded as a "scoring" sho—a shot over which the excellent player has maximum control.

fairway—The closely mown area between the tee and the green on par 4s and par 5s that is the preferred route for playing the hole.

fairway bunker—A hazard, either grass or sand, that is placed adjacent to or in a fairway.

fairway wood—Any of the wood clubs, other than the driver, designed for playing long shots from the fairway.

fat—The act of the lead edge of the clubhead digging into the ground too far behind the ball. This normally occurs when the angle of the clubhead into the ball is too steep and/or when the ball is positioned too far back in the stance.

feather—A shot in which a player hits the ball with less than the full value of a given club while apparently making a full swing at it. The shot is played by slowing down the speed of the swing and is executed for two reasons: to play a shot a certain distance with a lower trajectory and, mainly, to fool an opponent in match play.

fellow competitor—In stroke play competition, the player or players with whom a golfer is paired

flag—A banner or pennant hung from a stick or a pole that is placed in the hole. Typically a bright color, it is intended to be an easily spotted indicator of the hole position.

flagstick—A stick, pin, or pole with a flag (or other marker) attached to the top, showing the position of a hole.

flange—On some iron clubs, a protrusion from the back of the club. Some putters have a flange for additional weight. On a sand wedge, the flange causes the club to bounce off the sand rather than dig into the sand.

flex—The amount that a clubshaft bends when swung.

fore—Scottish in origin, it's meant to warn the group "before" (ahead of) you, but it's now used as a general warning to players anywhere on the course that an errant shot may be headed their way. If you hear this frequently where you play, look around for a new home course.

forecaddie—A caddie who stays ahead of the players to mark the lie of the balls in play.

forged iron—Irons that are hewn from a solid block of stainless steel. Forged irons are noted for their tremendous feel, but are also noted for their lack of forgiveness of mis hit shots. Sometimes referred to as forged blades.

forward press—In the full swing or with the putting stroke, the movement of the hands and wrists toward the target to initiate the swing.

fourball—A match between the best ball of two teams, each consisting of two players.

foursomes—A match between two teams, each consisting of two players playing a single ball by alternate strokes.

fried egg—Slang for the lie of a ball half buried in the sand, with the top half of the ball visible. So named for its resemblance to a sunny-side-up egg.

frog hair—A slang term for the fringe or *apron* around the green.

gallery—Collectively, the spectators at a golf tournament.

gamesmanship—Skill in winning matches by dubious methods without infringing on the Rules.

gap wedge—An iron with a loft between that of a pitching wedge and a sand wedge.

gimme—A short putt that is conceded in match play.

GIR—An acronym for "greens in regulation."

go to school—To learn the speed and line of a putt by observing another golfer's putt along the same line.

Golden Bear—Nickname for Jack Nicklaus, the greatest competitive golfer of all time.

grain—The direction the grass is growing toward on a putting green, which often affects the speed and the break of putts.

green—The closely mown putting surface where the hole is cut.

green fee—The money you pay to play at a golf course.

greenie—A side bet within a larger betting match. To win a *greenie*, which is only up for grabs on par 3 holes, you must do two things: Hit the green and be closest to the hole.

green-in-regulation—When your ball comes to rest on a green in at least two shots less than the par for that hole.

greenkeeper—The employee of a club or golf course who is responsible for the maintenance of the course. Nowadays the *greenkeeper* is often referred to as the "green superintendent."

grinder—A golfer who never loses the intensity of his concentration or resolve, regardless of circumstances.

grip—The end of the club, covered with rubber or leather, that you hold while swinging.

grip pressure—The amount of pressure you apply with your hands to the club.

groove—A line cut into the face of your club that helps get the ball airborne and create spin on the ball. Also, to practice your swing or a certain shot, resulting in consistent performance.

gross—Your score for a hole or a round before deducting handicap strokes.

ground the club—To touch the clubhead to the ground as you're addressing your ball.

ground under repair—Any place on the course that is undergoing maintenance work, or ground that has been determined to be in need of maintenance, and indicated by an outline of white paint on the ground, from which a player may receive a free drop.

hack—An unskilled golfer.

half shot—Any shot played with a swing that is approximately half as long as would be used for a full shot with the selected club.

halve—In match play, to play a hole in the same number of strokes as your opponent.

handicap—A compensation that allows players of all abilities to compete under equal circumstances. It is established by determining your average score over a number of rounds, always taking into account your most recent rounds, and the difficulty of the course being played.

hardpan—Firm ground, with little or no grass.

hazard—Sand bunker or water identified by a yellow stake.

heel—The part of the clubface that joins with the hosel.

high side—The side of a hole that faces the direction from which an approaching putt will break.

hit—To play a stroke, you have hit a shot.

hog back—A clearly defined ridge in a fairway or green.

hole—The round container, or cup, 4¼ inches in diameter, cut into the green.

hole-high—A shot that finishes level with the hole.

hole-in-one—A tee shot played into the hole in a single stroke.

honor—The right to hit first off the tee as determined by the player who had the lowest score on the previous hole.

hood—Tilting forward of the clubhead by moving the hands farther ahead of the ball, which reduces the effective loft of the club.

hook—A shot that curves from right to left.

hosel—The part of the clubhead, particularly on irons, that acts as a receptacle for the shaft.

impact—the moment when the clubhead strikes the ball.

improve your lie—To move the ball illegally into a better position for the next shot.

interlocking grip—For a right-hand player, the method of gripping the club with the right pinky finger interlocking with the left index finger.

intermediate target—A twig, a leaf, or a patch of grass on the same line as the eventual target, used to help align the player.

iron—A bladelike club generally made from steel.

Iron Byron—A mechanical ball-striking machine—named after golfer Byron Nelson—used to test golf clubs and golf balls.

island green—Any green completely surrounded by water.

jail—A lie from which it is nearly impossible to recover.

juice—Slang for spin on the ball.

junk—Collectively, smaller bets such as *greenies* and *sandies* that are contested in addition to a larger bet such as a Nassau.

kick—Random bounce taken by the ball after it hits the ground.

kickpoint—The point of maximum bend in a shaft.

King, The—Arnold Palmer's primary nickname.

knee-knocker—A putt of sufficient length to be challenging and that, particularly under pressure, might cause both mental and physical disorder.

knife—Slang name for the 1-iron.

knockdown shot—A low, driving shot struck with the irons to combat a headwind or to avoid overhanging limbs.

knockoff—A club that is a copy or forgery of an original design.

lag putt—A long putt struck with the intention of leaving the ball close to the hole in a spot from where the next putt will be easy.

laid off—When the clubface is pointed to the left of the target at the top of the swing.

lateral hazard—A water hazard that is parallel to the line of play and that is identified by red stakes.

launch angle—The angle at which the ball leaves the clubface at impact.

lay up—To intentionally play a shot short of a hazard or green.

lay the sod over it—Slang expression for hitting a shot *fat* and creating a divot so large that it covers the ball.

lead edge—The point where the bottom of the clubface meets the sole of the club. The part of the club you aim at the target.

leaf rule—An unofficial, "local" rule that allows you to drop a ball without penalty if you believe you can't find your ball because it is under a leaf or leaves.

lie—The position of the ball on the ground. Also, the angle at which the clubhead is set in relation to the shaft of the club is known as the lie of the club.

lift, clean and place—When the ground is exceedingly soft and muddy and the ball plugs upon hitting the ground, the players are sometimes allowed, under the Rules, to pick up the ball, wipe it clean, and place it without penalty in the general vicinity of the original spot.

line—The route a given shot is intended to follow.

line of putt—On the green, the path the ball is expected to take after being hit. The line of putt extends from the ball through the hole all the way to the other side of the green. This is important to know because it is illegal for the player or his caddie to touch the line of putt to indicate anything.

links—A seaside course.

lip—The edge of the hole.

lip-out—Any putt that hits a portion of the cup and spins out, failing to fall in.

Little Ben—Ben Crenshaw's nickname for his putter.

lob shot—A shot that you play high into the air with the intention of carrying it only a short distance and landing it softly.

local rules—Rules particular to a certain course, drafted to deal with circumstances unique to that layout.

loft—A measurement of the angle at which the clubface deviates from vertical.

long irons— Collectively, the irons with the least amount of loft. There are no set guidelines for which clubs make up the long irons, but it's safe to say that the 1-, 2-, 3-, and 4-irons are part of this group.

loop—To a caddie, a round of golf.

loopy—A swing that has any movements that take the club off plane.

loose impediments—Anything that is produced by nature—a twig, a loose flower petal, a small stone, goose dung—that may be removed from around the ball, or from the putting line, without a penalty.

low side—Any part of the green below the hole.

L wedge— Short for lob wedge, a club with sixty degrees or more of loft used for playing very short, very high shots.

mark—To place a coin or a small circular object behind the ball to indicate its position on the green.

marker—A coin or small circular object used to *mark* the ball's position on the green. Also, when an odd number of players qualify for the final two rounds of tournament play, the player assigned the task of playing with and keeping score for the competitor who would otherwise play alone.

mashie—An outdated iron club considered equal to the modern-day 5-iron.

mashie-niblick—An outdated iron club considered equal to the modern-day 7-iron.

match—A contest between two players or two teams made up of two players, and contested at *match play*. Also, a group competing in this manner.

match of cards—A method of breaking ties by comparing scorecards, with the lowest score on a particular hole winning the tiebreaker.

match play—The original form of keeping score in golf, and perhaps the most pure. The score is kept based on the number of holes won as opposed to the total score. It is still the preferred manner of play for most non tournament golfers and in nearly every betting game.

matched set—A set of clubs made by the same manufacturer and constructed to have a consistent progression of lofts, lies, lengths, etc.

medal—A prize awarded to the low scorer in a stroke-play tournament.

medalist—The player who shoots the lowest score during stroke-play qualifying for a match-play tournament.

medal play—identical to *stroke play*, the outcome being determined by the total number of strokes taken by players over the course of a round or rounds.

milk the grip—Repeated tightening and loosening of the hands on the grip of the club until you are ready to start the club back. This is done to keep tension out of the hands and therefore out of the swing.

misclub—To play the wrong club for a particular shot.

misread—to miscalculate the putting line.

muff—To play a shot poorly.

mulligan—A second attempt at the same shot allowed—without penalty—in a friendly match but not in formal competition.

Nassau—A three-part bet, with the same dollar or point value attached to each hole on the front nine, the back nine, and the total match.

natural—A birdie without the aid of handicap strokes in a match where you or others are getting handicap strokes.

net—Your score after handicap strokes are deducted for a hole or for the overall round.

neutral grip—A way of gripping the club so that neither hand is turned underneath the shaft.

niblick—An outdated iron club considered equal to the modern-day 9-iron.

ninety-degree rule—A regulation of motorized cart operation that requires the driver to cross the fairway in straight lines.

Norman, Greg—One of the most popular players in the history of the game. Nicknamed the Great White Shark, he has won two British Opens and is capable of phenomenal scoring performances.

offset—A club with a crook or slight bend in the hosel, placing the head slightly behind the shaft of the club; designed to help players who frequently slice the ball.

one-piece takeaway—When the arms, hands, wrists, and club move away from the ball together.

open stance—When the feet, knees, hips, and shoulders are pointed left of your target.

order of play—The order in which players should play their shots, the player farthest from the hole playing first. On the tee, the order of play is determined by the scores on the preceding hole, the lowest scores going first.

out of bounds—Ground that is not considered part of the golf course and from which you are not permitted to play under the Rules.

over-the-top—Swing fault in which the upper body improperly begins the downswing leading to an outside-to-inside swing path.

overclub—To use a club that produces too much distance for the particular shot.

overlapping grip—A manner of placing the hands on the club wherein the right pinkie finger is placed into the gap between the index and middle fingers of the left hand.

pace—The speed at which a putt is moving.

pace of play—The amount of time it takes a group to move around the course.

par—A standard of performance equal to the number of strokes it should take a scratch golfer to complete a particular hole.

peg—Slang for a wooden tee.

penalty stroke—A stroke added to a player's score because of a Rules violation or for hitting into a water hazard, out of bounds, or into an unplayable lie.

pendulum stroke—A putting stroke that keeps the wrists nearly motionless and that relies on the back-and-forth motion of the arms.

perimeter-weighted irons—A design that concentrates the bulk of the weight around the perimeter of the clubhead.

picker—A player who generally hits iron shots very cleanly, with little or no contact with the ground.

pill—Slang term for the ball.

pin—The flagstick, which marks the location of the hole on the green.

pin-high—When the ball comes to rest parallel with the hole, even if its not on the green.

pitch—A high-lofted short shot typically played with the intention of the ball hitting the green softly and rolling very little. Also, the act of hitting such a shot.

pitch mark—An indentation in the green made by the ball. Make sure you fix it.

play through—To pass through a group of slower golfers.

plugged—A ball being embedded in the ground.

poa annua—A weed that sometimes overgrows the grass on greens and fairways.

pop stroke—A style of putting that emphasizes use of the wrists with very little arm movement.

pot bunker—A deep bunker with a small circumference, the top of which is level with the general terrain.

practice green—A putting green that is not part of the actual course and is intended for use as a practice area and as a place for players to become familiar with the speed and texture of the greens on the course.

practice tee—The area at a golf course designed and laid out for playing practice shots.

pre-shot routine—Anything a player does in preparation to play a shot up to the point at which he starts to swing the club.

press—A supplemental wager made during a match.

pro-am—Short for professional-amateur, it's a format of play that teams a professional golfer with an amateur or amateurs.

pull—A shot that flies straight left of the target is a pull.

push—A shot that flies on a straight line but is right of the target.

putt—Any shot played toward the hole on the putting green.

putter—A club with a minimal amount of loft designed for playing shots along the ground on the putting green.

putting green—The closely mown area where the hole is cut.

putt out—To putt the ball into the hole.

quarter-shot—A shot played with a swing that is only one-quarter as long and aspowerful as a full shot.

quit—To decelerate through impact of a stroke.

Rae's Creek—A small stream that fronts the twelfth green at Augusta National Golf Club, then turns and runs along the thirteenth fairway before cutting in front of the thirteenth green.

ranger—A golf course employee who roams the course in a motorized golf cart making sure that players are keeping up with the pace of play.

rap—To strike a putt firmly.

read—To assess the green as a whole or the line of a single putt as it relates to thespeed, direction and texture of the grass.

recovery shot—A shot played from an undesirable position to a desirable position.

Redan Hole—A par 3 with a green set diagonal to the tee and a steep drop-off or swale off to one side of the green. The green positioning, the drop-off, and a bunker give the hole two lines of defense no matter where the hole is cut.

release—The uncocking of the wrists and rotation of the arms through impact.

relief—When a player is permitted to lift and drop the ball without penalty.

reverse C—A follow-through position in which the body loosely forms a reverse C— that is, the back is arched away from the target at the finish position.

reverse overlap grip—A putting grip in which the left index finger is placed over the first two or three fingers on the right hand.

reverse pivot—A movement in which the weight remains on the left side during the backswing and then is transferred to the right side on the downswing, or exactly opposite of the recommended technique.

rough—The part of the golf course that is not as closely mown as the fairway and is not a tee, a green or a hazard.

rub of the green—Bad bounces, deflections—any unanticipated misfortune that happens on the course.

Rules of Golf—Written and administered by the USGA or the R&A depending upon where you're playing, these are the official rules of the game.

run-up shot—A low shot played with the intention of the ball running up near the hole.

Ryder Cup—A biennial team match-play competition between professional golfers representing teams from the United States and Europe. Named for Samuel Ryder, the contest was first officially conducted in 1927, and was originally contested between the United States and Great Britain. The British team was expanded to include all of Europe in 1979, greatly increasing the level of competition. The site alternates between a U.S. course and a European venue, and the format of play includes foursomes (alternate-shot), four-ball (best-ball), and singles matches.

sand trap—A bunker.

sand wedge—A club designed specifically for playing short shots from the sand. The club typically has a loft of fifty-six degrees and a lie of sixty-three to sixty-five degrees.

sandbagger—A player who purposely posts false or inflated scores in order to achieve a handicap higher than what his ability warrants.

scats—A betting game typically played among three players, each hole worth a fixed amount of money. If one of the three players wins the hole outright, he wins the predetermined amount of money from the other two players. If there is a tie for low ball, the value of the hole carries over.

score—The total number of strokes played on a hole or a round.

scorecard—The card on which a player records the scores for the round.

scoring lines—The grooves on a clubface.

scramble—The act of hitting inconsistent shots yet still managing to make respectable scores. Also, a type of tournament play in which each of the four players on a team hits a tee shot. The group determines which ball is the best of the four, and each player plays the second shot from that spot. The team continues to play all its shots in this manner until holing out.

scratch—A player with a handicap of zero.

shaft—The long, cylindrical part of a golf club that connects the clubhead to the grip.

shag bag—A bag in which a player keeps practice balls.

shank—To hit the ball with the hosel of the club, causing it to fly directly to the right.

shape a shot—To intentionally make the ball curve in flight.

short game—Collectively chips, bunker shots, pitches, and putts.

short irons—The iron clubs with which short approach shots are intended to be played. Collectively the 8-iron, 9-iron, and wedges.

shot—A stroke recorded by striking the ball with a club.

shotgun start—Several groups on each tee of a course start a round so all the participants finish at roughly the same time. So named because back in the old days a gun would be fired to let the groups know it was okay to start the round.

shotmaker—A player capable of creating a variety of ball flights (e.g., a low hook, a high fade, a knockdown shot) and hitting these shots as the circumstances of a round dictate.

single—A match between two players.

skull—To contact the ball with the lead edge in the center of the ball, sending it lower and with more force than intended.

sky—To hit the ball much higher and shorter than intended.

slice—An out-of-control shot moving from left to right.

slope—A system that rates courses based on difficulty and used to assign accurate handicaps to players.

smother hook—A hooked shot that flies low to the ground and not very far.

snake—An extremely long putt that breaks in multiple directions.

snap hook—A shot that breaks off sharply to the left soon after being struck.

snowman—A score of 8 for a hole. So called from the numeral's resemblance to a snowman.

socket—The part of the clubhead into which the shaft is inserted.

sole—The bottom of a clubhead. Also, to set the club on the ground at address.

spade mashie—An outdated iron club considered equal to the modern-day 6-iron.

spike marks—Small pockmarks left on the green by spikes on golf shoes.

spikes—The metal cleats on the bottom of golf shoes.

spinach—Slang for rough.

spoon—An outdated term for a fairway wood that is sometimes used to describe a 3-wood.

square—A tie match. Also, the position of the clubface when perpendicular to the target line.

square grooves—Grooves etched into the clubface in the shape of a "U" as opposed to the traditional "V" shape.

Stableford—A system of scoring that awards points rather than strokes to the player based on scores in relation to par.

stance—The position of the feet when at address.

stiff—A shot hit very close to the hole. Also, a shaft that bends little during the swing.

stimpmeter—A hand-held ramp used to determine the speed (see speed) of a green.

stroke—The forward movement of the clubhead with the intent to hit the ball. Also, a shot added to the player's score as a result of a penalty.

stroke play—Competition based on the total number of strokes for a round or rounds.

strong grip—A grip in which the right hand is turned underneath the shaft and away from the target.

sucker pin—A hole location cut close to or hidden behind a hazard.

sweep—The action of picking the ball off the ground cleanly with a club while avoiding solid contact with the ground.

sweetspot—The spot on the clubface that, when contacted by the ball, produces the best possible result.

swing—To move the club into the ball.

swing key—A particular thought a player focuses on before his swing.

swing path—The path of the shaft as it is swung.

swing plane—The angle which the shaft follows throughout your swing.

takeaway—The initial phase of the backswing.

talk to the ball—Golfers are constantly searching for help, and seem to be under the delusion that talking to the ball (or yelling at it) will someone have an impact on the shot in progress. That's why we say things such as "Bite!" and "Sit down!" and "Chew!" Does the ball listen? It can't hurt.

tap-in—A very short putt. Also, to hole a very short putt.

target line—An imaginary line extending from the ball to your target.

tee—A small wooden peg used to prop up the ball for shots played from the tee. Also, the area from which tee shots are played.

tee off—To play a shot from the tee.

tee shot—A shot played from the teeing ground.

tempo—The rhythm with which a player swings the club.

Texas wedge—A shot played with a putter from off the green.

thin—A shot where the lead edge of the clubhead contacts the ball above its midpoint, causing a shot that flies lower and travels farther than intended.

three-quarter shot—A shot with a swing that is three-quarters the length of a full shot.

through the green—Anywhere on the course that isn't a teeing ground or a green.

tiger tees—An alternative way of referring to the championship tees.

tight—A hole with a narrow driving area. Also, a lie with very little grass underneath the ball, which is sitting close to the ground.

tips—The tees from which a course plays longest.

titanium—A specialty, lightweight metal made from sand and used to construct some shafts and clubheads.

toe—The end of the clubhead, particularly on the clubface, farthest from the shaft.

torque—The twisting of the shaft and the clubhead as a result of impact with the ball.

transition—The moment when the backswing changes into the downswing.

trap—An alternate term for bunker.

turn—The rotation of your body away from the ball. Also, the point between the ninth and tenth holes of a round.

turn it over—To make the ball curve from right to left. You can only turn it over from right to left.

uncock—To straighten the wrists during the downswing in preparation for impact.

underclub—To use a club that doesn't provide sufficient distance to execute a shot.

unplayable lie—A lie the player deems too difficult to play from.

up and down—Holing out from off the green in two shots, one of which is normally a putt.

upright—A swing in which the clubhead follows a steeper than normal path away from and into the ball.

utility wood—Any wood designed to play shots from difficult lies, such as from the rough.

Vs—The angles formed by your thumbs and forefingers when you grip the club.

waggle—A loose movement of the clubhead back and forth behind the ball that immediately precedes the takeaway.

water hazard—Any body of water on a golf course that is defined as a hazard.

weak grip—A grip in which the hands are turned more toward the target than in a neutral grip.

wedge—A high-lofted club used primarily for short shots within 100 yards of the green.

whiff—To swing and miss the ball completely.

winter rules—Rules in force, generally during cold conditions when course maintenance is difficult, that allow players to improve their lies through the green.

work the ball—To control the flight of the ball—that is, to intentionally draw it, fade it, hit it high, or hit it low

yardage marker—Anything placed on a golf course that indicates the total yardage for a hole or the yardage from specific locations to the hole.

yips—There is no precise definition for the *yips*, which are more a state of mind than anything else. The frequent or complete inability of a player to control the putter on short putts—the hands twitch and the ball goes nowhere near the hole.

Index

shafts of, 229–230
solid-head, 227, 229
styles of, 227
warm up with, 250
putting, 224–251
  aim in, 231–232
  alignment for, 246
  arms in, 227
  breakthrough tips for, 246–247
  drills for, 241, 315
  leaders, statistical annual, 368
  learning return putt in, 244
  line for, 242–245
  long putt strategy in, 242
  off the green, 175, 180–181
  practicing, 229, 247, 313
  preputt routine for, 235, 251
  science of, 279–281
  setup for, 234
  speed of, 231, 236, 237–239, 249, 250
  stroke essentials in, 230–235
  tempo in, 247
  three-foot, 216
  tips for, 233, 235, 239–242
  yips, coping with, 251

Quigley, Brett, 131

R&A (Royal and Ancient Golf Club of St. Andrews, Scotland), 325
Rawlins, Horace, 3
Ray, Ted, 4
ready position, 55–57
red stakes, 323
regripping, 86
"release," meaning of, 217
reverse pivot, 216
rhythm, pre-shot setup and, 71
right to left shots, 258–260
Roberts, Clifford, 6
Roberts, Loren, 26, 227, 290
Rosburg, Bob, 53
rough, 59
  fairway woods and, 134–136

flier lie in, 268, 269–270
fluffy lie in, 268
grass growth direction and, 266, 270–271
shotmaking from, 266–271
Royal and Ancient Golf Club of St. Andrews, Scotland, 325
Rules of Golf, 325–335
  in action, 331–335
  ball in water, 289–290, 330
  ball unfit for play, 330–331, 334
  club carrying limit, 27
  club length and, 45
  damaged balls, 44
  etiquette/common courtesies and, 322–325
  on hazards, 327–328
  irreparable harm to equipment, 335
  moved/deflected/stopped ball, 331, 332
  on moving loose impediments, 328–329, 333
  order of play, 326–327, 331
  playing wrong ball, 329–330, 331–332
  provisional balls, playing, 327
  stance building, 335
  on tee shot, 121
  teeing ground, 326, 327
  on unplayable balls, 329
Rummells, Dave, 100–101, 172
run-type, pitch shot, 187
Ryder Cup, 15

sand save, annual leading statistical percentages, 368–369
sand shot, 200–213
  buried lie and, 208–209, 210
  club selection for, 202–203
  controlling, 206–208
  fundamentals of, 203–206
  tips for assessing/playing, 211–213
  troubleshooting, 218
sand wedge, 27, 36–37

greenside sand play and, 202
pitch shot and, 185
Sarazen, Gene, 5, 7, 8, 53
Sawgrass Stadium Course (Fla.), 14
science of golf, 276–281
  linear and rotational energy, 278
  metal wood, 276–277
  putting, 279–281
  shaft flexibility, 278–279
  weather, 279
scoring average leaders, 368
scoring clubs, 32–34
  middle/short irons as, 162
Scott, Steve, 298
SENIOR PGA TOUR, 16–17
shaft, club, 22
  flexibility effects on, 278–279
  graphite or boron, 277
  Nelson's steel, 9
shanks, cures for, 215
shoes, non-metal spiked, 45
  sand traction of, 213
short irons/game, 172–197. See also middle/short irons
  basic rule of thumb for, 174
  bellied wedge and, 194–195
  chip shot, 176–178, 181–185
  coordinating target and swing in, 190–192
  flop shot and, 192–194
  pitch shot, 178–179, 185–190
  practice for, 169, 312–313
  pulling of, 214
  putting off the green, 175, 180–181
  shot selection in, 175
  shot trajectory and, 177, 190
  specialty shots, 192–195
shotmaking, 255–275. See also specific shots
  bump-and-run, 272–273

pre-shot routine and, 107,
108
snap hooks and, 107
stance width and, 106, 107
strategies for, 286–291
swing keys in, 113
tempo of, 108–109
terrain and, 121
at top, 112–113
trees and, 287
wind direction and,
122–123, 288–289
T. Woods', 110–111
your ball flight and, 287
teeing ground, 326, 327
television, golf and, 11–12
tempo
in putting, 247
of swing, 78, 79, 86
of tee shot, 108–109
Thomson, Peter, 13
Tolles, Tommy, 163
Tomasi, T. J., 219–220
touch, putting and, 249
TOUR. *See* PGA TOUR
tour winners, all-time, 369
Tournament Players
Championship, 14
Tournament Players Clubs, 14,
370
trajectory. *See also* loft, club
short game and, 177, 190
transition phase, swing, 85–88
beginners and, 167
trees
carrying, strategy for, 291
punch shot out of, 260–262
target and, 287
Trevino, Lee, 16, 17, 92
triceps push-up (strength training), 346
trouble shots. *See* shotmaking
trunk raise (strength training),
345
trunk rotation, 342–343
turning during swing, 81,
82–85, 101
reverse pivot and, 217
Tway, Bob, 203

uneven lies. *See* hilly lies
unexpected situation practice,
313
United States, golf in, 2–17
amateur era ends, 6
early icons, 8–11
Masters, PGA
Championship, 7–8
Nicklaus and, 12–13
PGA TOUR, 13–17
professional evolution of,
4–5
television and Palmer,
11–12
United States Golf Association,
325–326
unplayable balls, 329
upper body stretch, 341–342
U.S. Amateur, 3, 6, 7
U.S. Open, 3, 6, 9, 10, 11
1913, 4
1982, 14
winners, 356–359
"utility" woods, 135

Vardon, Harry, 4
Vardon grip, 53
Verplank, Bob, 169
visualizing shot, 64
with fairway woods/long
irons, 132
putt line and, 245
putting and, 250
takeaway and, 80

Wadkins, Lanny, 17, 70, 161,
163, 275
waggling club, 67, 68–69, 221
Waite, Grant, 39
Waldorf, Duffy, 82, 109
walk-type, pitch shot, 187
warm-up practice, 304–308
water
ball in, 289–290, 330
shotmaking from, 274–275
Watson, Tom, 13, 14, 17, 68,
150, 269
weather
etiquette and, 325

science of golf and, 279
wedges, 35–37
types, 202
weight shifts
backswing, 81–82
beginners and, 166–167
downswing and, 90
transition phase, 87
wind, 256, 271–272
carry and roll and, 122–123
direction, tossing grass and,
270
shotmaking and, 266
target strategy and, 288–289
Wood, Craig, 7, 9
woods, 28
driver *vs.* 3-wood, 217–218
metal, 30, 276–277
persimmon *vs.* metal, 29,
134
Woods, Tiger, 17
address position of, 220–221
on fixing slice or hook, 97
on practice range, 302
rough shot of, 216
tee shot of, 110–111
Woosnam, Ian, 66, 145,
220–221
Worsham, Lew, 11
wrist/forearm combo (strength
training), 345–346
wrong ball, playing, 329–330,
331–332

yardage books/markers, 162,
165

Zebelean, John, 276
Zoeller, Fuzzy, 30, 60
zone, playing in the, 146–147

Producer's Acknowledgments

This book was conceived, developed and produced by Mountain Lion, Inc., a book producer which specializes in bringing sports books to market. A book producer brings together and relies on the special skills of many people in preparing a book for manufacturing, distribution and marketing by the sponsoring publisher (in this case, Henry Holt and Company). The following individuals contributed to producing *The PGA TOUR Complete Book of Golf*, to whom we say, "Thanks."

- Mike Corcoran, writer who wrote the main text; John Ledesma, reporter who gathered the lion's share of the PGA TOUR players' comments.
- Patrick J. Cohn, Ph.D., sports and golf psychologist, who provided his insightful strategies and tactics for peak mental performance.
- Leonard Kamsler, Marc Feldman, Mike Plunkett and Tony Roberts—who collectively supplied the stop-action sequence, PGA TOUR action and landscape photography; and Barry Ross, who drew the illustrations.
- Joan Mohan of Mountain Lion Inc., who typed the manuscript and transcribed the player interviews; Max Crandall, who conceived the elegant page design of the book; Margaret Trejo, who transformed Max's ideas into finished pages; Mark Gola, managing editor of Mountain Lion Inc., who supervised the production, selected and edited the photographs and illustrations; Randy Voorhees, vice president of Mountain Lion Inc., who originated the idea for this project and brought together the PGA TOUR and Henry Holt and Company.

To the many other individuals who provided Mountain Lion with special assistance and support, we also say, 'Thank you."

- PGA TOUR folks who ably pitched in whenever needed: Chuck Adams, Director of Editorial Projects; Devon Brennan, Retail Licensing Coordinator; Wesley Haynes, Vice President Retail Licensing; Leo McCullagh, Vice President, Retail Licensing and Consumer Marketing; and John Morris, Vice President of Communications.
- Cindy Reid, Director of Instruction, Tournament Players Club at TPC Sawgrass.
- Bill and Mike Battle, Battle Enterprises.
- David Sobel, senior editor of Owl Books/Henry Holt and Company, who directed the project and championed it throughout.
- Tom Miller, PGA professional, Hopewell Valley Golf Club, Hopewell, NJ; Doug Errhalt, PGA professional, Jasna Polana TPC, Princeton, NJ; and Paul Kaster, member and club champion, Hopewell Valley Golf Club, who demonstrated many of the golfing techniques and physical fitness exercises.
- Teresa Carson and William Drennan, copyeditors; Eileen Delaney, proofreader; and Deborah Patton, indexer.

John J. Monteleone
Mountain Lion Inc.
Princeton, NJ
December, 1998

About the Authors

Michael Corcoran, formerly the editor-in-chief of *Golf Illustrated* magazine, and managing editor of ABC Sports/Jack Nicklaus Productions' The Wide World of Golf video series, has written for a wide variety of print and broadcast media. He lives in Pennsylvania, where he is currently executive editor of *Men's Health* magazine.

Patrick J. Cohn, Ph.D., a leading sports and golf psychologist, is contributor of the sections on *The Mental Game of Golf* that appear at the end of several chapters. He teaches mental game strategies and tactics to several players on the PGA TOUR and Nike Tour as well as collegiate golf teams. He is author of *The Mental Game of Golf: A Guide to Peak Performance* and *The Mental Art of Putting: Using Your Mind to Putt Your Best*; his articles have appeared in *Golf Magazine, Golfweek*, and *PGA Magazine*. Dr. Cohn writes a monthly column for *CBS SportsLine Golf Web*, appears on the Golf Channel's *Golf Academy*, and teaches at the Grand Cypress Golf Academy in Orlando. He is founder and president of Peak Performance Sports (www.peaksports.com), which is based in Orlando, Florida.

Photo Credits

AP/Wide World Photos: 5, 7, 9, 15

Marc Feldman: 135, 141, 157, 188, 209, 210

Dom Furore/*Golf Digest*: 110

Leonard Kamsler: 2, 8, 10, 11, 12, 13, 14, 16, 17, 35, 52, 63, 74, 76, 80, 81, 85, 87, 89, 91, 92, 93, 95, 114, 119, 123, 133, 152, 154, 161, 163, 164, 184, 194, 200, 207, 208, 226, 235 (middle), 236, 238, 254, 261, 264, 266, 269, 270, 273, 275, 284, 292, 294, 296, 307, 312, 373, 386

Tony Roberts: viii, ix, xiv, xv, 350

PGA TOUR Photo Services: xvi, xvii, 47, 73, 102, 103, 126, 128, 148, 150, 170, 172, 199, 222, 252, 302, 319, 320, 348

All illustrations were sketched and inked by Barry Ross.

All other images were photographed by Michael Plunkett and are property of Mountain Lion, Inc.